THEORIES IN
COGNITIVE PSYCHOLOGY:
THE LOYOLA SYMPOSIUM

THEORIES IN COGNITIVE PSYCHOLOGY: THE LOYOLA SYMPOSIUM

EDITED BY ROBERT L. SOLSO

LOYOLA UNIVERSITY OF CHICAGO

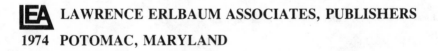 LAWRENCE ERLBAUM ASSOCIATES, PUBLISHERS

1974 POTOMAC, MARYLAND

DISTRIBUTED BY THE HALSTED PRESS DIVISION OF

JOHN WILEY & SONS

New York   Toronto   London   Sydney

Copyright © 1974, by Lawrence Erlbaum Associates, Inc.

Lawrence Erlbaum Associates, Publishers
12736 Lincolnshire Drive
Potomac, Maryland 20854

Distributed solely by Halsted Press Division
John Wiley & Sons, Inc., New York

Library of Congress Cataloging in Publication Data

Main entry under title:

Theories in cognitive psychology: the Loyola symposium.

  Includes bibliographical references.
  1. Cognition—Congresses. I. Solso, Robert L.,
1933–   ed. [DNLM: 1. Cognition—Congresses. BF311
L923t 1973]
BF311.T44   153.1   74–3098
ISBN 0–470–81228–1

Printed in the United States of America

CONTENTS

Preface   ix

SECTION I

1   CAN WE HAVE A THEORY OF MEANINGFUL MEMORY?
James J. Jenkins 1
    Forgetting   3
    Experiments on the Interaction of Tasks
      and Free Recall   9
    Reflections on the Experiments   15
    Current Directions   18
    A Final Illustration   18
    References   20

2   MEMORY AND THE EFFICACY OF CUES OR "YES, I KNOW!"
vs. "WHY DIDN'T I THINK OF THAT?" Robert L. Solso 21
    A "New Look" at Stimulus Selection
      and Cue Efficacy   22
    Retrieval and Cue Efficacy or You
      Can't Get There from Here   27
    References   42

3   **CONTINUITY OF PROCESSES ACROSS VARIANTS OF
     RECOGNITION LEARNING, Donald H. Kausler** **45**
     Historical Perspective   45
     Toward a General Theory of Recognition Learning   47
     Comparisons of Hit and Error Rates Across
        Task Variants   56
     Comparisons of Functional Relationships Across
        Task Variants   61
     Multiple Components of Multiple-Item
        Recognition Learning   67
     Summary   72
     References   72

4   **THEORETICAL IMPLICATIONS OF THE SPACING EFFECT,
     Douglas L. Hintzman** **77**
     Consolidation   81
     Rehearsal   83
     Voluntary Attention   86
     Encoding Variability   91
     A Methodological Digression   95
     Conclusions   96
     References   97

5   **SEARCH PROCESSES IN RECOGNITION MEMORY,
     Richard C. Atkinson, Douglas J. Herrmann, and Keith T.
     Wescourt** **101**
     Introduction   101
     Memory Search with Small Target Sets   109
     Memory Search with Large Target Sets   117
     Memory Search with Both Large and Small Target Sets   125
     Memory Search Moderated by Semantic Factors   129
     Memory Search Involving a Duplex Target Set   134
     Discussion   139
     References   144

6   **TRANSFORMATIONAL STUDIES OF THE INTERNAL
     REPRESENTATION OF THREE-DIMENSIONAL OBJECTS,
     Jacqueline Metzler and Roger N. Shepard** **147**
     Introduction   147
     Experiment I   153

Experiment II   169
Recent Experimental Findings   176
Theoretical Discussion   189
References   198

7   CRITIQUE OF PURE MEMORY, Frank Restle 203
Levels of Memory   204
The Nature of Organization   209
Cognitive Organization   214
Conclusions   215
References   217

8   DISCUSSION: SECTION I, Richard C. Atkinson, Douglas L.
Hintzman, James J. Jenkins, Donald Kausler, William
Macey, Jacqueline Metzler, Frank Restle, Roger N.
Shepard, and Robert L. Solso 219
References   230

SECTION II

9   AN INFERENCE MODEL FOR CONCEPTUAL RULE
LEARNING, L. E. Bourne, Jr. 231
Preliminary Issues   231
Processes in Conceptual Problem Solving   234
Interpretations of Rule Difficulty   238
A Model Based on Inference Operations   239
Summary and Conclusions   253
References   255

10   HOW DO PEOPLE DISCOVER CONCEPTS?
Roger L. Dominowski 257
The Scope of Theories of Conceptual Behavior   257
Methods of Data Collection   263
Experiment I. Hypotheses. How Many and How Sure   265
Experiment II. Reception Strategies for Simple And
    Conjunctive Concepts   269
Experiment III. Concept Identification While
    Thinking Aloud   276
Concluding Remarks   279

Protocols of Subjects Working Aloud   281
References   286

11   A TRANSFER HYPOTHESIS, WHEREBY LEARNING-TO-LEARN,
EINSTELLUNG, THE PREE, REVERSAL-NONREVERSAL
SHIFTS, AND OTHER CURIOSITIES ARE ELUCIDATED,
Marvin Levine 289
Introduction   289
The Transfer Hypothesis   292
Applications   293
Discussion   300
References   302

12   A SET ANALYSIS THEORY OF BEHAVIOR IN FORMAL
SYLLOGISTIC REASONING TASKS, James R. Erickson 305
Research on Syllogistic Reasoning   307
An Analysis of Syllogistic Reasoning   308
Applications of Models of Syllogistic Reasoning Data   313
A Model for Invalid Syllogisms   322
Discussion   327
References   329

13   THE ORIGINS OF LANGUAGE COMPREHENSION,
Janellen Huttenlocher 331
The Present Study   338
Related Studies   352
Discussion   354
References   367

14   DISCUSSION: SECTION II, Lyle Bourne, James Erickson,
Janellen Huttenlocher, Marvin Levine, Elizabeth Loftus,
Frank Slaymaker, and Gene E. Topper 369
References   376

Author Index 377
Subject Index 383

PREFACE

This book is intended to document some of the best recent theory and data in cognitive psychology. The reputations of its authors are indicative of the quality of its contents. By recording these contributions at this time we hope to direct the course of cognitive psychology and, perhaps, reveal to later generations of psychologists some of the pitfalls they should avoid.

Two areas of cognitive psychology are covered in this book: The first section contains papers on cognition and memory (in the most general sense); the second section, cognition and concept formation (in its most general sense). Few of the papers are easily classified, which, if we are to believe Thomas Kuhn, is one symptom of a paradigm shift. This new paradigm in psychology—which is really not cognition in the historical-philosophic sense at all—could be labeled neocognition, both to identify its distinction and its history. All contributors have freely drawn concepts and techniques from our intellectual predecessors, and one need apply only a small bit of imagination to find the work of Tolman, Ebbinghaus, Thorndike, Hull, Duncker, Hovland, and Piaget guiding our thoughts. However, these important historical concepts and techniques have not been used in the traditional way, but rather they have been applied in a novel way to the complex problems of how we remember, think, learn, perceive, transform information, and acquire language. The stimulating conclusion of this creative meld of techniques and problems is manifest in neocognition as expressed in this book.

The format of the symposium upon which this volume is based was similar to the first Loyola symposium on cognitive psychology. Abstracts of the drafts of chapters contained in this book were presented before an audience of students, faculty, and other interested people. At the conclusion of each day, a discussion was recorded. In addition to those who had presented abstracts of their papers, a Loyola graduate student and a faculty member joined the lively discussion. During the second day Elizabeth Loftus consented to moderate the discussion, and her skillfull performance is thankfully acknowledged. An edited version—what one author described as a closer approximation to standard English—of each day's discussion is included in this book at the conclusion of each section. Frank Restle honored my request to sit in on both discussion groups, as his research and expertise span a number of areas in the study of cognition. I am happily obligated to acknowledge help from a number of sources. Loyola University paid the bill. While most universities are eliminating all unnecessary (and some necessary) programs, foundation resources are not meeting the demand, and government-supported grants are drying up, Loyola, in her great vision, solely supported this open forum for *avant-garde* theory and research in cognitive psychology. As in the past, Gene Zechmeister gave me his sympathetic ear and wise advice—some of which I accepted. Ron Walker again facilitated all levels of convening this symposium, and his considerable role is gratefully acknowledged. Lyle Bourne was instrumental in helping me identify scholars in concept formation and problem solving. His assistance is warmly appreciated. My good friend Luca Koumelis prepared the illustrations for Chapter 2. Because her work was not recognized in the previous volume, I owe her double thanks now.

My fondest praise is reserved for my students. Their unbridled enthusiasm for the symposium, their aggressive pursuit of the ideas represented by our speakers, their conspicuous assistance in all of the numerous details will long be appreciated. Special thanks are due to John Buri, Kathleen Carlson, Donna Goetz, Bill Macey, Richard Ney, and Gene Topper. The help of three secretaries who labored on my behalf, always with less recognition than their talents and effectiveness deserve, is gratefully acknowledged here. They are Kathleen McCaffrey, Dolores Monteleone, and Zelinda Zingaro. Finally, the staff of LEA have labored diligently on this book and their effort is appreciated.

A personal remark: After being immersed in the development of the production of this book (and the symposium on which it is based) for nearly two years I can report the entire affair was a true labor of love. The opportunity to help provide a forum for the distinguished scientists who contributed to this book will never be forgotten, and their indelible impression as entirely compatible colleagues made the effort stimulating and personally rewarding.

ROBERT L. SOLSO

LIST OF CONTRIBUTORS

Numbers in parentheses indicate the pages on which the authors' contributions begin.

Richard C. Atkinson, Stanford University, Stanford, California (101, 219)

Lyle E. Bourne, Jr., University of Colorado, Boulder, Colorado (231, 369)

Roger L. Dominowski, University of Illinois at Chicago Circle, Chicago, Illinois (257)

James L. Erickson, Ohio State University, Columbus, Ohio (305, 369)

Douglas J. Herrmann, Stanford University, Stanford, California (101)

Douglas L. Hintzman, University of Oregon, Eugene, Oregon (77, 219)

Janellen Huttenlocher, Teacher's College, Columbia University, New York, New York (331, 369)

James J. Jenkins, University of Minnesota, Minneapolis, Minnesota (1, 219)

Donald H. Kausler, University of Missouri, Columbia, Missouri (45)

Marvin Levine, State University of New York, Stony Brook, New York (289, 369)

Elizabeth Loftus, University of Washington, Seattle, Washington (369)

William Macey, Loyola University, Chicago, Illinois (219)

Jacqueline Metzler, Stanford University, Stanford, California (147, 219)

Frank Restle, Indiana University, Bloomington, Indiana (203, 219)

Roger N. Shepard, Stanford University, Stanford, California (147, 219)

Frank Slaymaker, Loyola University, Chicago, Illinois (369)

Robert L. Solso, Loyola University, Chicago, Illinois (21, 219)

Eugene Topper, Loyola University, Chicago, Illinois (369)

Keith T. Wescourt, Stanford University, Stanford, California (101)

SECTION I

1

CAN WE HAVE A THEORY OF
MEANINGFUL MEMORY?[1]

James J. Jenkins
University of Minnesota

Many psychologists all over the world are bending their best efforts toward the development of an adequate theory of remembering. As papers in this book so richly illustrate, there is as yet no agreed-upon, satisfactory theory of human learning or memory. Some of us, indeed, even confess that we have no theory that can account for the findings that need to be explained.

It is awkward (and painful) to be in such a position in this day when everyone else seems to have at least a "model" to which he can appeal. This paper is an attempt to explain why I find myself in a "theory-less" position, and to suggest how I think all of us might be able to work out of it. I shall not be able to present a new theory, but perhaps I can enlist your support in the pursuit of one.

Concern with remembering is as old as concern with any branch of psychology. It is common knowledge that the Greek masters in rhetoric had well-developed systems of mnemonics, and, of course, every undergraduate in our courses today learns that immediately after the birth of experimental research in psychophysics, research in remembering and forgetting was initiated by Ebbinghaus. Currently, however, we have a paradox. Remembering is a field with a technology (mnemonics) that is good enough to sell (see your nearest book store). It has several journals of its own. It can lay claim to more experiments than almost any other area of psychology. But thought about memory has a marked tendency to slide back into a simplistic, mechanical theory that has its origins in Greek thought. In many respects, as Tulving and Madigan (1970) pointed out, Aristotle would be comfortable with most current theoretical attempts.

[1]Preparation of this paper was supported in part by grants to the University of Minnesota, Center for Research in Human Learning, from the National Science Foundation (GB-17590), The National Institute of Child Health and Human Development (HD-01136), and the Graduate School of the University of Minnesota.

The writer gratefully acknowledges his debt to his students and colleagues in the development of the ideas in this paper. In particular, he wants to thank David Walsh, Robert Till, Robert Verbrugge and Buford E. Wilson for their many contributions.

1

One must add that although this basic theory has been viewed as vastly unsatisfactory by many investigators, at the same time it is enormously resistant to change. The common associative theory of memory seems to be grounded in the world view of western thought. The world presents itself as a discrete series of events; we respond with discrete mental states (ideas) or behaviors (responses) in a series which copies some aspects of the world's series and which can be activated by some portion of that series at some later time. Of this general pervasive prototheory Ebbinghaus (1913) wrote in 1885:

> The amount of detailed information which an individual has at his command and his theoretical elaborations of the same are mutually dependent; they grow in and through each other. It is because of the indefinite and little specialized character of our knowledge that the theories concerning the processes of memory, reproduction, and association have been up to the present time of so little value for a proper comprehension of those processes. For example, to express our ideas concerning their physical basis we use different metaphors— stored up ideas, engraved images, well-beaten paths. There is only one thing certain about these figures of speech and that is that they are not suitable [p. 518].

But Ebbinghaus' research did not free us of the tyranny of the "figures of speech"; it served, rather, to add the aura of science and the quantitative trappings of statistics to the old metaphors. If we ask how Ebbinghaus could have failed, I believe we see that he was a victim of the presuppositions of the pervasive common theory he was trying to overcome. He accepted the notion that "things" became "associated" (as he had been well taught by the British Associationists in his days as a philosophy student). He operated on the reasonable assumption that he should avoid the contamination of the knowledge of "things" and their interassociations that the subject brought to the experiment. Therefore, to study learning and memorial processes by themselves, he decided to use unfamiliar "things"—nonsense syllables. In a sense, this decision which Ebbinghaus hoped would ensure his experimental success, effectively barred him from studying the most interesting aspects of memory—how the new materials relate to the knowledge that the subject brings to the experiment. Ebbinghaus so firmly closed the door against meaning that he could not see the importance of his own observation about the nonsense syllables:

> . . . the homogeniety of the series of syllables falls considerably short of what might be expected of it. These series exhibit very important and almost incomprehensible variation as to ease or difficulty with which they are learned. It even appears from this point of view as if the differences between sense and nonsense material were not nearly so great as one would be inclined a priori to imagine [p. 23].

One must conjecture that Ebbinghaus committed a particularly disastrous error. His method, his materials, and his orientation combined to hide the otherwise overwhelming effects of the most powerful variable in natural memorial functioning—the effects of knowledge. If one studies any field after first removing the variable that normally accounts for most of the variance, one is likely to obtain odd results that seem amiss or unusual in everyday life where that variable holds sway. And, to the extent that the excluded variable interacts in significant ways with the other variables, the findings from the laboratory studies will appear to us to be misleading or capricious when we view them in other settings.

As a one-time industrial psychologist, I know that when one works on man-machine systems, one is always told to study the major sources of the variance first, because (due to the nature of the cumulation of variable errors in systems) nothing else will make any realistic difference in the output of the system as long as the major source of the variance is left uncontrolled. If one takes this view of the experimental enterprise, one might conclude that Ebbinghaus and his successors have done a great deal of the refined work that we must do some day, but have failed to explicate the workings of the massive variable (or host of variables) that is central to remembering—the notion of knowledge. That is, while the work may eventually be of great value, it cannot be applied until we understand the major variable which Ebbinghaus tried to avoid studying.

Some hint of the power of knowledge as a variable is provided in the work of the last three decades on the topic of "meaningfulness." The term is ordinarily applied as if it were some attribute of the stimulus used in our research. But it is clear that meaningfulness is not any sort of physical attribute of a stimulus. It is customarily defined and measured in a Response-Response fashion. That is, one appraises meaningfulness by collecting one set of subject responses to some set of stimuli, and then using those responses to predict other behaviors, often far removed from the first. I would argue that this variable and others like it (i.e., association value, familiarity, and, probably, frequency) are indirect measures of a narrow aspect of subjects' knowledge. Obviously, such measures should not be treated in such a way that anyone could suppose that "meaningfulness" was an attribute of the stimulus itself.

Meaningfulness must be regarded as a variable to be explained, not as an explanation. The enormous range of meaningfulness that one finds in nonsense syllables and paralogs is correlated with many phenomena in learning and remembering. Setting forth those facts is not an explanation of them, it merely asserts that some powerful variable has been calibrated. The variable must be "unpacked" in some psychologically relevant way. In the case of nonsense syllables, for example, meaningfulness appears to be almost entirely a function of similarity to pronounced English words and of similarity to English orthography. This, in turn, suggests that the real source of variation in meaningfulness lies in the meanings encoded in words and in the knowledge of rule-systems governing both the syllable structure and the orthography that carry the subjects to word possibilities (Jenkins, 1966).

FORGETTING

Let us consider for a moment the consequences of trying to screen meaning and knowledge out of memory experiments. Certainly, the most famous finding of Ebbinghaus is the "curve of forgetting." As every *Psychology 1* student knows, Ebbinghaus demonstrated that one forgets 70 to 80% of what he learns within 24 hours. I seriously doubt that this is true in general.

There are two curious observations we must make about this finding. First, it flies in the face of experience. (But experience can be wrong. How often do we keep score? Maybe we must overlearn the things that we really want to remember?) Second, every experimenter who has tried to reproduce this effect knows that it doesn't work when you use naive subjects. On the first list they have learned, subjects are likely to *recall* 75 to 85% after 24 hours, instead of forgetting that amount!

However, if we persevere we can duplicate his results. The subjects, like Ebbinghaus himself, must be trained to behave "properly." With well-trained and experienced subjects, Ebbinghaus's generalization is verified. Indeed, if one is willing to keep after the subjects, one can get even poorer 24-hour recall by piling on more and more lists of the same kinds of materials (Underwood, 1957), until finally the subject has virtually no recall of the list that he learned to criterion the previous day (see Keppel, Postman, & Zavortink, 1968).

The customary explanation of this phenomenon is in terms of proactive interference, that is, it is supposed that the earlier learning interferes *in some way* with the recall of the current list. The nature of the interference is not specified. Notice that this (like "meaningfulness") is a finding begging to be explored, not an explanation in itself.

We might tell a different story about the phenomenon. Perhaps the subject is doing something different on the successive tasks and that what he is doing simply happens to lead to less successful 24-hour recall. The subject's immediate task is to reach some particular performance criterion—usually, to be able to recite the list or make the appropriate responses to stimuli. As he performs this task again and again, he learns that he can do this without going to the effort of making the materials meaningful, without noting "interesting" characteristics of the list, without bothering with mnemonics (which the speed of the list makes difficult), etc. As a result he stops "overpowering" the list as he did on the early trials and manages with minimal effort to give the short-term performance that he must give (because otherwise the experimenter won't let him go). For reasons that may or may not be important, the minimal procedures that give adequate performance on the short-term nonsense-syllable task have disastrous effects on the long-term task. However, performance on the long-term task has no consequences for the subject, so it does not make any difference (except to the psychologist who takes it seriously).

About ten years ago Lynn Brown and I conducted such a study of forgetting with paired-associate nonsense-syllable lists. Each day the subject tried to recall the list from the day before, and learned a new list which was tested for recall the next day. The study ran for 16 days, and we observed that 24-hour recall started at a very high level but by the 16th day had fallen to about 25%. We supposed at that time that the poorer recall might be a consequence of the faster learning, because it was obvious that the subjects were learning each list more rapidly than the one before. The average number of trials to learn the first list to criterion was 22, but the number of trials needed to learn the 16th list was less than 11.

To equate for number of trials and frequency of seeing the nonsense syllables, we ran a control group in which every day each subject was required to go through that day's list the same number of times as he had needed to learn the first list. This meant that on the average the subjects were receiving 100% overlearning by the time they got to the 16th list. (They were getting the list correct by the 11th trial but were required to complete 22 trials before they were allowed to leave.) We had hoped to determine the role of frequency of exposure in the 24-hour recall task. To our surprise, we found that even this remarkable overlearning had no appreciable effect on the course of 24-hour recall scores. The overlearning group was *just as poor* as the group that had learned each list to the usual criterion each day. The finding suggests that the change in *what* the subjects were doing was considerably more important than how much time they had to do it, or how many times they did it.

Like Ebbinghaus, many of us have continued to work with unrelated materials and nonmeaningful tasks. We attempt (again like Ebbinghaus) to force our subjects to disclose pure processes by eliminating meaningful contents. In essence, we guarantee that there is no way for subjects to do the kinds of things that they presumably excel in, or the kinds of things that they might do in ordinary learning situations, or the kinds of things that they have trained themselves to do in daily life. We make them assume the role of a highly-limited, special-purpose machine, and they accommodate us by doing so.

What, then, have we learned from the performance of trained subjects on these specialized tasks? How one answers that question depends on one's assumptions. If one believes that all learning and remembering is "cut from the same cloth," then it does not make any difference what the task constraints and materials are; we are learning about the process of learning and remembering. But if one believes that materials interact with strategies and processes, then one is in a much more difficult position. The most hopeful situation that one might hypothesize is that the phenomena are the same for all kinds of material (e.g., the same kinds of transfer and interference will be found), and that one only has to define the units on which the phenomena are observed to see the regularities in each new kind of material. In this case a general theory of learning and remembering must be set forth in detail so that one can specify in a clear but abstract fashion what the appropriate units are for any kind of material of interest, as well as what the general phenomena or "laws" are.

How likely is it that either of these common assumptions about learning and remembering is true? Rather unlikely, I fear. Just reflect for a few minutes on what the differences are in a particular task, like serial learning, as we change materials.

Suppose that we start with a 15-item list of triple consonants (CCCs). The rules of the game say that these assemblies of letters and the order in which the triplets appear should be "random" to avoid any possibility that there is some "other way" to perform the task. In practice, what is normally done is to generate sets of CCCs and have other subjects work through them (doing meaningfulness rating, association-value rating, etc.), in order that we may weed out the triples that are "good sequences," acronyms, alphabetical sequences, rhymes, etc. In short, we take out, as far as possible, all the useful constraints except those that may be idiosyncratic to the individual subject. We have now assured that the subject who is trying to "learn the list" must master 15 "mini-sequences," the CCC combinations, and then assemble those sequences into a chainlike structure, the list.

The procedures that we have followed virtually guarantee that this task is unrelated to anything that subjects are normally asked to do (except perhaps learning the alphabet). The only way that facts about this task can be related to ordinary problems is to have a theory of such problems that gives them an analysis in terms of associative chains of discrete elements. That is, to apply our knowledge it would be necessary to be able to consider the more complex activities as just large collections of simple chains. But this is just what the linguists, ethologists, and Piagetians have been telling us we cannot do. Scholars from these and other fields have won increasing agreement over the last two decades that associative-chain analyses are inappropriate—or even wildly incorrect. To the extent that these scholars and their arguments are judged correct, the applicability of the learning and remembering data from our simple experiments is drastically limited to very simple situations.

If we now move up to the level of even the lowly nonsense syllable, it becomes apparent at once that we engage a richer set of constraints. First of course, we arrange that the triplets are drawn from two classes of letters, the so-called consonant and vowel letters. We fix an order sequence, CVC, and are immediately introduced to the effects of "structure." We note the effects of new variables that are apparently dependent on the orthography, syllable structure, and lexicon of English. For example, if we ask the subjects to pronounce the "syllables," we see that an elaborate, learned rule-system is brought into play. Consider the following instances: The consonant letter "C" is read by subjects as /s/ in front of the letters "i" and "e" and as /k/ in front of the letters "a," "o," and "u" (e.g., CIL, CEL, CAL, COL, CUL). The letter "X" tends to be read as /z/ when it comes first and as /ks/ when it comes last (e.g., XIL, LIX). The vowels tend to be given the "short" pronunciation (LIX is read "licks" not "likes"), and so on. Given this conversion to syllable form, the meaningfulness variables come into play with great force. Some syllables are "real" words known to the subject (POD); some are "real" but unknown (DOP); some are similar to real words in spelling or pronunciation (LIX); etc.

Of course we set to work again to screen out the influence of these important variables so we can go back to "basic learning work." But the variable is so powerful that we cannot just discard a few easily learned combinations. We find that we have a continuum from unpronounceable combinations that defy orthographic rules all the way up to real words. The variable is as great in its impact on learning and retention as the difference between our best and poorest subjects.

Obviously, it calls for study and analysis, but the tradition of our field is to "control for it"—get it out of our experiments—or to account for it in some mechanical way (like letter frequency counts), which implies that the source of the variable is in the stimulus in some sense and not in the knowledge that the subject brings to the experiment.

The naive subject tries to "make sense" of the nonsense syllables (and remembers much more than he needs for a long time). The practiced subject (I suggest) abandons these strategies that buy him little in terms of his immediate task, and he becomes an efficient machine for this specialized behavior.

If we move from nonsense syllables to words, we find still another situation. The problems of integration of the individual sequences that constitute "items" have now disappeared. The subject brings that knowledge to the experiment as a result of years of experiences with English. The orthographic rules, the linguistic constraints on syllable structure, the existence of this particular assembly as an item in the lexicon, the denotations and connotations of the term, its usual part of speech status, and "standard" circumstances under which the word is used are available to the subject for potential use in regenerating the word, relating it to other words, or whatever the task seems to demand. As before, we may require that the subject learn some given sequence of these materials, a sequence that is carefully chosen so as to avoid meaningful subsets. But surely his resources in this case are far greater than the resources he had available for this portion of the task with CCCs. And, perhaps, just as many more dimensions are available to him for constructing the list structure, so also there are many more dimensions that may be important in determining transfer and interference from many more "unrelated" tasks.

If at this point we assign some other arbitrary task that we often use, such as free recall, we will be impressed with the fact that the subject is trying with all of his might to get some order and structure into the materials we have given him to work with. The phenomena of associative and category clustering appear and, where there are no clear relations in the materials, we see the subject generate his own subjective organizations.

If we give the subject time to organize or if we pick items that are already related, we will be impressed with the subject's ability to make use of mnemonics, existing associative relationships, visualization, logical relations, etc. In short, we see (perhaps for the first time in our hypothetical series) the enormous influence of instructions and materials, on the one hand, and knowledge and skills, on the other, in creating involved and complex interactions as the subject attempts to solve the learning and retention problems.

As we go to more complex materials such as phrases, sentences, and paragraphs, we have an opportunity to see more complicated integrative phenomena. If possible events are described, we expect to see in the learning and retention we study a variety of effects that derive from what the subject knows or believes about the world. If inevitable consequences follow the states of affairs described in our materials, we may expect the subjects to anticipate them and "recall" them. If sentences are ungrammatical, we may see normalizing effects. If sentences are grammatical but anomalous, we may expect the grammatical structure to be preserved while the anomalies furnish problems of sense. If the sentences are grammatical and reasonable but unrelated to each other, we may expect to see phenomena limited to sentences as "objects." But if sentences are related, we may see the total event or episode as the "object," and the sentence effects may be subordinated or completely overridden by the phenomena relevant to appropriate paraphrase in the service of understanding ideas. The phenomena that we see in these experiments are considerably different from those we focused on earlier, with the list of triple consonants.

How can we hope to cope with the staggering range of phenomena that we see as we change tasks and materials? Three kinds of proposals may be considered to deal with this diversity. First, it can be argued that the phenomena of learning and remembering are the same (in some underlying sense) for all materials. It is only the surface description that is different. Presumably this view would say that the classic phenomena of learning and retention (e.g., proactive interference) will be found in the "appropriate" units at the higher levels.

A second view is that the phenomena are emergent and therefore different in kind from level to level. This view should argue that each phenomenon must be studied separately at its own appropriate level.

A third view might try to find a middle ground between the first two by arguing that each level differs in the kind of knowledge that may be employed and in the way that such knowledge interacts with the kinds of tasks that are possible at each level. In general, this view should argue that new and more complicated phenomena will be seen at each level, but that they might be predictable from the study of the relevant structures of knowledge and the way that these structures could be employed in the performance of tasks.

Many psychologists either hold the first position as being the most parsimonious or have chosen it indirectly by limiting themselves to a particular level and a particular kind of phenomenon. They stand on the plausible ground that one must first understand one piece of the whole thoroughly. If one cannot achieve that, then one cannot hope to understand the whole eventually.

Another group has chosen to make content-free processing models, in the hope that the content being processed is not crucial to the enterprise, or that new content just adds more to the basic processers.

Those in the Gestalt tradition, of course, argue that only holistic approaches will be fruitful and seem to feel that perceptual and memorial processes will turn out to be much alike in the long run.

As an investigator who has struggled with learning and remembering at several levels, and who has even done perceptual scaling with verbal materials, I confess that I have difficulty finding a secure place to stand. I would *like* to assert that the phenomena of each level are duplicated at the next level *if* one knows how to make the right kind of general description of the phenomena *and* if one can perform the necessary projection operations on the other levels. But in the dark hours of the night when my optimism is at a low ebb, I entertain the thought that the phenomena are emergent, and that they do indeed depend on our understanding specific interactions of instructions, tasks, materials, knowledge, and skills.

In the cheering light of day, it appears to me that some middle course is the most defensible one. I cannot see how a simple list of relevant phenomena or a diagram of content-free processing is going to be sufficient for the task. But I cannot believe that the organism is so complicated as to be unpredictable if we try to deal with what it knows. I think that we are going to have to work out ways of representing knowledge and its relation to classes of tasks that we are interested in. We are going to have to discover what skills can be brought into the service of memorial tasks, and how they are so brought. We are going to have to give descriptions of the conditions of acquisition and the requirements of criterial tasks that will enable us to determine what the subject did and what good having done that will be to him later.

While I have great respect and admiration for the investigator who stays at one level, I think we must spread our net more widely, rather than more narrowly, if we are to understand learning and remembering. My colleague, John Flavell, who is studying the emergence of memory in children, argues persuasively that remembering can involve any or all of the cognitive processes and capabilities. We group "memory" tasks together because of our concern with the intention to remember and our concern with the accuracy of the hoped-for result, but there may be no limit on the mechanisms employed in the service of that intention to produce that result. Remembering may be no more than a highly abstract task description and may not implicate any particular mechanism or have much commonality from one instance to another as the materials and circumstances involved are changed.

EXPERIMENTS ON THE INTERACTION OF TASKS AND FREE RECALL

In an effort to give some substance to this rather nebulous argument, I am going to present a series of studies that have served to focus our attention on the problems I have been discussing. The experiments are interesting examples, because they are well within the learning-remembering tradition and use ordinary materials. They are experiments on intentional and incidental learning with a free-recall criterion using single English words. There is nothing mysterious, complicated, or *avant-garde* about them. We should all be at home with such studies. Yet, I will argue these experiments pose problems for us that are not solved by our analyses of nonsense-syllable experiments (i.e., that the word level is different), and that they show the extraordinary power of particular kinds of orienting tasks in affecting performance on a criterial task.

The story begins about 1966 with research by Tom Hyde (then a student at Minnesota, now on the staff at Case Western Reserve). Hyde was interested in the question of whether associative clustering in the free recall of lists of related words was influenced by the orienting tasks performed by the subjects while the words were being presented. Would a subject who was paying attention to meaning show more clustering in recall than a subject who was concentrating on some other aspect of the words, their orthographic form, for example? The question was of interest for several reasons. First, there was the general question of whether one had to "notice" the associations for them to affect the structure of recall. Second, there was the question about the locus of the clustering effect. Was it an input, storage, or output phenomenon? Third, there was the question as to the effect of the intention to recall, and whether it interacted with the clustering effect.

The results of many experiments were summarized in our first publication (Hyde & Jenkins, 1969). They can be briefly summarized here. When the subject performed a meaningful task (rating each word for pleasantness or unpleasantness), both the total amount of recall and the proportion of associative clustering were as great as the recall and clustering shown by the group of intentional learners who performed no special orienting task at all! The groups that were required to process the word they heard as an orthographic object (estimate letter length or say if the word had an "e" or a "g" in it) showed very poor recall and little clustering.

The groups that performed orienting tasks were divided in the traditional way between those who knew that they would be asked to recall later and those who were uninformed. Prior knowledge of whether recall would be required had little effect on either the recall or the clustering. In addition, we ran the study under short (2 sec) and long (4 sec) presentation times and with a double presentation (twice at 2 sec each), and under each condition we found the same results.

We concluded then (as the literature had concluded long before) that "intention to learn" was not a very important variable (see Postman, 1964). On the other hand, it was clear that the contrast between tasks requiring meaningful analysis and tasks requiring nonmeaningful analysis was very powerful in determining the structure and amount of recall. (Structure and amount were confounded in this study of course.)

Our colleagues raised the question as to whether the subjects who performed orthographic processing were not penalized somehow. After all, they had to retrieve the spelling of each word and deal with an analysis of the word into subunits (letters). Obviously, it could be argued that this was a disadvantage in number of elements considered and inappropriateness of the analyzed elements for the recall task. To answer this objection, Carroll Johnston and I (Johnston & Jenkins, 1971) conducted a study which contrasted a meaningful operation with a "formal" operation that did not require analysis into letters. For the meaningful task, we had subjects give adjectives that were appropriate to the nouns in the list, and nouns that were appropriate to the adjectives. For the nonmeaningful or formal task, subjects were directed to supply rhymes for the words in the list, thus encouraging them to treat the word as a complete unit but directing their attention to its sound as opposed to its meaning. We were pleased that the results were similar to those of the first experiments. The group that gave relevant nouns and adjectives showed as much associative clustering as the intentional control group, and nearly as much total recall. The rhyming subjects showed little clustering and little recall.

It now seemed clear that we had a major effect on our hands. The differences we were finding in clustering and recall were on the order of two-to-one between meaningful and nonmeaningful orienting tasks. Further, there was the remarkable absolute level of recall to consider. The incidental subjects doing the pleasantness-rating task were recalling as much as intentional subjects who were performing no orienting tasks at all. While we had been prepared to find little effect of "intention to learn" when we contrasted two groups doing orienting tasks, we had not really expected that doing a meaningful task could compensate for both intention and the presumed loss of time that the task entailed. That was a surprise.

Furthermore, a close study of the data suggested that the excellent recall of the groups that were performing the meaningful tasks was not entirely due to increased utilization of the associative structures available in the materials. The meaningful tasks seemed to be associated with an absolutely higher level of recall of individual words.

Hyde and I proceeded to more experimentation, this time using both associatively related and unrelated lists of words (i.e., a list that offered obvious associative structures and a list that offered no obvious structures). We also broadened the variety of orienting tasks to give us a better indication of the general nature of tasks that were advantageous and disadvantageous. We added *estimating the frequency of usage* of the word as a meaningful task. (The semantic nature of this task can be debated; we already knew that Postman, Adams, and Bohm (1956) had found high clustering in recall with this orienting task, so it was easy for us to persuade ourselves that it must be meaningful. We suppose that it involves thinking about the meaning of the word and estimating how often one encounters that meaning or referent.) We added two tasks that entailed determining the part of speech of the word (giving it a label as a part of speech, and fitting it into a semantically impoverished sentence, "It is _____" *vs* "It is the _____"). And we used the old standbys, pleasantness rating, *e*-checking (checking for the letter e), and length estimation.

The results confirmed the earlier work and aided in its interpretation. The nonsemantic tasks produced poor recall in both the related and the unrelated lists and resulted in low proportions of associative clustering in the related list. The semantic tasks were as good or nearly as good as the intentional learning instruction in producing recall on both lists and resulted in high clustering on the related list.

The intentional-incidental difference was nonexistent on the unrelated words and just barely significant on the related list (i.e., "intention" interacted with the orienting tasks only on the list that afforded associative structures).

The overall best description of the list effect is that the presence of the organizational structure in the "related" list acted as an enhancing agent in detecting (or magnifying) differences, so on the related list all effects were more dramatic. But the basic point of the experiment emerged clearly; difference in the two types of orienting tasks, (semantic *vs* nonsemantic), resulted in a major difference in amount recalled, even when there was no obvious organizational structure in the materials.

It is of some interest to note that the syntactic tasks affected recall in the same way as the orthographic or meaningless tasks; subjects performing all these tasks were generally poor in both recall and clustering. The popular belief that parts of speech are defined semantically (e.g., "A noun is the name of a person, place, or thing") finds no support in these data. It is also important to note that popular word associates, such as those used in this experiment, usually share the same part of speech classification. One might therefore suppose that this orienting task would facilitate associative clustering even if it did not assist in overall recall, but no such facilitation was observed. (For a full report of these experiments, see Hyde and Jenkins, 1973.)

By this time we had a good deal of feedback from colleagues who offered two common explanations for our findings. One explanation was that the semantic orienting tasks were easier than the nonsemantic orienting tasks. It was argued that this difference permitted the semantic subjects *more time* to rehearse or think about the words. The other explanation was just the opposite: The semantic orienting tasks required *more effort,* and thus the subjects worked on the words more, attended more, and processed more. All this effort, then, resulted in better recall. The first hypothesis we can call the *time* hypothesis, and the second hypothesis we can term the *effort* hypothesis. Both hypotheses threatened to involve us in a tedious effort to measure "time" or "effort" of tasks; an effort we were reluctant to undertake.

David Walsh (Walsh & Jenkins, 1973) came up with an ingenious (if brute force) solution to the dilemma of being doubly damned on task difficulty. He proposed that we combine the orienting tasks in pairs without increasing the interstimulus interval. If *time* were the crucial variable, then all combined tasks would produce poorer recall than that associated with either of the component tasks alone. For example, if pleasantness rating (said to be easy) were combined with *e*-checking (said to be difficult), then the joint task must be more difficult and more time consuming still. The resulting recall should therefore be poorer than the recall for *e*-checking alone. If, on the other hand, *effort* were important, then combining tasks should increase the level of recall. The subject would be required to work harder, notice more things about the words, and process them in more ways. This should result in better recall. (One could make additional comments about multiple encodings here, too). In brief, one hypothesis predicted the combined tasks should result in poorer recall than either single task, and the other hypothesis predicted that the combined tasks should result in better recall than either single task.

We, of course, stuck to our guns (and our biases) and merely asserted that semantic processing was good for recall and nonsemantic processing was not. Combining two nonsemantic tasks, then, should result in no improvement in recall, but combining a nonsemantic task with a semantic task should raise the level of recall to the level of the semantic task alone.

Walsh and I (Walsh & Jenkins, 1973) ran a series of studies using a list of low frequency, unrelated words. We ran each orienting task singly, as well as all possible pairwise combinations. We also examined both orders of task presentation (e.g. pleasantness rating followed by e-checking, and e-checking followed by pleasantness rating).

The results were clear cut. Both the time hypothesis and the effort hypothesis were defeated. The semantic task increased the recall associated with the nonsemantic task when it was coupled with one, but the nonsemantic tasks did not act together to increase recall over either one alone. (The order of the tasks when they were coupled together made no difference in amount recalled.) It seems safe to conclude that it is the semantic processing itself that is important in our experiments, not some parameter of the task, like time or effort, that is independent of the content or type of processing involved in the task.

Following the technique of the Walsh and Jenkins (1973) study, Hyde (1973) performed an independent test of the time and effort hypotheses with somewhat different tasks on an associatively related list of words. He obtained the same results. Recall was facilitated by each semantic orienting task, regardless of whether the task was performed alone or in combination with another task. Performing two semantic tasks in the same time interval conferred no advantage in recall over a single semantic task, and performing a semantic task and a nonsemantic task in the same interval conferred no disadvantage. The pattern in associative clustering was essentially the same as the pattern in recall.

We emerged from these experiments with considerably more confidence in the designation that we were applying to our independent variables (the semantic tasks) and with an expanded list of tasks. At this point our knowledge of task effects was as follows:

Facilitative tasks (those resulting in recall and clustering at approximately the level of an intentional learning group with no orienting task)

    Rating words for pleasantness (versus unpleasantness)

    Rating words for activity (versus passivity)

    Writing relevant adjectives or nouns

    Estimating frequency of usage

Non-facilitative tasks (those resulting in one half to one third as much recall and clustering as the facilitative tasks)

    Letter checking (''e'' or ''g'' usually)

    Estimating letter length of words

Writing rhyming words
Syllable counting
Voice identification (four voices)
Identifying part of speech
Testing word in sentence slot

By this time there did not remain many good counterhypotheses about controlling variables. One we did hear, however, was that the "set" of the subjects had been altered by the orienting tasks in some global way that affected recall. This is somewhat vague, but it appears to express the concern that the instructions for the semantic tasks created a general learning set that was not created by the nonsemantic instructions. In some versions, this hypothesis is not testable, but in its most specific form it is.

Robert Till took the suggestion that tasks be varied from one word to another within the same list. (I believe that this suggestion was made by Endel Tulving in a conversation about these experiments. Since it works so well, it is a pleasure to attribute it to him in any event.) Till developed a "cuing" technique for the orienting tasks. The subject is given a list of tasks (say two to four), each of which is designated by a letter. After he is instructed in performing the tasks named by the letters, he hears a list of words presented via tape recorder. Each word is followed in a half second by a letter designating what task is to be performed on that word. The subject performs that task and waits for the next word. Since the pairing of tasks and words is arbitrary, all possible pairings may be distributed to the same group of subjects randomly. Thus, when the subjects hear "TABLE (pause) A," one subject sees that he is to rate the word for pleasantness, another subject sees that he is to check if there is an "e" in the word, another subject estimates letter length, etc. The next word may be "SICKNESS (pause) C." The first subject now estimates letter length, the second rates for pleasantness, and the third checks to see if the word has an "e" in it. In this fashion, all subjects perform all tasks, and all tasks may be counterbalanced over all positions and words. If desired, each subject can be used for his own control, or the word-position unit may be taken as the control item and all tasks compared with words held constant.

The result of the experiment was most encouraging. With a list of unrelated words, Till and Jenkins (1973) found that the results originally seen in the between-subject experiments were readily obtained in within-subject experiments. Each subject recalled about twice as many of the words that he had rated for pleasantness as he did words on which he had performed *e*-checking or length estimation.

Richard Jenkins and I repeated Till's work with three semantic tasks (rating for pleasantness-unpleasantness, importance-unimportance, and strength-weakness) and one nonsemantic task (the venerable *e*-checking) and found the same result. Ratings that required semantic processing were associated with about twice as much recall as the nonsemantic task. The effect was consistent both within subjects and within words.

Till went further with the cuing technique and showed that one can "break up" the associative clustering in a list of associates by having the subject perform one task (semantic) on one word of the pair and another task (nonsemantic) on the other word of the pair. If the same task is performed on both pair members, clustering is high when the task is semantic but low when the task is nonsemantic (see Till & Jenkins, 1973).

Recently Till, Randy Diehl, and I have been asking whether the tasks have to be *identical* to facilitate clustering or just of the *same type*. The answer now seems to be that if any two semantic tasks are performed on the members of an associative pair, we will observe associative clustering in recall. (That is, if one rates one pair member for "pleasant-unpleasant" and the other pair member for "important-unimportant," associative clustering is facilitated. Clustering is at the same level that it is when both pair members are rated for pleasantness or both rated for importance.) The important ingredient seems to be that the tasks bring the semantic properties of the word into consideration, not that the tasks be identical.

Buford E. Wilson, who is currently a postdoctoral fellow at our Center, has run a number of interesting variations and extensions of these experiments. For example, he has run repeated trials of presentation and recall with the subjects repeating the orienting task each time the words are presented and attempting recall before the next list presentation. As expected, the pleasantness-rating group starts with the highest recall (even above the intentional group with no orienting task), but the intentional group passes all the orienting task groups on the second trial. All the groups show rapid learning of the list, however, as measured by the rapid increase in average recall over the four trials.

An interesting finding in Wilson's research is that the index of subjective organization grows more rapidly in the intentional group than in the groups performing orienting tasks. Thus, it may be suggested that the major effect of the orienting tasks (on a list of unrelated words) is to make the words available for recall but not necessarily to provide an organization for recall.

REFLECTIONS ON THE EXPERIMENTS

Perhaps at this point we should stop and ask what inferences we can draw from this series of experiments that bear on the general problems we were originally discussing.

First, it is surely clear that memory is not an automatic consequence of being exposed to external events. Further, it is not an automatic consequence of having responded to the events. Still further, it is not an automatic consequence of having intended to remember the events.

Perhaps no one believes anymore that memory is automatic, or that responding guarantees memory, or that intention to learn is a major variable in recall, but it seems prudent to set the record straight. It seems most parsimonious to say that events in the world *offer opportunities* for certain kinds of activities and make possible certain kinds of experiences. The events alone do not in any reasonable sense *cause* these activities or experiences. The argument is parallel to that of Gibson's (1966) on perception. The world affords support for certain kinds of experiences, but the organism has to "pick up" the relevant aspects of the world. This assumes the organism must be appropriately equipped (by tuning, attention, past history, etc.) to have the appropriate experience, and it assumes that the events in the world have structures that afford such opportunities to the organism.

Second, it appears to be the case (surprisingly) that orienting tasks are quite powerful in "setting the switches" with respect to the kind of experience that a word will provide to a subject. In our experiments, we have often used time intervals that would have permitted the subject to perform his assigned orienting task and (if he were in an "intentional" group) go on to do anything that seemed fruitful for recall during his remaining time. (The fact that compound tasks that include a semantic task yield good recall argues that the subjects who have a single nonsemantic task *could* do much better if they put their time to efficient use.) We must conclude that the subjects do not know what to do, or simply do not change what they are doing without the demands of a specific task. One would suppose that this is not a limitation on what people *can* do (witness the compound task) but rather a limitation on what they *do* do.

Third, some orienting tasks serve memory as well as, or better than, the activities that subjects engage in when they are asked to learn and are given no orienting task. In almost all of our experiments, for example, the pleasantness-rating task has produced slightly better recall than the instruction to learn (with no task to perform). While it may turn out that pleasantness rating is the best possible orienting task, it seems unlikely that we should have blundered on this phenomenon and found the single best case at the same time. Thus, the possibility is open to us that we can direct a subject to perform certain tasks on a set of materials and by this direction produce better recall (even unintentionally) than the subject could produce for himself intentionally. (This is obviously similar to the claim of the various mnemonic "systems" but since they demand intention to learn and seem to be essentially arbitrary and meaningless, we ought to be able to do better than such systems when we come to understand the fifth point below.)

Fourth, in this set of experiments content-free and process-free variables such as time, effort, and "intention to learn" seem to have little or nothing to do with remembering. It may be, of course, that the absence of these variables is a condemnation of the "unnaturalness" of the experiments, rather than a denial of the role of these variables in the course of human learning. All that we can say here is that such variables play no appreciable role in the experiments, compared to the nature of the orienting task.

Fifth, in the studies we have conducted so far, considering the meaning of an item in the course of executing an orienting task is far and away the most important thing one can do with respect to effective recall. Other experiences that focus on the orthographic, phonetic, acoustic, or syntactic knowledge of the subject are only weakly available to the subject as he faces the criterial recall task.

At the present time it is not clear why meaning should dominate recall in this fashion. Craik and Lockhart (1972) have suggested that semantic judgments require processing at "deeper levels" and hence leave "more permanent traces." I am very reluctant to accept the implication that processing is unidirectional and that "depth" and "lasting" qualities are necessarily related. I am sympathetic to their position but cannot believe that things will turn out to be as simple as they postulate.

A different hypothesis might be that it is just the nature of the human mind that when symbols are employed, meanings are ordinarily computed and forms are ordinarily discarded. In a symbol, it is true by definition that meanings are crucial and forms are secondary (and arbitrary). Meaning must somehow be "carried," but form as the "carrier" may normally be "dumped" rather than retained to overtax and clutter up the system. Thus, what we see in the experiments may be a reflection of what is normally demanded of the species and, perhaps, what has been evolutionarily shaped along with our general capacity to symbolize.

A third hypothesis is the most prosaic. It may be that we are working with a special class of subjects who have developed skill at manipulating, storing, and retrieving meaningful semantic information (if you will forgive those metaphors in a presentation that is supposed to be indifferent to the information-processing point of view). Perhaps it is merely a matter of practice and skill. Thus, when we ask these subjects to recall items after they have pursued some sort of meaningful task, they can readily do so merely because they are accustomed to doing exactly that. Only rarely do our subjects try to retrieve a voice, a set of words that share the presence or absence of "e," sets of words that are n-letters long, words by part-of-speech categories, etc.

If it is really the case that we are dealing with a skill and that recall could just as well be based on any other set of noticeable features, then it should be of great interest to apply our experiments to experts who specialize in crossword puzzles, clerks who alphabetize for a living, puzzle-solvers who spend time doing anagrams, gamesmen who play Scrabble, etc. Similarly, it would appear to be interesting to work out other criterial performances where we might expect to observe differences in favor of other orienting tasks.

Finally, a fourth hypothesis (somewhat like the second) might be that the meaning code is the most efficient and powerful representation of an event because the cognitive systems are most efficiently organized in the service of just such codes. The meaning codes stand in the middle, so to speak, of the network of systems that can be employed to produce imagery, to paraphrase, to describe functions, to list attributes, to retrieve associates, to perform linguistic analysis, to construct rhymes, etc. The business of the code is to deal with meanings in whatever way is required, so this code has access to all other systems in the sense that they are ordinarily employed in the service of a meaningful end. Thus, the chief difference between the various orienting tasks may be one of richness made available by the analysis needed to perform the task. The nonsemantic tasks may be poor for recall and clustering because they are weak, specialized, or impoverished codings of the event in the world. They serve the immediate purpose, and the orienting task is discharged. But regardless of the effort, difficulty, or time consumed, they are still weak representations. They do not have access to the variety of systems; they do not hold a central position in the semantic domain where retrieval normally starts in daily life.

CURRENT DIRECTIONS

Well, where do we go from here? Impressed with the "naturalness" of our findings to date, we are pressing on in the direction of finding more powerful demonstrations of the effects of *comprehension of meaning* on what one remembers and how it is organized. The research is turning up fascinating evidence in a variety of experimental settings.

Buford E. Wilson and John Bransford have informally shown that the recall power of pleasantness rating can be improved by asking for pleasantness rating *in a given situation*. ("Rate each word as to how pleasant or unpleasant it would be if you were on a desert island.") Bransford and Nancy McCarrell have completed a study that shows that one remembers words better when one has validated some unusual use for the referent (for example, answering the question "Can a brick be used as a door stop?" as opposed to the question, "Does a brick have corners?"). We are flirting with the notion that the construction of a meaning, or the evaluation of a personal aspect of a meaning are the important ingredients in having an experience that will be remembered, but we have not yet been able to show that the meanings must be personal constructions. We are half-way convinced that Arnheim's (1969) distinction between synthetic and analytic aspects of meaning is important in determining remembering (and surely our best tasks are those that he would call synthetic), but we do not yet have a crucial case that is convincing.

A FINAL ILLUSTRATION

I would like to close with an experiment that illustrates how we are trying to think about comprehension as a function of particular forms and contents of communications. This ingenious experiment has just been completed by Robert Verbrugge and Nancy McCarrell. These investigators asked themselves what it was that a listener would have to understand if he were trying to comprehend a metaphorical sentence. Consider a metaphor like, "Skyscrapers are the giraffes of a city." This sentence presumably requires the listener to select some relation that is appropriate to both the *topic* of the sentence, "skyscrapers," and the *vehicle* of the metaphor, "giraffes." Such a relation is called the *ground* of a metaphor. Here the *ground* would have to be something like "tall compared to surrounding things." In contrast, in a sentence like "Skyscrapers are honeycombs of glass," the *topic* is "skyscrapers," the *vehicle* is "honeycombs" and the *ground* that the listener must find would be something like "partitioned into hundreds of small units."

The success of their suppositions was shown by a cued-recall test, where subjects were cued with either appropriate or inappropriate *grounds* for the metaphors that they had heard. It should be noted that all the cues could be applied to the *topics* of the sentences that all subjects had heard. With appropriate *grounds* the subjects retrieved 10 out of 14 sentences appropriately matched to cues. With inappropriate *grounds,* the subjects retrieved only 3 out of 14 sentences. It seems clear that comprehension of the sentences did in fact entail the supposed relation, and that the relation made possible the retrieval of the sentence. It is also clear from further work that obtaining the one relation had the effect of blocking the relation involved in the other metaphor, that is, taking "skyscraper" in one way prevented the subject from recognizing a cue for it aimed at a different attribute.

Perhaps this last experiment is an illustration of how we can try to work our way into a better formulation of remembering meaningful events. Notice that it is rooted in an effort to understand what one must do to comprehend a metaphor. It is aimed, therefore, at a very special kind of experience as a target. It supposes how one must use his knowledge (of syntax, of metaphorical style, of the topic and the vehicle) to extract a relationship necessary for comprehension. It then makes the further assumption that the "content" of this implicit relation can be used to cue that particular sentence for recall.

It is a "risky" kind of experiment. No one has worked out the paradigm for studies of this kind. The success of these experiments depends on a host of reasonable but untested assumptions. The experiment is specifically directed at an *interaction* of the task (trying to comprehend the sentences), the materials (sentences), the metaphorical relations (topic, vehicle, and ground), and a particular form of criterial task (cued recall).

Because it is such a risky experiment, it is both powerful and weak. It is a powerful demonstration that complex, specified interactions can be experimentally employed to give novel results. But it is weak in that it is a single demonstration based on intuitive understanding of the language, the process of metaphor, the task of comprehension, and the task of cued recall. Thus, the experiment is both a demonstration and a challenge. It demonstrates that complex interactions can be intuitively understood. It challenges us to make those intuitions explicit in theories that are general enough in scope that we can apply them widely to many classes of cognitive phenomena to increase both our understanding and our predictive power.

At this point I am optimistic about the possibility of general theories of remembering meaningful materials. I think these theories will ultimately include descriptions of our systems of skill and knowledge and specify how the information in these systems interacts with tasks and materials as they come together in the confluence of behaviors that we are willing to classify as remembering.

REFERENCES

Arnheim, R. *Visual thinking*. Berkeley: University of California Press, 1969.

Craik, F. I. M., & Lockhart, R. S. Levels of processing: A framework for memory research. *Journal of Verbal Learning and Verbal Behavior*, 1972, **11**, 671–684.

Ebbinghaus, H. *Memory: A contribution to experimental psychology*. (Translated by H. A. Ruger & C. E. Bussenius.) New York: Teachers College Press, Columbia University, 1913. (Originally published: Leipzig: Duncker & Humblot, 1885.)

Gibson, J. J. *The senses considered as perceptual systems*. Boston: Houghton Mifflin, 1966.

Hyde, T. S. Differential effects of effort and type of orienting task on recall and organization of highly associated words. *Journal of Experimental Psychology*, 1973, **79**, 111–113.

Hyde, T. S., & Jenkins, J. J. Differential effects of incidental tasks on the organization of recall of a list of highly associated words. *Journal of Experimental Psychology*, 1969, **82**, 472–481.

Hyde, T. S., & Jenkins, J. J. Recall for words as a function of semantic, graphic, and syntactic orienting tasks. *Journal of Verbal Learning and Verbal Behavior*, 1973, **12**, 471–480.

Jenkins, J. J. Meaningfulness and concepts: Concepts and meaningfulness. In H. J. Klausmeier & C. W. Harris (Eds.), *Analyses of concept learning*. New York: Academic Press, 1966.

Johnston, C. D., & Jenkins, J. J. Two more incidental tasks that differentially affect associative clustering in recall. *Journal of Experimental Psychology*, 1971, **89**, 92–95.

Keppel, G., Postman, L., & Zavortink, B. Studies of learning to learn: VIII. The influence of massive amounts of training upon the learning and retention of paired-associate lists. *Journal of Verbal Learning and Verbal Behavior*, 1968, **7**, 790–796.

Postman, L. Short-term memory and incidental learning. In A. W. Melton (Ed.), *Categories of human learning*. New York: Academic Press, 1964.

Postman, L., Adams, P. A., & Bohm, A. M. Studies in incidental learning: V. Recall for order and associative clustering. *Journal of Experimental Psychology*, 1956, **51**, 334–342.

Till, R. E., & Jenkins, J. J. The effects of cued orienting tasks on the free recall of words. *Journal of Verbal Learning and Verbal Behavior*, 1973, **12**, 489–498.

Tulving, E., & Madigan, S. A. Memory and verbal learning. *Annual Review of Psychology*, 1970, **21**, 437–484.

Underwood, B. J. Interference and forgetting. *Psychological Review*, 1957, **64**, 49–60.

Walsh, D. A., & Jenkins, J. J. Effects of orienting tasks on free recall in incidental learning: "Difficulty," "effort," and "process" explanations. *Journal of Verbal Learning and Verbal Behavior*, 1973, **12**, 481–488.

2
MEMORY AND THE EFFICACY OF CUES
or
"YES, I KNOW!" vs. "WHY DIDN'T I THINK OF THAT?"

Robert L. Solso
Loyola University of Chicago

"Temple"–"Cathedral"	*"Chinese"–"Gong"*
"Tower"–"Steeple"	*"Shrine"–"Pagoda"*

"Pagoda! You've got it!" "Yes, I know" boasts the winner. "Why didn't I think of that?" puzzles the loser. Embodied in this game, where one member of a team gives a verbal cue to his partner in the hope that the partner will guess the concealed word, is a complex interplay between memory and cues. Embodied in this paper, in hopefully a less cryptic message than the password puzzle, is a selected review of the memory-cue interplay with particular attention to the saliency of cues and an hypothesis regarding inter- and intra-structural associative cuing.

In the brief history of experimental psychology that has dealt with the conditions of learning, the topics of frequency of association, reinforcement, drive, transfer, and many others have received considerable attention. And although the pace of developing reliable laws of learning has been tortuously slow, it would be an error to suggest that no real progress has been made. However, the role of the stimulus in acquisition and recall has been regarded as simply a necessary or even an assumed component of the learning process. This benign neglect is understandable in light of the need to develop workable laws between simply-controlled independent variables and responses. With an increased sophistication in technique and, more importantly, an increased emphasis on looking at psychological processes on an expanded scale, we have been forced to study the role of the stimulus as it relates to the entire spectrum of cognitive psychology. The importance of cue efficacy, as a focal point for the understanding of a comprehensive range of psychological processes has recently received serious attention by Ellis (1973) who suggested that how stimuli are perceived, selected, and encoded is a component of the important paradigm shift we hear so much of in contemporary psychology. And yet, as Thomson (1971) laments, ". . . despite the extensive research in the field of verbal learning and memory, there is a dearth of studies whose purpose has been the identification of effective retrieval cues [p. 1]." The first part of this paper will focus on the process by which subjects select stimuli and later use selected stimuli as a means to recover encoded information.

The efficacy of the cues used to recover the word "pagoda" is predicated on several assumptions which will serve as a model for memory structure and the means by which the encoded thing is to be released. These assumptions include (a) the word "pagoda" is stored in a memory trace of the person, (b) "pagoda" is variously associated with other items also stored in the person's memory and not as an isolated entity, (c) items that are associated are conceptualized as forming a network of strong and weak semantic associates among verbal units arranged in a hierarchy, and finally, (d) the efficacy of a cue to item retrieval is dependent on the proximity of the cue to the stored item in the memory structure. Cues closely associated to the item to be remembered are better retrieval stimuli than cues distantly associated with the to-be-remembered item. In addition to simple within-structural recall between cues and associated items, some cues may function at the same time to stimulate multiple structural attributes, which may cause the person to form a synthesis of the combined associations. Responses synthesized from several associative structures are affiliated with the mysteries of the creative process, but from an analytic standpoint they are simply special forms of retrieval whose contingencies are found in a novel arrangement of situational stimuli acting on associatively stored information. More will be reported on this later, but in the next section we shall review some contemporary work on the stimulus and suggest how this information may play a wider role in information processing and retrieval.

A "NEW LOOK" AT STIMULUS
SELECTION AND CUE EFFICACY

A rich stock of information about cue efficacy can be found in the abundant literature on stimulus selection. The development of this phenomenon grew out of Underwood and Schulz's (1960) observation that subjects, while forming paired associates, selected a portion of the nominal stimulus (experimenter-defined stimulus) as a functional stimulus (subject-defined stimulus). The fractionation of stimuli seemed to be related to the meaningfulness of the stimulus. As they wrote, "As the stimulus elicits fewer and fewer immediate associates, the subject must work harder at the task of finding some component of the stimulus which elicits an associate and which might mediate the response . . . It appears that if the three-letter stimulus is not integrated—or does not suggest an immediate association—the subject merely selects a particular part of the stimulus on which to base his association [p. 298].'' This exploratory remark opened a new trail of research effort now identified as stimulus selection.

Of the two hundred or more stimulus-selection experiments reported since Underwood and Schulz's observation, most have attempted to isolate subject-defined factors which identify the salient features of a stimulus field. Remarkably little consideration of psychological theory has clouded the purely empirical search for salient features, and no major *cause celebre* has emerged. Journeymen workers in verbal learning have been content to establish lawful relationships between cue saliency as measured by means of a transfer paradigm and the meaningfulness of the stimuli, position of stimuli, relation of the stimuli to the response, and other factors.

Perhaps verbal learners were too busy filing reports on each unsolved cell in the stimulus-selection matrix to realize that not only were they identifying salient *learning* stimuli, they were also identifying salient *retrieval* stimuli. This ''new look'' in stimulus selection places it in the context of wider psychological phenomena which, in addition to learning, has implications for memory, retrieval, encoding, and, indeed, the entire spectrum of cognitive psychology. Embedded in the numerous studies of stimulus selection we may find the nature of cue efficacy. It is curious that few verbal learning researchers perceived the ''new look'' in stimulus selection in their interpretation of data, but were satisfied with the exploration of functional stimuli. The real impact on psychology of these experiments may be in relating stimulus selection to encoding, memory, and decoding. Also, verbal learning is well overdue for a little serendipity.

Stimulus selection, as viewed from the standpoint of a cognitive theory, has one champion in Richardson (1972) who recently suggested that stimulus selection may be considered a type of encoding. The next section will contain a summary review of stimulus-selection components, with the over-all view being to fit them into the ''new look'' in stimulus selection.

Cue Efficacy and Meaningfulness of Stimuli

Throughout the last 12 years, cue selection as a function of meaningfulness has occupied a central position in the stimulus-selection literature. The rationale of this hypothesis is that subjects confronted with a compound stimulus composed of a high- and a low-meaningful term will tend to select the higher-meaningful term as a functional stimulus and more or less disregard the second, lower-meaningful stimulus term. The first direct test of this hypothesis was done by Underwood, Ham, and Ekstrand (1962) whose experiment proved to be a procedural prototype for many subsequent research papers. In their experiment, compound stimuli were composed of a verbal element surrounded by a color. After paired-associate acquisition with the compound stimulus, stimulus selection was measured by a transfer task in which one stimulus component (e.g., the verbal element) was given to one group, and the other stimulus (e.g., the color) was given to a second group. The assessment of stimulus selection by transfer data was problematic for Underwood et al., as differences in second-list acquisition may be attributed to the efficacy of one class of stimuli as contrasted with the other. Conceivably, cue efficacy could be independent of stimulus selection. It should be noted that Underwood et al. were aware of this factor and ran additional subjects with the single stimulus alone, to provide a more accurate base for interpreting transfer results. The results of this experiment yielded convincing evidence for stimulus selection as a demonstrable acquisition mechanism.

A spate of experiments validated the basic hypothesis of stimulus selection as a function of meaningfulness. Cohen and Musgrave (1964) used sets of high-meaningfulness CVCs (100% AV) and low-meaningfulness CVCs (10% AV) and single vowels as response terms in a six-item anticipation-learning task. By using CVCs of known meaningful value, it was possible to specifically test the hypothesis of stimulus selection as a function of meaningfulness but, in addition, they reported that the position of two independent verbal elements tandemly presented favors the selection of the left element. Supporting evidence for mean-ingfulness as a powerful determinant in stimulus selection has also been reported by Houston (1964), James and Greeno (1967), Lockhart (1968), Solso (1968, 1971, 1972), and Young, Teeters, and Zelazny (1966).

All other factors being held constant, higher-meaningful stimuli have a higher probability of being selected as functional stimuli than lower-meaningful stimuli with cue saliency being measured in terms of cue efficacy. If this were the only factor in stimulus selection, experimentation could cease; however, stimulus selection is a many factored thing. An experiment by Solso (1971) examined one side of the complex problem of stimulus selection. In this experiment the degree that the principle of stimulus selection as a function of meaningfulness generalized to complex stimuli was examined. Trisyllable stimuli of varying meaningfulness (100% AV, 90% AV, and 25% AV) were paired with digits, and then all possible combinations of single, dual, and triple trigrams were presented in a standard stimulus-selection transfer paradigm. The results corroborated the principle of highest-meaningful stimuli being selected over lower-meaningful stimuli and hence higher-meaningful stimuli were better retrieval cues.

Presumably, subjects confronted with stimuli of different meaningfulness react by (a) differentiating between the stimuli of the compound, and (b) tentatively selecting one stimulus for purposes of the functional stimulus. The fluency with which these reactions are performed is contingent on several known variables, among which is the relative meaningfulness of stimuli.

We can safely conclude that subjects select the highest meaningful cue as a functional stimulus during the encoding process and that retrieval is enhanced if cued with the highest meaningful stimulus. Why is cue efficacy tied to cue mean-ingfulness? Two explanations are offered. Initially, higher-meaningful stimuli are more readily encoded into memory structure than low-meaningful stimuli. Meaningfulness is commonly based on subjects' associations to the verbal stimuli, and it is likely that memory structures are more hospitable to stimuli of similar associative frameworks than to stimuli of different or impoverished associative frameworks. If a reduced number of associates are found in the subject's memory (as in the case of low-meaningful stimuli) he must form associates or the item must be adopted by an existing structure. The second factor in cue efficacy and meaningfulness is predicated on the inference that the higher-meaningful term was initially encoded. The cue consonant with the encoding stimulus should maximize recovery of that term in the same sense that A-B; A-B transfer is superior to A-B; A'-B or A-B; C-B transfer. In addition to the encoding-decoding constancy rule it is suspected that higher-meaningful items are more easily recovered from memory structure even if low-meaningful items are equally well learned. This speculation needs validation and may tell us more about the relationship between stored items and the recall of these items.

Position and Stimulus Selection. Two lines of inquiry have examined position as a determinant of the stimulus selected: The first line has used two distinctive verbal elements as stimuli; the second has used a single verbal element, usually a trigram, as a stimulus. In the former case the verbal elements are normally tandemly presented. Cohen and Musgrave (1964) report that the first position is favored in stimulus selection while James and Greeno (1967) using the same lists as Cohen and Musgrave but with slightly modified instructions, surprisingly did not find any effects of position in either the original learning stage or the transfer stage. In a subsequent study, Cohen and Musgrave (1966) reported that the first stimulus has a higher probability of being selected. In their experiment, compound stimuli composed of several levels of stimulus meaningfulness and in varying levels of meaningful difference between the stimuli were used. It is reasonable to assume that if the verbal elements which compose a compound stimulus are composed of sets drawn from widely different meaningfulness levels, then the selection mechanism based on meaningfulness is activated; but as the verbal elements in each set more closely approximate each other and presumably stimulus competition based on meaningfulness increases, then other stimulus-selection mechanisms, such as position, become activated.

In the second case, stimulus selection as a function of the position a letter holds in a trigram has yielded wide agreement that the first position favors the selection of that letter as a functional stimulus. This finding has been documented by Jenkins (1963), Postman and Greenbloom (1967), and Richardson and Chisholm (1969).

The efficacy of a cue seems to be related to its position in relationship to other cues. In recent work at the Loyola laboratories we have demonstrated that redintegration of words is more favorably cued by the initial letter than by letters in other positions.

Stimulus Competition and Stimulus Selection. Consider the possibility of a subject confronted with two stimuli of similar meaningfulness and selecting one stimulus on one trial and then selecting the other stimulus on a subsequent trial. It is conceivable that this vacillation of learning tactics would result in a reduced rate of acquisition when contrasted with acquisition with a single stimulus. This phenomenon called stimulus competition has been observed by several researchers.

Stimulus competition, as manifested in a reduction of the acquisition rate, was perhaps first reported by Cohen and Musgrave (1964), although they did not discuss their data in terms of stimulus competition. Six stimulus conditions, in which all possible combinations of high- and low-meaningfulness stimulus pairs can be derived, were used as stimuli. These groups were HH, HL, LH, LL, L, and H and, unlike the contextual-cue studies discussed above, were composed of only verbal material, not colors. Following a stimulus-competition model, in which competition increases as a function of the increased similarity between the cues in a compound stimulus, one would predict that in the HH or LL condition (the cues approximating each other in terms of their selectability) stimulus competition would be very high, and in the H or L condition competition would be low. If stimulus competition is high, then it is expected that acquisition rates would be retarded as subjects are caught in a conflict between two desirable or undesirable stimuli. The result of this conflict may be a vacillation between the selection of the vying stimuli, which may reduce the opportunity for response acquisition and associative learning.

The concept of stimulus competition was directly tested by Solso (1968) when compound stimuli composed of colors and verbal items of known meaningfulness level were used. In this experiment evidence was presented for the deleterious effect of stimulus competition on learning. A subsequent experiment (Solso & Trafimow, 1970) was conducted in which high-meaningful stimulus cues were paired with stimuli ranging from high to low meaningfulness. The results indicated that learning decreased as a function of the decrease in disparity between the meaningfulness of the items in the compound stimulus. This was offered in support of a stimulus competition model. Furthermore, it was suggested that stimulus selection was a separate and identifiable stage, which preceded response acquisition and associative learning. The position that subjects adopt some strategy in the selection stage has received support from Harrington (1969) who has suggested that in the early stages of acquisition with compound stimuli, subjects learn a pattern and then select a stimulus. It is conceivable that pattern learning and stimulus competition are functionally identical concepts. Laws which govern these processes are badly needed.

The preceding review of stimulus-selection research may provide an inductive base from which generalizations about cue efficacy may be drawn. Three hypotheses of stimulus selection were examined: stimulus selection and meaningfulness, stimulus selection and position, and stimulus selection and competing stimuli. Several important conclusions germane to cognitive psychology are suggested. The human organism is surrounded by a cluttered stimulus field out of which it is continuously filtering out all but the most salient of cues. Selected cues may be associated with other items and serve as potent retrieval cues. The bases for stimulus selection includes, among other stimulus factors, the meaningfulness of the terms, the position of stimuli, and the competitiveness of the stimulus field. Finally, stimulus-selection data may form an inductive basis for predicting cue efficacy as it relates to memory retrieval.

After stimuli have survived an initial filter and their trace is situated in some type of memory structure, what is their fate? The next section contains some speculation regarding the associative history of selected stimuli.

RETRIEVAL AND CUE EFFICACY
OR
YOU *CAN'T* GET THERE FROM HERE

Indeed, why didn't our password loser think of pagoda? After all, he had three highly meaningful cues: "temple," "Chinese," and "tower". Perhaps he was confronted with the same problem the tourist faces when he asks a native for directions and gets the answer, "You can't get there from here." The implication is either that the cues "temple," "Chinese," and "tower" fell victim to our loser's filtering of stimuli (and his response of "steeple" to the final cue of "tower" would suggest he disregarded at least one cue) or that the associative pathways between the cues and "pagoda" were too weak to disclose the correct response. The previous section of this paper dealt with the issue of stimulus selection; this section will consider the associative aspects of cue efficacy.

Cue efficacy is reciprocally dependent on the structure in which associations are stored. Data reported by Tulving and his associates (Thomson & Tulving, 1970; Tulving, 1966; Tulving & Osler, 1968; Tulving & Pearlstone, 1966; Tulving & Thomson, 1971) support the contention that cues are most efficacious if they are similar to subject-defined or experimenter-defined encoding methods. The cogent factor in Tulving's encoding-specificity hypothesis is his assertion that retrieval cues are effective *only* if the cue corresponds to a part of the encoding pattern. The principle is illustrated in the following colorful passage by Thomson and Tulving (1970):

> . . . Thus, the cue "white" cannot provide access to stored information about the occurrence of BLACK as a TBR word, if BLACK has been encoded as part of the "train-BLACK" complex, or as part of a unique event in a series of unique events. The two lexical units, BLACK and BLACK, are identical, but the encoded engram of the unique event BLACK, in the context of "train," and in the context of a specific set of TBR events, may be as different from the pattern of neural excitation corresponding to the generalized concept of BLACK as a beautiful and talented actress receiving an Oscar is different from any one of millions of stars twinkling in the endless night [p. 261].

The status of the encoding-specificity hypothesis is not without critics, many of whom subscribe to some form of an associative-continuity hypothesis. Proponents of this second hypothesis argue that cue efficacy is related to organizational principles of the subject's general verbal store. Bahrick (1970) has hypothesized a two-phase model for prompted recall which consists of independent retrieval and recognition process. As will be seen later, this two-phase model closely resembles the search-and-match hypothesis represented in the present paper. The associative-continuity hypothesis is illustrated by Bahrick (1970) in the following example:

> . . . the individual who wants to recall the name of the girl he took to a high school prom, but fails in his initial effort, may produce a list of girls' names from his general memory store until he retrieves a name which he recognized as the correct one. If he also happens to remember that the name began or ended with a certain syllable and restricts the repertoire of retrieved names in accordance with this cue, the likelihood of successful retrieval is increased [p. 215].

The polemics are easily distilled: Bahrick's girl has faded into a murky past along with wilted flowers, crew cuts, and bland associates, while Tulving's starry girl remains clearly *in situ*.

The encoding-specificity hypothesis vs. the associative-continuity hypothesis issue will remain alive for some time, partly because it is widely held that subjects encode retrieval cues throughout their life history *and* during their experimental history. Given the ubiquity of proximal and parallel exposure to and selected encoding of cues, it is logically correct to infer the following antinomy: (*a*) *specific* cues were present and encoded, and (*b*) *specific* cues were present and *not* encoded. The inference that cues present during the encoding process act as potent retrieval stimuli is well substantiated and is virtually unchallenged among theorists in this field. The *necessity*[1] for specific retrieval cues to be present (and presumably active) during storage in order to be effective as a retrieval cue poses a hopelessly snarled experimental web in which serious researchers are destined to bind themselves with their own data. Inferences about the efficacy of retrieval cues are based on dependent variables or in the things they retrieve. The mere physical presence or absence of a cue does not *guarantee* that it will or will not be encoded. Since laboratory encoding is intertwined with extralaboratory experience, the problem of cue efficacy and encoding is compounded by the variance generated by two inferences: the nature of encoding during experimentation and the nature of encoding during the subject's extraexperimental experiences. If a cue was effective in memory retrieval, then one could infer it was encoded; if a cue was not effective, then it was not encoded. The logic of this theorization is "heads I win, tails you lose" and is of dubious worth in the history of psychology. We might ask how long scientists will puzzle over questions with no answers, especially in light of Tulving's own complaint (Tulving & Madigan, 1970) that the ". . . psychological study of how people

---

[1]Tulving (Tulving & Osler, 1968) is unequivocal on this point: "Specific retrieval cues facilitate recall *if and only if* the information about them and about their relationship to the TBR words is stored at the same time as the information about the membership of the TBR words in a given list [p. 599]." (The italics in the quote are mine.)

learn and remember things has kept countless thinkers, scholars, researchers, teachers, and students gainfully occupied without yielding any dramatic new insights into the workings of the human mind . . . [p. 437]." Perhaps if the subject's entire lexical-associative history could be carefully documented, the variance of the latter inference would be reduced. Such a laborious task is well beyond common patience and technology.

Furthermore, an interpretation of a rigid form of the encoding-specificity hypothesis (cf. Thomson & Tulving, 1970, who said "retrieval of event information can only be effected by retrieval cues corresponding to a part of the total encoding pattern representing the perceptual cognitive registration of the occurrence of the event [p. 261]") leaves little room for creative synthesis of encoded material.

Multiple Encoding: Instantaneous or Protracted?

In addition to the problem of single-dimension encoding, recent theorists have pondered the question of multiple encoding. Conspicuous among these theorists are Underwood and Wickens who both conceptualize memory to be made up of several attributes but differ as to when and how the encoding takes place. Wickens (1972), using a release from proactive inhibition (PI) method, has concluded that multiple encoding of a symbol occurs within a split second. The release from PI argument is based on an ingenious technique developed by Wickens in which subjects are asked to learn three common category words. Immediately following the presentation of the word triads, a distractor task of 20-seconds length is presented, followed by recall, and then the entire cycle is repeated with three different words of the same class. The fourth trial is different for an experimental group; they are given three words drawn from another class while the control subjects are given three words from the same old class. A remarkable increase in recall of the new class of items on the fourth trial has been reported by Wickens. By varying the nature of the classes, Wickens is able to elucidate the encoding attributes of words and has concluded that most words have multiple-component values but also may remain insensitive to other attributes. Wickens' (1972) final conclusion is that the *initial* encoding of a word is "rich and multiple—as it would need to be for distinguishing between words and nuances of words [p. 213]." He then expands his conceptualization of memory attributes by speculating about the decoding process, which may prove to be the most controversial issue and generate considerable research in the remainder of this decade. "Not all dimensions are used in the recall process, for the presence of certain salient characteristics may mitigate against the simultaneous use of others [p. 213]."

Underwood's (1972) reaction to Wickens' conceptualization is contained in his own triad: The PI technique primes encoding and may spuriously inflate the number of encoding attributes elicited when a single word is presented with unrelated words; no evidence is presented by Wickens that multiple encoding takes place during the brief experimental task; multiplicity and automaticity of encoding eliminates the intentional-incidental dichotomy. Of the three criticisms, the first is sure to be supported by empirical data (in addition to the references cited by Underwood) while the last criticism, at least to Underwood's apparent satisfaction, is patently clear in light of the long history of intentional-incidental learning experiments. The second criticism is problematic, as no strong empirical evidence is available to discredit or support the criticism. Of course, there is a world of common knowledge which alternately validates and invalidates the spontaneity of encoding. On a purely sensory level, it seems unlikely that each of the multitude of sensations detected during every split second of our receptive life immediately permeates all of the numerous semantic nuances of that sensation. Indeed, the considerable evidence presented in the earlier section of this paper on stimulus selection would indicate that complete bundles of sensory information are not encoded, if we accept the efficacy of a decoding cue as truly reflecting the encoding process. The validity of Underwood's second criticism may ultimately be demonstrated in the neurophysiologist's laboratory sometime in the next century, but until then we impatient psychologists can make decisions based on parsimoniousness of theories; a simple one will be offered later.

Underwood's criticism of Wickens' assertion that words are multiply encoded does not deny that some words are multiply encoded but rather one part of the quarrel is over when the encoding occurs. The dispute closely resembles the Tulving-Bahrick dispute, in that Bahrick does not deny that cues encoded during the acquisition phase are effective retrieval cues, but is skeptical as to the *necessity* for cues to be encoded during acquisition to function as facilitory retrieval cues.

Multiple Encoding and Cue Efficacy: You *Can* Get There From Here

In our studies at Loyola, we have examined the effect of multiple cuing on retrieval, with the hope of shedding some light on the multiple encoding notion. Recently, Solso and Biersdorff (1973) prompted recall by means of three cues; the initial letter of the target or to-be-remembered (TBR) word, a word which rhymed with the TBR word, and a word which had as its associate the TBR word. Following prompting (see Table 1 for an example of the words and cues) with a single cue, all possible combinations of two cues were presented to different groups of subjects. And finally, all three cues were given to different groups of subjects. Two experiments were reported which, in addition to minor procedural differences, differed in that one group was prompted immediately after seeing TBR words and the other groups were given an opportunity for free recall of TBR words and prompting was confined to only those words not initially recalled. Within both experiments control groups who had never been exposed to the TBR words during the experiment were cued in a like manner to the experimental groups.

Although the *a priori* probability that the associative cue would elicit the TBR word was low ($p \approx .10-.20$), it proved to be the best single cue. Of greater importance is the efficacy of multiple cuing. Recall of TBR words in both experiments

TABLE 1

Examples of Words and Cues in Solso and Biersdorff Study

Target Words	Cues		
	Initial	Rhyme	Associate
Cold	C	Mould	Winter
Dirt	D	Hurt	Earth
Horse	H	Coarse	Chariot
Talk	T	Hawk	Whisper

increased in a spectacular fashion; in some instances nearly doubling single-cuing recall, while triple cuing resulted in almost complete recovery of the TBR word. The data were interpreted as supporting a multiple-encoding hypothesis but unfortunately are equivocal as to when encoding took place.

Solso and Biersdorff offer this interpretation of their data:

> . . . multiple cuing may serve the function of restricting the search area for the location of situational verbal items. The logic of this argument is that target words which were previously encoded in complex long-term memory structure, were freshly rehearsed and held in Ss' immediate memory. Prompting by means of a single cue may have caused Ss to spew out their implicit associative responses (IARs) to the *prompter*. Each IAR is then compared with items in immediate memory until a match between an IAR and a freshly rehearsed item is recognized. Other theorists (Shiffrin & Geisler, 1973) have proposed a similar model for the elicitation of complexly structured information stored in long-term memory. Multiple cuing may greatly restrict the nature of IARs common to two cues. For example the word ''chariot'' as an associative cue leads to a hierarchy of IARs which may include ''race,'' ''cart,'' ''carriage,'' ''lariat,'' ''Roman,'' and ''horse'. The IAR hierarchy of the compound stimulus ''chariot,'' again as an associative cue, restricted by the letter ''H'' as an orthographic cue includes comparatively few responses, among which are the words ''horse'' and ''Hur'' (or ''Heston'' if one is a film aficionado). Three cues, ''chariot,'' ''H,'' and ''course'' as a rhyming cue, restrict the number of compatible IARs to only one. By restricting the search and match words the probability of reconstruction of the to-be-remembered word is greatly enhanced. In the present experiments triple cuing allowed reconstruction of the word even if the *S* did not see the word. Such a theoretical position does not deny that some verbal items may be multiply encoded upon perception, but does account for the facilitory nature of multiple cuing which does not presume verbal items to be necessarily encoded into attributes during the experimental situation [pp. 13–14].

This position is similar to Underwood's assertion that multiple encoding of a word may occur at some time in the subject's life history but that multiple cue efficacy need not be tied to experimental encoding.

The efficacy of multiple cuing reported in the Solso and Biersdorff experiment leads to the speculation that through novel placement of cues one can extract different information than the subject has encoded. The interpretation is not contrary to the doctrine of *tabula rasa,* to which most behaviorists adhere, but rather acknowledges that human subjects think! And that thinking entails a creative synthesis of previous associations and impressions.[2] If one accepts this simple interpretation—which has its historical roots in mental chemistry—then the nature of retrieval stimuli as a source of identifying cognitive features assumes singular prominence. The *arrangement* of cues largely determines if a person responds with "Yes, I know!" (YIK) or "Why didn't I think of that?" (WDITOT), and he need not be programmed with associates identical to retrieval associates in order for him to know. It is postulated that retrieval cues generate their own associates and that the process leading to "Yes, I know" consists of forming associates to retrieval stimuli and matching their associates to stored items. The successful operation of this process of search and match is contingent on the aptness and generative capacity of the cues plus the structure of the memory. Of course, the thing to be recalled must have left *some* trace in the subject's memory, but its location in a structural web may be remotely related to the form of the decoding cues.

The frequent use of "mental forestry" as a metaphor for memory structure may help elucidate the above point, and I, as well as my immediate intellectual predecessors and distant biological ancestors, don't mind going out on a limb. Associations, darting through the spatiotemporal labyrinth of cortical memory may plainly be likened to moving from one part of a tree structure to another. The shorter the distance (e.g., from a twig to a branch being shorter than from moving from a leaf to a branch, or "a collie is a dog" being shorter than "a collie is an animal") the more rapidly subjects can trace their associations (cf. Bower, 1970; Collins & Quillian, 1969; Landauer & Freedman, 1968; and Loftus, Freedman, & Loftus, 1970, for complete details.) Laws which govern intrastructure travel are being quickly developed. But how are associations formed *between* memory structures? To continue with the arborization of memory, the above description deals with what can be called terrestrial association, i.e., they are above the surface and clearly visible, however other associative networks, subterranean if you choose, form the root structure of the knowledge tree. These later structures differ from their fresh-air counterparts only in that they have the capacity to associate with other structures. Thus, it is possible that cues, seeming specific to one structure are in fact surreptitiously touching numerous other structures. Cues, which were once thought to be specific to a fairly vivid structure, may now generate new associative links with other structures. A less verdant description of the above model will be presented in a later section of this paper.

Cue Efficacy and Memory Structure

It is a tough job to keep up with all the new theories of memory as the past decade has produced a bumper crop. And although it may be entirely fitting—indeed, even expected—that among the contributions to this volume a fresh model

---

[2] "Let no one say I have said nothing new: The arrangement of the material is new." — Pascal.

will emerge, it will *not* appear in this chapter. What is proposed is a simplified model designed to elucidate two essential aspects of the cognitive process discussed in this chapter. These two aspects are the selection of cues and interstructural association based on salient cues and stored information. First, consider the nature of cues and memory structure.

The consideration that some stimuli are selected from a field of stimuli to operate as functional stimuli is rarely criticized. Various theorists have postulated a selective filter, sensory register, stimulus analyzing mechanisms, etc., that generally serve the function of filtering out distracting stimuli and admitting salient stimuli. The considerable data on stimulus selection referred to earlier has identified many salient features of cues. It is presumed that the efficacy of cues in recall is related to their similarity to the encoded item. Cue efficacy is also related to the number of items it generates and to the probability the generated item will form a consonant link with the encoded article. This notion is stated in two interdependent theorems:

THEOREM 1: Cue efficacy is inversely related to the number of responses it generates.

THEOREM 2: Cue efficacy is directly related to the probability that it will generate an encoded attribute of the to-be-remembered thing.

If a stimulus generates many responses, then all other factors being equal (e.g. hierarchical arrangement of IARs), the efficacy of the cue to retrieve encoded material is necessarily reduced (Theorem 1). On the other hand, if the number of responses generated by the retrieval cue are few, there is a correspondingly reduced probability that the encoded attribute of the to-be-remembered item will be among the generated responses. This curiosity will be examined in terms of the interstructural associative paradox in a later section of this paper, but now a slightly expanded version of memory structure will be presented.

Memory structure is conceptualized as performing two functions: the incorporation of sensations and the generation of responses. The first of these functions,

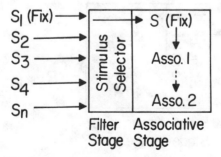

FIG. 1. Incorporative phase of associative memory.

the incorporative stage, is illustrated in Fig. 1, and consists of only three components: stimuli, stimulus filter, and stimulus associations. Of the numerous stimuli which achieve threshold value, only a small fraction reach the associative stage as most fall victim of a stimulus-filtering system. Some of the stimulus-selection factors have been documented in the earlier part of this paper. Of the few stimuli which reach the associative stage it is postulated that in the human adult most are encoded into an already well-constructed configuration of associations. However, it is not held that *all* of the nuances of the stimuli are realized, consciously or unconsciously. The incorporative stage of a verbal item is illustrated by presenting to a subject the word "Fix." Presuming that the verbal element passes through the initial filter, it is then encoded into an already existing structure of associatively related thoughts. In the present example, "Fix" may be encoded into the structure that is related to repair or mend. The number of structures in which a verbal element is encoded is dependent on many considerations, of which time and intention are among the most conspicuous. With the continuous stimulation and reaction to stimuli typical of normal human encounter, the associative complexity of specific sensations is presumed to be minimal. It is unlikely that more than one or two separate structural encodings of the word "Fix" would occur in the ongoing panorama of events which require attention and reaction.

The generative or decoding phase is the stage in which stored information is disclosed. Response generation originates from stimuli and the more consonant the stimulus with the encoded item, the better the recovery of the item. However, the encoding properties need not be identical to the decoding properties in order to function as retrieval cues. In effect, cross-talk across channels is possible. Cross-structural associative cuing, although not generally as effective as within-structural associative cuing, nevertheless may serve as a retrieval cue. Retrieval by means of cross-structural cues will be discussed in the next section, but now consider retrieval by means of within-structural cuing. Apparently the most salient cue is identical to the thing to be remembered. In the above example and illustrated in Fig. 2 is cuing with the word "Fix." Recovery of "Fix" to the

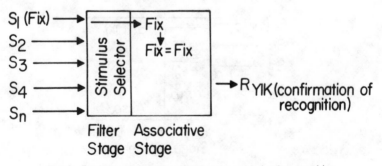

Fig. 2. Generative phase of associative memory: simple recognition.

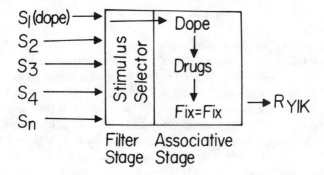

FIG. 3. Generative phase of associative memory: associative recall.

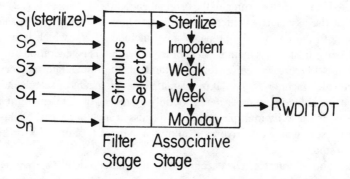

FIG. 4. Generative phase of associative memory: non-confirmation of associative link.

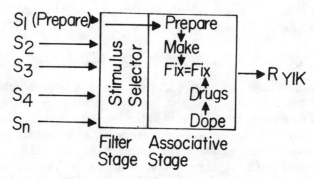

FIG. 5. Generative phase of associative memory: cue structure and memory structure different.

stimulus "Fix" involves only a cursory search and the recognition of the identity of the two items.

Intrastructural associative cuing requires more extensive search as illustrated in Figure 3 in which the cue word "Dope" is associatively related to "Fix." The immediate associates, conceptualized as implicit associative responses (IARs), to "Fix" may include "Dope," "Drugs," and "Fix." The response of "Fix" is recognized as identical to the encoded word and, hence, in response to "Fix" a "Yes, I know" (YIK) is generated. Conversely, the failure to respond, a "Why didn't I think of that" (WDITOT) is illustrated in Fig. 4 in which the cue "Sterilize" (as used in neutering an animal) produces a series of IARs which do not include "Fix." In this example, interassociative cuing is obfuscated by the IARs being only tangentially related to the target word "fix" in the subject's memory structure.

Interstructural associative cuing, in which a cue primarily related to one nest of associations may recover a response embedded in another nest of associations, is illustrated in Fig. 5. Returning to the original encoding of "Fix" (Fig. 2) it can be seen that the associative structure included "Dope," "Drugs," etc. The IAR hierarchy to the cue word "prepare" may include "Fix" which is principally encoded in our subject's memory in another structure. The generation of the word "Fix" to "Prepare" is compared with items in the immediate memory of the subject which includes "Fix." It is postulated that by means of search and match, subjects are able to remember items not only by means of intrastructural associative cues, but also by multiple cuing, as discussed in another part of this paper, which is particularly effective as it allows a subject to gain a fix on multiply encoded items.

In the above example, cues seem to function paradoxically as the breadth of IARs generated by a stimulus need to be wide enough to include the encoded term, but the search-and-match procedure is directly related to the number of IARs. Multiple cuing of the sort reported in the Solso and Biersdorff study greatly facilitates recovery by affecting both components, i.e., multiple cuing, limits the number of IARs and, at the same time may generate cogent links between and within structures. A more detailed description of the inter- and intrastructural associative paradox is found in the next section.

Cue Efficacy and the Interstructural Associative Paradox (ISAP)

Interstructural association and cue efficacy seem to be governed by two processes: (a) the number of alternative implicit associative responses (IARs) generated by the cues and (b) the probability that the cues will form a compatible link between structures. Conceptually, the number of IARs and the probability of linking two structures are correlates of each other, but paradoxically they are functionally opposite. That is, as the number of alternative IARs increases, retrieval is prolonged, whereas the probability of congruous interstructural links being generated is directly related to the number of IARs available.

The interstructural associative paradox is analogous to trying to find a book in an unindexed library. Consider this problem: You are to search through five libraries to find *Main Street* by Sinclair Lewis. The first library has only 10 books, the second library has 100 books, the third 1000 books, the fourth 10,000 books, and the fifth, 100,000 books. How will you find the book? If you search through the first library only a simple scan is required to exhaust the population, but, unfortunately, the probability is slim that *Main Street* will be among the 10 books. Conversely, if you search through the fifth library, the search will be arduous, but the probability that the book is among the searched items is high.[3] So it is with interstructural associative cuing. The greater the number of IARs the higher the probability a nexus between structures will be in the population, while the greater the IARs the more protracted the search.

So far structural analysis of encoded material has been applied to a narrow range of verbal components. However, the model conceptualized in this paper is considered to be much more pervasive and capable of describing more complex cognitive function. Several diverse examples have been selected to illustrate the flexibility of the model.

A pioneer in mathematical communication theory, G. E. Shannon, developed a technique for prediction and entrophy of printed English (Shannon, 1951). Entrophy is a statistical parameter which embodies the information load contained in each letter in language text. The growth of entrophy and prediction of language was necessitated by the need to decode cryptic messages during World War II, and a wealth of information about verbal processes is available but infrequently cited, in cryptological literature.[4] Shannon recognized that anyone who is fluent

---

[3] A retrieval index may be calculated based on the probability the item is among the generated items times the number of items in the search area, i.e., $RI = p \cdot N$.

[4] An entertaining poem by e. e. cummings demonstrates a type of auditory entrophy in which commonly heard utterances help in the decoding of his message. People who try to decode this poem nearly always read it aloud, probably as a feedback mechanism.

oil tel duh woil doi sez
dooyuh unnurs tanmih eesez pullih nizmus tash,oi
dough un giv uh shid oi sez. Tom
oidoughwuntuh doot,butoiguttuh
braikyooz,datswut eesez tuhmih. (Nowoi askyuh
woodundat maik yurarstoin
green? Oilsaisough.)—Hool
spairruh luckih? Thangzkeed. Mairsee.
Muh jax awl gawn. Fur Croi saik
ainnoughbudih gutnutntuhplai?

HAI

yoozwidduhpoimnuntwaiv un duhyookuhsumpnruddur
givusuhtoonunduhphugnting

in a given language has an enormous knowledge of the statistical composition of that language, as well as knowledge of its idioms, cliches, and grammar. The "implicit" knowledge, especially in a highly redundant language as English, allows us to reconstruct whole words or phrases if only a fragment of the original message is available. In an informal study, Shannon had subjects guess a letter of a phrase; if the person's guess is correct he is informed and he continues to guess the item. If his guess is wrong he is given the letter and then proceeds to guess the next item, and so on. As the person has more and more letter cues, the probability of reconstructing the next letter is enhanced. One typical result of this technique is illustrated below with the correct phrase above and the guesses below: The dash indicates a correct guess.

Text: MANY BRAVE HEARTS ARE ASLEEP IN THE DEEP SO BEWARE

Guesses: MA–Y BRAV– H–A––– ––– ASL––– I– ––– –––– –– ––––––

The errors, Shannon notes, occur most frequently at the beginning of words and "syllables where the line of thought has more possibility of branching out [p. 6]." In the reconstruction of this message we can detect a parallel process to the recovery from memory of previously encoded material. Specifically, the number of IARs generated by the cues (in the present example, previous letters, context, and familiarity with the phrase) is inversely related to the correct recovery of the correct word. Perhaps the most striking example of the principle is seen in trying to generate a second letter to the letter "q": The constraint on alternatives is massive. Contrast this with the generation of alternative responses to the letter "i."

In a second more direct example of the model, Solso, Topper, and Macey (1973) used anagrams as a source of stimuli. The rearrangement of letters to form a word has been demonstrated by Dominowski and Duncan (1964) and others to be a partial function of the frequency of the bigrams (BF) in the solution word. Shannon's assertion that language users carry with them statistical knowledge of the language is apparently applicable to anagram studies. The role BF plays in anagram solving is in the initial formation of bigram units which may then serve as word fragments in reconstructing the solution word. The higher the statistical probability that one letter will be followed by another (e.g., SH>HS), the higher the probability subjects will form those bigrams in anagram problems. However, after word fragments have been formed, a second process is undertaken in the solving of anagrams. The subject must now match the bigrams (or larger letter sequences) with words stored in his memory. This two-stage process of forming word fragments and matching them with words in memory, suggested by Solso, et al., is similar to a search-and-match model of memory recovery. The anagram model, like the memory recovery model, is paradoxical in that bigram formation is a direct function of BF but once the bigram is formed the match stage may be protracted if the subject is required to search through a large store of words containing the formed bigrams. The matching stage of anagram solution seems to be related to bigram versatility (BV), defined as the number of different words in which a given bigram occurs. In a separate study Topper, Macey, and Solso (1973) counted BV. Although BF and BV are high correlates of each other, some noticeable anomalies between relative BV scores and relative BF scores were noted in the normative data and were later used to make visible the two stages of anagram solution. For example, the bigram "OF" has a high frequency of occurrence in the English language derived largely from the preposition "of." However, the BV is low; only a few different words contain the bigram "OF." Theoretically, anagram solution time should be relatively fast if (a) the solution word bigrams appear frequently in the language and (b) the solution word bigrams are confined to a low number of different words. We suggested that BF determines the formation of bigrams and BV determines the size of the set of words the subject must search through in order to match the letters of the anagram with a word stored in his memory. Returning to our example of the password loser (WDITOT), he may also fail to solve an anagram if the solution word contains low-frequency bigrams while the distribution of bigrams encompasses many words. Our winner (YIK), on the other hand, may be confronted with the opposite set of anagram conditions, i.e., high BF and low BV. Our data support this notion.

A third illustration of the model is in the answering of questions. In the first Loyola Symposium on Cognitive Psychology, Norman (1973) outlined the basic rudiments required for answering a question. These are simple inference, knowledge of causality, understanding of basic laws, general knowledge of the world, and an understanding of what the person asking the question already knows. Norman describes simple retrieval question-answering by means of the following algorithm: (a) Search the memory for the structure equivalent to the question; (b) if successful, report: (c) if unsuccessful, report "I don't know." However, as Norman suggests, the above algorithm has a fundamental difficulty called the paraphrase problem. That is, the information may actually be stored in the memory but in a different format from that of the question. The problem of information retrieval and cue efficacy seems to haunt a wide range of cognitive functions and dysfunctions. Let us presume that the information is stored in memory but that the initial reaction to the question is "I don't know." In Norman's conceptualization this may correspond to the first stage of answering questions, i.e., a rapid, cursory search about the information. If this fails to reveal the answer, the response is determined by why the search failed. If the answer is illogical (e.g., What is Charles Darwin's phone number?) the subject may want to know what the joke is. However if the question asks for a remotely rehearsed item (e.g., name all the students in your third-grade class) the subject may try to retrieve more information about fellow third-grade pupils. For example, he may try to picture the classroom and identify where each member sat as a recall mnemonic. Particularly germane to the associative-recall hypothesis, which links one

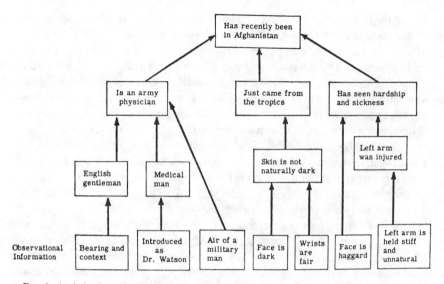

FIG. 6. An inductive scheme based on Sherlock Holmes' first meeting with Dr. Watson (used by permission of F. J. McGuigan and Prentice-Hall, Inc.).

structure with another, is Norman's (1973) conclusion: "In a network representation of memory, everything is eventually connected to everything else; so that if two items exist somewhere in memory, there must be some path connecting them, although that path may be nonmeaningful [p. 138]."

Given time and efficacious cues, the path between two items is not only possible but may also become highly meaningful. The only prerequisite for the formation of highly meaningful, indeed, inspirational, mental pathways is that the items to be associated are stored (preferably in some structure) and that the configuration of cues maximize the growth of the structural interrelationship.

The final diverse example of cue efficacy and interstructural association can be seen in inductive schema. A dramatic example of inductive logic is reported by McGuigan (1960) in citing a passage from *Sherlock Holmes*. It is recognized that few of us have the inductive talent of the great detective and, in truth, if we acted on the sketchy information provided in the protocol of Doyle's novels we would probably more closely resemble Inspector Clouseau[5] than Mr. Holmes. Nevertheless, an inductive schema based on the first meeting between Sherlock Holmes and Dr. Watson will provide a neat icon to illustrate cue efficacy and interstructural association. McGuigan extracted a passage from *Sherlock Holmes* and then composed Fig. 6, which represents the salient facts contained in the passage. In the passage cited by McGuigan, Holmes is introduced to Dr. Watson and immediately states "You have been in Afghanistan, I perceive." Holmes describes his train of thoughts (which ran so swiftly through his mind that he

[5]As portrayed by Peter Sellers in *A Shot in the Dark*.

arrived at the conclusion without being conscious of intermediate steps) as being predicated on the observable facts at the base of the inductive pyramid in Fig. 6. Of course, if the story line needed an opium smuggler from Macao, the same basic facts could lead to the invincible Sherlock Holmes bashing away at Dr. Watson's arm and spilling out a kilo of white stuff. With full awareness of the frailties of this inductive schema, let us examine it in light of some of the thoughts expressed in this paper.

The first stage of Mr. Holmes' swiftly developing train of thoughts started with selection of salient stimuli. Undoubtedly, a myriad of sensations were available to him, of which only a few passed through an initial filter to figure into his thoughts. For example, the fact that Dr. Watson had 12 gromlets on his left shoe had no conscious impact on Mr. Holmes, but if Dr. Watson was wearing a wooden shoe, or a sandal, or an open toed pump, or had no shoe at all, it may have been selected as a basis for an inductive conclusion. The inductive structure describes only a portion of the observational information and excludes a considerable body of well-structured information Mr. Holmes had stored in his mind. Among this information may have been the important knowledge that Afghanistan had been invaded by the British forces through India and, depending on the exact data portrayed in the novel, the British occupation of Afghanistan had ended.

The second stage of this thought process is much more complicated. According to ideas expressed in this paper, and elsewhere, each bit of observable information which has passed through the sensory screen generates a hierarchy of IARs. A small number of these associates are represented in Fig. 6 but undoubtedly many more IARs were generated. Of these multiple IARs, links were made between common elements. For example, the common denominator ''is an army physician'' was believed to be a common associate of the observation ''Bearing and Context,'' ''Introduced as Dr. Watson,'' and ''Air of a military man.'' We can aptly apply the associative paradox to this problem in that the greater the number of associations, the greater the effort to search through them to match common associates with other structural associates; while at the same time the greater the number of associates, the greater the probability common elements between structures will be among the generated associates.

The preceding four diverse examples of the associative paradox are not intended to represent an empirical validation of the hypothesis but rather are offered to illustrate how the associative paradox may apply to the study of language, problem solving, and logic, with the purpose of providing research workers a different perspective on these problems.

SUMMARY

Two principle hypothesis have been elucidated in this chapter. The first is that stimulus-selection data, in addition to revealing information about the saliency of cues, is also applicable to the structure of memory, the decoding processes, and the synthesis of stored information. This ''new look'' in stimulus selection will hopefully provide future experimenters with a solid analytic basis for their inferences regarding the efficacy of cues.

The second hypothesis is that cue efficacy is governed by two factors, which has a paradoxical effect on retrieval. These factors are that as the number of implicit associations to a stimulus increases, there is a corresponding increase in the probability that an associative link between the cue and the encoded thing will be included in the sample of associations while, with the increased number of associations, the more protracted will be the search for an appropriate link between the encoded thing and the cue. Multiple cuing was conceptualized as having a potent effect on retrieval as it reduced the number of formed associations and simultaneously provides the subject with an appropriate link between cues and to-be-recalled item. Finally, the interstructural associative paradox was applied to a variety of widely-divergent cognitive processes.

REFERENCES

Bahrick, H. P. Two-phase model for prompted recall. *Psychological Review,* 1970, **77**, 215–222.

Bower, G. H. Organizational factors in memory. *Cognitive Psychology,* 1970, **1**, 18–46.

Cohen, J. C., & Musgrave, B. S. Effect of meaningfulness on cue selection in verbal paired-associate learning. *Journal of Experimental Psychology,* 1964, **68**, 284–291.

Cohen, J. C., & Musgrave, B. S. Effects of formal similarity on cue selection in verbal paired-associate learning. *Journal of Experimental Psychology,* 1966, **71**, 829–838.

Collins, A. M., & Quillian, M. R. Retrieval time from semantic memory. *Journal of Verbal Learning and Verbal Behavior,* 1969, **8**, 240–247.

Dominowski, R. L., & Duncan, C. P. Anagram solving as a function of bigram frequency. *Journal of Verbal Learning and Verbal Behavior,* 1964, **3**, 321–325.

Doyle, A. C. *Sherlock Holmes.* Garden City, New York: Garden City, 1938.

Ellis, H. C. Stimulus encoding processes in human learning and memory. In G. H. Bower (Ed.), *The psychology of learning and motivation.* Vol. 7. New York: Academic Press, 1973.

Harrington, A. L. Effects of component emphasis on stimulus selection in paired-associate learning. *Journal of Experimental Psychology,* 1969, **79**, 412–418.

Houston, J. P. S-R stimulus selection and strength of R-S association. *Journal of Experimental Psychology,* 1964, **68**, 563–566.

James, C. T., & Greeno, J. G. Stimulus selection at different stages of paired-associate learning. *Journal of Experimental Psychology,* 1967, **74**, 75–83.

Jenkins, J. J. Stimulus "fractionation" in paired-associate learning. *Psychological Reports,* 1963, **13**, 409–410.

Landauer, T. K., & Freedman, J. L. Information retrieval from long-term memory: Category size and recognition time. *Journal of Verbal Learning and Verbal Behavior,* 1968, **7**, 291–295.

Lockhart, R. S. Stimulus selection and meaningfulness in paired-associate learning with stimulus items of high formal similarity. *Journal of Experimental Psychology,* 1968, **78**, 242–246.

Loftus, E. F., Freedman, J. L., & Loftus G. F. Retrieval of words from subordinate and superordinate categories in semantic hierarchies. *Psychonomic Science,* 1970, **21**, 235–236.

McGuigan, F. J. *Experimental psychology: A methodological approach.* Englewood Cliffs, N.J.: Prentice-Hall, 1960.

Norman, D. A. Memory, knowledge, and the answering of questions. In R. L. Solso (Ed.), *Contemporary issues in cognitive psychology: The Loyola symposium.* Washington: Winston, 1973.

Postman, L., & Greenbloom, R. Conditions of cue selection in the acquisition of paired-associate lists. *Journal of Experimental Psychology*, 1967, **73**, 91–100.

Richardson, J. Encoding and stimulus selection in paired-associate verbal learning. In A. W. Melton and E. Martin (Eds.), *Coding processes in human memory*. Washington: Winston, 1972.

Richardson, J., & Chisholm, D. C. Transfer of cue selection based on letter position. *Journal of Experimental Psychology*, 1969, **80**, 299–303.

Shannon, C. E. Prediction and entropy in printed English. *Bell System Technical Journal*, 1951, **30**, 50–64.

Shiffrin, R. M., & Geisler, W. S. Visual recognition in a theory of information processing. In R. L. Solso (Ed.), *Contemporary issues in cognitive psychology: The Loyola symposium*. Washington: Winston, 1973.

Solso, R. L. Functional stimulus selection as related to color versus verbal stimuli. *Journal of Experimental Psychology*, 1968, **78**, 382–387.

Solso, R. L. Stimulus selection among trisyllable stimuli. *Journal of Experimental Psychology*, 1971, **88**, 289–291.

Solso, R. L. Stimulus selection: A suggested taxonomy. *The Journal of General Psychology*, 1972, **87**, 231–244.

Solso, R. L., & Biersdorff, K. Recall under conditions of cumulative cues. Unpublished manuscript, Loyola University of Chicago, 1973.

Solso, R. L., & Trafimow, E. S. Stimulus competition as a function of varying stimulus meaningfulness. *Psychonomic Science*, 1970, **18**, 103–104.

Solso, R. L., Topper, G. E., & Macey, W. H. Anagram solution as a function of bigram versatility. *Journal of Experimental Psychology*, 1973, **100**, 259–262.

Thomson, D. M. Encoding variability and retrieval. Paper presented at the meeting of the Midwestern Psychological Association, Detroit, May, 1971.

Thomson, D. M., & Tulving, E. Strength of cue in encoding and retrieval. *Journal of Experimental Psychology*, 1970, **86**, 255–262.

Topper, G. E., Macey, W. H., & Solso, R. L. Bigram versatility and bigram frequency. *Behavioral Research Methodology and Instrumentation*, 1973, **5**, 51–53.

Tulving, E. Subjective organization and effects of repetition in multitrial free-recall learning. *Journal of Verbal Learning and Verbal Behavior*, 1966, **5**, 193–198.

Tulving, E., & Madigan, S. A. Memory and verbal learning. *Annual Review of Psychology*, 1970, **21**, 437–484.

Tulving, E., & Osler, S. Effectiveness of retrieval cues in memory for words. *Journal of Experimental Psychology*, 1968, **77**, 593–601.

Tulving, E., & Pearlstone, Z. Availability versus accessibility of information in memory for words. *Journal of Verbal Learning and Verbal Behavior*, 1966, **5**, 381–391.

Tulving, E., & Thomson, D. M. Retrieval processes in recognition memory: Effects of associative context. *Journal of Experimental Psychology*, 1971, **87**, 116–124.

Underwood, B. J. Are we overloading memory? In A. W. Melton & E. Martin (Eds.), *Coding processes in human memory*. Washington: Winston, 1972.

Underwood, B. J., Ham, M., & Ekstrand, B. Cue selection in paired-associate learning. *Journal of Experimental Psychology*, 1962, **64**, 405–409.

Underwood, B. J., & Schulz, R. W. *Meaningfulness and verbal learning*. Philadelphia: Lippincott, 1960.

Wickens, D. D. Characteristics of word encoding. In A. W. Melton & E. Martin (Eds.), *Coding processes in human memory*. Washington: Winston, 1972.

Young, R. K., Teeters, T. D., & Zelazny, C. Transfer as a function of stimulus selection. *Psychonomic Science*, 1966, **6**, 163–164.

3

CONTINUITY OF PROCESSES ACROSS VARIANTS OF RECOGNITION LEARNING[1]

Donald H. Kausler
University of Missouri, Columbia

HISTORICAL PERSPECTIVE

It takes little discriminatory skill to detect the seemingly "new look" in verbal learning research that emerged during the past decade. If we were able to plot frequency distributions of studies along an "involvement of cognitive processes" dimension, we would undoubtedly find some degree of overlap between the distributions of the 1960's and the 1950's. Nevertheless, the d' value would surely be large, and the hit rate for recognizing "new" versus "old" research would be high.

Many of our colleagues (e.g., Melton & Martin, 1972) attribute the "new look" to a revolution, one that fulfills the criteria of a Kuhnian paradigm shift. According to this conceptualization, information theory and psycholinguistics have been the primary inciters to revolt, while classical associationism has been the guillotine's principal victim. By contrast, others (e.g., Greeno & Bjork, 1973) perceive the "new look" to be an evolutionary, rather than revolutionary, product. Thus, the current scene is regarded as being an extension of the mathematical learning theories of the 1950's, which, in turn, were extensions of still earlier developments in the Hullian era. Whatever instigated the "new look," the point raised here is that the look is less new than it is truly old (a fact which in itself may be symptomatic of a paradigm shift; Kuhn, 1962). After decades of preoccupation with the meaningfulness of nonsense syllables, the unlearning mech-

[1]John H. Mueller contributed substantially to this chapter, in terms of both helpful criticism and pertinent suggestions.

anism of interference theory, the functional stimulus in serial anticipation learning, etc., we seem to have slipped, in a healthy state of regression, to many of the problems and issues that were part of verbal learning's early history. The pioneer is the Ebbinghaus who distinguished between storage and retrieval as memory phenomena (cf. Ebbinghaus, 1885, p. 1), rather than the Ebbinghaus (1885) who burdened us with the doctrine of remote associations, or the Ebbinghaus (1902) who ordered free-recall research to stifle itself shortly after Kirkpatrick's (1894) introduction of the free-recall method. The regression carried with it a return of James' (1890) primary-secondary memory distinction, the Höffding (1891) problem, the Ranschburg (1902) effect, Bartlett's (1932) reconstructive memory concept, and so on. Most importantly, at least for present purposes, the regression restored recognition to its proper place as a core problem area in the psychology of verbal learning and memory.

Historically, recognition entered the experimental literature of verbal learning as a means of providing a more sensitive measure of amount learned (or retained) than that offered by the active recall of items. Early researchers established a methodology that later became widely adopted by today's "new lookers." The methodology calls for the study of a free-recall list, followed by a recall test, and then a recognition test. By means of this sequence, Hollingworth (1913) demonstrated that correct recognitions were consistently greater than correct recalls, with the superiority being greater for words as items than for nonsense syllables as items. Such demonstrations confirmed McDougall's (1904) contention that item strength varies continuously, and that recognition of items is more sensitive to lower levels of strength than is recall. The "lower threshold" concept of recognition became a major reason for the widespread use of recognition measures in research on long-term retention. Beginning with Luh's (1922) study, recognition scores succeeded in revealing memory for items that were considered lost when evaluated by standard recall scores. Prior to the "new look" period, recognition had been reduced largely to the obsequious role of a "lower threshold" dependent variable.

By contrast, the "new look" has given recognition a much needed face lifting. Thus, recognition and recall are now commonly viewed as differing at the process level, rather than at the threshold level. Recall presumably requires a retrieval process that is obviated in recognition (cf. Kintsch, 1970). The hoary study-recall test-recognition test sequence has shifted, accordingly, to become a means of segregating the storage of items from the retrieval of the same items. But we discover again that the "new look" is really a return to another, long neglected, part of our heritage. Some of our most prestigious forefathers (James, 1890; Müller, 1913) alerted us to the wisdom of a two-process theory relating recognition to recall. Somehow their signal faded away in the noise created by years of threshold-oriented research.

Our present concern, though, is with still another approach to recognition. The contemporary period has seen recognition, through several methodological variations, become a major learning task *per se*. Subjects are directed to recognize "target" items, rather than to recall them. Measuring the recognition of target items and the false recognition of distractors serves as the objectives for the experimental operations. Here too we find an impressive, but relatively noninfluential, historical background. Strong (1912) introduced a methodology in which target items (full page advertisements) were presented singly, and then tested for recognition within a matrix composed of both "old" and "new" items. His dependent variables were the adjusted percentages of subjects correctly recognizing old items as "old" and incorrectly recognizing new items as "old." Interestingly, the adjustments were based on confidence ratings given each "old" decision—a definite ancestor to contemporary confidence measures. Except for an occasional study (e.g., Peixotto, 1947; Seward, 1928), little more was done with the single-item recognition learning task until Shepard and Teghtsoonian (1961) aroused the "new look" generation by displaying the task's efficacy for investigating memory processes in general.

A few years later, Underwood, Jesse, and Ekstrand (1964) added the final chapter to the capture of recognition's past history by reintroducing McClelland's (1942) verbal discrimination (VD) method.[2] In McClelland's method, multiple items (usually pairs), rather than single items, are presented for study. One of the paired items in each compound is arbitrarily designated a "target," or "right" (R), item, and the other a distractor, or "wrong" (W), item. Each pair occurs on a test phase, and the target member is selected by the subject. Labeling the multiple-item method "verbal discrimination learning" was an unfortunate choice. Single-item recognition learning tasks usually involve verbal items, thus making such tasks require "verbal discriminations" to the same extent as multiple-item tasks. Moreover, the "verbal" discriminations demanded in many multiple-item studies (e.g., Ross, 1972) are actually between paired pictures, rather than paired words. Finally, it must be mildly jolting to the anti-VD members of the verbal-learning-memory establishment when they read newspaper headlines proclaiming VD to be on the rise. At any rate, the multiple-item method, like its single-item counterpart, has shown considerable promise as a means of gaining insights into the mysteries of memory.

TOWARD A GENERAL THEORY OF RECOGNITION LEARNING

Prerequisites

As described above, the multiple-item task is characterized by pairwise discriminations between two old items. That is, both R and W intrapair components are old in the sense of having been exposed during a study phase. In a popular

---

[2]Actually, the method had been used in the years intervening between McClelland's research and that of Underwood et al. (e.g., Postman, 1962; Underwood & Viterna, 1951). However, these studies were directed at issues other than recognition learning *per se* (e.g., massed versus distributed practice).

version of the single-item recognition learning task (e.g., Shepard, 1967), the subject must also discriminate between two items during the test phase, but now only the target member of each pair is old. Thus, the discrimination is between "old" and "new," rather than "right" and "wrong." Given the obvious commonality in task structure between single-item and multiple-item recognition learning, we should expect to find some degree of continuity between their processes as well. However, with the notable exception of Underwood's (e.g., 1972) frequency theory, contemporary theories (e.g., Anderson & Bower, 1972; Kintsch, 1967, 1970; Norman & Wickelgren, 1965) of recognition learning are restricted to the analysis of processes underlying single-item tasks. What appears to be an adequate account of recognition learning in the context of single-item tasks may encounter serious problems when it is generalized, as it must be, to the multiple-item situation. A good example is the contextual association theory of Anderson and Bower (1972). Here is the essence of the theory, as summarized recently by Bower (1972):

> A recent paper by Anderson and me (1972) touches on this topic of list differentiation in the course of theorizing more generally about recognition memory. A critical viewpoint of our theory is that we conceived of list identification as analogous to a paired-associate learning task, in which items as stimuli are becoming associated to list tags or list markers as responses. A list marker or tag denotes a particular subset of list-context elements (thoughts, cognitive events, cues) active at the time a particular item occurs. We elaborated upon what we meant by list-context cues, the set of stimulus events that combine to identify for the subject that time block of item presentations he calls List i, $i = 1, 2, 3, \ldots$. For instance, one simple list context cue is a subjective count or label, as "first list," "second list," and so on, sustained by the subject throughout presentation of a given list. Thus at the time the item *cat* appears in List 1, the subject may be in a particular state of arousal, may be thinking of his stupidity, that this is the first set of items, and worrying about how well he will be able to remember them. The combination of these several cognitive elements that happened at a particular time (when *cat* was presented) during List 1 serves to identify a list marker [p. 106].

Clearly, "A significant consequence of this context-retrieval theory is that the task of item recognition is not really different in kind from that of list discrimination (Anderson & Bower, 1972, pp. 101–102)." There is ample evidence to indicate that subjects can identify not only the specific list (within a series of lists) that a given item occurred in (e.g., Hintzman & Waters, 1970), but also the relative position within that list (Hintzman, Block, & Summers, 1973). In effect, Anderson and Bower's theory assumes that the process mediating single-item recognition is equivalent to the process mediating list identification—correctly recognizing an item as being old is the same as identifying that item's inclusion in a recently studied list. The equivalence eliminates the necessity of postulating a special strength of familiarity principle solely for the purpose of explaining recognition of individual items. While admitting to the efficacy of a strength principle, Anderson and Bower (1972), nevertheless, proceeded to reject it for the following reason:

> As long as both models handle equally well the simple recognition task, there is no way to disprove this dualistic claim. However, on grounds of parsimony one would say that there is no need for a special theory for a special circumstance when a more general theory subsumes the special circumstance and many others. Besides its lack of parsimony, this attempt to give a special status to the pure recognition paradigm ignores the fact that all recognition experiments are implicitly list or set discrimination experiments [p. 102].

The difficulty, of course, is that not all recognition experiments are implicitly list discrimination experiments. The major exception is the multiple-item experiment. Contextual elements active at the time a given R item occurs are also likely to be active when its W item counterpart occurs. Consequently, identifying the R item solely on the basis of list-inclusion cues would be a highly unreliable, if not impossible, process. A theory incorporating a strength-of-familiarity principle is seemingly more general than Anderson and Bower's contextual-association theory, at least in the sense of its capacity for spanning a broader spectrum of recognition-learning experiments. List differentiation would appear to be the better candidate than multiple-item recognition for representing a special circumstance that requires a special process, such as the contextual mechanism proposed by Anderson and Bower.

A general theory of recognition learning should be as relevant for the multiple-item task as it is for single-item tasks. Our choice for such a theory is a modification of contemporary frequency theory. The modification is based on the feature component hypothesis that has worked so well when applied to single-item experiments (e.g., Anisfeld & Knapp, 1968; Kollasch & Kausler, 1972). One of our objectives in this chapter will be to examine the appropriateness of a feature analytic-frequency tagging theory for multiple-item tasks. The assumed continuity between the two main variants of recognition learning leads us to hope for some degree of success.

Process Analysis

Words are viewed as having featural components (e.g., phonemic, orthographic, and semantic) stored in permanent memory. When a given word, A, is presented for study as an item on a single-item recognition task; responses to that word yield frequency-of-response tags (f) that are stored with specific featural components of that word ($a_w a_x$, and so on).[3] The primary sources of response tags are the representational (perceptual) and rehearsal responses identified by frequency theory (Ekstrand, Wallace, & Underwood, 1966). Not all features of Word A are necessarily attended to and processed during the study phase (Anisfeld & Knapp, 1968). Therefore not all components carry frequency tags

---

[3]Recency tags represent a reasonable alternative for single-item recognition learning. In effect, a recency tag is indistinguishable from a frequency, or familiarity, tag in this case. However, recency tags would have little relevance for multiple-item recognition learning. Since W and R intrapair items would both carry recency tags, they would not provide discriminatory cues. For the sake of parsimony, frequency-of-response tags are preferred here for both task variants.

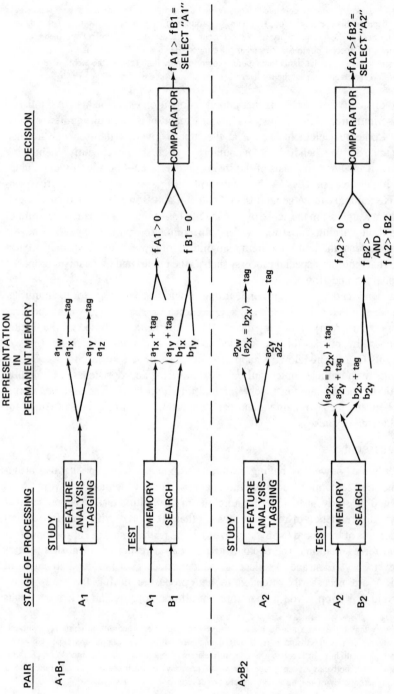

FIG. 1. Feature tagging (study) and memory search (test) sequence for a single-item recognition learning task in which there is either nonsharing (top panel) or partial sharing (bottom panel) of tagged features between a study word (A_1 and A_2) and its paired test distractor word (B_1 and B_2).

with them into a later test phase. Those components that are tagged represent collectively the strength of that item's memory trace (symbolized here as f_A). The number and type (e.g., sensory versus semantic) of tagged features are presumed to be contingent upon the time available for processing (Shulman, 1971) and the nature of the rehearsal activity *per se* (Craik & Lockhart, 1972).

During the test phase, the subject encounters a pair of words, A and B, from which he is to select the old target item. As shown in Fig. 1, a search of the representations of Words A and B in permanent memory reveals that $f_A > f_B$ for the two pairs represented. In Pair A_1B_1 the distractor, Word B_1, is a new item that appears for the first time during the test phase. It may be seen that the features of Word B_1 (b_{1w}, b_{1x}, and so on) do not overlap at all with the features of Word A_1 that were processed and tagged during the study phase (a_{1x}, a_{1y}). In effect, $f_{B1} = 0$, and f_{A1} should be substantially greater than f_{B1}. There is the possibility that a distractor may share one or more features with a tagged study item, even though the distractor came from a pool of unrelated words. This is illustrated for Pair A_2B_2 in Fig. 1. Here one of the features of Word B_2 (b_{2x}) is identical to one of the tagged features of Word A_2 (a_{2x}). For example, A_2 might be the word *pane*, and a_{2x}, a_{2y} might be its phonemic features. If B_2 happened to be a rhyming word, such as *sane*, there would be a partial overlap in tagged features. A search of memory during testing retrieves the information that $f_{B2} > 0$. The intrapair discrimination between A_2 and B_2 should therefore be more difficult to make than the discrimination between A_1 and B_1.

Finally, a distractor may be selected so that it deliberately shares features with a study item. This is illustrated for Pair A_3B_3 in Fig. 2. Here two of the features of Word B_3 (b_{3x}, b_{3y}) are identical to the two tagged features of Word A_3 (a_{3x}, a_{3y}). This would be the case if Word B_3 happened to be a homonym of Word A_3 (i.e., *pain*). The consequence would be that $f_{B3} = f_{A3}$, and selection of the previous study item would be a matter of guessing. The underlying assumption, of course, is that the study item had been processed only at the phonemic level. If other features of the study item (e.g., a_{3w}), such as its semantic information, had also been processed and tagged, the overlap would no longer be total—and f_A would once more be greater than f_B. Whatever the circumstances, there is a general rule—if the disparity between f_A and f_B is discriminably great enough, the subject correctly selects Word A on this basis.

The test phase need not follow the paired old item-distractor item format. With other procedures the nature of the decision process is modified somewhat, but the basic reliance on the strength of tagged features is unaltered. When test items are presented one at a time, the subject must evaluate each f_A (test item = A word) or f_B (test item = B word) relative to some absolute criterion value. For each f_A and f_B value confronted by the subject, the decision "old item" is given whenever the criterion is exceeded. Otherwise, the one-item-at-a-time format possesses the same potential for varying the degree of feature sharing between A and B words as the paired-item testing format. For example, we might have the

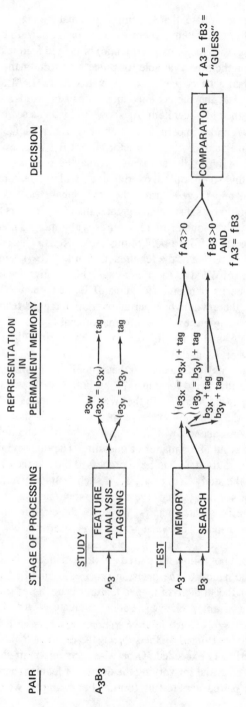

FIG. 2. Feature tagging (study) and memory search (test) sequence for a single-item recognition learning task in which there is complete sharing of tagged features between a study word (A_3) and its paired test distractor word (B_3).

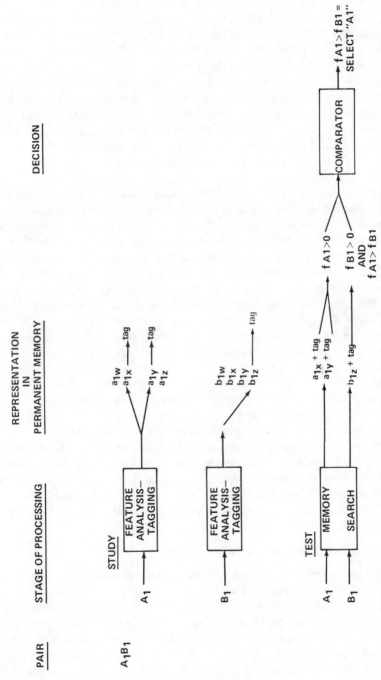

FIG. 3. Feature tagging (study) and memory search (test) sequence for a multiple-item recognition learning task in which features of both the right (A_1) and wrong (B_1) words are tagged during the study phase.

equivalent of A_3 study words. During the test phase, the subject would receive either A_3 words or their B_3 counterparts. That is, some of the singly presented test words would be new (B_3). On the basis of feature sharing, there should be a number of f_B values that exceed the criterion value. Thus, the false alarm rate should be much greater than when the A and B words are largely void of shared features (i.e., A_1 and B_1 test words). The one-item-at-a-time test method has the advantage of separating errors of recognition into misses (identifying old words as new) and false alarms (identifying new words as old). We shall return to this advantage later. On the other hand, the paired-item test method approximates more closely that of multiple-item recognition learning, and for this reason studies employing the method will be given preferential treatment in this paper.

The complexity of the situation is increased considerably when Word B is exposed simultaneously with Word A during a study phase, as it is in the multiple-item recognition task. For example, in the first trial of the standard anticipation method the subject sees A_1 and B_1 ("unrelated") words together, but without knowledge of A_1's correctness. He is forced to guess which word is the R item, before he receives informative feedback cuing him as to A_1's correctness. The likely consequence is the processing and tagging of at least part of Word B_1's features, as well as part of A_1's features. However, Word A_1 is responded to more frequently than Word B_1 via rehearsal of the former following feedback (Ekstrand et al., 1966), resulting in $f_{A1} > f_{B1}$. Words A_1 and B_1 occur together again during the anticipation phase of the second trial. At this point a search of the representations of the two words in permanent memory is conducted (see Fig. 3). The probability of Word A_1 being selected as the intrapair R item is, as in the test trial of single-trial recognition learning, a function of the magnitude of the disparity between f_{A1} and f_{B1}. Additional trials on the task continue to result in more responses per trial to A_1 than to B_1. Accordingly, the disparity in strengths continues to increase until f_{A1} is discriminably and consistently greater than f_{B1}.

In theory, the difficulty of intrapair discriminations should increase when paired A and B words share features, just as it does in the A_3B_3 situation described earlier in connection with the single-item task. We should again begin to approximate the situation where $f_A = f_B$. Parallel functions of this kind would, in fact, represent a major source of evidence for the continuity of processes across task variants.

Contrast with Traditional Frequency Theory

There are important differences between the present analysis and that of frequency theory, even though frequency of responding to individual items plays a central role in both approaches to recognition learning. Frequency theory, as formalized most precisely by Ekstrand et al. (1966), identifies words *qua* words as the recipients of frequency-of-responding units. By contrast, featural components of words are viewed as the beneficiaries in the modification proposed here. The distinction matters little for A_1B_1 combinations. That is, the account of hit rates is as appropriate from the perspective of frequency-tagged unrelated whole words as it is from the perspective of frequency-tagged bundles of features that make up those unrelated words. Only when there is overlap between intralist members, as with A_3B_3 combinations, do we find a significant contrast. Ekstrand et al. clearly accept the concept of an implicit associative response as the underlying causal factor for the variations in hit rates that occur when intralist members are related to one another. Overlap is therefore defined in terms of the occurrence of one item as an implicit associate to another item. More recently, Shaughnessy and Underwood (1973) clarified the nature of the mechanism further by equating an implicit response with the displaced rehearsal of the associatively related item. For example, if *pretty* is an A_3 item and *beautiful* is its B_3 counterpart, direct rehearsal of *pretty* is presumed to yield "displaced" rehearsal of *beautiful* (a natural-language word associate of *pretty*) as well. Thus, f_{B3} should gain parasitically in value as f_{A3} increases directly.

There is an imposing body of evidence that conflicts with the implicit associative-response hypothesis. This evidence has been recently reviewed by the present author (Kausler, 1974) and will only be touched upon here. One of the most convincing bits comes from studies relating error rates to the degree of pre-experimental associative connection between A_3 and B_3 words (as determined by word association norms). The implicit associative-response hypothesis predicts that f_B should become increasingly greater as the A_3-to-B_3 normative relationship increases, thereby generating increasingly more false recognitions of B_3. The evidence supporting this prediction is, at best, inconsistent. Single-item studies have characteristically employed the one-item-at-a-time testing procedure. Grossman and Eagle (1970) reported a zero correlation between the rate of false alarms and associative strength over a fairly narrow range of normative values. Kausler and Settle (1973) replicated Grossman and Eagle's procedure and materials, and again found a zero correlation between error rate and associative strength. However, they did find a modest correlation between confidence ratings and associative strength. A near zero correlation was also found by Mueller (1973). The range of associative strength employed in the last study was considerably greater than in the earlier studies. On the other hand, Cramer (e.g., 1972) has managed to confirm the positive correlation expected from the implicit associative-response hypothesis. A number of investigators (e.g., Barch & Whalen, 1970; Eberlein & Raskin, 1968; Fulkerson & Kausler, 1969; Lovelace & L. Schulz, 1971; Zimmerman, Shaughnessy, & Underwood, 1972) have discovered a null effect when associatively related words make up the intrapair combinations of a multiple-item task (although an adverse effect for associative relatedness was found by Palermo and Ullrich, 1968, and by McCarthy, 1973). Since associatively related words are likely to share semantic features, a feature-analytic hypothesis seemingly predicts an adverse effect on intrapair discriminations as well. However, since semantically related words are unlikely to share other kinds of features, increments in f_{B3} values may be avoided by a compensatory process whereby only these nonoverlapping features are attended to (to be elaborated upon later). The implicit associative-response hypothesis encounters even more serious problems in explaining the absence of an associative strength-acquisition rate relationship when the linkage occurs between either interpair R members or interpair W members (Mueller, Kanak, & Flanagan, 1973).

There is one other important difference between the present approach and traditional frequency theory. The difference, which centers on the multiple-item task, will be the subject of our final section. In the meantime, our next step is to examine the available evidence that supports the continuity of processes between single-item and multiple-item recognition learning. The continuity is suggested, of course, by the similarity of operations defining the two task variants, and its presence would imply the necessity of a general theory of recognition learning. Two kinds of evidence will be reviewed. The first deals with variations in basic hit rates and error rates that occur across task variants; the second deals with the functional relationships between critical independent variables and hit rates across task variants.

COMPARISONS OF HIT AND ERROR RATES ACROSS TASK VARIANTS

While there are obvious similarities in the operations defining single-item and multiple-item tasks, there is also one key difference. The difference rests in the study phase of the two tasks. The effect of exposing the target item alone versus the effect of exposing it with a distractor raises much more than a minor methodological question. From our previous analysis it may be seen that the disparity between f_A and f_B extant at the time of testing should be greater when A was studied alone than when it was yoked to B. Accordingly, we expect to find a much higher hit rate (i.e., the mean percentage of subjects correctly identifying target items on a test phase) for single-item than for multiple-item tasks. The differential in rates follows, in fact, from the general continuity of processes across task variants.

Since most single-item experiments involve only one study-test sequence, the proper contrast is with the hit rate on the anticipation phase of the second (or first nonguessing) trial of multiple-item experiments. Moreover, to avoid potential confounding effects, the comparisons should be restricted to studies in which the number of A words (i.e., list length) is equal for the two tasks, and the sets of A and B words are identical across tasks. Surprisingly, there seem to have been no studies that permit a fully valid comparison when the A and B words are unrelated. However, it is possible to compare hit rates for different studies employing the same list length, but with different samples of words as A and B items. For example, Newby and Young (1972) reported a hit rate of 93.3% (estimated from their Fig. 1) for a single-item task containing 15 A items. The comparable hit

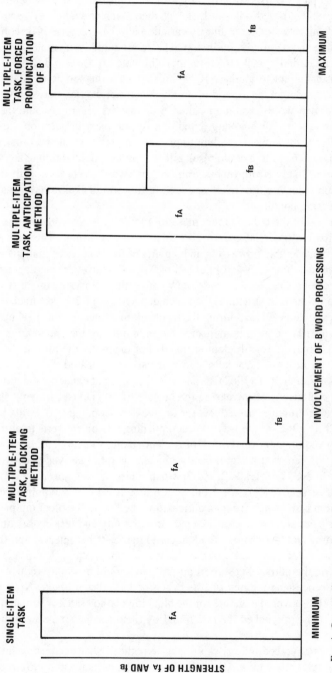

FIG. 4. Comparative strengths of f_A and f_B as a function of task structure, given the assumption that the degree of processing an A word is invariant with respect to the degree of processing a paired B word.

rate for the 15 pair VD lists employed by Kausler, Fulkerson, and Eschenbrenner (1967) was 68.7% (based only on List 1 of their transfer sequence).

In general, hit rates reflect primarily variation along a "degree of B word feature processing and tagging" continuum. The continuum, as illustrated in Fig. 4, is anchored at one end by task structures that eliminate exposure to B words during a study phase. Failure to attain a 100% hit rate with this single-item structure could stem from coincidental, and often idiosyncratic, overlap between the features of several A words, and their paired B distractors. Testing would then approximate an $f_A = f_B$, or guessing, condition for the pairs in question. Another possible factor is the subject's failure to process and tag several A words during the study phase. The failure could result either from lack of attention to a given A word, or, more likely, from time-sharing of that word's rehearsal with the rehearsal of a previous A word. In either event, testing would again approximate the $f_A = f_B$ guessing condition.

The other end of the continuum comes close to being represented by the standard "anticipation-first trial guessing" method of VD learning. This task structure assures considerable processing and tagging of the features of many B words during the anticipation-guessing intervals of Trial 1. However, the degree of B word involvement is increased even more when additional processing of B words is demanded by the task structure. One such demand is to force pronunciation of B words, as well as A words, during the feedback intervals of Trial 1 (Kausler & Sardello, 1967). The concomitant decrement in hit rate for the anticipation intervals of Trial 2 may be readily demonstrated. For example, the hit rate was less than 60% for Kausler and Sardello's 15-pair list, as compared to the hit rate of 68.7% for Kausler et al.'s (1967) 15-pair list. The present conceptualization also suggests several means of increasing the hit rate for a VD task. In general, any variation in task structure that reduces the degree of responding to B words should increase hit rate. One simple way of accomplishing this objective is to eliminate the guessing requirement on Trial 1 of the anticipation method. Fulkerson and Johnson (1971) reported a significantly greater hit rate, as averaged over the anticipation intervals of Trials 2 and 3, when guessing was absent (83%) than when it was present (74%). An even more dramatic way of accomplishing the same objective is to switch from an anticipation method to the blocking method. In the latter method there is a clear separation of study and test phases on each trial. The study and test phases are identical to the feedback interval and the anticipation interval, respectively, of the VD anticipation method. Identification of the A word on the initial exposure of an AB pair should markedly reduce attention to, and processing-tagging of, the B component. Accordingly, Newby and Young (1972) discovered a hit rate for the blocking method (85%; estimated from their Fig. 1) that approached the rate found by them for the single-item method (93.3%).

Implicit in the preceding analysis is the hypothesis that decreasing hit rates for choosing A words within AB test-pairs result from increasing false recogni-

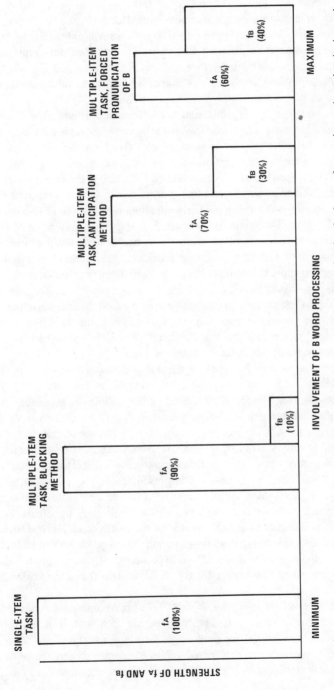

Fig. 5. Comparative strengths of f_A and f_B as a function of task structure, given the assumption that the degree of processing an A word varies inversely with the degree of processing its paired B word.

tions of B words as R items. A corollary of this hypothesis is that the extent of frequency tagging determining f_A is relatively unaffected by the conditions extant during the study of A words. Stated differently, f_A is invariant with respect either to single-item versus multiple-item task variation, or, when only multiple-item tasks are considered, to anticipation versus blocking variation (see Fig. 4). Recognition errors attributable to false recognition of B words (i.e., false alarms) should be sensitive to such variations.

There is, however, a very different way of conceptualizing the interaction between A and B words. The total capacity for processing-tagging the information indigenous to AB pairs may be constant, given a fixed rate exposing those pairs. Consequently, whatever segment of that capacity is expended on B words would necessarily be compensated for by a correlated reduction in the amount of processing-tagging given to A words. In other words, a gain in f_B is gained at the expense of a loss in f_A. The result for variation along the "degree of B feature processing and tagging" continuum is depicted in Fig. 5. It may be seen that for each point along the continuum the alternative conceptualizations predict the same amount of disparity between f_A and f_B. However, the present hypothesis does yield one important prediction that differs markedly from the prediction yielded by the previous hypothesis. Recognition errors attributable to the nonrecognition of A words should no longer remain constant across methodological variations. This prediction follows from the reduction in f_A that occurs in the transition from minimal to maximal processing of B words. Therefore, misses should increase, rather than remain invariant, while false alarms increase.

The appropriate means of contrasting these hypotheses calls for a testing procedure in which A and B words are exposed individually in a random order. This is the one-item-at-a-time procedure described earlier. While the procedure is often used in single-item recognition learning experiments (e.g., Grossman & Eagle, 1970, Experiment 1), it has not been fully adapted for use in conventional VD experiments. It simply requires intrapair R and W items to be presented individually in a randomized order, with subjects being instructed to identify each item's "rightness" or "wrongness." Our present interest is in the comparison of miss rates and false alarm rates following a single-item study phase and a blocking-method multiple-item study phase. The constant f_A hypothesis predicts that the miss rate should be roughly equal for the two task variants, whereas the variable f_A hypothesis predicts that the miss rate should be higher for the multiple-item than for the single-item task. Both hypotheses, of course, predict that the false alarm rate should be higher for the multiple-item than for the single-item task.

Fortunately, a recent study by Ross (1972) approximated the desired procedure. Furthermore, his study involved the same A and B items (abstract pictures, rather than words) for both single-item and multiple-item conditions, thus satisfying our requirements noted earlier. Separate groups (seventh-grade children) received A items either without (single-item task) or with (multiple-item task) paired B items during a study phase. The latter condition resembled the blocking method in that each intrapair A (or "right") item was pointed to by the experimenter. The A and B items were then tested individually, but linked items (e.g., A_1B_1 in Fig. 3) apparently occurred successively, rather than in random order. In agreement with the constant hypothesis, the percentage of misses for A items (i.e., identifying them as either "new" or "wrong") was nearly identical for single-item (20%) and multiple-item (19%) tasks. Moreover, the percentage of false alarms for B items (i.e., identifying them as "old" or "right") was much greater for the latter task (13%) than for the former (6%).

COMPARISONS OF FUNCTIONAL RELATIONSHIPS ACROSS TASK VARIANTS

General Overview

One of our most potent tools for identifying continuity of processes across tasks is to search for commonality of functional relationships. In general, our confidence in continuity increases directly with the number of common functional relationships that performance on the tasks in question bear with relevant independent variables (cf. Kausler, 1974, for elaboration, and for application to continuity between paired-associate and serial anticipation learning tasks). Conversely, evidence for differential intertask processes accumulates to the extent that the tasks evince disparate functional relationships. It is, in fact, the existence of disparate functional relationships for such traditional item attributes as meaningfulness that supports the necessity of distinguishing between recognition and recall at the process level (Kausler, 1974; Kintsch, 1970).

The covariation between level of meaningfulness and hit rate offers a conventional starting point for examining further the question of intertask continuity of recognition processes. The single-item recognition hit rate for high-frequency (H) A words is generally below that for low-frequency (L) A words. A prototypal study is that of Shepard (1967). The hit rate for H A words, tested pairwise with H B words, was 82%, whereas the comparable rate for L A words, tested pairwise with L B words, was 92%. Unfortunately, the evidence is more equivocal for multiple-item tasks. In support of continuity, some researchers (e.g., Lovelace & Pulley, 1972; Rowe & Paivio, 1971) also found faster acquisition for L A–L B pairs than for H A–H B pairs. However, others (e.g., Ingison & Ekstrand, 1970; R. Schulz & Hopkins, 1968) failed to find any effect of differential meaningfulness levels on multiple-item acquisition. Meaningfulness in its various guises is probably not a very effective variable for confirming commonality of functional relationships in recognition learning. The problem rests in the basis for expecting an inverse relationship in the first place. Presumably, H A words share more tagged features with randomly paired H B words (as in the A_2B_2 pair of Fig. 1) than do L A words with randomly paired L B words. As a result, the average intrapair disparity between f_A and f_B should be greater for low-meaning-ful than for high-meaningful words.[4] Since the inverse relationship is contingent upon randomly determined featural overlaps, occasional null effects should not be too surprising.

A far better strategy is to vary intentionally and systematically the degree of featural overlap between A and B words for both single-item and multiple-item tasks. At one end of the continuum we find tasks patterned after the A_1B_1 pairs of Fig. 1; at the other end, patterned after the A_3B_3 pairs of Fig. 2. In between we could have tasks in which there is a more moderate amount of featural overlap, as in the A_2B_2 pairs of Fig. 1. In theory, f_B should increase directly as the number of features shared between intrapair members increases. The hit rate for both single-item and multiple-item tasks should decrease concomitantly—in agreement with our general conceptualization of recognition learning (see p. 51). However, intertask continuity of processes does not necessarily mean complete identity of processes. The multiple-item task permits the operation of a compensa-tory process that is unlikely to occur with the single-item task. Since the A and B words forming intrapair R and W items are studied together, the subject has the opportunity to attend selectively (or to process at a different level in terms of Craik and Lockhart's, 1972, analysis) to those features of Word A that are *not* shared by Word B (e.g., the a_{3w} feature in Fig. 2). Selective attention is especially likely to be primed when all of the intralist pairs are characterized by the same feature-sharing rule (e.g., all paired words are synonyms of one another, or all paired words are homonyms of one another). The distinctive features of A words may then receive a greater degree of processing and frequency tagging than the shared features. Returning to our earlier example, the tagged features for *pane* would be those that distinguish it semantically (or perhaps orthographically) from *pain*. The consequence could be a return to the f_A to f_B ratio expected for "unrelated" A and B words. In other words, the hit rate would not depart markedly from that found for a control list composed of "unrelated" word pairs.

There is an alternative to the intrapair method of introducing feature sharing between the R and W items of a VD list. The alternative has the advantage, so to speak, of greatly mitigating the contribution from the compensatory process described above, thereby making it more directly comparable to the single-item task. The modified method calls for an interpair, rather than intrapair, arrange-ment of feature-sharing words (Fulkerson & Kausler, 1969; Kausler & Olson, 1969). Each A word is the R item of one pair, while its B word counterpart is the W item of a different pair (e.g., *pane* as the R item of Pair *j* and *pain* as the W item of Pair *k*). A list constructed in this manner should yield the reduction in hit rate generally expected from our theory whenever B words share tagged features with A words. Since the related words are not exposed together, a strategy focus-

---

[4]An additional factor considered by frequency theory (Ekstrand et al., 1966) is a Weber's law principle that will not concern us in this chapter.

ing on the processing-tagging of only distinctive features is unlikely. The magnitude of f_B for an interpair related list, averaged over all pairs of the list, should be considerably greater than the magnitude of f_B for either an intrapair-related list or a control list, again averaged over all pairs. Our principle remains, "The less the disparity between f_A and f_B, the more difficult the intrapair discrimination."

In the remainder of this section we will review briefly some of the evidence relating both single-item and multiple-item recognition learning to varying degrees of feature sharing between A and B words. Phonemic, orthographic, and semantic features will be considered separately as sources of generating featural overlap.

Phonemic Features

Our review will be restricted to only those studies employing complete phonemic overlap of A and B words (i.e., homonymity). Homonyms have a special significance in research on recognition learning. They are usually associatively unrelated to one another. Consequently, their effects on recognition phenomena can be explained by the feature-analytic hypothesis, but not the implicit associative-response hypothesis.

In terms of single-item recognition learning, our review will be further restricted by considering only those studies employing the study-pairwise test (A study word paired with a B distractor word) methodology. Initially, Buschke and Lenon (1969) reported the expected lower hit rate for the single-item task when the B words were homonyms of their directly paired A words than when they were unrelated featurally (34.5% and 45.9%, respectively; corrected for guessing). Cermak, Schnorr, Buschke, and Atkinson (1970) found a comparable decrement (hit rates of 55% and 65%, as estimated from their Fig. 1; corrected for guessing) when their subjects were instructed to concentrate on the "sound" of each A word during the study phase. Additional confirmation of a reduced hit rate with intrapair homonymity came from a study by Bruder and Silverman (1972). However, the reduction in hit rate was somewhat less than the 10% observed in the Buschke and Lenon and Cermak et al. studies.

Our search for a parallel functional relationship in the multiple-item situation is rewarded when we examine the two studies employing homographs in an interpair condition. Both Kausler and Olson (1969) and L. Schulz and Lovelace (1972) discovered such a list to be markedly more difficult to learn than a control list. The intrapair homonymity condition also produced a learning decrement for the multiple-item task in Kausler and Olson's study, but the decrement was significantly less pronounced than in their interpair condition. Bruder and Silverman (1972) found a similar decrement under a fast exposure rate, but not under a slow rate (in fact, the homonym condition was superior to the control condition). To complete the picture, Buschke and Lenon (1969) found a null effect for intrapair homonymity. Taken together, the pattern of results for the intrapair list condition supports our postulation of a compensatory process that reduces the difficulty of discriminating between pairwise related items by directing the processing-tagging of item information to other than shared features.

Interestingly, the case for continuity across task variants is made even stronger by the demonstration of a similar compensatory process in single-item recognition learning that is activated under certain conditions. Suppose subjects are primed to process and tag the semantic features of each of a series of A study words. Since the phonemic features for many of these words are likely to receive little processing and frequency tagging, the identical features for their B counterparts encountered on the test phase would have little strength. Consequently, f_B should be well below the level of f_A for most pairs, and intrapair discriminations should be relatively easy. The appropriate demonstration occurred in the previously cited study by Cermak et al. (1970). Priming of semantic processing was accomplished in one of their conditions by instructing subjects to concentrate on the "dictionary meaning" of each A study word as it was presented. The hit rate was 90% for both homonym and control test pairs. In addition, the high hit rate obtained under semantic priming indicates the greater efficacy of the processing-tagging mechanism for semantic features than for phonemic features. It will be recalled that the hit rate for their control list under "sound" instructions was only 65%.

Orthographic Features

The general importance of a word's orthography as a viable source of "taggable" features was revealed in a study by Zechmeister (1972). Words scaled high in orthographic distinctiveness yielded a significantly higher hit rate than words scaled low in distinctiveness (single-item recognition learning, paired-item testing). Since the orthographic features of A words are seemingly processed and tagged during study phases, B words sharing these orthographic features should receive substantial increments in their f_B values. Thus, performance on single-item and multiple tasks should show parallel inverse relationships with the extent of orthographic overlap between A and B words.

An effective means of testing the expected inverse relationship has been through the use of homonym word pairs that vary widely in their orthographic distinctiveness. The degree of featural overlap should be much greater for pairs of low distinctiveness (e.g., *real, reel*) than for pairs of high distinctiveness (e.g., *earn, urn*). Accordingly, acquisition should be more difficult for the former condition than for the latter. Once more, continuity across tasks has been manifested— the inverse relationship between degree of orthographic overlap and rate of acquisition shows up clearly for both the single-item (e.g., Raser, 1972) and the multiple-item task (e.g., Kausler, 1973b).

The preceding studies, while supportive of continuity, nevertheless present some interpretative problems. The contrast in acquisition rates between low and high levels of distinctiveness may be statistically significant for each task variant, but this fact alone does not necessarily assure parallel intertask functional relationships. Conceivably, the magnitude of the contrast between low and high levels of distinctiveness may be much greater for one task than for the other. More importantly, the change in learning proficiency over the levels of distinctiveness between "low" and "high" may be quite different for one task than for the other—if such intermediate levels had been related to learning proficiency. For example, the overall functional relationship might be linear for single-item recognition learning and negatively accelerated for multiple-item recognition learning. What is needed is a set of materials scaled continuously for distinctiveness. Acquisition rates over a number of levels of the independent variable could then be determined separately for the task variants. Hopefully, commonality of the independent-dependent variable relationship would emerge.

A study directed at this objective was recently completed in our laboratory. We (Kausler & Pavur, 1974) began by scaling the 20 consonants of the alphabet in terms of the graphic distinctiveness between their upper and lower case forms. This was accomplished by having subjects rate each of the 20 pairs on a 9-point scale, and then determining the mean rating for each upper-lower case pairing (the means have quite acceptable reliability when measured by agreement between independent samples of subjects; rho = .93). The 20 pairs then served as the items for single-item and multiple-item tasks that were administered to separate groups of subjects. For the single-item task the 20 nominal consonants were study items (together with 20 two-digit numbers as filler items). Of these, 10 were displayed in upper case form and 10 in lower case form. On the test phase the upper-lower case forms of each consonant were presented together, and the subjects had to select the "old" member of every pair. For the multiple-item task (blocking method) the upper-lower case forms were presented as study pairs with one member of each pair identified as being "right." On each test phase the pairs were presented again, and the subjects were asked to select the "right" member of every pair. There were two study-test cycles for the single-item task, and eight for the multiple-item task.

In agreement with our previous analysis, hit rates were slightly higher for the single-item task than for the blocking version of the multiple-item task. The difference was larger for pairs of low distinctiveness than for pairs of high distinctiveness (when split at the median). The rates, as averaged over Trials 1 and 2, were 84.4% (high) and 79.4% (low) and 82.6% (high) and 74.5% (low) for the single-item and multiple-item tasks, respectively. More important at the moment, however, are the cross-task commonalities in covariation between total errors and distinctiveness ratings. These covariations are shown in Fig. 6 (with distinctiveness grouped into five levels of four consonants each). Both functions are peculiarly nonmonotonic. Our concern, though, is mainly with the striking correspondence between the two functions over the entire range of distinctivess. The correspondence is illustrated further by the moderately high correlation (rho = .64) between cross-task error rates when the entire set of 20 consonants provides the data points. Such correspondence would surely not emerge without having a high degree of overlap between the processes underlying the two task variants.

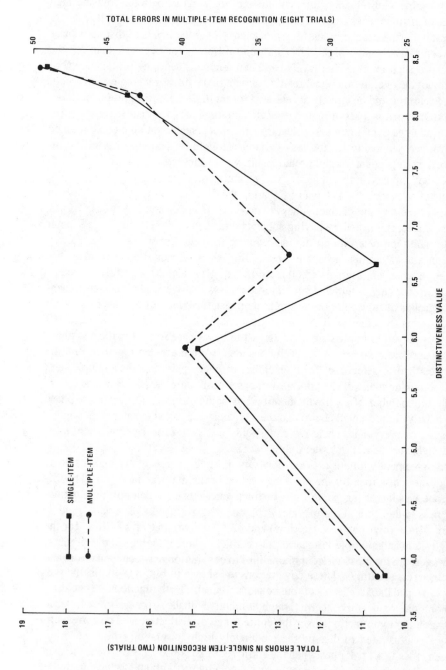

Fig. 6. Error rate as a function of rated distinctiveness between study and test distractor items (upper-lower case forms of consonants) for both single-item and multiple-item recognition learning tasks.

Semantic Features

Manipulation of semantic featural sharing is complicated by the likely associative overlap between many words sharing semantic features. Our preference is to consider only those studies that succeeded in clearly manipulating semantic features independently of associative relatedness. As with phonemic features, this manipulation is best accomplished by means of employing a special population of words. In this case, it is homographs, rather than homonyms. Since homographs usually have complete overlap of sensory features, discriminations between their separate forms can be made solely on the basis of their distinctive meanings.

Only gross comparisons between the basic task variants are possible. These comparisons reveal that hit rates for both single-item and multiple-item tasks are sensitive to variations in semantic feature sharing. In a well-known study by Light and Carter-Sobell (1970) the study items were homographs that were modified by paired adjectives selected so as to prime one specific meaning of each item (e.g., "strawberry" *jam*). The tagged semantic features were presumably those primed by the modifier (e.g., *jam* as a sweet preserve). In one test condition the homographs were modified by words that primed meanings consistent with the previously tagged meanings (e.g., "raspberry" *jam*). In another condition the homographs were modified by words that primed the alternate meanings (e.g., "traffic" *jam*). The hit rate was significantly higher in the first condition than in the second (73% to 63%). The lower hit rate in the second condition resulted from the reduction in the number of tagged features that were retrieved during the test phase (e.g., the semantic features corresponding to *jam* as objects pressed together were *not* tagged during the study phase). The value of f_A entering into comparison with a standard for deciding the "oldness" of the test item was therefore reduced. A comparable effect for the multiple-item task was demonstrated recently by the present author (Kausler, 1973a). The task structure called for the double functioning of homographs. Intrapair discriminations were easier to make when the words paired with a given homograph primed different meanings (e.g., *net-tennis* and *income-net* as R-W pairs) than when they primed the same meaning (e.g., *net-tennis* and *catch-net* as R-W pairs). The value of f_B for pairs containing the homographs as W items was presumably less in the first condition than in the second, thus enhancing the disparity between f_A and f_B for those pairs. The lower f_B stems from the fewer semantic features that are taggd elsewhere in the list when nominally identical A words are rehearsed.

MULTIPLE COMPONENTS OF MULTIPLE-ITEM RECOGNITION LEARNING

We turn in this final section to the promised discussion of the remaining difference between traditional frequency theory and the present analysis of recognition learning. While the difference deals primarily with multiple-item learning, it also has considerable relevance for the broader question of continuity with single-item learning.

For some years now it has been known that subjects reveal extensive associative learning between the W and R components of the pairs within a standard VD list (e.g., Spear, Ekstrand, & Underwood, 1964). Frequency theorists generally consider this phenomenon to be a curious, but irrelevant, variant of incidental learning (Wallace, 1973). The associations are simply the product of rote contiguity learning, promoted by the juxtaposed rehearsal of intrapair W and R components. The irrelevance centers on the effect, or rather lack of effect, that this so-called incidental learning has on the intentional task of discriminating between intrapair W and R components. Intentional learning is viewed solely in terms of accrued frequency units to single W and R items. By contrast, the present author has long been identified with a "multiple component" theory of multiple-item recognition learning (Kausler & Boka, 1968; Kausler et al., 1967). The original version of the theory postulated that intrapair associations may, under certain circumstances, interact with intrapair frequency judgments to determine the efficacy of selecting R items. One such circumstance is met when a new list contains the re-paired W and R items of a previously learned list. The significant increment in error rate that occurs for a re-paired list has been attributed to interference generated by competing intrapair associations (Kanak & Dean, 1969). A similar increment in error rate has been observed for a single list in which the W and R items are re-paired on each trial (Zimmerman et al., 1972). Another circumstance is met when a new list contains the old W items of a previously learned list that are now paired with new R items. Both negative transfer for the intentional learning of the second list (Kausler et al., 1967) and retroactive inhibition for first-list intentional learning (Eschenbrenner, 1969) have been attributed to interference from competing intrapair associations.

Our current preference, however, is for a different version of multiple component theory. The revision has the advantage of maintaining continuity with single-item recognition, and, in fact, has its origin in recent developments within this area. For this reason, we shall consider these developments first.

The effects of context on single-item recognition has attracted recent attention. Like many other contemporary issues, concern with context is really a return to a topic well known to our ancestors (e.g., Meyer, 1914). The experimental procedure calls for exposing each to-be-remembered item with a simultaneously present "context," or cue, item (e.g., DaPolito, Barker, & Wiant, 1972; Tulving & Thomson, 1971; Winograd, Karchmer, & Russell, 1971). A recognition test is then administered under varying conditions, including presenting to-be-remembered items without their previous context, with their previous context, or with an altered context (i.e., with a new word). In each case the subject decides "old" or "new" when the to-be-remembered item is identified as a test probe. Tulving and Thomson found the hit rate to be greatest when the context was reinstated. Conversely, the hit rate was significantly impaired when the context was either absent or altered. Generalization of their results is limited by the fact that their context items were words associatively related to the to-be-remembered words. However, comparable context effects were demonstrated by Winograd et al. and DaPolito et al., even though the cue words and the to-be-remembered words were associatively unrelated to one another. The possibility of a further restraining factor was introduced by Winograd et al. in that the effect occurred only when subjects were instructed (during the study phase) to form a bizarre image combining the cue word and the to-be-remembered word. The results of DaPolito et al.'s study indicated that even this restraining factor may not be necessary for the context effect to be manifested. In their case the to-be-remembered word was presented with two context words. The hit rate was 86% when the context was fully reinstated (i.e., both context words were present), 63% when the context was only partially reinstated (i.e., a new word replaced one of the two context words), and 60% when the context was completely absent.

Winograd et al. (1971) proposed an interesting hypothesis for the mechanism underlying the context effect. Labeling the to-be-remembered word "A" and the context word "B," their hypothesis takes the following form: ". . . Rather than represent what the subject has encoded by A-B, that is, as an association or link between two separate elements, we suggest an alternative presentation, AB. That is, AB is to be taken as a way of indicating that a compound image is stored as a functional unit, with each part undoubtedly altered by its incorporation into that whole [p. 204]."

What interests us is the concept of a functional unit incorporating A and B words. Apparently, this unit, AB, is stored in memory, along with frequency-of-response tags to the featural components of the separate A and B words. An "old" decision to the A test probe is then contingent upon two factors: (a) the extent to which f_A exceeds some criterion value, and (b) the extent to which the AB unit present at the time of testing matches the AB unit stored in memory. Failure to identify the A word as "old" is a frequent consequence when the AB units do not match, even though the value of f_A equals that found when they do match. Generalization of this conceptualization to the multiple-item task is readily accomplished. Here the W item may be viewed as a context, or B, word that enters into an AB unit with the to-be-remembered, or A, word. Thus, for each pair the multiple components accruing strength during list practice are f_A, f_B, and f_{AB}.

In the standard, single list condition of multiple-item learning it seems unlikely the f_{AB} component carries much weight in the intrapair discrimination process, unless the AB unit itself somehow identifies the A word (e.g., as the actor of a compound image). Otherwise, the unit probably serves as some initial familiarity check, from which processing proceeds to tease apart the separate f_A and f_B components. The situation changes drastically, however, when the list condition departs markedly from that of a standard single list (as illustrated in Fig. 7). Here the initial familiarity check may reveal that f_{AB} does not exceed some criterion value. This is the situation confronting the subject when he encounters a list that

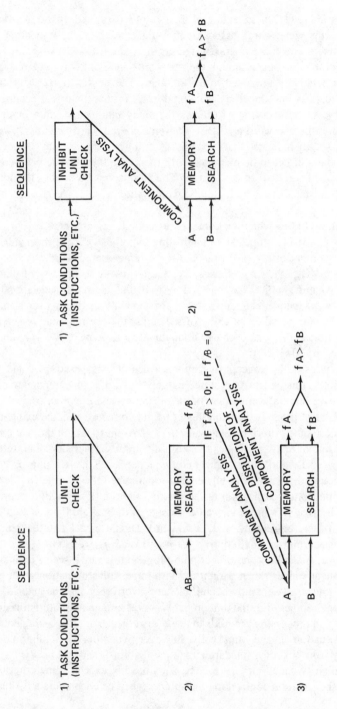

FIG. 7. Left panel: Processing sequence involving a familiarity check of a stable AB functional unit ($f_{AB}0$; e. g., consistently paired A and B words) or an unfamiliar AB functional unit ($f_{AB}0$; e. g., re-paired A and B words). Right panel: Processing sequence when the initial familiarity check is inhibited by special instructions (e. g., informing subjects of a re-paired set of A and B words).

is made up of either re-paired A and B words or old B words paired with new A words. In both cases the initial familiarity check disrupts the analysis of individual item information that would otherwise cue the correct response, and an increase in error rate follows. For a re-paired list f_A should remain discriminably greater than f_B, at least for most pairs, even though the A and B words had not appeared together before. Similarly, for an old-new transfer list f_B should be discriminably greater than f_A for all pairs at the start of second list practice, thereby enabling subjects to select the right word by avoiding the word with the greater frequency strength (Rule 2 of Ekstrand et al.'s account of VD learning).

From the preceding discussion it should be clear that the initial familiarity check involving the $A\!B$ unit is ordinarily an automatic process. It is, in fact, this automaticity that leads to increments in error rates for our aberrant list conditions, increments that are otherwise difficult to explain in terms of the concepts of traditional frequency theory. However, it is also likely that the familiarity check is subject to cognitive control. The most direct way of introducing a control process is to inform subjects in advance of the list's other-than-standard composition. The expected consequence is the inhibition of the familiarity check for each aberrant unit. Instead, the subject turns directly to the processing of the informationally rich individual A and B components. The behavioral result should be the mitigation of the expected increment in error rate.

The clearest evidence for the above hypothesis comes from a study by Zimmerman et al. (1972; Experiments IV and V). Their experimental subjects received four trials on a single list in which the A (R) and B (W) items were re-paired on each trial. Subjects who were not instructed as to the nature of the re-paired list made significantly more errors than control subjects who received constant pairings of A and B items across trials. On the other hand, subjects who were fully informed as to the list's aberrant nature did not differ in error rate from control subjects (in fact, the former group was slightly superior). A similar instructional phenomenon occurs when the re-pairing is for a transfer list. Wallace and Nappe (1971) found a lower error rate on their re-paired transfer list than the rate found by Kanak and Dean (1969). Subjects were fully instructed about the new list in the former study, but not in the latter. Finally, Wallace, Remington, and Beito (1972) failed to find any pronounced retroactive inhibition for a first list that was followed by an old-new second list. Again, their subjects were fully informed about the nature of the second list. As a result, the $A\!B$ units of the first list remained intact throughout second-list practice. It is the disruption of these units by the presence of new, but partially overlapping, units in the second list that presumably produces retroactive inhibition.

Frequency theory, as modified and extended in this chapter, seems capable of serving as a general theory of recognition learning. Most importantly, it accommodates the continuity of processes that is manifested across the methodological variants of recognition learning. It also has the potential for accommodating a number of the phenomena of multiple-item recognition learning that are viewed as falling outside of the boundary conditions of traditional frequency theory (cf. Wallace, 1973).

SUMMARY

A general theory of recognition learning must account for the phenomena of both single-item and multiple-item (or verbal discrimination) learning. The need for a general theory is apparent in the continuity of processes across the major methodological variants of recognition learning. Two kinds of evidence for process continuity were reviewed. The first concerned the predictable variation of hit rates that accompanies systematic variation of task structure. The second concerned the commonality of functional relationships between critical independent variables and hit rates that is found for single-item and multiple-item tasks.

The general theory proposed in this chapter is a modification of the traditional frequency theory. Featural components, rather than words *qua* words, are viewed as the recipients of frequency-of-response tags. Sharing of tagged features between related words, rather than displaced rehearsal of related words through implicit associative responses, is identified as the mechanism underlying false alarms. Finally, with regard to multiple-item recognition learning, the processing and frequency tagging of intrapair information involves a functional unit incorporating the component items, as well as the separate components themselves. The latter process is analogous to the one presumed to be operative in single-item recognition learning when context items accompany the to-be-remembered items.

REFERENCES

Anderson, J. R., & Bower, G. H. Recognition and retrieval processes in free recall. *Psychological Review*, 1972, **79**, 97–123.

Anisfeld, M., & Knapp, M. E. Association, synonymity, and directionality in false recognition. *Journal of Experimental Psychology*, 1968, **77**, 171–179.

Barch, A. M., & Whalen, C. H. Intrapair relations in verbal discrimination learning. A paradoxical finding. Paper presented at the meeting of the Midwestern Psychological Association, Cincinnati, 1970.

Bartlett, F. C. *Remembering: A study in experimental and social psychology*. Cambridge: Cambridge University Press, 1932.

Bower, G. H. Stimulus-sampling theory of encoding variability. In A. W. Melton & E. Martin (Eds.), *Coding processes in human memory*. Washington: Winston, 1972.

Bruder, G., & Silverman, W. Effects of semantic and phonetic similarity on verbal recognition and discrimination. *Journal of Experimental Psychology*, 1972, **94**, 314–320.

Buschke, H., & Lenon, R. Encoding homophones and synonyms for verbal discrimination and recognition. *Psychonomic Science*, 1969, **14**, 269–270.

Cermak, G., Schnorr, J., Buschke, H., & Atkinson, R. C. Recognition memory as influenced by differential attention to semantic and acoustic properties. *Psychonomic Science*, 1970, **19**, 79–81.

Craik, F. I. M., & Lockhart, R. S. Levels of processing: A framework for memory research. *Journal of Verbal Learning and Verbal Behavior*, 1972, **11**, 671–684.

Cramer, P. Evidence for a developmental shift in the basis for memory organization. Paper presented at the annual meeting of the Psychonomic Society, St. Louis, 1972.

DaPolito, F., Barker, D., & Wiant, J. The effects of contextual changes on component recognition. *American Journal of Psychology,* 1972, **85**, 431–440.

Ebbinghaus, H. *Über das gedactnis: Untersuchungen zur experimentellen psychologie.* Leipzig: Duncker and Humbolt, 1885.

Ebbinghaus, H. *Grundzuge der psychologie.* Leipzig: Von Veit, 1902.

Eberlein, E., and Raskin, D. Intrapair and interpair associations in verbal discrimination learning. *Psychonomic Science,* 1968, **11**, 145–146.

Ekstrand, B. R., Wallace, W. P., & Underwood, B. J. A frequency theory of verbal-discrimination learning. *Psychological Review,* 1966, **73**, 566–578.

Eschenbrenner, A. J., Jr. Retroactive and proactive inhibition in verbal discrimination learning. *Journal of Experimental Psychology,* 1969, **81**, 576–583.

Fulkerson, F., & Johnson, J. E. Methodological variables in verbal discrimination learning. *Psychonomic Science,* 1971, **22**, 68–69.

Fulkerson, F., and Kausler, D. H. Effects of intrapair and interpair bidirectional associates on verbal-discrimination learning. *Journal of Verbal Learning and Verbal Behavior,* 1969, **8**, 307–310.

Greeno, J. G., & Bjork, R. A. Mathematical learning theory and the new "mental forestry." *Annual review of psychology,* 1973, **24**, 81–116.

Grossman, L., & Eagle, M. Synonymity, antonymity, and association in false recognition responses. *Journal of Experimental Psychology,* 1970, **83**, 244–248.

Hintzman, D. L., Block, R. A., & Summers, J. J. Contextual associations and memory for serial position. *Journal of Experimental Psychology,* 1973, **97**, 220–229.

Hintzman, D. L., & Waters, R. M. Recency and frequency as factors in list discrimination. *Journal of Verbal Learning and Verbal Behavior,* 1970, **9**, 218–221.

Höffding, H. *Outlines of psychology.* London: Macmillan, 1891.

Hollingworth, H. C. Characteristic differences between recall and recognition. *American Journal of Psychology,* 1913, **24**, 533–544.

Ingison, L. J., and Ekstrand, B. R. Effects of study time, method of presentation, word frequency, and word abstractness on verbal discrimination learning. *Journal of Experimental Psychology,* 1970, **85**, 249–254.

James, W. *Principles of psychology.* Vol. 1. New York: Holt, 1890.

Kanak, N. J., & Dean, M. F. Transfer mechanisms in verbal discrimination. *Journal of Experimental Psychology,* 1969, **79**, 300–307.

Kausler, D. H. Homographs as double function items in verbal discrimination learning. *Journal of Experimental Psychology,* 1973, **98**, 214–216. (a)

Kausler, D. H. Orthographic distinctiveness of homonyms and the feature tagging hypothesis of verbal discrimination learning. *American Journal of Psychology,* 1973, **86**, 141–149. (b)

Kausler, D. H. *Psychology of verbal learning and memory.* New York: Academic Press, 1974.

Kausler, D. H., & Boka, J. A. Effects of double functioning on verbal discrimination learning. *Journal of Experimental Psychology,* 1968, **76**, 558–567.

Kausler, D. H., Fulkerson, F., & Eschenbrenner, A. J., Jr. Unlearning of List one right items in verbal-discrimination transfer. *Journal of Experimental Psychology,* 1967, **75**, 379–385.

Kausler, D. H., & Olson, R. D. Homonyms as items in verbal discrimination learning and transfer. *Journal of Experimental Psychology,* 1969, **82**, 136–142.

Kausler, D. H., & Pavur, E. Orthographic distinctiveness of consonants and recognition learning. *Journal of Experimental Psychology,* 1974, in press.

Kausler, D. H., & Sardello, R. J. Item recall in verbal-discrimination learning as related to pronunciation and degree of practice. *Psychonomic Science,* 1967, **7**, 285–286.

Kausler, D. H., & Settle, A. V. Associative relatedness versus synonymity in the false recognition effect. *Bulletin of the Psychonomic Society,* 1973, **2**, 129–131.

Kintsch, W. Memory and decision aspects of recognition learning. *Psychological Review*, 1967, **74**, 496–504.

Kintsch, W. Models for free recall and recognition. In D. A. Norman (Ed.), *Models of human memory*. New York: Academic Press, 1970.

Kirkpatrick, E. A. An experimental study of memory. *Psychological Review*, 1894, **1**, 602–609.

Kollasch, S. F., & Kausler, D. H. Recognition learning of homophones. *Journal of Experimental Psychology*, 1972, **92**, 432–434.

Kuhn, T. S. *The structure of scientific revolutions*. Chicago: University of Chicago Press, 1962.

Light, L. L., & Carter-Sobell, L. Effects of changed semantic context on recognition memory. *Journal of Verbal Learning and Verbal Behavior*, 1970, **9**, 1–11.

Lovelace, E. A., & Pulley, S. J. Verbal-discrimination learning: Familiarization of common and uncommon words. *Canadian Journal of Psychology*, 1972, **26**, 97–105.

Lovelace, E. A., & Schulz, L. S. Intrapair associations in verbal discrimination learning. *Psychonomic Science*, 1971, **24**, 157–158.

Luh, C. W. The conditions of retention. *Psychological Monographs*, 1922, **31**, (3, Whole No. 142).

McCarthy, S. V. Verbal discrimination learning as a function of associative strength between noun pair members. *Journal of Experimental Psychology*, 1973, 97, 270–271.

McClelland, D. C. Studies in serial verbal discrimination learnng: I. Reminiscence with two speeds of pair presentation. *Journal of Experimental Psychology*, 1942, **31**, 44–56.

McDougall, R. Recognition and recall. *Journal of Philosophical Psychology and Scientific Methods*, 1904, **1**, 229–233.

Melton, A. W., & Martin, E. Preface. In A. W. Melton & E. Martin (Eds.), *Coding processes in human memory*. Washington: Winston, 1972.

Meyer, H. Bereitschaft und wiederkennen. *Zeitschrift für Psychologie*, 1914, **70**, 161–221.

Mueller, J. H. False recognition as a function of encoding strategies. Unpublished manuscript, University of Missouri, 1973.

Mueller, J. H., Kanak, N. J., & Flanagan, J. L. Implicit associative response strength in verbal discrimination. *American Journal of Psychology*, 1973, in press.

Müller, G. E. Zur analyse der gedachtnistätigkeit und des vorstellungsverlaufes. *Zeitschrift für Psychologie*, Erganzungsband **8**, 1913.

Newby, R. W., & Young, R. K. Presentation of correct and incorrect items in verbal discrimination learning. *Journal of Experimental Psychology*, 1972, **96**, 471–472.

Norman, D. A., & Wickelgren, W. A. Short-term recognition memory for single digits and pairs of digits. *Journal of Experimental Psychology*, 1965, **70**, 479–489.

Palermo, D. S., & Ullrich, J. R. Verbal discrimination as a function of associative strength between the word-pair members. *Journal of Verbal Learning and Verbal Behavior*, 1968, **7**, 945–952.

Peixotto, H. E. Proactive inhibition in the recognition of nonsense syllables. *Journal of Experimental Psychology*, 1947, **37**, 81–91.

Postman, L. The effects of language habits on the acquisition and retention of verbal associations. *Journal of Experimental Psychology*, 1962, **64**, 7–19.

Ranschburg, P. Über Hemmung gleichzeitiger Reizwirkungen. *Zeitschrift für Psychologie*, 1902, **30**, 39–86.

Raser, G. A. False recognition as a function of encoding dimension and lag. *Journal of Experimental Psychology*, 1972, **93**, 333–337.

Ross, B. M. Frequency theory in immediate recognition of nonverbal material. *Journal of Experimental Psychology*, 1972, **92**, 117–122.

Rowe, E. J., & Paivio, A. Word frequency and imagery effects in verbal discrimination learning. *Journal of Experimental Psychology*, 1971, **88**, 319–326.

Schulz, L. S., & Lovelace, E. A. Interpair acoustic and formal similarity in verbal discrimination learning. *Journal of Experimental Psychology*, 1972, **94**, 295–299.

Schulz, R. W., & Hopkins, R. H. Presentation mode and meaningfulness as variables in several verbal-learning tasks. *Journal of Verbal Learning and Verbal Behavior*, 1968, **7**, 1–13.

Seward, G. H. Recognition time as a measure of confidence. *Archives of Psychology*, 1928, **16**, (Whole No. 99) 1–54.

Shaughnessy, J. J., & Underwood, B. J. The retention of frequency information for categorized lists. *Journal of Verbal Learning and Verbal Behavior*, 1973, **12**, 99–107.

Shepard, R. N. Recognition memory for words, sentences, and pictures. *Journal of Verbal Learning and Verbal Behavior*, 1967, **6**, 156–163.

Shepard, R. N., & Teghtsoonian, M. Retention of information under conditions approaching a steady state. *Journal of Experimental Psychology*, 1961, **62**, 302–309.

Shulman, H. G. Similarity effects in short-term memory. *Psychological Bulletin*, 1971, **75**, 399–415.

Spear, N. E., Ekstrand, B. R., & Underwood, B. J. Association by contiguity. *Journal of Experimental Psychology*, 1964, **67**, 151–161.

Strong, E. K., Jr. The effect of length of series upon recognition. *Psychological Review*, 1912, **19**, 447–462.

Tulving, E., & Thomson, D. M. Retrieval processes in recognition memory: Effects of associative context. *Journal of Experimental Psychology*, 1971, **87**, 116–124.

Underwood, B. J. Recognition memory. In H. H. Kendler & J. T. Spence (Eds.), *Essays in neobehaviorism: A memorial volume to Kenneth W. Spence*. New York: Appleton-Century-Crofts, 1972.

Underwood, B. J., Jesse, F., & Ekstrand, B. R. Knowledge of rights and wrongs in verbal-discrimination. *Journal of Verbal Learning and Verbal Behavior*, 1964, **3**, 183–186.

Underwood, B. J., & Viterna, R. O. Studies of distributed practice: IV. The effect of similarity and rate of presentation in verbal-discrimination. *Journal of Experimental Psychology*, 1951, **42**, 296–299.

Wallace, W. P. Verbal discrimination. In C. P. Duncan, L. Sechrest, & A. W. Melton (Eds.), *Human memory: Festschrift for Benton J. Underwood*. New York: Appleton-Century-Crofts, 1973.

Wallace, W. P., & Nappe, G. W. Re-pairing "right" and "wrongs" in verbal discrimination learning. *Journal of Experimental Psychology*, 1971, **87**, 355–360.

Wallace, W. P., Remington, R. K., & Beito, A. Retroactive inhibition as a function of transfer paradigm in verbal discrimination. *Journal of Experimental Psychology*, 1972, **96**, 463–465.

Winograd, E., Karchmer, M. A., & Russell, I. S. Role of encoding in cued recognition memory. *Journal of Verbal Learning and Verbal Behavior*, 1971, **10**, 199–206.

Zechmeister, E. B. Orthographic distinctiveness as a variable in word recognition. *American Journal of Psychology*, 1972, **85**, 425–430.

Zimmerman, J., Shaughnessy, J. J., & Underwood, B. J. The role of associations in verbal-discrimination learning. *American Journal of Psychology*, 1972, **85**, 499–518.

4
THEORETICAL IMPLICATIONS OF THE SPACING EFFECT[1]

Douglas L. Hintzman
University of Oregon

Interest in the effects on memory of the temporal distribution of study trials goes back to some of the very first memory experiments. Jost (1897) noted a facilitative effect of the spacing of learning trials in Ebbinghaus's data, and set out to study it systematically. More than sixty years later, Underwood (1961) was compelled by a large body of experimental evidence to conclude that "Facilitation by distributed practice in verbal learning occurs only under a highly specific set of conditions, and the magnitude of the effect when it does occur is relatively small [p. 230]." Today, with interest focused more on the learning of individual items than on the acquisition of multi-item lists, and with study and test trials for a particular to-be-remembered item routinely separated, the conclusion is quite different. The effect on retention of the spacing of repetitions is large, and the number of different conditions under which it occurs is truly remarkable.

To me, the ubiquity of the phenomenon is a source of both fascination and frustration—fascination, because it seems that a finding that is so general must be telling us something important about memory; frustration, because it is difficult to study a phenomenon that you cannot manipulate. Since the relevant literature is growing rapidly, it appears that my fascination with the spacing effect is shared by a number of other investigators. This seems like a good time to review some of

[1]The research reported herein was performed pursuant to a grant from the Office of Education, US Department of Health, Education, and Welfare. Contractors undertaking such projects under government sponsorship are encouraged to express freely their professional judgment in the conduct of the project. Points of view or opinions stated do not, therefore, necessarily represent official Office of Education position or policy.

the salient facts about the spacing effect and to relate them to the more prominent attempts to explain it. That is what I will try to do here.

First, it must be understood which phenomena are included under the rubric "spacing effect" in the following discussion and which are not. Suppose a to-be-remembered item is presented for study twice (the first and second presentations will be referred to as P_1 and P_2, respectively); and later, a long-term retention test is given. If the length of the P_2-Test interval is held constant and that of the P_1-P_2 interval is varied, the spacing of the two study presentations affects performance on the test: When the P_1-P_2 interval is short, retention is poorer than when the P_1-P_2 interval is long. More specifically, performance on the test appears to improve as the spacing interval increases from 0 to about 15 sec, while increases in spacing beyond 15 sec have little effect. While it is possible that the temporal parameters of the spacing effect may differ somewhat depending on materials and other experimental manipulations (and may be different for non-human primates than for man; Robbins and Bush, 1973), the rough value of 15 sec will serve to restrict the present discussion to a set of findings which appear, at least to me, to be examples of the same phenomenon.

The spacing effect would not be so interesting, of course, if it could be derived from other laws of memory. But the effect is an anomaly in at least three respects. First, note from the preceding description that retention decreases as P_1 becomes more recent. This violation of the law of recency has been pointed out by a number of authors, probably first of all by Jost (1897). Second, since the amount of time for which an item is presented is the same regardless of spacing, the phenomenon is an apparent violation of the total-time law, which holds that retention depends only on study time and not on how that time is distributed. This point has been discussed by Underwood (1970). Third, if massed repetitions are relatively infrequent in a list, they should be especially striking to the subject, and so a von Restorff or isolation effect—which would increase rather than decrease retention of the massed-repetition items—should occur. But even when asked to judge the number of times in a row an item occurred, subjects respond as though successive repetitions were hardly noticed at all (Hintzman & Block, 1970).

In the preceding description of the spacing effect, the nature of the to-be-remembered material and the type of retention test were left unspecified. This was deliberate, since the spacing effect appears to occur in virtually all memory tasks. It has been found in paired-associate learning (e.g., Greeno, 1964), in free recall (e.g., Melton, Reicher, & Shulman, 1966), in recognition memory (e.g., Hintzman & Block, 1970; Kintsch, 1966), and in the distractor paradigm (e.g., Peterson, 1963). Dependent variables have included not only the probability of recall or recognition but also recognition latency (Hintzman, 1969a) and judged frequency (Hintzman, 1969b; Underwood, 1969). A spacing effect is found whether presentation is all auditory or all visual (Melton, 1970), or modalities are mixed in the same list (Hintzman, Block, & Summers, 1973). To-be-remembered materials have included nonsense syllables (e.g., Kintsch, 1966), words (e.g., Melton, 1967), sentences (e.g., Underwood, 1970), and pictures (Hintzman & Rogers, 1973). The spacing effect is found over a wide range of presentation rates (Melton, 1970) and occurs regardless of whether levels of spacing are manipulated within a list or between lists (Underwood, 1969). Further, the effect is not limited to two presentations, but increases in magnitude the more presentations have been given at the same spacing (e.g., Underwood, 1969).

The spacing effect is sufficiently general that failures to obtain it under the appropriate conditions are, potentially, of considerable theoretical importance. The investigator who fails to obtain the effect would probably be wise to suspect sampling error, ceiling effects, or a flaw in the experimental design. Barring discovery of some artifact, replication of the negative outcome and establishment of its boundary conditions would be highly desirable.

The generality of the spacing effect will be taken quite seriously here. It will be assumed throughout this paper that the cause of the spacing effect in all cases, regardless of the task and type of material, is essentially the same. This assumption is not necessarily true, of course. Different mechanisms might produce superficially similar effects in different memory tasks. However, in the interest of parsimony and in the absence of clearly contradictory information, it seems reasonable to seek a single general explanation that holds for all tasks in which the spacing effect has been demonstrated.

While the description of the spacing effect given previously is generous in its inclusion of a variety of tasks and materials, it also excludes a number of phenomena from consideration. For example, by specifying that the spacing effect asymptotes at a P_1-P_2 interval of around 15 sec, the description excludes as irrelevant the research comparing massed and distributed learning of serial and paired-associate lists, which occupied so many investigators from Jost (1897) through Underwood (1961). In such experiments, a trial was routinely defined as including one presentation of each member of the list, and so the interpresentation intervals for individual items were seldom as short as 15 sec.

The statement that the spacing effect asymptotes at about a 15-sec spacing interval likewise excludes from consideration two phenomena that have been found in spacing experiments which seem mutually contradictory and appear to be of limited generality. First, in free recall, a continued increase in performance over spacing intervals much longer than 15 sec is often observed (e.g., Melton, 1970). In the literature, this continued increase has been referred to as the "Melton" or "lag" effect. The terminology, however, is somewhat confused. Many authors distinguish between the lag effect and the "massed-vs.-distributed practice" effect. The former compares different spacings of one or more intervening items, while the latter simply contrasts spacings of zero (massed practice) with all spacings greater than zero (distributed practice). D'Agostino and DeRemer (1972) have shown that some such distinction is valid. Their experiments suggest that long lag effects, such as that obtained by Melton, are peculiar to free recall, while the massed-vs.-distributed practice effect is obtained with both free recall and cued recall. As the term "spacing effect" is used here, it is to be identified primarily with what the free-recall literature calls the "massed-vs.-distributed practice" effect—although as the previous description implies, a "short-lag" effect, over P_1-P_2 intervals of less than 15 sec, should be considered part of the same phenomenon. The Melton lag effect, since it is apparently peculiar to free recall, should not be.

The finding which is contradictory to the Melton lag effect, and which is also excluded by the present definition, is a decrease in performance over spacing intervals beyond 15 sec. A rather impressive decrease was found in continuous paired-associate learning by Peterson, Wampler, Kirkpatrick, and Saltzman (1963), and by Young (1971). A similar decrease was obtained with a study-test paired-associate procedure by Madigan (1969, Exp. II), and a small but statistically significant decrease was found using a frequency-judgment task by Hintzman et al. (1973). Since it is impossible to say at present just what conditions are necessary to produce the inverted-U spacing curves that were obtained in these studies, and since the finding seems to be the exception rather than the rule, decreases in the spacing curve beyond a 15-sec interval, like increases beyond that point, will generally not be considered in the following discussion. It is the initial increase with spacings of 0 to 15 sec that all tasks seem to have in common, and so that is the phenomenon with which this paper will be concerned.

Finally, by specifying a test of long-term retention, the preceding description of the spacing effect avoids problems concerning the interaction between lengths of the P_1-P_2 and the P_2-Test intervals. The experiments of Peterson and his colleagues which first demonstrated the spacing effect in long-term retention also showed that the effect was reversed when retention was tested immediately (Peterson, Hillner, & Saltzman, 1962; Peterson et al., 1963). That is, short-term retention benefited more from massed than from spaced repetitions. The finding is an important one not only with regard to the spacing effect, but also in connection with the question of whether a valid theoretical distinction can be drawn between short-term and long-term memory processes. Unfortunately, with the exception of Rumelhart (1967), other workers have largely ignored Peterson's finding. We do not know whether the facilitative effect of massed repetitions on short-term retention is general or peculiar to paired-associate learning; and we do not know whether it can be explained adequately in terms of concepts ordinarily applied to short-term memory experiments (e.g., less proactive interference in the case of massed repetitions). So while admitting the potential importance of the effect of spacing on short-term retention, the position taken here is that we do not yet know enough about the phenomenon to decide just what facts about it a general theory of the spacing effect could or should explain.

As I see it, then, the primary task of a theory of the spacing effect is to explain the fact that long-term retention of a to-be-remembered item increases as the interval between P_1 and P_2 of the item increases from 0 sec to approximately 15 sec in duration. The explanation should be general enough to explain those cases where the effect occurs and where it does not, regardless of the particular experimental paradigm. Presumably, if a theory can be found which meets this relatively modest goal, it can be expanded later to account for other phenomena.

With these preliminary matters out of the way, let us turn to a discussion of particular theories of the spacing effect.

CONSOLIDATION

Explanations of the spacing effect which rest on a hypothetical consolidation process have been presented by Peterson (1966) and by Landauer (1969). For present purposes we may define consolidation as an autonomous increase over time in the retrievability of a memory trace, taking place independently of the physical presence of the stimulus the trace represents. Since an increase in retrievability over time is not what the data generally show, consolidation theories attribute the consolidation process to a long-term memory trace of the event and assume that over short intervals consolidation is masked by a decrease in retrievability of a temporary, short-term trace. Commonly, it is further assumed that the short-term trace is the source of consolidation; that is, information is assumed to be continually transformed, at a rate proportional to the momentary short-term trace strength, from the short-term state to the more permanent long-term state. In explaining the spacing effect it must be assumed that different occurrences of the same item are handled by the same consolidation mechanism and, at short spacings, compete for its use. If P_2 comes before consolidation of P_1 is complete, the result is less total consolidation, and therefore a weaker long-term memory trace, than is obtained if the spacing between presentations is longer. In order to explain the spacing effect as it has been described here, the consolidation process must be assumed to take about 15 sec.

The consolidation hypothesis, as an explanation of the spacing effect, has not been favored by most investigators. One reason, no doubt, is that attempts to confirm the existence of a consolidation process in animal experiments have not been completely successful (see, for example, Miller & Springer, 1973). However, a more important reason may be the fact that consolidation is assumed to be an involuntary process, outside the subject's direct control. The Zeitgeist in human memory research currently emphasizes voluntary control processes such as encoding strategies and rehearsal, and theories couched in such terms are therefore generally favored over those in which autonomous processes play key roles. Thus Melton (1970), in commenting on papers given at a symposium on spacing effects in 1969, said, ". . . I find it comforting that no one in the symposium appealed to consolidation as an explanation of observed distributed practice effects, but all sought instead to find understanding from hypotheses about the information-processing activities of the subjects [p. 604]." Melton's preference for explanation in terms of voluntary, as opposed to involuntary, processes reflects an attitude that is dominant today.

Animal experiments and the Zeitgeist aside, is there any evidence of an empirical nature that would lead one to reject consolidation as an explanation of the spacing effect? It seems natural, in the context of the consolidation hypothesis, to assume that at short spacings, P_2 interrupts the consolidation of P_1 and recruits ongoing processing activity for itself. In order to determine whether it is retention of P_1 or that or P_2 which suffers at short spacings, Hintzman et al. (1973) differentially tagged P_1 and P_2 of words with modality information, and on a later retention test asked subjects to give combined modality and frequency judgments. Both auditory and visual presentation were used, and in different conditions P_1 and P_2 were either in the same or different modalities. Four different spacing intervals were used. Frequency judgments were affected by spacing both when P_1 and P_2 modalities were the same and when they were different; and the magnitude of the effect was about the same in both cases. In those conditions where the two modalities were different, modality judgments were most consistent with the hypothesis that later retrieval of P_2 suffers from repetition at short lags, while retrieval of P_1 is unaffected. Thus evidence obtained by tagging semantically identical events with different modality attributes suggests that P_2 does not interrupt consolidation of P_1—rather, the inference is in the opposite direction.

The outcome is not crucial, however. For while it does seem more natural to imagine that P_2 should interrupt the consolidation of P_1, it is also compatible with the consolidation hypothesis to imagine that the ongoing consolidation of P_1 prevents adequate consolidation of P_2. The result eliminates one version of consolidation theory, but does not disconfirm all attempts to explain the spacing effect in terms of a consolidation process.

Another experimental outcome that seems inconsistent with the consolidation hypothesis has been reported by Bjork and Allen (1970). In their experimental conditions, a word triplet was presented twice. P_1 was followed by a distractor task which was relatively easy in one condition and relatively difficult in another. The distractor task was followed by P_2, which was always followed in turn by a distractor of intermediate difficulty. Finally, a recall test was given. Recall was not worse in the condition in which the P_1-P_2 interpolated task had been difficult than in the condition in which it had been easy. In fact, it appears from the data that the difficult interpolated task may have produced slightly better recall performance than did the easy task. If, as is commonly assumed, a distractor task occupies short-term-store capacity in direct proportion to its difficulty, then this outcome is difficult for the consolidation theory outlined previously to explain. If consolidation is directly related to short-term trace strength, then less consolidation and hence poorer long-term recall should result from the difficult P_1-P_2 interpolated task than from the easy one.

To escape this dilemma, a theorist might drop the consolidation-as-transfer notion, as some have done for other reasons. Wickelgren and Berian (1971), for example, have assumed that a study trial establishes both a short-term trace and a "potential" long-term trace. Consolidation—the transformation of the potential trace into a retrievable trace—does not depend in any way on the strength or even on the existence of the short-term trace. If the function of the short-term trace is simply to fill in as the long-term trace becomes retrievable, as in the Wickelgren and Berian model, the properties and magnitudes of the two traces can be independent. Difficulty of the distractor task need not affect consolidation.

While several versions of consolidation theory can be rejected on the basis of the experimental evidence reviewed here, it appears that one could still defend as an explanation of the spacing effect a consolidation theory which assumes (a) that ongoing consolidation of P_1 blocks consolidation of P_2, and (b) that consolidation of the long-term trace is independent of the strength and quality of the short-term trace.

REHEARSAL

According to the second theory we will consider, the spacing effect is produced by a voluntary rehearsal strategy of the subject. This notion is similar to the consolidation hypothesis in that it postulates continuing processing of information in the absence of the stimulus; but it differs in that the processing is assumed to be under the subject's voluntary control. For present purposes we may define rehearsal as the voluntary retrieval and reprocessing of a memory trace when the stimulus it represents is no longer present. In the model of Atkinson and Shiffrin (1968), it is assumed that a small number of items (the rehearsal set) can be rehearsed concurrently, and that rehearsal, by prolonging an item's stay in short-term memory, increases the amount of information about the item that is transferred to long-term memory. In a more recent version of the model, it is assumed that information is transferred to long-term memory only at the time a rehearsal takes place (Atkinson & Shiffrin, 1971). In either version, the spacing effect can be explained by assuming: (a) that the probability of the trace of P_1 is a member of the rehearsal set decreases with time since P_1, and (b) that the subject will not concurrently hold two copies of the same item in the rehearsal set. It follows that the total amount of rehearsal given an item, and thus its total long-term trace strength, will be greater if P_2 comes when P_1 is no longer being rehearsed than if P_2 comes immediately after P_1.

The work of Rundus (1971), investigating the rehearsal patterns of subjects who were instructed to rehearse aloud during presentation of free-recall lists, supports this explanation of the spacing effect. In an experiment in which the spacing of repetitions was varied, subjects were observed to rehearse words that had short P_1-P_2 intervals fewer times than words that had longer P_1-P_2 intervals. Much of the differential rehearsal, Rundus's data show, took place during the spacing interval. This suggests a rather trivial explanation of the spacing effect: Long P_1-P_2 intervals give the subject more time to rehearse P_1 before P_2 occurs than do short intervals, and this fact alone could produce the effect of spacing on later retention. The experiment of Hintzman et al. (1973), in which P_1 and P_2 were differentially tagged with modality information, appears at first to be inconsistent with this notion. The modality-judgment data from that study suggested that it is retention of P_2 that increases with spacing, while only P_1 can be rehearsed during the P_1-P_2 interval. This apparent difficulty can be overcome, however, by assuming that when the spacing interval is short the subject tends to keep on rehearsing P_1 even after P_2 has occurred. Of course, one must suppose that the modality tag which identifies the remembered presentation on the modality-judgment test is part of the information that is rehearsed.

More difficult for the rehearsal hypothesis is the finding of Bjork and Allen (1970) that a difficult task interpolated between P_1 and P_2 does not lead to poorer recall than an easy interpolated task. The problem is similar to that faced by the consolidation hypothesis, but it cannot be solved in the same way. The fact that a distractor task interferes with short-term retention in proportion to its difficulty led us earlier to reject the notion that consolidation is the transfer of information from short-term to long-term memory, and to propose instead that the consolidation of the long-term trace may be independent of the short-term store. Rehearsal, however, as a conscious activity involving processing capacity, cannot reasonably be assumed to be unaffected by the difficulty of a distractor task. Therefore the assumption of a strong faciliative effect of rehearsal during the P_1-P_2 interval appears to be in fundamental disagreement with the Bjork and Allen (1970) result.

It might be argued that the differential rehearsal takes place after P_2, rather than during the spacing interval; but there is a serious difficulty with such a proposal. Rehearsal involves retrieval; and so differential rehearsal following P_2 might properly be considered a manifestation of the spacing effect, rather than an explanation of it. An argument in terms of differential rehearsal following P_2, therefore, appears to be a circular one, in which the phenomenon to be explained has become an explanation of itself. But rather than debate this issue further, let me present some empirical results that seem to be even stronger evidence against rehearsal as a general explanation of the spacing effect.

Shaffer and Shiffrin (1972) have claimed that subjects do not rehearse complex visual scenes. This conclusion was based on their finding that recognition memory for pictures was affected by stimulus "on" time, but not by the blank "off" time which followed presentation. Subjects apparently were not rehearsing the immediately-preceding picture during the blank interval—at least not in a way that measurably affected retention. The importance of the Shaffer and Shiffrin conclusion for the present paper lies in the argument that if pictures are not rehearsed, and if rehearsal is the cause of the spacing effect, then a spacing effect should not be found in memory for complex visual scenes.

Hintzman and Rogers (1973) tested this prediction. Color vacation slides were presented either 0, 1, 2, or 3 times, and for the pictures that occurred 2 and 3 times, the spacings were 0, 1, or 5 intervening items. Presentation was at a 3-sec rate, including an interstimulus interval of .8 sec. Following presentation of a 190-slide sequence, subjects were shown the pictures one at a time and asked to judge the number of times each had occurred. The results, shown in Fig. 1, demonstrate a clear effect of spacing, much like that found using verbal materials. In further work with the same task, Hintzman and Rogers (1973) compared the effects on retention of empty P_1-P_2 intervals vs. intervals filled with the presentation of other items. The results showed that it makes little difference whether a given P_1-P_2 interval is empty or filled; the effect of spacing on picture memory is primarily a matter of time. This outcome suggests that the spacing effect is not produced by the information-processing activities of the subject during the P_1-P_2 interval. In particular, it is evidence against facilitative rehearsal of pictures during empty spacing intervals, and so is in complete agreement with the conclusion of Shaffer and Shiffrin (1972) that pictures are not rehearsed. The important point to be considered here is that despite the lack of evidence for picture rehearsal, memory for pictures is subject to the spacing effect.

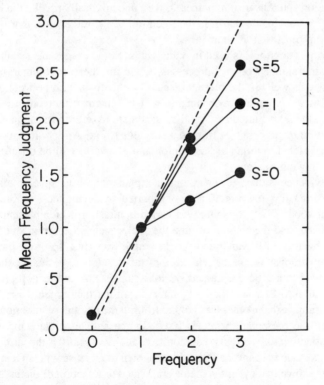

FIG. 1. Effect of spacing (0, 1, or 5 intervening items) on the judged frequency of occurrence of pictures (Hintzman & Rogers, 1973).

In a sense, because it postulates a process under the subject's conscious control, the rehearsal explanation of the spacing effect has more degrees of freedom than the consolidation theory has. It might be expected, therefore, that it would be less falsifiable. However, because rehearsal is a process that has been identified with several different experimental operations, there are many ways the rehearsal hypothesis can be disconfirmed. In the studies of Bjork and Allen (1970) and Hintzman and Rogers (1973), manipulations that affect rehearsal did not have the effects on retention that the rehearsal hypothesis predicts. It appears that rehearsal cannot play the key role in an adequate, general theory of the spacing effect.

VOLUNTARY ATTENTION

Both the consolidation and rehearsal hypotheses attempt to explain the spacing effect in terms of continued processing that goes on when the to-be-remembered stimulus is no longer present. An alternative explanation is that less attention is paid P_2 when it occurs shortly after P_1 than when the P_1-P_2 interval is longer. Attention explanations of the spacing effect have the advantage that, unlike the consolidation and rehearsal hypotheses, they unequivocally predict the Hintzman et al. (1973) conclusion that it is the retention of P_2, rather than that of P_1, that suffers from repetition at short lags.

The term "attention" is used in many ways. Some usages are meant to imply only certain voluntary control processes, while in others, involuntary processes are included as well. In the present discussion the distinction between voluntary and involuntary attention mechanisms will be an important one to maintain. Therefore, the term "attention" will be used here to refer to the subject's voluntary direction of processing effort to a stimulus event. An involuntary attention hypothesis, stated in terms of habituation and recovery, will be discussed in the section following this one.

What evidence is there for an attention explanation of the spacing effect? One study favoring this interpretation was reported by Shaughnessy, Zimmerman, and Underwood (1972). Spacing was varied in a task in which presentation was subject-paced, and the amount of time the subjects chose to spend studying each item was measured. It was found that less time was given to immediate than to delayed repetitions. While the relevance of this result to experiments that are not subject-paced might be questioned, it does suggest that subjects prefer to give more attention to P_2 when the P_1-P_2 interval is long than when it is short. Presumably, subjects have other ways of controlling the amount of attention given an item when the presentation rate is fixed. In the case of picture memory, differential attention to P_2 might be demonstrated fairly directly if the number of eye movements made in scanning P_2 could be shown to increase with spacing. Loftus (1972) has shown that eye movements are related to retention of pictures in a way that suggests they may be an overt indicator of interest.

In another relevant investigation, Elmes, Greener, and Wilkinson (1972) compared the free recall of words that occurred after P_2 of massed-repetition items with that of words that occurred after P_2 of spaced-repetition items. The words that followed massed repetitions were recalled better than those that followed spaced repetitions. It is interesting to compare this study with attempts to demonstrate a facilitative effect on the recall of items immediately preceding, rather than following, massed-repetition items. An effect on the preceding item would suggest that the subject was using the massed P_2 to rehearse. According to Greeno (1970), such an effect is not found. The Elmes et al. (1972) result suggests instead that a massed repetition may be treated by the subject as a rest opportunity, which somehow enables him to devote more processing capacity to the next word in the list. The phenomenon is worthy of further study, and it would be especially valuable to know whether it occurs in other memory tasks.

While the Shaughnessy et al. (1972) and Elmes et al. (1972) studies favor an attention explanation, it is more critical for evaluation of the hypothesis to determine whether or not the process underlying the spacing effect is voluntary.

How can a voluntary process be distinguished from an involuntary one? Both, of course, must be lawfully related to various independent variables. The difference has to do with the kinds of independent variables that affect each. Voluntary processes are highly flexible and are governed by the subject's beliefs, expectations, and past exierence in the task. Involuntary processes, on the other hand, are relatively inflexible and can be changed by experience only gradually if at all. A fairly straightforward operational distinction between voluntary and involuntary processes, then, can be formulated in terms of instructional variables: Assuming that a subject's beliefs and expectations can be controlled through experimental instructions, an experimental outcome that has been demonstrated to be vulnerable to instructional manipulation may be said to be voluntary. An outcome that cannot be so manipulated, even by instructions specifically aimed at altering the voluntary process imagined to be responsible, may be said to be involuntary. Convincing evidence for the voluntary-attention explanation of the spacing effect, according to this analysis, must rest on demonstrations that the effect can be eliminated or sharply attenuated by appropriate experimental instructions or other manipulations of the subject's strategies.

An experiment by D'Agostino and DeRemer (1973, Experiment I) attempted to control the amount of attention given to sentences by requiring the subjects to read each sentence aloud, form a visual image of the subject-object interaction conveyed by the sentence, and spend the remainder of the 10-sec exposure time describing the image to the experimenter. There were two different recall tasks, described to the subjects beforehand, but the subjects did not know which one they would be given. In one, the object phrases of the sentences were to be free recalled; in the other, the subject phrase of each sentence was given as a cue for recall of the object phrase. An effect of the spacing of repetitions was found in free recall, but not in cued recall. The fact that the two tasks produced different results is difficult to interpret. The cued-recall result appears to support the attention hypothesis, since controlling the attention given P_2 should eliminate the spacing effect. The free-recall result, however, indicates that the effect was not completely eliminated. The D'Agostino and DeRemer (1973) outcome suggests that the assumption made earlier, that the cause of the spacing effect is the same in all tasks, may be in error. In defense of the assumption, however, it should be mentioned that performance in their cued-recall task was so high (over 80% at all lags) that a ceiling effect may have washed out the effect of spacing in that condition.

In a recent unpublished experiment, Jeffery Summers and I attempted to test the attention hypothesis by manipulating the attention given to second occurrences of repeated items. The stimuli were scenic pictures. The P_1-P_2 spacings were 0, 1, 5, and 15 intervening items, and presentation was at a 3-sec rate. Half the pictures at each spacing were accompanied at P_2 onset by an audio signal, and half were not. The subjects were told that when a tone occurred, it meant that the picture would be worth 4¢ on the retention test; when no tone occurred the picture was worth only 1¢. Tones did not occur during P_1 for any of the repeated pictures. Figure 2 shows the effect of this manipulation on frequency judgments. The two data points for single presentation items indicate that pictures occurring once accompanied by a tone were given higher frequency judgments than were those which occurred alone. The two spacing curves show that a tone at the time of P_2 had a similar effect. Apparently, the intended manipulation of degree of attention given to P_2 was successful. However, the effect of the tone did not interact with the effect of spacing. If spaced repetitions are ordinarily given nearly maximum attention and massed repetitions are given very little, then a manipulation of the amount of attention paid to P_2 would most likely have its greatest effect at shorter spacing intervals. The failure to find an attenuation of the spacing effect when P_2 was accompanied by the tone is certainly not conclusive, but an obvious interpretation is that the spacing effect involves a different mechanism than the one that was affected by our instructions regarding differential payoffs.

A similar attempt to manipulate voluntary processing effort was behind the free-recall experiments of Elmes, Sanders, and Dovel (1973). Their attention manipulation made use of the isolation, or von Restorff, effect. Both massed- and spaced-repetition items were presented in each list. In some lists, several massed items were isolated by being presented in a distinctive way—a distinctive voice in auditory lists, distinctive letters in visual lists. In other lists, several spaced items were isolated in the same manner. The massed items that had been isolated were found to be recalled better than spaced items from the same list—and this result led the investigators to associate the spacing effect with voluntary processing activities of the subject. However, the facilitative effect of isolation on the recall of spaced items, in other lists, was even greater than that on the recall of massed items. That is, the Elmes et al. (1973) data reveal that the spacing effect

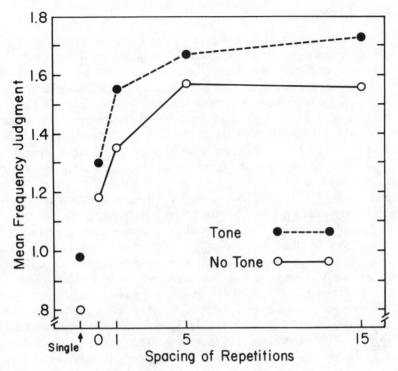

FIG. 2. Effects of an incentive manipulation at P_2 on the function relating judged frequency of pictures to spacing (Hintzman & Summers, unpublished study).

was not attenuated by isolation—if anything, it was enhanced. According to the present argument, this is not the outcome that would lend support to the hypothesis that voluntary processing activities of the subject underlie the spacing effect.

There are two final points to be made regarding the attention hypothesis. The first is that, in order to be complete, such an account of the spacing effect should explain why the subject chooses not to attend to P_2 at short spacings. This is easy for a two-process theorist, who can simply assume that the subject follows a rule of devoting full attention only to items not already represented in short-term memory. For a one-process theorist, a plausible general rule might be more difficult to state. The second point refers back to the previous discussion of the generality of the spacing effect. Is it likely that the strategies adopted by subjects in such a variety of different memory tasks would invariably include the same voluntarily-chosen tactic? While such a commonly-used tactic might exist, it must be agreed that the case in favor of control-process explanations of the spacing effect would be much stronger if tasks could be found in which the absence of the effect were a reliable phenomenon.

HABITUATION

The habituation hypothesis is like the voluntary-attention hypothesis in that it explains the spacing effect as due to deficient registration of P_2 when the P_1-P_2 interval is short. But it is also like the consolidation hypothesis, in assuming that the underlying mechanism is not under the subject's voluntary control. The basic idea is that when the to-be-remembered stimulus occurs, some internal representative of the stimulus, the activation of which is necessary for an enduring memory trace to be stored, becomes adapted—that is, its threshold for activation is raised. This could be interpreted in an all-or-none learning framework as a decrease in the probability of storage of a new trace, or in an incremental framework as a decrease in the strength of any new trace that is formed. Adaptation or habituation may be assumed to continue for as long as the stimulus is present, and recovery to begin when the stimulus ceases. The spacing effect follows directly from these assumptions; if P_2 of the to-be-remembered item comes before recovery from the effect of P_1 is complete, later retention will be poorer than it will be if P_2 is delayed. Habituation and recovery apparently cannot be identified with the neural refractory period, since a recovery time of around 15 sec—far longer than the refractory period of a neuron—is needed to explain the spacing effect; however, the two processes may be thought of as roughly analogous. And likewise, the analogy with the behavioral habituation studied in lower animals, suggested by the present choice of terms, should be considered as only a rough one. In the present use of the term, it is the "response" of storing a particular kind of memory trace that is habituated.

Habituation has been given little consideration as an explanation of the spacing effect. Underwood (1969) pointed out that the phenomenon of verbal satiation might provide a clue regarding the cause of the spacing effect; and Posner and Warren (1972) suggested that habituation found in EEG records might be related to the effect of spacing on retention. But there appear to have been no efforts to explore systematically the implications of such a hypothesis. In part, this may be because habituation, like consolidation, is assumed to be an involuntary process, and explanations in terms of involuntary processes are out of step with the Zeitgeist. I shall argue, on the basis of the evidence currently available, that the possibility that the spacing effect is due to habituation and recovery should be given more serious consideration.

First, it should be noted that the habituation hypothesis, like the voluntary-attention hypothesis, clearly implies that P_2 is the locus of the spacing effect, and this was the conclusion of the modality-tagging experiment of Hintzman et al. (1973). Second, when materials that the subject cannot rehearse are used, the recovery process should depend only on time and should be independent of whether the P_1-P_2 interval is filled with the presentation of other items or is empty. The experiments of Hintzman and Rogers (1973) described earlier confirmed that the effect of spacing on picture memory is primarily a function of time.

Third, when materials that the subject can rehearse are used, a paradoxical effect is predicted. Rehearsal, by maintaining habituation, should prevent full recovery and therefore retard acquisition during subsequent study trials. Such a process could have produced the Bjork and Allen (1970) finding that a difficult distractor task between P_1 and P_2 actually led to slightly better retention than did an easy task. It appears consistent with the habituation hypothesis, then, to suppose that rehearsal immediately preceding a study trial can have an inhibitory effect on retention of P_2 that outweighs its facilitatory effect on retention of P_1.

Also in accord with this notion is a rather striking result obtained by Horowitz and Newman (1969) in a paired-associate learning task. In their experiments, presentation of a stimulus-response pair took 5 sec; the first 4 sec were allotted to stimulus presentation, and the remaining 1 sec to presentation of the response term. In one condition, the stimulus term was presented four times. An example of events during the 5-sec interval would be: *GZK, GZK, GZK, GZK, farm.* In the other condition, the stimulus occurred two times, with the middle two intervals blank; for example: *GZK, ---, ---, GZK, farm.* Learning in the latter condition was much more efficient than in the former condition. Although several different interpretations of this finding are possible, it is quite consistent with the habituation mechanism we are considering here. In one condition, the stimulus term has been presented repeatedly just prior to its nearly contiguous occurrence with the response term. An associative relationship between the habituated stimulus and the response should be difficult to learn. In the other condition, recovery is allowed before near-contiguous presentation of both members of the pair, and so learning should be easier.

It should be noted that the term habituation, as it is used here, does not imply that immediate repetition of a stimulus will make all responses to the stimulus weaker. It is only a particular kind of internal response—that of storing a long-term memory trace of the event—that is affected. Testable predictions are not too difficult to generate from a habituation-recovery hypothesis. We are currently doing some experimental work designed to provide evidence for or against this explanation of the spacing effect.

ENCODING VARIABILITY

The theory of encoding variability has been developed and applied to verbal learning primarily by Martin (1968, 1972). It has been suggested as an explanation of the spacing effect by several investigators—among them, Melton (1967, 1970), Madigan (1969), and Bower (1972). The basic assumption is that there are several different ways in which a given to-be-remembered item can be encoded, and that the more different encodings that have been given for the item during the study phase of the experiment, the more different ways there are in which it might be retrieved on the retention test. If it is assumed in addition that the encoding of P_2 is more likely to be different from that of P_1 the longer the P_1-P_2 interval is, then the effect of spacing on recall and recognition is explained. The greater the spacing, the more different ways there are in which the item can be retrieved.

The term "encoding" can be interpreted in several ways, and this ambiguity, ironically, is itself an illustration of what is usually meant by "variable encoding." That is, it is most commonly assumed that the dimensions along which encoding varies are semantic ones. Where words are concerned, the idea is that different presentations of the same word may be given different interpretations. If they are, then retention is enhanced. If not, then multiple presentations should be no better than a single presentation.

As a test of this version of the encoding-variability hypothesis, Madigan (1969) measured free recall of words presented twice at different spacings under conditions in which accompanying "cue" words, intended to bias the interpretation of the to-be-remembered word, were either the same on P_1 and P_2 or were different (e.g., *fever-CHILL, fever-CHILL* vs. *fever-CHILL, snow-CHILL*). As predicted, the spacing effect was flatter in the varied-cue condition than in the same-cue condition. A similar manipulation of Johnson, Coots, and Flickinger (1972), which used adjectives to bias clearly different meanings of homographs (e.g., *sport-FAN, electric-FAN*), produced a similar but statistically insignificant outcome. And D'Agostino and DeRemer (1973, Exp. II) measured the free recall of object phrases of sentences, comparing a condition in which a given object phrase was embedded in the same sentence on both occasions with one in which the two sentences were different (e.g., *The lion devoured the raw meat* and *The chef cooked the raw meat*). Again, the finding was essentially the same: a typical spacing curve when the same sentence was repeated, and a flattened curve when the sentences were different.

While this is the outcome expected by encoding-variability theory, it cannot be considered strong evidence in the theory's favor. Since the encoding, by definition, is the way the to-be-remembered item is represented in memory, almost any theory of the spacing effect would predict the same result. Two clearly different encodings of the same orthographic pattern should no more show a spacing effect than the presentation of two different words. And conversely, if two stimuli which are quite different physically are encoded in the same way, a spacing effect should occur. That this is so is demonstrated by the fact that when the subjects are bilingual and the "repetition" is a translation of the P_1 word, a spacing effect—although somewhat attenuated—is obtained (Glanzer & Duarte, 1971); and also by the finding that the spacing effect is equally great whether the P_1 and P_2 modalities of a word are the same or different (Hintzman et al., 1973).

More critical for the encoding-variability hypothesis is the prediction that retention in the case where different encodings are biased on P_1 and P_2 should be better than that in which the same encoding is biased on both presentations, and that this difference in performance should be present regardless of the P_1-P_2

spacing. In all three studies cited above (D'Agostino & DeRemer, 1973, Exp. II; Johnston et al., 1972; Madigan, 1969), retention in the different-encoding condition was superior to that in the same-encoding condition only at a spacing of 0. Apparently, it is only in a highly contrived situation, as when a homograph is presented in two blocks of semantically related words which either bias the same meaning or different meanings (e.g., *meter-inch-FOOT* and *measure-yard-FOOT* vs. *meter-inch-FOOT* and *arm-leg-FOOT*), and all the words are then free recalled, that a difference in favor of the different-encoding condition is obtained at all spacings (Gartman & Johnson, 1972). This finding could be predicted from what is known about categorization in free recall, and while it is an excellent demonstration of variable encoding, it is probably irrelevant to questions concerning the adequacy of encoding variability as a general explanation of the spacing effect.

Let us next consider two problems with the rules of retrieval assumed by the encoding-variability hypothesis. The first has to do with the recognition of the item as old at the time of P_2. To quote Martin (1972), "If he [the subject] varies his encoding of the stimulus from Trial 1 to Trial 2, then we must expect him to fail to recognize that stimulus on Trial 2 [p. 65]." It would seem to follow, since the subject must vary his encoding in order for a spacing effect to be produced, that the spacing effect will only be found where recognition on P_2 is far from perfect. In one experiment using high-frequency English nouns, recognition performance was uniformly high at all P_1-P_2 lags (approximately 96% correct)—nevertheless, the spacing between P_1 and P_2 affected recognition latencies on P_3 (Hintzman, 1969a). And in the picture memory experiments of Hintzman and Rogers (1973), an increase in P_1-P_2 spacing from 0 to 15 sec was found to have a considerable effect on judged frequency. Given what is known about recognition memory for pictures (e.g., Shepard, 1967), it is thoroughly implausible to imagine that recognition accuracy on P_2 could have decreased appreciably in a 15-sec period. It is apparent that if the encoding-variability hypothesis is to be used as a general explanation of the spacing effect, the subject's use of different encodings on P_1 and P_2 cannot be identified as easily as Martin's statement implies.[2]

The second problem with the retrieval rules of the theory has to do with judgments of frequency. Note that in the case of recognition memory the explanation offered by the theory is internally consistent. If P_1 is given one encoding and P_2 is given another, then later recognition performance is enhanced because if either of these two encodings is given the item on the test, it will be recognized. On each presentation, whether during the study phase or the test phase, it is assumed

---

[2]Markov models which can explain the spacing effect only if a substantial number of items are assumed to be in an "unlearned" state when P_2 occurs (e.g., Greeno, 1967; Young, 1971) also have difficulties with the fact that the effect is found with easily-remembered materials such as pictures. Such models, intended primarily to deal with paired-associate recall, were thought to be of too limited generality to be given serious consideration here.

that only one encoding is given the item. However, in the case of frequency judgments, the rule must be changed. For in order to know that an item occurred two or three or four times, the subject would have to encode the test item simultaneously in several different ways. Thus in the case of the frequency-judgment task, different rules must be assumed to apply during the study and test phases of an experiment. During the study phase, encodings must be singular, while during the test phase they must be multiple. Surprisingly, although several authors concerned with the encoding-variability hypothesis have had subjects give frequency judgments (e.g., Gartman & Johnson, 1972; Madigan, 1969), this difficulty with the theory does not appear to have been discussed.

But let us grant for the moment the inelegant assumption that the encoding process is different during a frequency-judgment test than during presentation. Is there any evidence that holding the verbal context the same on repeated presentations attenuates the remembered frequency of occurrence of a word, as would be expected if multiple meanings were the basis for judged frequency? In an unpublished experiment done several years ago, I tested this prediction. A list of 320 words was presented visually, at a 3-sec rate, to 54 subjects. Words were presented in the list either 0, 1, 2, 3, or 5 times; and repetitions of the 2-, 3-, and 5-presentation words always occurred at a spacing of five intervening items. In the Varied Context condition, these repeated words were preceded and followed by filler words which changed on each presentation. In the Constant Context condition, the repeated words occurred together in phase, so that a given word was preceded by the same word and followed by the same word on almost every presentation. On the frequency-judgment test, which the subjects had not been led to expect, the words occurred in random order. The mean judged frequencies for words that occurred 0 and 1 time were .14 and 1.19, respectively. Those for the 2-, 3-, and 5-presentation words in the Varied Context condition were 1.99, 2.49, and 3.58, while the corresponding means for the Constant Context condition were 2.46, 2.66, and 3.59. Judgments were slightly higher when the context was held constant than when it was varied ($p < .05$). This outcome is the opposite of that predicted by the variable-encoding hypothesis. Internal inconsistency of the theory aside, then, encoding variability does not appear to provide an adequate account of frequency judgments.

Considering, in addition to all these difficulties, the fact that where verbal auditory stimuli are concerned, repeated massed presentation is precisely the condition that reliably produces variable encoding (the verbal transformation effect; e.g., Warren, 1961), the evidence seems to weigh rather heavily against the hypothesis that the number of different semantic encodings given a stimulus is the key to our understanding of the spacing effect.

There is another possible interpretation of the variable-encoding hypothesis, however, which focuses on nonsemantic components of the memory trace. Anderson and Bower (1972) have outlined a theory which assumes that when a word or other item is encoded into memory its meaning becomes associated with a bundle of contextual elements. The elements represent, roughly speaking, the state of the subject's stream of consciousness at the time the word is presented. Each time the word occurs, a new bundle of contextual elements can become associated with the meaning of the word. These associations between meaning and cognitive context are what, when retrieved on a later retention test, inform the subject that the word occurred recently and in the experimental setting; and this, of course, is crucial information for accurate performance on most memory tasks. The more different appropriate contextual associations a test item retrieves, the more evidence the subject has for deciding that it occurred in the experimental context, and therefore the more likely he is to produce it on a recall test or call it "old" on a test of recognition memory. On a frequency-judgment test, it can be assumed that the subject's strategy is to estimate the number of different contextual bundles that are associated with the test item. If, in addition, one makes the plausible assumption that an immediate repetition tends to sample the same contextual elements, then the spacing effect is explained. The temporal parameters of the spacing effect should depend on the rate of turnover of contextual elements in consciousness (cf., Bower, 1972).

A version of the variable-encoding hypothesis emphasizing nonsemantic rather than semantic dimensions of encoding would appear to have some promise. Such an account might have difficulty explaining why the spacing effect is not attenuated when P_1 and P_2 of a word are in different modalities (Hintzman et al., 1973), but this depends on whether modality information is assumed to be part of the context. The hypothesis, obviously, is difficult to assess as long as the nature of the contextual elements involved is not specified.

A METHODOLOGICAL DIGRESSION

Since so much of the experimental work connected with the encoding-variability hypothesis has been done using free recall, this seems like a good opportunity for some remarks regarding methodology. My point is that while free recall is a perfectly appropriate task to use in studying organizational factors in memory, it is a poor one for studying the effects of such variables as frequency, recency, isolation, and the spacing of repetitions. The virtues and failings of the task both lie in its most distinguishing feature: the lack of experimenter control over the order of recall. The problem has been uncovered in a number of recent investigations, but it has been put most succinctly by Rundus (1973): "Recall of some of the items of a [free-recall] list reduces the probability of recall for the remaining list items [p. 49]."

The importance of this conclusion is obvious. Any variable that affects recall order will have a spurious effect on recall probability. And since most investigations of free recall have not reported order information, we have only a rudimentary understanding of what variables affect order and how they affect it. Apparently, a number of conclusions drawn from free-recall studies need to be re-examined;

and for most purposes it would seem wise to use tasks such as paired associates, recognition memory, or frequency judgments, in which the experimenter has control over test order. With regard to spacing, it seems possible that the Melton lag effect may be an artifact of recall order. As was indicated earlier, the effect appears to be peculiar to free recall, and this observation is confirmed when free and cued recall are directly compared (D'Agostino & DeRemer, 1972).

CONCLUSIONS

A number of assumptions have been made here with which not everyone will agree. The central assumption is that the cause of the spacing effect is the same in all memory tasks. For this reason, certain spacing phenomena which are of limited or uncertain generality have been given little attention, and the spacing effect has been defined in a restricted way. At the same time, experiments meeting restricted criteria of spacing and retention intervals have been considered relevant regardless of the particular task or materials involved. The assumption of a common underlying cause cannot be defended on strictly logical grounds, since different processes, operating in different situations, could produce what appears to be the same phenomenon. Nevertheless, my goal has been to assess the relative merits of certain theoretical attempts as completely general explanations of the spacing effect, and the following conclusions should be interpreted in that light.

Given the evidence reviewed above, I suggest the following ranking of the five hypotheses under consideration—starting with the least likely to survive as an adequate general explanation of the spacing effect and ending with the one that appears most promising.

The rehearsal hypothesis, since it refers to a process that has been related to several experimental manipulations, is the most falsifiable; and that is its undoing. Both the Bjork and Allen (1970) study using verbal materials and rehearsal-preventing tasks of differing difficulty and the Hintzman and Rogers (1973) study using nonrehearsed materials produced outcomes clearly at variance with the rehearsal explanation of the spacing effect. Despite its *a priori* plausibility, therefore, the rehearsal hypothesis appears to be the most difficult to defend.

Two versions of the encoding-variability hypothesis can be identified, and they must be considered separately. The most common version, which assumes that the dimensions along which encoding varies are semantic, suffers from internal inconsistencies regarding retrieval rules, a number of apparent empirical disconfirmations, and no strong evidence that would favor it as an explanation of the spacing effect. Unless someone can put the pieces together in a way that works, the survival of this version seems unlikely. The second version of the encoding-variability hypothesis identifies the dimensions along which encoding varies with elements of the cognitive context, as discussed by Anderson and Bower (1972).

This version is very different from the semantic one, and appears to be more promising. Its implications need to be worked out in detail.

The most common version of consolidation theory, which identifies consolidation as the transfer or copying of information from short-term into long-term memory, is contradicted, as is the rehearsal hypothesis, by the Bjork and Allen (1970) result. A version of the consolidation hypothesis which assumes no connection between short-term memory and consolidation of the long-term trace, and which holds that ongoing consolidation of P_1 blocks the consolidation of P_2, still seems tenable.

The voluntary-attention hypothesis has some supporting evidence. But the fact that the spacing effect occurs in such a wide variety of tasks, and the apparent inertia of the effect in the face of attempts to control attention, argue against a voluntary control-process explanation. More work should be done making use of instructional manipulations and other methods of controlling the processing activities of the subject, however, before any firm conclusions are drawn.

The habituation hypothesis I put at the top of the list partly as an act of perverse defiance of the Zeitgeist with its current emphasis on control-process explanations, and partly because it seems to have at least as much chance of being correct as any of the other hypotheses under consideration. Since the habituation hypothesis has been largely ignored, and there have been few if any attempts to put it to empirical test, it is difficult to evaluate. Perhaps my putting the hypothesis at the top of the list will encourage a few investigators to take it more seriously as an explanation of the spacing effect.

REFERENCES

Anderson, J. R., & Bower, G. H. Recognition and retrieval processes in free recall. *Psychological Review,* 1972, **79**, 97–123.

Atkinson, R. C., & Shiffrin, R. M. Human memory: A proposed system and its control processes. In K. W. Spence & J. T. Spence (Eds.), *The psychology of learning and motivation: Advances in research and theory.* Vol. 2. New York: Academic Press, 1968.

Atkinson, R. C., & Shiffrin, R. M. The control of short-term memory. *Scientific American,* 1971, **225**, 82–90.

Bjork, R. A., & Allen, T. W. The spacing effect: Consolidation or differential encoding? *Journal of Verbal Learning and Verbal Behavior,* 1970, **9**, 567–572.

Bower, G. H. Stimulus-sampling theory of encoding variability. In A. W. Melton & E. Martin (Eds.), *Coding processes in human memory.* Washington: Winston, 1972.

D'Agostino, P. R., & DeRemer, P. Item repetition in free and cued recall. *Journal of Verbal Learning and Verbal Behavior,* 1972, **11**, 54–58.

D'Agostino, P. R., & DeRemer, P. Repetition effects as a function of rehearsal and encoding variability. *Journal of Verbal Learning and Verbal Behavior,* 1973, **12**, 108–113.

Elmes, D. G., Greener, W. I., & Wilkinson, W. C. Free recall of items presented after massed- and distributed-practice items. *American Journal of Psychology,* 1972, **85**, 237–240.

Elmes, D. G., Sanders, L. W., & Dovel, J. C. Isolation of massed- and distributed-practice items. *Memory & Cognition,* 1973, **1**, 77–79.

Gartman, L. M., & Johnson, N. F. Massed versus distributed repetition of homographs: A test of the differential-encoding hypothesis. *Journal of Verbal Learning and Verbal Behavior*, 1972, **11**, 801–808.

Glanzer, M., & Duarte, A. Repetition between and within languages in free recall. *Journal of Verbal Learning and Verbal Behavior*, 1971, **10**, 625–630.

Greeno, J. G. Paired-associate learning with massed and spaced repetitions of items. *Journal of Experimental Psychology*, 1964, **67**, 286–295.

Greeno, J. G. Paired-associate learning with short-term retention: Mathematical analysis and data regarding identification of parameters. *Journal of Mathematical Psychology*, 1967, **4**, 430–472.

Greeno, J. G. Conservation of information-processing capacity in paired-associate memorizing. *Journal of Verbal Learning and Verbal Behavior*, 1970, **9**, 581–586.

Hintzman, D. L. Recognition time: Effects of recency, frequency, and the spacing of repetitions. *Journal of Experimental Psychology*, 1969, **79**, 192–194. (a)

Hintzman, D. L. Apparent frequency as a function of frequency and the spacing of repetitions. *Journal of Experimental Psychology*, 1969, **80**, 139–145. (b)

Hintzman, D. L., & Block, R. A. Memory judgments and the effects of spacing. *Journal of Verbal Learning and Verbal Behavior*, 1970, **9**, 561–566.

Hintzman, D. L., Block, R. A., & Summers, J. J. Modality tags and memory for repetitions: Locus of the spacing effect. *Journal of Verbal Learning and Verbal Behavior*, 1973, **12**, 229–238.

Hintzman, D. L., & Rogers, M. K. Spacing effects in picture memory. *Memory & Cognition*, 1973, **1**, 430–434.

Horowitz, L. M., & Newman, W. An interrupted stimulus can facilitate PA learning. *Journal of Verbal Learning and Verbal Behavior*, 1969, **8**, 219–224.

Johnston, W. A., Coots, J. H., & Flickinger, R. G. Controlled semantic encoding and the effect of repetition lag on free recall. *Journal of Verbal Learning and Verbal Behavior*, 1972, **11**, 784–788.

Jost, A. Die Assoziationsfestigkeit in Iher Abhängigheit von der Verteilung der Wiederholungen. *Zeitschrift für Psychologie*, 1897, **14**, 436–472.

Kintsch, W. Recognition learning as a function of the length of the retention interval and changes in retention interval. *Journal of Mathematical Psychology*, 1966, **3**, 412–433.

Landauer, T. K. Reinforcement as consolidation. *Psychological Review*, 1969, **76**, 82–96.

Loftus, G. R. Eye fixations and recognition memory for pictures. *Cognitive Psychology*, 1972, **3**, 525–551.

Madigan, S. A. Intraserial repetition and coding processes in free recall. *Journal of Verbal Learning and Verbal Behavior*, 1969, **8**, 828–835.

Martin, E. Stimulus meaningfulness and paired-associate transfer: An encoding variability hypothesis. *Psychological Review*, 1968, **75**, 421–441.

Martin, E. Stimulus encoding in learning and transfer. In A. W. Melton & E. Martin (Eds), *Coding processes in human memory*. Washington: Winston, 1972.

Melton, A. W. Repetition and retrieval from memory. *Science*, 1967, **158**, 532.

Melton, A. W. The situation with respect to the spacing of repetitions and memory. *Journal of Verbal Learning and Verbal Behavior*, 1970, **9**, 596–606.

Melton, A. W., Reicher, G. M., & Shulman, H. G. A distributed practice effect on probability of recall in free recall of words. Paper presented at the meeting of the Psychonomic Society, Chicago, October, 1966.

Miller, R. R., & Springer, A. D. Amnesia, consolidation, and retrieval. *Psychological Review*, 1973, **80**, 69–79.

Peterson, L. R. Immediate memory: Data and theory. In C. N. Cofer & B. S. Musgrave (Eds.), *Verbal behavior and learning: Problems and processes*. New York: McGraw-Hill, 1963.

Peterson, L. R. Short-term verbal memory and learning. *Psychological Review*, 1966, **73**, 193–207.

Peterson, L. R., Hillner, K., & Saltzman, D. Time between pairings and short-term retention. *Journal of Experimental Psychology*, 1962, **64**, 550–551.

Peterson, L. R., Wampler, R., Kirkpatrick, M., & Saltzman, D. Effect of spacing presentations on retention of a paired-associate over short intervals. *Journal of Experimental Psychology*, 1963, **66**, 206–209.

Posner, M. I., & Warren, R. E. Traces, concepts, and conscious constructions. In A. W. Melton & E. Martin (Eds.), *Coding processes in human memory*. Washington: Winston, 1972.

Robbins, D., & Bush, C. T. Memory in great apes. *Journal of Experimental Psychology*, 1973, **97**, 344–345.

Rumelhart, D. E. The effects of interpresentation intervals on performance in a continuous paired-associate task. Institute for Mathematical Studies in the Social Sciences Technical Report No. 116. Stanford: Stanford University, 1967.

Rundus, D. Analysis of rehearsal processes in free recall. *Journal of Experimental Psychology*, 1971, **89**, 63–77.

Rundus, D. Negative effects of using list items as recall cues. *Journal of Verbal Learning and Verbal Behavior*, 1973, **12**, 43–50.

Shaffer, W. O., & Shiffrin, R. M. Rehearsal and storage of visual information. *Journal of Experimental Psychology*, 1972, **92**, 292–296.

Shaughnessy, J. J., Zimmerman, J., & Underwood, B. J. Further evidence on the MP-DP effect in free-recall learning. *Journal of Verbal Learning and Verbal Behavior*, 1972, **11**, 1–12.

Shepard, R. N. Recognition memory for words, sentences, and pictures. *Journal of Verbal Learning and Verbal Behavior*, 1967, **6**, 156–163.

Underwood, B. J. Ten years of massed practice on distributed practice. *Psychological Review*, 1961, **68**, 229–247.

Underwood, B. J. Some correlates of item repetition in free-recall learning. *Journal of Verbal Learning and Verbal Behavior*, 1969, **8**, 83–94.

Underwood, B. J. A breakdown of the total-time law in free-recall learning. *Journal of Verbal Learning and Verbal Behavior*, 1970, **9**, 573–580.

Warren, R. M. Illusory changes of distinct speech upon repetition—the verbal transformation effect. *British Journal of Psychology*, 1961, **52**, 249–258.

Wickelgren, W. A., & Berian, K. M. Dual trace theory and consolidation of long-term memory. *Journal of Mathematical Psychology*, 1971, **8**, 404–417.

Young, J. L. Reinforcement-test intervals in paired-associate learning. *Journal of Mathematical Psychology*, 1971, **8**, 58–81.

5

SEARCH PROCESSES
IN RECOGNITION MEMORY[1]

Richard C. Atkinson, Douglas J. Herrmann, and Keith T. Wescourt
Stanford University

INTRODUCTION

This paper is concerned with a theoretical account of some phenomena in the field of recognition memory. Many tasks have been used to study the recognition process (for a review see McCormack, 1972, and Kintsch, 1970), but we will focus on a particular procedure that has been extensively investigated in recent years. This task, introduced by Sternberg (1966) and often referred to as "memory scanning," involves a series of discrete trials. On each trial a test stimulus is presented, and the subject is required to decide whether or not the stimulus is a member of a previously defined target set. The subject is instructed to make a positive ("yes") response if the test stimulus is from the target set, and a negative ("no") response otherwise. The target sets in the experiments to be discussed range in size from just a few to as many as 60 items (usually words). When the set is large, subjects are asked to memorize it prior to the sequence of test trials; when the set is relatively small, it is presented at the start of each trial and followed shortly thereafter by the test stimulus. Under either condition errors are infrequent and the principal data are reaction times (RT).

In this paper we examine a series of experiments on memory scanning in terms of an extremely simple set of models that are all variants of one basic model. The models incorporate only those assumptions necessary for treatment of the phe-

[1]This research was supported by grants from the National Institute of Mental Health (MH21747) and the National Science Foundation (NSFGJ-443X3). The second author was on a Research Training Fellowship from the Social Science Research Council during the period this paper was written, and the third author was on a National Science Foundation Graduate Fellowship.

101

nomena under analysis. It should be noted, however, that the models can be regarded as special cases of a more general theory of memory (Atkinson & Shiffrin, 1968, 1971; Atkinson & Wickens, 1971; Atkinson & Juola, 1973, 1974). Thus, their evaluation has implications not only for the experiments examined here, but for the theory of which they are special cases. Before discussing specific studies, it will be useful to provide a brief overview of the theory.

Elements of the Memory System

The elements of the memory system are diagrammed in Fig. 1. The system is divided into a memory storage network and control processes. The sensory register (SR), short-term store (STS), and long-term store (LTS) comprise the memory storage network. Information from the environment enters the system

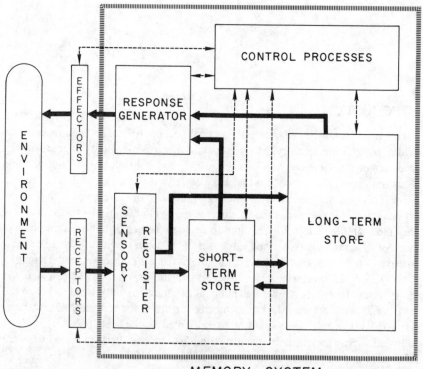

MEMORY SYSTEM

FIG. 1. A block diagram of the memory system. Solid lines indicate paths of information transfer. Dashed lines indicate connections that permit comparison of information arrays residing in different parts of the system; they also indicate paths along which control signals may be sent which modulate information transfer, activate rehearsal mechanisms, set decision criteria, alter biases of sensory channels, initiate the response generator, etc.

through the SR and is retained there briefly while pattern recognition is initiated. The STS is a working memory of limited capacity from which information decays fairly rapidly unless maintained by control processes such as rehearsal or imagery; the contents may be thought of as the "current state of consciousness" for the subject. The LTS is a large and essentially permanent memory bank. Information stored there is normally never lost, but the effectiveness of retrieval processes determines its availability for further use. Although the different components of the memory storage network are represented as separate boxes in the figure, these need not correspond to different neurological systems; rather, the different components of the system may simply represent different phases of activation of a single neurological system. The control processes regulate the flow of information between components of the network and the application of particular storage and retrieval processes within components. Control processes are adaptive with regard to the environment and demands of a task, and are in part under the conscious control of the subject. They include selective attention, rehearsal, choice of retrieval cues, and all types of decision strategies.

Representation of Information Within the System

Information enters the system from the environment at the SR. This information, if attended to, is processed by pattern-recognition routines. The function of these routines is to transform various exemplars of the "same" stimulus into a unitary representation within the particular physical modality (e.g., auditory or visual) of the input. We will refer to these representations of a stimulus as its *perceptual code*. A perceptual code is specified in terms of a set of primitive features and does not convey information about the referents or meanings of the stimulus. The code may be thought of as an ordered list of features sufficient to locate the stimulus in an n-dimensional space; the dimensions of the space represent the ranges of values of an orthogonal set of perceptual features.

We are not concerned in this paper with variability in the pattern recognition process that generates a perceptual code, because the tasks considered here do not involve perceptually ambiguous stimuli. In other situations, however, where stimuli are perceptually ambiguous, variability of the perceptual codes output by the pattern-recognition process may be a significant determiner of subsequent processing. In such cases, prior context may affect pattern recognition: Information already in the system creates expectations about information about to enter. These expectations are realized by feedback processes that change parameter values within the pattern-recognition process. Thus, a particular sensory pattern may result in different perceptual codes entering the system as context is varied; for example, an "ill-formed" stimulus being seen as the number "13" or the letter "B" (Bruner & Minturn, 1955). The experiments reported in this paper involve presenting subjects with words in a consistent context and in a consistent typeface;

thus our analyses will tend to ignore the variability that is possible in initial stages of perceptual processing.[2]

Perceptual codes represent stimuli along perceptual dimensions. It is the case, however, that stimuli may convey information at a second level. This is particularly evident for words; they have assigned meanings with little or no dependence on their physical form. Stimuli are therefore represented within the memory system in a second form; we will call these representations *conceptual codes*. As in the case of perceptual codes, a conceptual code may be thought of as an ordered list of features specifying a point in an n'-dimensional space, where the dimensions of the space correspond to some set of primitive conceptual features (Fillenbaum & Rapoport, 1971). The conceptual code for a word does not represent its definition or full meaning. Rather, a distinction may be made between the defining and characteristic features of meaning (Lakoff, 1972; Rips, Shoben, & Smith, 1973). In this view, conceptual codes primarily represent a subset of the characteristic features of meaning. Such features indicate the classes of conceptual relations that may be entered by the concept representing a word. Reference to the conceptual dependency theory of language understanding developed by Schank (1972) can make this more substantive. Consider the conceptual code for some verb. It indicates the class of ACTs (primitive actions) that the verb maps into, the classes of "picture-producers" (concrete nouns) that form conceptual dependencies with the verb, and perhaps those aspects of the verb's meaning that differentiate it from other verbs mapping into the same ACT class.

Conceptual codes available to the memory system are permanently stored and organized within a functional partition of LTS that will be referred to as the conceptual store (CS). Each conceptual code and the array of perceptual codes linked to it form what will be called a CS-node. Thus, the sight of an actual dog, the auditory perception of the spoken word, the display of the printed word, etc., each has a perceptual code; the linking of these perceptual codes to a single conceptual code form a CS-node. It is the case that synonymous stimuli will have their various perceptual codes linked to a single conceptual code, and homographic or homophonic stimuli will result in identical perceptual codes being linked to different conceptual codes.

Perceptual and conceptual codes are the basic elements of *memory structures* stored within a second partition of LTS that we call the event-knowledge store (EKS). Events and episodes are recorded in EKS by linking together copies of codes or parts of codes that correspond to the patterns of stimuli entering the system from the environment. The EKS may be represented as an n''-dimensional space, where the dimensions are all those that characterize perceptual and con-

---

[2]Although we develop the memory system here on the basis of tasks involving words as stimuli, analogous processes are assumed to operate in the coding of visual scenes and nonverbal auditory stimuli. The sensory patterns produced by such stimuli are analyzed by the pattern recognition process and the resultant perceptual codes are then available for further processing. Just as for words, these codes characterize nonverbal stimuli as lists of primitive physical features.

ceptual codes and also include other dimensions (i.e., $n'' > n + n'$). These other dimensions correspond to the temporal and spatial features between stimuli that underlie events and also to features (such as "superset," "subset," and "has-as-part") that relate concepts to other concepts. Each memory structure is stored at a point in the EKS space. The position of this point in the n''-dimensional space may be a function of a subset of the features within the memory structure, but may also reflect features of codes processed at the time the structure was formed but not included in the structure. In this sense, the location of a memory structure in EKS is less determined by its contents than is the location of a node in the CS.

We wish to emphasize that the CS and EKS are not assumed to be independent structures. It seems intuitive that structures in CS evolve over a period of time as a result of repeated experience with some stimulus in a number of different episodes. These episodes provide a basis for inferring that a particular stimulus enters only particular classes of conceptual relations. For example, a bird tends to be an actor for only certain types of acts, and similarly, an act such as eating tends to have a restricted class of objects—namely, those that are "edible." Such generalizations develop with experience and are represented in the conceptual code that is linked to particular perceptual codes. Obviously, the perceptual code generated by the presentation of a novel stimulus, such as "durp," will not be located at any existing node in CS. However, if "durp" were to become the name of a new soft drink, a CS node for it would eventually be formed. The conceptual code at this node would be a list of features such as "liquid," "non-acting-picture-producer," "object-of-INGEST-ACT," etc. (These and any other "features" used in this paper are not intended as actual primitives but are used for illustrative purposes only.)

We next consider the processes by which information in LTS is retrieved. The organization of CS in terms of feature dimensions provides a basis for a content-addressable retrieval process (Shiffrin & Atkinson, 1969). Thus, the retrieval of information from CS can be quite rapid, requiring no "conscious" search. Once a CS node is located, all the codes stored there become available to the system. Difficulties may occur in this process only if perceptual input is "noisy," or if the perceptual code is stored at more than one CS node. In the former case, the perceptual code may be incomplete, requiring an examination of several nodes (possibly leading to errors based on physical similarity). In the latter case, only one of the nodes may be the "correct" one, in which case conceptual features of the context may serve to locate the appropriate node. The utilization of context in searching CS is obvious when we consider that homophonic and homographic words are seldom recognized as ambiguous in context. Puns and many jokes have their effect because they create a context that deliberately locates two senses for an ambiguous word.

The location of a memory structure in EKS is also a directed search process, but it is not strictly content-addressable like the CS search process. Since the original placement of a memory structure may reflect only partially the features of its member codes, it will often be the case that several memory structures in EKS will need to be examined. The initial avenues of entry into EKS will be determined by the features of the retrieval context (Tulving & Thomson, 1973). Subsequent search may be directed by features of codes retrieved from other memory structures. Such a search will be relatively slow and will often become "conscious" as memory structures are examined and further dimensions of search are selected.

Application to Memory Scanning

The distinctions made here between perceptual codes, conceptual codes, CS nodes, and memory structures in EKS are not arbitrary. Rather, they reflect the subject's ability to process information at different levels of complexity (Craik & Lockhart, 1972). Two exemplars of a word, one in capitals and the other in lower case, may be judged "different" or "same" depending on whether the decision criteria involve physical or semantic similarity; in the former case, a comparison between two perceptual codes is the basis of the decision, whereas, in the latter case, two different perceptual codes associated with the same CS node lead to the judgment that the words mean the same. A somewhat analogous same-different decision is made in EKS if a subject must judge whether or not a given pair of test words are both members of a previously memorized list. In this case, a match must be sought between the codes for the two test words and the codes in the EKS structure associated with the memorized list.

In subsequent sections of this paper, we consider a series of memory-scanning experiments and analyze them in terms of models derived from the theory outlined above. To introduce these analyses, it will be helpful to provide a brief overview of how the theory is to be applied. We consider first the case where the target set is very large and stored in long-term memory, and then the case where the target set involves only a few items and is in short-term memory.

In the long-term case, the list of target words must be memorized prior to the sequence of test trials. As the subject attends to each word during learning, a perceptual code is produced by the pattern-recognition process. That code is then mapped onto the appropriate CS node. At that time, alternative perceptual codes and/or the conceptual code may be copied into STS. Because STS has limited capacity, the addition of new codes as more words are studied results in the loss of codes already in STS. We suppose that control processes act to organize the words on the target list, that is, the subject attempts to maintain in STS codes that are similar along some dimensions. This array of codes is then copied into a memory structure in EKS. The location of this structure can be thought of as a point in EKS defined by values on each of the dimensions of EKS; of course, for any particular structure many dimensions may not be specified. The values that define the point will be those that are common to codes in the memory structure;

they will also be determined by the context in which the list is learned (psychology experiment, etc.) and temporal factors. For simplicity, we usually assume that the entire target list is represented by a single memory structure located at a particular point in EKS. Obviously, this need not always be the case. There may be situations where a trade-off exists between one large structure and several smaller ones that are dispersed. In an experiment to be considered later (involving categorized memory lists) a single memory structure is formed for the entire list plus separate structures for each category sublist.

Once the memory structure for the list has been formed in EKS, the test phase of the experiment can begin. The subject's task is to compare a coded representation of the test stimulus against the codes in the memory structure, to determine if the probe is a target or a distractor. In our experiments the subject has no difficulty in locating the memory structure in EKS; this is evident by the fact that he can recall the list with no difficulty at any time during the experiment. Thus, we assume that contextual and temporal cues permit the search process to locate the memory-list structure rapidly and with little variability.

When a test word is presented, initial processing generates a perceptual code which is quickly mapped onto the appropriate CS node (see Fig. 2). Prior to extracting a code from the CS node to scan against the list's memory structure in EKS, the monitoring process may apply a special test. The test measures the activity level of the node associated with the test word; the node's activity level is a function of how frequently and how recently the node was accessed. We refer to the activity level of a CS node as its *familiarity value*. The node does not contain

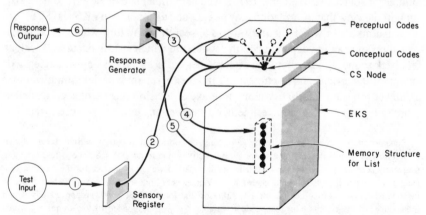

Fig. 2. A block diagram illustrating the processes involved in determining whether or not a test stimulus is a member of a "large" target set stored in LTS. Component processes are as follows: (1) input of test stimulus to sensory register; (2) pattern-recognition process leading to a mapping of test stimulus onto a perceptual code, and in turn access to the conceptual code; (3) immediate decision to respond based on familiarity; (4) selection of code to be scanned against memory structure in EKS; (5) decision to respond based on scan of the list's memory structure; (6) response output.

information about whether or not the test word was on the memory list, but its activity level does indicate the familiarity of the word.[3] Under some conditions, the location of a node with a relatively high or relatively low familiarity value may lead the subject to respond immediately without searching EKS. If the retrieved familiarity value is above a "high criterion" value, the subject may assume that the item was recently presented and thus is very likely to be a member of the target list; for a familiarity value below a "low criterion," he assumes that the item has not been recently presented and thus is unlikely to be on the target list. In the former case, the subject makes a quick positive response; in the latter case, a quick negative response. For intermediate familiarity values, an appropriate code is extracted from the CS node and compared with codes of the list's memory structure in EKS. The success of the comparison will lead to either a positive or negative response, thereby terminating the trial.[4]

Similar processes are assumed to operate when the target set is small (1 to 5 items) and varies from trial to trial. In this case, the target set is represented in STS as an array of perceptual and/or conceptual codes. When a test word is presented, precisely the same process described above is involved in estimating the item's familiarity value. If the retrieved familiarity value is above a high criterion or below a low criterion, the subject makes an immediate response; otherwise, a code for the test stimulus is extracted from its CS node and compared with the set of codes in STS. Thus, the process underlying recognition of information in EKS and STS is the same. However, differences between the memory stores may cause different codes to be preferred in each; evidence for this comes from a number of sources (Broadbent, 1970). The experiments to be described here also support the view that information may be encoded differently in EKS and STS.

Decisions about which memory stores to search and in turn which information structures to examine depend upon the context in which testing occurs, as well as feedback to the subject about the effectiveness of prior processing strategies. For example, the specific instructions used in an experiment will determine whether a subject relies on familiarity alone to make a decision or executes an extended search of memory. If the experimenter's instructions emphasize speed, then fa-

---

[3]Stated more precisely, the familiarity value must be considered as current activity level *relative* to baseline level such that the relative increase in activity due to accessing a node is less for more frequently accessed nodes. This interpretation is necessary if we are to account for the fact that subjects do not generally false alarm to their names or other very high-frequency words when these are inserted as distractors in a recognition test. Atkinson and Juola (1973; p. 602) report a study which included word frequency as an independent variable. Subjects responded to low-frequency words (both targets and distractors) faster than to high-frequency words. This means that low-frequency target words had higher familiarity values than high-frequency target words, but that low-frequency distractors had lower values than high-frequency distractors. The former relation depends on low-frequency words getting a greater boost in familiarity during study, and the latter relation depends on high-frequency words having more fluctuations from baseline activity due to extra-experimental events.

[4]See Mandler, Pearlstone, and Koopmans (1969) for a similar conception of recognition memory.

miliarity will play a key role; if accuracy is emphasized, then the slower memory search will occur. Thus, the high and low criteria for judging familiarity are determined by the speed-accuracy trade-off that the subject regards as acceptable.

The theory has been described in very general terms, and we turn now to specific applications. The first application deals with experiments employing small target sets (1 to 5 items) stored in STS. The second application involves large memory sets (60 or more items in some cases) stored in EKS. The third application considers scanning experiments where the target set involves some items stored in STS and others in EKS; experiments of this sort permit us to make direct comparisons between search rates in EKS and STS, and to examine the parallel versus serial search of these stores. The last two applications deal with target lists that are categorized; the questions of interest are how and under what conditions the category information may be used in making a response decision. Because the memory system is stratified so that information can be represented in several different stores (and in different memory structures within a store), performance in even simple tasks often depends upon a complex "mixture" of underlying processes. Our goal is not to build the simplest possible model for the set of experiments examined, but rather to analyze these experiments within the framework of a theory that is applicable to a wide range of phenomena.

MEMORY SEARCH WITH SMALL TARGET SETS

The first experiments to be considered involve the search of short-term memory; the specific studies are variants on the type of scanning task investigated by Sternberg (1966, 1969a, 1969b, 1971). On each of a series of trials, the subject is presented with a memory set of from one to six words; the words in the memory set are "new" in the sense that they have not been presented on any prior trials of the experiment. When the subject has the memory set in mind, a test word is presented visually; the subject makes a positive response if the test word is in the memory set, and a negative response otherwise. The typical finding is that reaction time for both the positive and negative responses are linearly increasing functions of memory-set size, and that the slopes of the two functions are roughly equal.

The theoretical account of this type of experiment is schematically represented in Fig. 3. The memory set is temporarily stored in STS. When the test word is presented, it is encoded and mapped onto its CS node. Although the CS node does not contain a tag or marker indicating that the test word was in the memory set, it does have information about the familiarity of the word. If the subject finds a very high familiarity value, he gives an immediate positive response; if he finds an extremely low value, an immediate negative response is given. If the familiarity value is intermediate, the subject must then take the test word and scan it against the memory set in STS. If the scan yields a match, a positive response is made; otherwise, a negative response. When the familiarity value is intermediate,

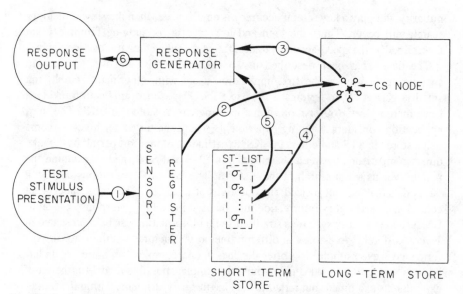

FIG. 3. A schematic representation of the search-and-decision processes in a short-term recognition memory study. A test stimulus is presented (1) and then matched to a CS node (2). The familiarity value associated with the node may lead to an immediate decision (3) and response output (6). Otherwise, a code is extracted and scanned against the target list in STS (4), which leads to a decision (5) and subsequent response (6). Path (1), (2), (3), (6) represents a much faster response process than Path (1), (2), (4), (5), (6), and it is independent of the size of the STS set.

the speed of the response is much slower and depends on the number of words in the memory set. Thus, for very high or very low familiarity values, the subject makes a fast response that does not depend on the memory-set size; for intermediate values a slower response occurs that is an increasing function of memory-set size.

The observed response latency averaged over trials is then a mixture of fast decisions based on familiarity alone (independent of memory-set size) and slower decisions based on a search of STS (dependent on memory-set size). The likelihood of bypassing the search of STS depends on the distribution of familiarity values associated with targets and distractors. Figure 4 presents familiarity distributions associated with a target word and a distractor. When a test word is presented, a familiarity value is sampled from the appropriate distribution. If the familiarity value is above a high criterion c_1, the subject makes an immediate positive response; and below a low criterion c_0, an immediate negative response. Otherwise, a search of STS is executed. It is assumed that the subject never makes an error if a search of STS occurs; however, if the search is bypassed, then an error will occur whenever the test word is a target with a familiarity value below c_0 or a distractor with a familiarity value above c_1. Note that the proportion of test words that lead to a search of STS depends on the placement of the criteria. The probability distribution of familiarity values, x, for targets and dis-

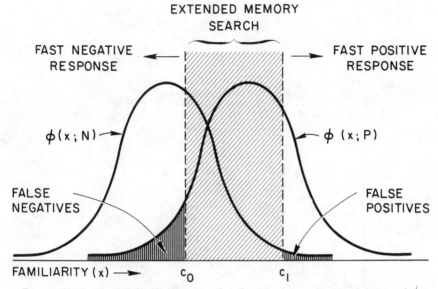

FIG. 4. Distributions of familiarity values for distractor items, $\phi(x;N)$, and target items, $\phi(x;P)$.

tractors will be denoted as $\phi(x;P)$ and $\phi(x;N)$, respectively; for present purposes these distributions will be assumed to be unit-normal with means μ_P and μ_N. (We use P for the target distribution because a positive response to a target is correct, and N for the distractor distribution because a negative response to a distractor is correct.) Later it will prove useful to know the probability of having made a search of STS given that the subject generated a correct response; this probability is denoted as s for targets and s' for distractors. As shown in Fig. 4, the probability that a correct response to a target involved a search of STS is the probability of a positive response based on a search of STS divided by the overall probability of a positive response; namely,

$$ s = \frac{\int_{c_0}^{c_1} \phi(x, P)\, dx}{\int_{c_0}^{\infty} \phi(x, P)\, dx} \tag{1} $$

Similarly, the probability that a correct response to a distractor involved a search of STS is

$$ s' = \frac{\int_{c_0}^{c_1} \phi(x, N)\, dx}{\int_{-\infty}^{c_1} \phi(x, N)\, dx} \tag{2} $$

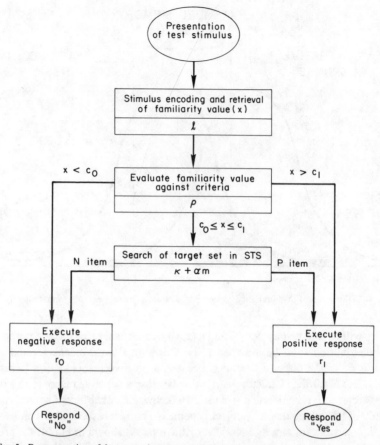

FIG. 5. Representation of the processing stages underlying recognition performance when the target set resides in STS. When stimulus familiarity is greater than c_1 or less than c_0, a rapid positive or negative response is executed; otherwise, the encoded test stimulus is scanned against the contents of STS, leading to the appropriate response.

The preceding discussion can be summarized by referring to the flow chart in Fig. 5. Noted in the figure are the times associated with each stage. Certain stages must be executed for all probes; namely, encoding (l), evaluation of the familiarity value (ρ), and response execution (r_0 for a negative response and r_1 for a positive response). For probes of an intermediate familiarity value, the additional stage of searching STS is necessary. It is assumed that this search takes time $\kappa + \alpha m$ where m denotes the size of the memory set; κ is the time to initiate the search of STS, and the search is proportional (with parameter α) to the size of the memory set. This linear search function corresponds to the exhaustive case of the serial-scanning model proposed by Sternberg (1969a). While Sternberg's model has proved to be extremely valuable in interpreting a variety of memory-search experiments, good fits between the model and data do not require that the underlying process be either serial or exhaustive (for a discussion of this point see Townsend, 1971, and Murdock, 1971). Thus the use of a linear search function does not commit us to specific assumptions about whether the search is serial or parallel, self-terminating or exhaustive.

In terms of the time constants given in Fig. 5, expressions can be written for the latency of various types of responses. First note that an error to a target item takes time $l + p + r_0$, whereas an error to a distractor takes time $l + \rho + r_1$.[5] Expressions for correct responses are more complicated. We let $t(P)$ denote the response time for a correct response to a target (i.e., the time for a positive response) and $t(N)$ denote the response time for a correct response to a distractor (i.e., the time for a negative response). Recalling the definitions of s and s', we can write the following expressions:

$$t(P) = (1 - s)\left[l + \rho + r_1\right] + s\left[l + \rho + \kappa + \alpha m + r_1\right]$$

$$= (l + \rho + r_1) + s(\kappa + \alpha m), \tag{3}$$

$$t(N) = (1 - s')\left[l + \rho + r_0\right] + s'\left[l + \rho + \kappa + \alpha m + r_0\right]$$

$$= (l + \rho + r_0) + s'(\kappa + \alpha m). \tag{4}$$

Examining these equations, we see that both $t(P)$ and $t(N)$ increase linearly with set size. In many experiments (see Sternberg, 1969a), the slope of the negative and positive functions are roughly equal, and this would be the case when s equals s'. The condition under which s equals s' requires that c_1 and c_0 be set symmetrically (i.e., the tail of the target distribution below c_0 must equal the tail of the distractor distribution above c_1). The linear predictions for $t(P)$ and $t(N)$ are based on the assumption that the criteria do not vary with m; a correlated implication of this statement is that error rates also do not vary with m. Of course, in some experiments (especially where m is fixed over a block of trials), it is possible that the subject adjusts c_1 and c_0 as a function of the memory-set size. For example, when m is large the subject may anticipate a slow response and compensate by adjusting the criteria to generate more fast responses based on familiarity alone. Under these conditions errors would increase with m, and RT curves would be curvilinear.

The predictions outlined above are consistent with a number of experimental

[5]The model predicts that error latencies are "fast" since they are the result of decisions based upon familiarity alone: Whenever the memory set is searched, it is assumed that a correct response always occurs. While this assumption is reasonable for the tasks described here, it is the case that "slow" errors (resulting from a failure in the search process) will occur in other situations. Such errors would be expected when acquisition of the memory set is less than perfect. They might also occur when instructions emphasize speed of response; subjects in this case could establish an upper bound on the time they will search the stored memory set before "guessing."

results (Atkinson & Juola, 1973, 1974). In this sense, the model has proved to be quite satisfactory. However, these goodness-of-fit demonstrations have not directly tested the role of familiarity in a short-term-memory scanning task. With this in mind, Charles Darley and Phipps Arabie designed and ran a study at Stanford University which attempted to experimentally manipulate familiarity. The study was basically like the prototype experiment described at the beginning of this section. Memory-set size varied randomly from trial to trial, taking on values from 2 to 5 items. Each memory set involved new words (i.e., words that had not been used on any prior trial); the test word was a target on half the trials and a distractor on the other half. The only difference from the prototype experiment described at the outset of this section was that distractors were not always new words, thus permitting the experimenters to manipulate their familiarity values.

In accord with prior notation, the presentation of a target as the test word will be called a P-trial to indicate that a positive response is correct; the presentation of a distractor will be called an N-trial to indicate that a negative response is correct. In this experiment the distractors were of three types: new words never presented before in the experiment (denoted N_1 since the word was presented for the first time); words that had been presented for the first time in the experiment as distractors on the immediately preceding trial (denoted N_2 since the word was now being presented for the second time); and words that had been presented for the first time on the immediately preceding trial both as a member of the memory set and as a positive test word (denoted N_3 since the word was now being presented for the third time). Thus, there were four types of test words (P, N_1, N_2, and N_3), and we assume that different familiarity values are associated with each. Figure 6 presents a schematic representation of the four familiarity distributions. The mean of the P-distribution should be the largest since the test word on a P-trial is a member of the current memory set and should be very familiar; likewise, the mean of the N_1-distribution should be smallest because N_1 words are completely new; the other two means should be intermediate since N_2 and N_3 words appeared on the prior trial. Also displayed in the figure are the criteria c_0

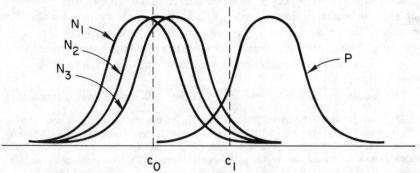

FIG. 6. Distributions of familiarity values for the three types of distractor items (N_1, N_2, N_3) and for target items (P).

and c_1, which are assumed to be the same for all trial types. This assumption is reasonable since the subject cannot predict the type of test that will occur, and thus he has no basis for varying the criteria. As can be seen from Fig. 6, an increasing amount of the distribution falls between c_0 and c_1 as we move from N_1 to N_2 to N_3. In terms of the mathematical formulation, s' defined in Eq. 2 increases from N_1 to N_2 to N_3. Accordingly, the likelihood of searching STS in-

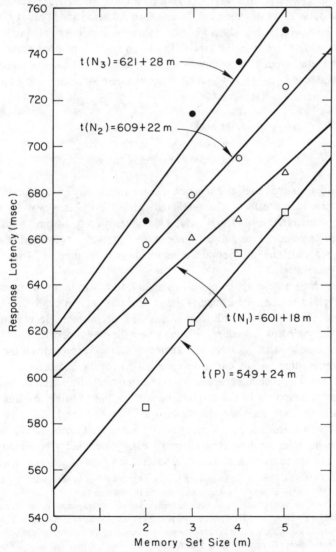

FIG. 7. Mean response latencies for the four probe types as a function of the size of the memory set. The straight lines fitted to the data represent theoretical predictions.

creases and thus the slope of the $t(N_i)$ function increases from N_1 to N_2 to N_3; for the same reason the intercept of the $t(N_i)$ function also increases from N_1 to N_2 to N_3.

The latency data for the four types of probes are presented in Fig. 7. Note that latency increases with set size and is ordered such that P is fastest, and N_1, N_2, and N_3 are progressively slower. The straight lines in the figure represent theoretical predictions of the model. The derivation of theoretical equations and methods of parameter estimation are described in Atkinson and Juola (1974) and will not be reviewed here. It should be noted that the model not only predicts the response-time data, but also the probability of an error as response time varies over the four trial types. The complete set of parameter estimates is reported in Atkinson and Juola (1974), but several are given here since they play a role in later discussions, namely,

$$(l + \rho + r_1) = 499 \text{ msec} \qquad \kappa = 70 \text{ msec}$$

$$(l + \rho + r_0) = 563 \text{ msec} \qquad \alpha = 34 \text{ msec}$$

The results displayed in Fig. 7 indicate that the familiarity manipulation had a large and predictable effect. The predicted slope for P items was 24 msec, whereas the predicted slopes for N_1, N_2, and N_3 items ranged from 18 msec, to 22 msec, to 28 msec. If the subject ignored the familiarity value and searched STS on every trial, then all four functions would have a slope of 34 msec (the estimated value of α).[6]

Other experimental manipulations also should lead to variations in familiarity. The prototype experiment described at the start of this section can be viewed as involving an infinite pool of words from which the experimenter selects stimuli on each trial. Compare this procedure with one where the pool is restricted (say to 10 words), and on each trial stimuli are drawn without replacement from the pool. In the first procedure, words are never repeated during the course of an experiment; in the second procedure, repetitions occur frequently from trial to trial. The second case corresponds to the original memory-scanning study by Sternberg (1966) where the item pool was the digits from 0 to 9.

When no words are repeated, the familiarity index for targets should be substantially higher than for distractors, thereby making familiarity an effective dimension on which to make a decision. When a small pool of words is used, the

[6]Inspection of response time (in the final block of trials) for individual subjects indicates that they are bimodally distributed as would be expected from the theory; one mode, associated with a fast response based on familiarity alone, and the other mode for slower responses based on extended searches of memory. Analysis of RT distributions is complicated by the fact that there are too few observations on each subject, and further, that response times over-all tend to decrease during the course of the experiment. To fit the observed distributions one would have to elaborate the model to include assumptions about the distributions associated with each stage in the process, and about over-all decreases in response time with practice.

familiarity value of all items will be raised, thus tending to wash out differences in familiarity between targets and distractors. Under these conditions the familiarity index will be less useful and a search of STS will be required more frequently. Support for this view comes from a study by Rothstein and Morin (1972) who ran just this type of comparison. They reported steeper slopes and higher intercepts for RT functions when the memory sets were selected repeatedly from a small pool. The repeated presentation of items increases the familiarity of all items to a high level, thereby reducing the usefulness of the familiarity measure as a basis for responding. Consequently, the probability of searching STS should be high, causing the slope of the RT function to be near its maximal value.

In addition to the relative familiarity of targets and distractors, another factor influencing the likelihood of searching STS is the placement of a subject's criteria. For example, if the subject is instructed to avoid errors, the appropriate strategy would be to set c_0 and c_1 relatively far apart, thereby insuring that a search will be conducted on most trials. Since the time necessary to complete a search depends on memory-set size, both over-all latency and set-size effects should be increased. Alternatively, if response speed is emphasized in the instructions, the criteria c_0 and c_1 should be placed close together so that most responses will be based on familiarity alone. In this case, over-all latency would be decreased and minimally influenced by set size.

William Banks of Pomona College ran such an experiment in our laboratory with the anticipated results. An entirely new set of words was presented on each trial as the memory set; set sizes were 2, 3, 4, 5, and 6 and varied randomly over trials. Targets and distractors occurred equally often, and the distractors always involved new words. Subjects served in two experimental conditions: accuracy instructions and speed instructions. The RT data for correct responses are presented in Fig. 8. If the criteria are being adjusted as suggested above, then the model predicts that the slope and intercept of the RT functions under accuracy instructions should be greater than under speed conditions. The results shown in Fig. 8 support this prediction; also, the pattern of error data is consistent with the model. Similar results have been reported by Weaver (1972) with memory sets of letters and a wider range of set sizes. It should be noted that Swanson and Briggs (1969) and Briggs and Swanson (1970) have found no differences in slope of the RT-set size function across speed and accuracy conditions. Comparison of their payoff matrices with those of Banks and of Weaver, however, suggests that Briggs's and Swanson's incentive system was not strong enough to cause subjects to adjust their criteria and rely more heavily on the familiarity measure.

MEMORY SEARCH WITH LARGE TARGET SETS

A recognition task comparable to the one discussed in the last section can be formulated for very large target sets. Prior to the test session, the subject is required to learn a long list of words to a criterion of perfect recall; this list serves

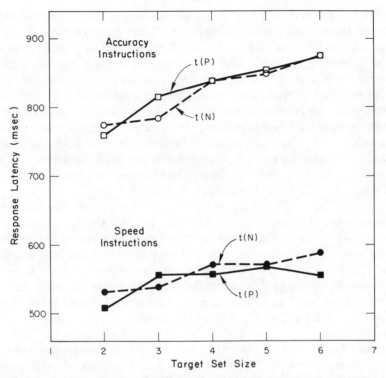

FIG. 8. Mean response latencies for P-items and N-items for five target-set-size conditions in an experiment manipulating instructions to subjects, emphasizing accuracy in one condition and speed in another.

as the memory set for the remainder of the experiment. The test session involves a series of trials where either a target word or a distractor is presented; the subject is instructed to make a positive response to an item from the list and a negative response otherwise. A number of studies have been done using this technique with target sets ranging from 10 to 60 words. These studies have been reviewed elsewhere (Atkinson & Juola, 1973) and interpreted in terms of the model presented here.

In this paper we will consider only one such study, which manipulated the size of the memory set (16, 24, and 32 words) and the number of times targets and distractors were presented during the test sequence; for a detailed account of the experiment see Atkinson and Juola (1974). Figure 9 presents RT data from the final block of test trials as a function of target set size; some words (whether targets or distractors) were presented for the first time during this final trial block, while others had been presented earlier in the test sequence and thus were receiving a repeated presentation. The left-hand panel presents RTs for correct responses to targets and distractors receiving their initial presentation in the final

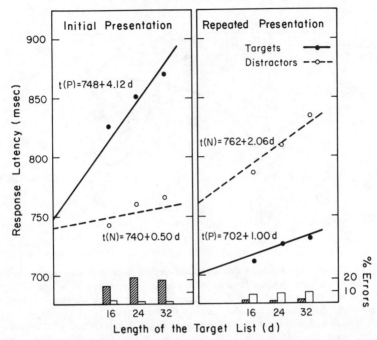

FIG. 9. Mean response latencies and error percentages as functions of target list length. The left panel presents data for initial presentations of target and distractor words, and the right panel presents data for repeated presentations. Incorrect responses to target words are indicated by the shaded bars, and errors to distractors by the open bars. The straight lines fitted to the data represent theoretical predictions.

block of test trials; the right-hand panel, for words receiving a repeated presentation. In both panels RTs increase with the size of the memory set; however, the slopes of the functions are much less than is observed when smaller memory sets are involved. It is interesting to note that repeating an item has a different effect if that item is a target word as compared with a distractor. Positive responses are slower and show a steeper slope to the initial presentation of a target word as compared to a repeated presentation of a target word; in contrast, negative responses are faster and have a more shallow slope to the initial presentation of a distractor than to a repeated presentation of one.

The model to be applied here is the same as the one developed in the last section. The only difference is that the memory set exceeds the capacity of STS, and it is assumed to be stored in EKS. Figure 10 presents a flow diagram of the process. The test item is encoded and the appropriate CS node is accessed, leading to the retrieval of a familiarity value. If the familiarity value is above c_1 or below c_0, the subject gives a fast response. Otherwise, the subject retrieves a code for the test word to use in scanning the memorized list in EKS. Thus far the model is identical to that for the short-term case presented in the last section. How-

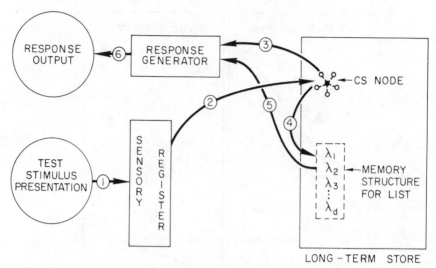

LONG - TERM   STORE

FIG. 10. A schematic representation of the search and decision processes in long-term recognition memory. A test stimulus is presented (1) and then encoded and matched to an appropriate CS node (2). The familiarity index associated with the node may lead to an immediate decision (3) and in turn to a response (6). Otherwise, an extended search of the stored target list is initiated (4), which eventually leads to a decision (5) and a subsequent response (6). Path (1), (2), (3), (6) represents a much faster response process than path (1), (2), (4), (5), (6), and one that is independent of target-set size.

ever, the code used to search the EKS may not be the same as that used in the short-term memory search. For example, Klatzky, Juola, and Atkinson (1971) present evidence that alternative codes for the same test stimulus can be generated and compared with either verbal, spatial, or conceptual representations of memory-set items. After retrieval of the appropriate code, a search of the memory set is executed, leading in turn to a correct response. Note that a response based on familiarity follows the same path as was proposed for familiarity decisions in the short-term case. However, when a search of EKS is required we assume that the time to initiate the search (κ) and the search rate per memory set item (α) will not be the same as in the short-term case; this difference in the search rate may be due either to the storage of different types of codes in STS and EKS, to differing search and comparison processes within the stores, or to both. Restated, the parameters l, ρ, r_1, and r_0 are the same in the long-term and short-term cases; these cases differ only with respect to the values of κ and α. Thus, Eqs. (3) and (4) apply here, except that the estimates of κ and α should differ for experiments involving large memory sets.

For the conditions of this particular experiment, the criteria c_1 and c_0 are assumed to be fixed and independent of the size of the memory set. The effect of repeating a word during the test sequence is to boost its familiarity value; this boost in familiarity is assumed to occur for both repeated targets and repeated

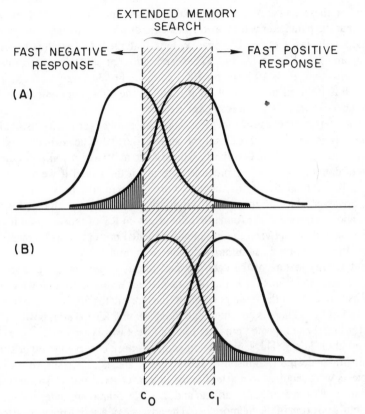

FIG. 11. Distributions of familiarity values for distractor and target items when presented for the first time (Panel A), and when receiving a repeated presentation (Panel B).

distractors. Figure 11 illustrates the familiarity distributions for targets and distractors when presented for the first time (top panel), and for targets and distractors when receiving a repeated presentation (bottom panel). Note that the likelihood of searching EKS is less on the repeated presentation of a target word than on the initial presentation of a target word; in contrast, the reverse holds for distractors. In terms of s and s' defined in Eqs. (1) and (2), s is less for a repeated presentation of a target and s' is greater for a repeated presentation of a distractor. Of course, the greater the likelihood of searching EKS, the steeper the slope of the RT function (i.e., the slopes of the target and distractor functions approach α as s and s' approach one, respectively).

A quantitative application of the model sketched above leads to the predicted functions displayed in Fig. 9. The slopes and intercepts for targets and distractors show the appropriate relationships for initial and repeated items. In addition, the theory accurately predicts error rates and RTs for errors. The details of the model and its fit to these data are presented in Atkinson and Juola (1974). It is important to note that the parameter estimates for this case differ from the short-term study discussed in the last section. The time, κ, to initiate the EKS search is 137 msec, as compared to 70 msec for the STS search; in contrast, the search rate per memory-list item, α, is 10 msec for EKS compared to 34 msec for STS. Thus, the search is initiated more rapidly if it involves the STS, but comparison time per memory-set item is much faster for EKS.

To summarize, the same model is applicable to experiments using large memory sets as well as for those using small sets; the difference is in the extended search on those trials where familiarity is not used to make a decision. The complex pattern of data in Fig. 9 is interpretable in terms of the model if we assume that there is a boost in familiarity whenever a word is presented for test.[7] It should be noted, however, that the increase in familiarity is short-lived. Juola, Fischler, Wood, and Atkinson (1971) found that the effect on RT of repeating an item diminished as the lag between the initial and repeated presentations increased, indicating that the boost in familiarity decays over time.

An interesting feature of the data reported in this section is the absence of a serial-position effect in RTs. If the time to make a response to a target word is plotted as a function of the serial position of that word in the original study list, the result is a flat line. There is absolutely no trend relating RT to serial position; that is true for initial and repeated presentations of target words separately, as well as for the combined data. The same phenomenon has been observed in other studies using a similar design (Atkinson & Juola, 1973) and is rather surprising since the subjects were required to master the list in a strict serial order. Theoretically, this means that both familiarity effects and the EKS search are independent of a target item's position in the memory list. The absence of a serial-position effect in these experiments, however, does not mean that organizational factors influencing the acquisition of a target set will not affect RTs in the recognition phase of the experiment. In one study reported by Atkinson and Juola (1973), the set of target words was organized and learned as a semantic hierarchy; under these conditions RTs on the recognition tests varied as a function of the placement of the word in the original hierarchy.

Another example, more closely related to the experiment reported in this section, is a study conducted by Susan LeVine at Stanford University. Her test

[7]An increase in familiarity is not restricted to presenting the word in a test sequence. We have run a study similar to the one described in this section, except that the target set involved 25 words and distractor words were never repeated during the sequence of test trials. The test sequence involved two blocks of 50 trials each with a brief break between trial blocks. During the break subjects were given written instructions regarding a task they supposedly were going to participate in immediately after completing the second block of test trials; subjects were required to read the instructions twice, once silently and once aloud. In actual fact, 10 words in the instructions served as distractor words in the second block of test trials. Comparing RTs for distractor words that had been in the instruction set with those that had not yielded a statistically significant difference. Distractor words used in the instructions were responded to more slowly, as would be expected if their familiarity value was increased by including them in the instruction set.

sequence involved a target set of 48 words; half of the test trials involved target words and half distractors. The unique aspect of the study was the method for memorizing the target set. The subject memorized the 48 words as 24 paired associates and used an anticipation procedure. Eight of the paired associates were tested and studied on every trial of the training session, eight pairs on every other trial, and eight pairs on every third trial; thus, by the end of learning some pairs had been brought to a "high" acquisition level, others to a "medium" level, and others to a "low" level. In the recognition phase of the experiment, there were 96 trials; 48 trials tested individual words from the study list (positive trials) and 48 involved words not previously studied (negative trials). The RTs for correct responses to target words are presented in Fig. 12 along with error rates; the RT for correct responses to distractors was 758 msec with an error rate of 3 percent. Inspection of Fig. 12 indicates that RT is faster to a word that was a response member of a paired associate as compared with a stimulus member. Even for those words that have been perfectly mastered (i.e., high acquisition set), the stimulus versus response role of a word had an effect on recognition performance.

It is interesting to note that RT is related to the acquisition level; the more times a word was presented during study, the faster the RT. The fact that RT varied

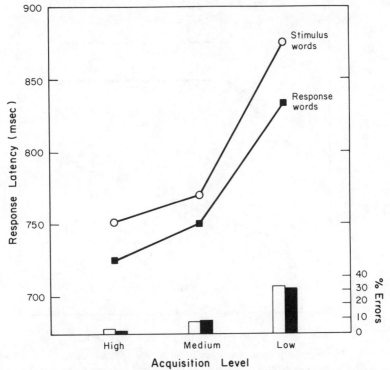

Fig. 12. Mean response latencies and error percentages across three conditions of acquisition for targets that were either stimulus or response members of paired associates.

with acquisition level suggests that the list-length effects in the prior study might be explained in the same way. One could assume that in mastering a memory list, the longer the list the lower the acquisition level at the start of the test series. Thus, the effect of list length on RT might be explained by a lower degree of mastery of the longer lists, rather than by a longer EKS search as we have done. This type of explanation could be accommodated by the theory, but we rejected it because of the error-rate data. In the paired-associate study, error rates increased as the acquisition level decreased (see Fig. 12). However, in the list-length study, both error rates and their reaction times were constant over list lengths; nevertheless, reaction times for correct responses increased with list length. For this reason we assumed in the theoretical analysis that all lists were equally well learned, that familiarity distributions were invariant over list lengths, and that the RT effects were to be explained by a longer (but equally accurate) search of the longer lists. This is an important point and emphasizes that we do not regard the linear search function postulated in this and the previous section as critical to the theory; rather, different search functions can be postulated depending on the organization

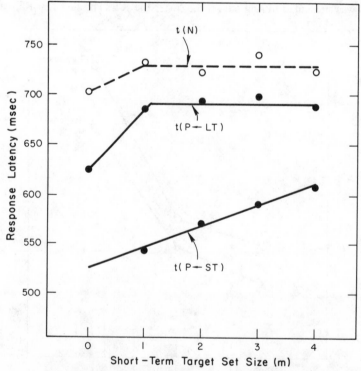

Fig. 13. Mean response latencies for targets ($P \leftarrow ST$, $P \leftarrow LT$) and distractors (N) as a function of ST set size in an experiment involving short- and long-term target sets. The straight lines fitted to the data represent theoretical predictions.

of the target list and the feature sets by which target items are coded in EKS. For the experiments considered in this paper a linear function appears to provide a good approximation.

MEMORY SEARCH WITH BOTH LARGE AND SMALL TARGET SETS

The experiments reported in this section involve a mix of the procedures discussed in the previous two sections. Prior to the test session, the subject memorizes a list of 30 words (designated the LT set) to a criterion of perfect mastery. In addition, each trial of the test session begins with the presentation of a short list of words (designated the ST set) that have never been shown before in the experiment. The test phase of the trial involves the presentation of a word, and the subject is required to make a positive response if the word is a member of either the LT set or the current ST set, and a negative response otherwise; thus a target is a word from either the LT or ST set, and a distractor is a word never previously used in the experiment. The size of the ST set varies from 1 to 4; half of the targets are from the ST set and half from the LT set. In addition, on some trials no ST set is presented, and then the target is necessarily from the LT set. Over trials, targets and distractors occur equally often.

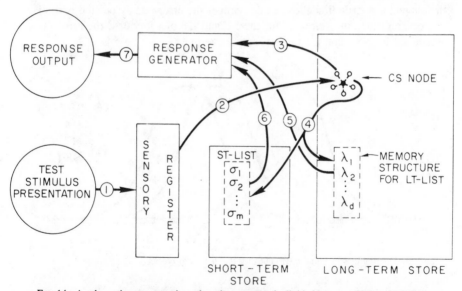

FIG. 14. A schematic representation when the target set is divided between STS and LTS. A test item is presented (1) and then matched to its CS node (2). The familiarity index of the node may lead to an immediate decision (3) and response output (7). Otherwise, appropriate codes are extracted from the CS node, and then used to simultaneously search STS and LTS (4). A decision about the test item is eventually made, based on the search of LTS (5) or of STS (6) and a response output (7).

Results from experiments by Wescourt and Atkinson (1973) and Mohs, Wescourt, and Atkinson (1973) are displayed in Fig. 13. RTs for targets and distractors are plotted as a function of m, the ST-set size; $t(P \leftarrow ST)$ and $t(P \leftarrow LT)$ denote the latency of a correct positive response to an ST and LT item, respectively, and $t(N)$ denotes a correct negative response to a distractor. Inspection of the figure indicates that $t(P \leftarrow ST)$ increases with the size of the ST set. In contrast, $t(P \leftarrow LT)$ and $t(N)$ seem to be independent of ST-set size as it varies from 1 to 4; however, the presence or absence of a ST set ($m = 0$ versus $m > 0$) has a marked effect on these two response times.

The model for this experiment is essentially the same as the one developed in the previous sections. A flow chart of the process is presented in Fig. 14. The LT set is assumed to reside in EKS, and each ST set is temporarily stored in STS. The recognition process first involves a check of the test word's familiarity value, which may lead to an immediate response. If not, a search of the EKS and STS will be required before a response can be emitted.

As described earlier, the decision to respond on the basis of familiarity alone is a function of the criteria c_0 and c_1. Figure 15 presents a diagram of the familiarity distributions for ST-set words, LT-set words, and distractors. The relative positions of these distributions are not determined a $priori$, but are inferred from error rates associated with the three types of test items (i.e., the tail of the distractor distribution above c_1 determines the error rate associated with distractors; and the tails below c_0 for the ST and LT distributions, the error rates associated with ST and LT targets, respectively).[8]

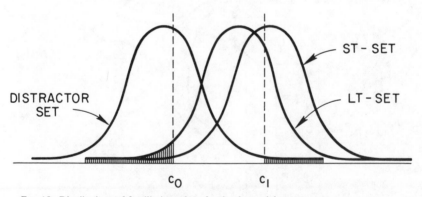

FIG. 15. Distributions of familiarity values for the three trial types.

[8]An experiment has been conducted by Richard Mohs in which elements of the LT set are included in the ST set on some trials; the time for a positive response to these items can be denoted as $t(P \leftarrow ST \ \& \ LT)$. The average response times in the experiment were ordered as follows: $t(P \leftarrow ST \ \& \ LT) < t(P \leftarrow ST) < t(P \leftarrow LT) < t(N)$. These results would be expected if the presentation of LT-set words within ST sets cause an additional boost of familiarity value for them.

When the retrieved familiarity value of a test word does not suffice for a decision to be made, then a search of STS and EKS is required. In this case, the principal issue is the order in which the two stores are searched. For example, the search could be first conducted in STS and if a match is not obtained, then continued in EKS. This scheme seems plausible since information in STS tends to be lost rapidly. However, if the two stores were searched in this order (and the time to search STS depended on the size of the ST set), then both $t(P \leftarrow LT)$ and $t(N)$ should increase as m goes from 1 to 4. Clearly, the data in Fig. 13 do not support this sequential search scheme. An alternative approach is to assume that STS and EKS are searched in parallel, and that if a match is found in either store, a positive response will be made; if both searches are completed and no match is established, then a negative response will be made.

The flow chart for the parallel-search process is shown in the right-hand panel of Fig. 16; the left-hand panel is for those trials on which the ST set is omitted and illustrates precisely the model developed in the previous section of this paper.

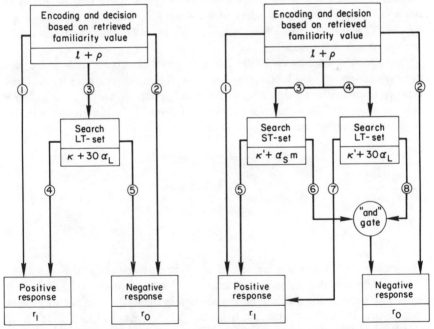

FIG. 16. Schematic representations of the processing strategies in searching the memory stores. The model when an ST set is omitted is shown in the left-hand panel; arrows (1) and (2) represent fast responses based on familiarity alone, whereas (4) and (5) represent responses after a search of EKS has occurred. In the right-hand panel a parallel-search model is presented for those trials on which an ST set is present. The arrows (1) and (2) represent fast responses based on familiarity. When a search is required, the ST and LT sets are searched simultaneously (3,4). If a match is found in the ST set (5) or in the LT set (7), a positive response will be made. If a match is not established in either set (6,8), a negative response will be made.

As indicated in the figure, the time κ' to initiate the search of both the EKS and STS (i.e., when $m > 0$) is assumed to be different from the time κ to initiate search of EKS alone (i.e., when $m = 0$). Once the search of a store is initiated, its rate is independent of whether or not any other store is being searched. We let α_S and α_L denote the search rates for the two stores. Thus, when an ST set is present, it takes time $\kappa' + \alpha_S m$ to search the STS store and time $\kappa' + 30\alpha_L$ to search EKS. When the ST set is omitted, it takes time $\kappa + 30\alpha_L$ to search EKS. Recall that the LT set is of size 30.

Since both stores are searched simultaneously when $m > 0$, the total search time will depend on which search required the most time. For the sizes of the ST and LT sets considered here, we assume that the STS search is always completed prior to the completion of the EKS search. Consequently, the search of STS will yield a match in time $\kappa' + \alpha_S m$ and the search of EKS will yield a match in time $\kappa' + 30\alpha_L$. If the test item is a distractor, then both searches will have to be completed (which takes time $\kappa' + 30\alpha_L$) before a negative response can be initiated. Thus, $t(P \leftarrow ST)$ will increase as m goes from 1 to 4, but both $t(P \leftarrow LT)$ and $t(N)$ will be independent of the size of the ST set. However, $t(P \leftarrow LT)$ and $t(N)$ will be faster when no ST set is present than when one is present, if κ is less than κ'.

A quantitative application of the model sketched out above leads to the predicted functions in Fig. 13. Not presented in the figure are error rates for the three types of test stimuli, but they also are accurately predicted by the model. (For a detailed account of this work, see Atkinson and Juola, 1974.) In fitting the model to these data, certain parameter estimates prove to be interesting:

$$\kappa' = 207 \text{ msec}$$

$$\kappa = 140 \text{ msec}$$

$$\alpha_S = 35 \text{ msec}$$

$$\alpha_L = 10 \text{ msec}$$

The κ and α_L recovered here are very close to the corresponding estimates made in the last section dealing with long-term target sets; similarly, the estimate of α_S is very close to the estimate of α recovered in the analysis of the short-term memory study. Finally, κ', the time to initiate the joint search of EKS and STS, is significantly above κ, the time to initiate the search of EKS alone.

In the model, we assumed that α_L is independent of the size of the ST set; any difference in the search of EKS on trials with and without an ST set is simply due to κ' and κ, respectively. Independent support for this assumption comes from an experiment conducted by Keith Wescourt. The experiment exactly replicated the procedure described in this section, except for positive test words: All positive test words were drawn from the LT set and the ST set was never tested. Subjects had to maintain 0 to 4 items in STS for recall at the end of the trial; however, they were told (and it was always the case) that the test word would be either an LT item or a distractor. Under these conditions, the latency of a positive response to an LT item and of a negative response to a distractor did not display a jump from the $m = 0$ condition to the $m > 0$ conditions; rather, both latency functions were constant as the ST-set size varied from 0 to 4. The parameters κ and α_L estimated in the prior experiment can be used to predict these data; the parameter κ' was not required since only EKS needed to be searched even on those trials where an ST set was present. The existence of a load in STS *per se* had no effect on RT; what did affect performance in the original experiment was the relevance of the STS load for the scanning decision.

MEMORY SEARCH MODERATED BY SEMANTIC FACTORS

A number of studies, using both small and large memory sets, have shown that semantic factors can influence RT. In this section, recognition experiments involving semantic variables are considered, and the theory is employed to explain how they can affect search and decision processes.

A frequently used paradigm requires a subject to memorize a target set composed of sublists, where words on each sublist are from a given category. The number of sublists will be denoted by c, and the length of each sublist by d; thus, the target set is composed of $c \cdot d$ words. For example, with $c = 2$ and $d = 3$, the target set might be

$$[(\text{BEAR, LION, HORSE}) (\text{CARROTS, PEAS, BEANS})]$$

a total of six words from the categories *animal* and *vegetable*. Once the target set has been memorized, tests are initiated. On a test trial, one of three types of words is presented: (1) a word on the memory list (P-item) to which the subject is required to make a positive response; (2) a word not on the memory list but from a category represented on the list (N-items) to which the subject is required to make a negative response; and (3) a word not on the memory list and not a member of any of the categories represented on the list (N*-items) to which the subject also is required to make a negative response. In the above example, a P-item might be LION, an N-item might be DEER, and an N*-item might be NAIL. A target word (P-item) is presented with probability ½, a related distractor (N-item) with probability ½ η, and an unrelated distractor (N*-item) with probability ½$(1 - \eta)$. When $\eta = 1$, only P and N items are presented; when $\eta = 0$, only P and N* items; and when $0 < \eta < 1$, a mix of P, N, and N* items. The dependent variables of principal interest are again latencies of correct responses to P, N, and N* items and will be denoted as $t(P)$, $t(N)$, and $t(N^*)$, respectively.

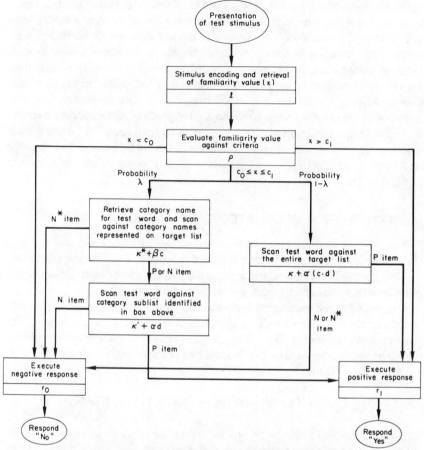

FIG. 17.   Representation of the processing stages underlying recognition performance when semantic factors may influence search in EKS. The subject may execute a rapid response based on familiarity or alternatively may search EKS. In the latter case, semantic information may be utilized to direct search on some proportion of trials; on other trials this information is ignored and the entire target set is scanned.

The theory as it applies in this situation is summarized in Fig. 17. A word is encoded (time l) and its familiarity value is retrieved and evaluated (time ρ). If the familiarity value is above c_1, an immediate positive response is made; below c_0, an immediate negative response. If the familiarity value is intermediate, the subject has two options. With probability λ he categorizes the test item and then scans its category name against the category names represented on the memory list. If no match occurs (N*-item), a negative response is made; if a category-name match occurs, the subject then searches the appropriate category sublist of the memory set, making either a positive response (P-item) or a negative response (N-item). Alternatively, with probability $1 - \lambda$ the subject ignores the semantic information in the test item and searches the entire memory list.

Given that the subject does categorize the test item, the time to retrieve its category name is κ^*, and the search rate among the c category names is β; thus, the time for this stage is $\kappa^* + \beta c$. If the categorizing stage determines that the word is an N^*-item, a negative response occurs. Otherwise, the subject next searches the sublist of the memory set identified by the categorization process; it takes time κ' to initiate the search, and its rate is α yielding time $\kappa' + \alpha d$ for this stage. Given that the subject does not categorize the item, the search of the entire memory list is presumed to take $\kappa + \alpha(c \cdot d)$; that is, time κ to initiate the search which proceeds at rate α for the total set of $c \cdot d$ items.

Figure 18 illustrates the familiarity distributions associated with P, N, and N^* items. While not critical to the model, the N distribution is shown in the figure to have a higher mean than the N^* distribution. The reason is that there is evidence to suggest that distractor items that are related to items on the memory list have a higher familiarity value than unrelated distractors (Juola et al., 1971; Underwood, 1972). This relation between the distributions would be expected if there were a spread of "activation" in the CS space in the areas of target-word nodes (Meyer & Schvaneveldt, 1971). Using Eq. (1), the quantity s can be defined for the P distribution. Similarly, using Eq. (2), the quantities s_N' and s_{N^*}' can be defined for the N and N^* distributions. Once this has been done, the following expressions can be written for the time to make a correct response to each of the item types:

$$t(P) = (l + \rho + r_1) + s\left\{\lambda\left[(\kappa^* + \beta c) + (\kappa' + \alpha d)\right] + (1 - \lambda)\left[\kappa + \alpha(c \cdot d)\right]\right\} \quad (5)$$

$$t(N) = (l + \rho + r_0) + s_N'\left\{\lambda\left[(\kappa^* + \beta c) + (\kappa' + \alpha d)\right] + (1 - \lambda)\left[\kappa + \alpha(c \cdot d)\right]\right\} \quad (6)$$

$$t(N^*) = (l + \rho + r_0) + s_{N^*}'\left\{\lambda\left[\kappa^* + \beta c\right] + (1 - \lambda)\left[\kappa + \alpha(c \cdot d)\right]\right\}. \quad (7)$$

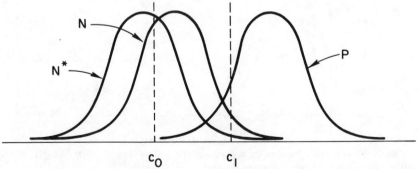

FIG. 18. Distributions of familiarity values for the two types of distractor items (N^*, N) and for target items (P).

How does the subject select between his two options: Should he first categorize a test item or search the entire memory list? We offer no theory to explain this selection and propose to estimate λ from the data. However, if all parameters of the process are fixed and the subject is trying to minimize his average response time over all trial types, then λ should be selected as follows: If the quantity $\left[(\kappa^* + \beta c) + \frac{1}{2}(1 + \eta)(\kappa' + \alpha d)\right]$ is greater than $\left[\kappa + \alpha(c \cdot d)\right.$, set λ equal to 0; otherwise set λ equal to 1.[9] Stated somewhat differently, an optimal setting for λ depends on an interplay of search parameters with the structure of the list (the values of c and d) and the nature of the test schedule (the value of η). Although estimates of the various search parameters vary from study to study (see Juola & Atkinson, 1971), the data indicate that (a) β is about three times as large as α, and that (b) κ^* and κ are fairly close to each other with κ' somewhat smaller.

Figure 19 presents unpublished data from two separate experiments, one conducted by Homa (1972) as part of a Ph.D. thesis at the University of Wisconsin, and the other as a pilot study at Stanford University. For the data displayed in the figure, $\eta = \frac{1}{2}$ and $c = 2$; the Homa data are for d equal to 2, 3, and 5, whereas

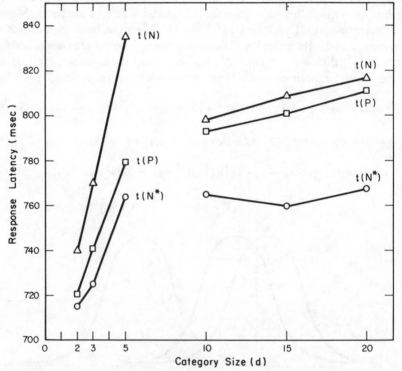

FIG. 19. Mean response latencies for positive items (P) and for semantically related (N) and unrelated (N*) negative items as a function of category size (d).

[9] A similar proposal has been made by Naus (1972).

the Stanford data are for d equal to 10, 15, and 20. No attempt will be made to generate quantitative predictions for these data; it is evident that appropriate parameter values can fit the results. The main point to consider is the effect of d on $t(N^*)$. In the Homa data, $t(N^*)$ is increasing and at about the same rate as $t(N)$, which indicates that λ is close to zero; thus, when d is relatively small, the subject is scanning the entire memory list and not attempting to categorize test items. For the Stanford data, $t(N^*)$ is relatively constant over the three values of d while $t(N)$ shows a sizable increase; this finding, of course, implies that λ must be equal to one (i.e., that the subject is categorizing each test item and processing the item accordingly).

These results are what one might expect if the subject is attempting to set λ optimally. When d is small, the slow scan of the category names is not warranted, but when d becomes large, there is an advantage to categorizing and, only if necessary, making a search of the appropriate sublist. Thus, the subjects appear to be selecting a value of λ in accordance with the specific parameters of the search task.[10]

There are other results that can be cited to support the λ-process proposed here. For example, Homa has data where $c = 12$ and $d = 1$ for which the estimate of λ is zero. On the other hand, Tarrow Indow (personal communication) has data for $c = 1$ and d varying from 5 to 27; these data are consistent with the view that λ is zero for small values of d, but increases to one for d greater than 10 or 12.

We have not provided a quantitative fit of the model to the data presented here. The reason is that the task is quite complex from a theoretical viewpoint; the subject has alternative strategies to apply, which means that different subjects may be electing different mixes of strategies in a given experimental condition. Hence, a quantitative evaluation of the model requires carefully designed experiments and a large sample of data for each subject. It is clear, however, that the basic outline of the theory is correct. An individual subject may or may not retrieve a category name for a test item, depending on the structure of the memory list (the values of c and d) and the nature of the test sequence (the value of η).[11]

The experiments considered in this section have all used words for the stimulus materials. Comparable experiments have been run using letters and digits to distinguish between P, N, and N* items. For example, the memory set might be

[10]The model proposed here assumes that the subject selects between one of two search strategies with probability λ. Another approach is to assume that both searches (the search by categories and the search of the entire list) are initiated simultaneously and that the one finishing first determines the subject's response latency; this type of assumption is in accord with a model proposed by Naus, Glucksberg, and Ornstein (1972). Under certain conditions, the simultaneous search model generates the same predictions as the model developed in this paper. Thus, the particular interpretation that we offer is open to question, and an argument can be made for a simultaneous search.

[11]Studies can be run that vary the length of sublists within a memory list. For example, the memory list can involve three categorized sublists with one having 4 words, the second 8 words, and the third 12 words for a total set of 24 (i.e., $c = 3$, $d_1 = 4$, $d_2 = 8$, $d_3 = 12$). Applications of the theory to these experiments is straightforward, but the equations are cumbersome.

composed of three letters, with the test involving a letter from the memory set (P-item), a letter not in the memory set (N-item), or a digit (N*-item). Results from these experiments have been somewhat variable. There are studies (Williams, 1971; Lively & Sanford, 1972) where the estimate of λ is significantly greater than zero for small memory sets of three or four items. For other studies, as we shall see in the next section, the estimate of λ is very close to, if not exactly, zero. It appears that when words are used as the stimulus materials, the estimate of λ is invariably zero for small memory sets; but when letters versus numbers are used, λ is sometimes greater than zero. Of course, when letters versus digits are used, it is conceivable that the subject may be classifying the probe on the basis of perceptual features; clearly, when words are used, there is no possibility for category classification based on perceptual cues, but with letters versus digits such a possibility may exist depending on the type font and displays used. A greater readiness to classify on the basis of perceptual factors than on semantic factors is consistent with the viewpoint developed in this paper, which distinguishes between perceptual codes and conceptual codes. Since a test stimulus will be represented in the memory system as a perceptual code before it can be represented as a conceptual code, strategies that allow accurate responding by processing perceptual codes will be preferred in those tasks where response speed is an important task demand.

MEMORY SEARCH INVOLVING A DUPLEX TARGET SET

In this section we examine an experiment that has similarities to the ones considered in the previous two sections; nevertheless, its theoretical analysis requires separate treatment. The experiment is one in a series of studies conducted by Charles Darley at Stanford University dealing with duplex target sets. His research on this problem is in an early stage, and the theoretical treatment given here may prove to be premature. The task is of such intrinsic interest, however, that some discussion of it seems warranted at this time.

On each trial the subject is presented with a target set composed of two subsets —one of letters and the other of digits. The target set is presented visually, with one subset on the left and the other on the right; whether letters or digits are on the left is determined randomly on each trial. The sizes of the two subsets are also randomly determined from trial to trial, each independently taking on the values 1, 2, or 3; the digits are drawn from the numbers 1 through 9 and the letters from a restricted alphabet with the vowels deleted. When the subject has the target set in mind, a test stimulus, which is either a letter or digit, is presented. The subject is required to make a positive response if the probe is from the target set, and a negative response otherwise. For example, the target set might be ((D,B,K)(8,6)); if any of these five items is presented at test, the subject should make a positive response; otherwise, a negative response. The subset that corresponds to the test stimulus will be called the *memory set* and the other the *load*

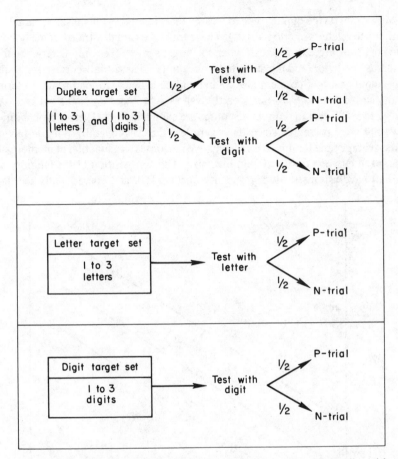

FIG. 20. Design of an experiment with duplex target sets. The upper panel describes trials presenting both a set of letters and a set of digits. The two lower panels describe trials presenting a homogeneous set of either letters or digits.

set. We let d_M denote the size of the memory set and d_L the size of the load set. In terms of the above example, if the test stimulus is a letter, then $d_M = 3$ and $d_L = 2$; if the test stimulus is a digit, then $d_M = 2$ and $d_L = 3$. Of course, until the test stimulus appears the subject does not know which array is the memory set and which is the load. The top panel of Fig. 20 presents a schematic account of a trial; letters and digits are tested equally often, and positive and negative trials are equally probable. The question of interest is how the scan of a memory set in STS is influenced by the size of a load set also in STS.[12]

[12]In this experiment, the subject was required to recall aloud the load set after he made his RT response; errors in this recall were extremely rare. The requirement to recall the load set does not seem to be an important factor, for Darley has run another study where the recall was omitted with results comparable to those to be reported here.

Mixed in with the duplex-type trials are others involving only a single target set (either 1 to 3 letters or 1 to 3 digits). These trial types are illustrated in the bottom two panels of Fig. 20; note that when the target set involves only letters, the test stimulus is a letter (and the same holds for digits). These trials correspond to the procedure used by Sternberg (1966) and will be called zero-load trials. In terms of the above notation, d_M takes on the values 1 to 3 and $d_L = 0$.

Average RT data for correct responses are shown in Fig. 21; error probabilities have not been presented since they were less than 3% overall. What is plotted is the average time for positive and negative responses as a function of memory-set size; each curve is for a different load size. The composition of the memory set did not have a statistically significant effect on RT, and consequently the data

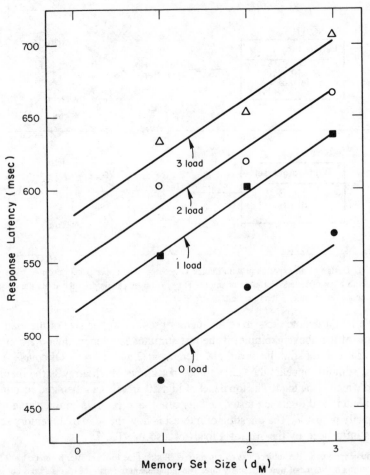

FIG. 21. Mean response latencies (combining positive and negative trials) for four conditions of memory-load size as a function of three target set sizes.

have been averaged over both memory sets composed of letters and memory sets composed of digits. For example, in Fig. 21 the observed value of 601 msec for a memory set of two and a load of one is an average which includes positive and negative responses and memory sets of letters and of digits.

The results displayed in Fig. 21 indicate that the load has a clear effect on RTs, but only on the intercept of the functions. It appears that all four RT functions have approximately the same slope. The subject cannot simply be classifying the test stimulus as a letter or digit and then restricting the search to appropriate subset. If this were the case, the obtained equality of the slopes for the four functions would be predicted, but predictions for their intercepts would be incorrect. The three load functions would all have the same intercept, which would be above that

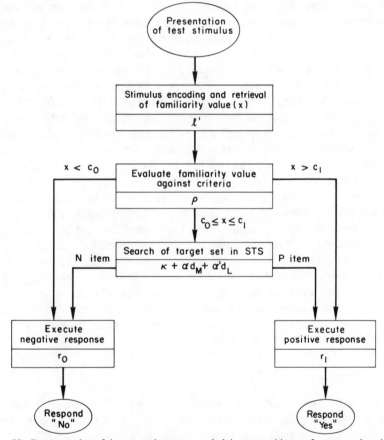

FIG. 22. Representation of the processing stages underlying recognition performance when there are two target sets in STS. A rapid response may be executed based on stimulus familiarity; otherwise, the encoded test stimulus is scanned against the contents of STS. The time of the search is a function of both target and load-set sizes.

for the zero-load functions; the intercept difference would reflect the time needed to determine which subset to search. A better fit to the data is not obtained by adding the assumption that maintaining a load set decreases the search rate for the memory set in proportion to load size. If this were the case, the three load functions would still all have the same intercept, and only their slopes would increase with load size.

It appears that the subject makes no attempt to limit the search by categorizing the test item but rather searches the entire target set; categorization would take time and is not warranted if that time is greater than the time required to search the load set. If target-set sizes were greater than those employed here, a categorization strategy might be used; in that case, a model like the one presented in the previous section would be appropriate.

Figure 22 presents the model for this experiment. As in previous sections, the familiarity distribution for a target item is assumed to have a mean above that for a distractor item, and to be independent of the size of the target set. First, the test stimulus is encoded and its familiarity value checked against the criteria c_0 and c_1. Given a high or low familiarity value, the appropriate response is immediately executed. Otherwise, a search of STS occurs. The time to initiate the search of STS is κ. The search rate for items in the target set from the same class as the test item is α, and the search rate is α' for items from the other class. Thus, the search of STS on a duplex trial takes time $\kappa + \alpha d_M + \alpha' d_L$. When no load is present, the same process applies and is precisely the one presented in the second section of this paper (see Fig. 5). The only difference is with regard to the time parameter for encoding the test stimulus. In the zero-load conditions, the subject knows that the test stimulus will be from the same class as the target set; being able to anticipate which class the test stimulus will be from may facilitate the encoding process. To provide for this possibility, we let l represent the encoding time for the zero-load case in accord with previous notation and use l' for the load case. Otherwise, all parameter values are identical for the load and zero-load conditions; the target and distractor distributions for familiarity values, criteria values, and α are assumed to be the same on all trials.

For the zero-load case the equations for RT are identical to Eqs. (3) and (4). The proportion of positive and negative trials was equal in this experiment, and hence, averaging Eqs. (3) and (4), yields

$$t_M = (l + \rho + \bar{r}) + \bar{s}(\kappa + \alpha d_M) \tag{8}$$

Here t_M denotes average RT to a memory set of size d_M in the zero-load condition. The quantity $\bar{r} = (r_1 + r_0)/2$ and $\bar{s} = (s + s')/2$, where s and s' are as defined in Eqs. (1) and (2). Similarly, for the load conditions

$$t_{M,L} = (l' + \rho + \bar{r}) + \bar{s}(\kappa + \alpha d_M + \alpha' d_L) \tag{9}$$

where $t_{M,L}$ denotes average RT to a memory set of size d_M with a load set of size d_L. Note that t_M is a linear function of d_M with intercept $(l + \rho + \bar{r} + \bar{s}\kappa)$ and slope $\bar{s}\alpha$. Similarly, $t_{M,L}$ is a linear function of d_M with intercept $\left[(l' + \rho + \bar{r} + \bar{s}\kappa) + (\bar{s}\alpha'd_L)\right]$ and the same slope $\bar{s}\alpha$.

Fitting Eqs. (8) and (9) to the data using a least-squares method yields the predicted functions given by the straight lines in Fig. 21.[13] There are only four identifiable parameters and their least-squares estimates are as follows:

$$(l + \rho + \bar{r} + \bar{s}\kappa) = 443 \text{ msec}$$

$$(l' - l) = 41 \text{ msec}$$

$$(\bar{s}\alpha) = 40 \text{ msec}$$

$$(\bar{s}\alpha') = 33 \text{ msec}$$

Note that α is greater than α'; that is, the search rate for target items in the same class as the test stimulus is slower than the search rate for items in the other class. This relation is what would be expected if the time to establish a mismatch between two letters is slower than between a letter and a digit (and vice versa). Such a difference is consistent with representations of items as codes comprised of features. In general, fewer feature comparisons are necessary to find a mismatch between items in different classes than between items in the same class.

There are other interpretations that can be given to these data. For example, one might assume that the subject first decides which subset to search and then dumps the load set from memory before starting the search. If the time to dump the load set is a linear function of its size, this interpretation (properly formulated) generates the same predictions as the one presented above. For reasons that are too lengthy to discuss here we do not favor the latter interpretation. Nevertheless, until there is more research using this type of task, it will be difficult to choose between these and other explanations. In our view, however, familiarity plays the same role in the load and zero-load conditions, and an adequate model will have to take this factor into account.

DISCUSSION

The model described in this paper asserts that recognition memory involves the operation of a set of processes. The information processing stages that occur in a particular recognition task are determined by the physical parameters of the

[13]The model also has been fit to the data with the positive and negative RTs kept separate. The fits are comparable to those displayed here, but were not presented to simplify the discussion. It should be noted that the slope of the four positive functions was about 47 msecs, whereas the slope of the four negative functions was about 33 msecs. In the theory, this means that s is greater than s'. Similarly, the intercept of a negative function tended to be higher than the intercept of the corresponding positive function, indicating that r_0 is greater than r_1.

experimental situation and by subjects' strategies. These strategies develop in accord with subjects' perceptions of task demands and abilities to apply alternative strategies. The experiments reviewed here support the model's major contention: Recognition decisions may be made quickly on the basis of partial information (familiarity), or they may be made more slowly, and more accurately, on the basis of an extended memory search. The data indicate that performance in a memory-scanning task represents a mixture of these two processes. Several factors have been shown to influence which of these processes subjects will tend to rely upon.

Besides these data, introspective reports seem to support the type of model developed here. Subjects report that sometimes they find themselves making immediate responses to a probe without "knowing for sure" whether or not it is a target item; on other trials, they report recalling portions of the target set before knowing how to respond. Subjects are almost always aware of their errors, indicating that although they may respond on the basis of familiarity, they continue processing by searching memory and thereby check their decision.

Limitations of the Mathematical Model

While we feel that the theory has wide applicability, certain qualifying comments need to be made about the specific models outlined in the previous sections. These models are reasonable approximations for the situations that have been investigated, but they do not reflect the full complexity of the theory. In particular, the assumption of independence of processing stages may not be justified. This assumption is reasonable in some cases, but generally processing in memory involves interactions between operations in different components of the system; processing operations selected at one stage can influence subsequent stages by restricting the number of alternative processes available, by altering the operating characteristics of these processes, or by both. The selection of internal codes could have such effects on subsequent stages of search and comparison when these depend on the nature of features comprising codes.

A second assumption made in the mathematical models is that the time to execute a memory search is a linear function of the target-set size. Corollary to this is the assumption that the search functions for both positive and negative probes are identical. There is no *a priori* reason for these assumptions; it is simply the case that much of our data are in accord with them. It is not necessary, however, that the search-and-comparison functions increase linearly with target-set size to account for the observed linear increase of RT. Both linear and nonlinear RT functions can be obtained from models that have mixtures of fast familiarity-based responses (which have times independent of target-set size) and slower responses based on extended searches (which have times either independent of or related nonlinearly to target-set size). This is the case, for example, if set size affects the mixture of the two processes; in terms of the model, the criteria that determine when familiarity-based decisions are made might vary as a function of target-set size. Under these conditions, a linear RT function can be obtained, but, in general, nonlinear functions would be expected.[14] Similar reasoning can be applied to the assumption that the scan time for both positive and negative probes is the same. Certain types of interactions between the encoding and search stages or between the search and decision stages may occur for positive and negative probes. In general, interactions would lead to differences between positive and negative probes, but in particular cases such differences may not be observed. For example, if negative probes are encoded more slowly than positive probes, but are scanned against the target set more rapidly, then the trade-off on times between stages might result in identical observed RTs for positives and negatives. The models presented here assume a linear search time that is the same for positive and negative probes, because it simplifies matters and still gives good fits to the data.

The Division of LTS

In describing the theory we proposed that LTS has two components, the conceptual store and event-knowledge store. Subdividing LTS is not a new idea (see, for example, Tulving, 1972). However, the distinctions between CS and EKS are different from the type of distinctions made in other theories. The main difference is that the CS is not a true lexicon or "semantic memory." It functions primarily as a high-speed interface between the perceptual processes and EKS. The conceptual code at each node in CS provides a very limited subset of information about a concept's full "meaning." One way to view this subset is that it provides information about the concept's relations to broad conceptual categories rather than to its relations with other specific concepts. Conceptual codes may be utilized initially to form the conceptual relations that characterize complex stimulus ensembles; subsequently, their dimensions suggest entry points into EKS where more detailed information about a concept may be located. The CS may be regarded as more analogous to an index for an encyclopedia rather than a dictionary. This index has the property of being organized on the basis of both the physical and conceptual elements of its entries, thereby allowing fast access to the stored information. While the particular description of the CS presented here does not depend directly upon any of our experimental results, it is consistent with research demonstrating that there are different levels of information representation (Posner, 1969, 1972). In addition, an experiment by Juola (1973) indicates that the familiarity of a stimulus does not depend on the specific mode of presentation; this supports our view of a CS node where the various perceptual representations of a concept are linked to one another. At an intuitive level, the CS also seems to be the type of memory required for the parsing of input by theories of language understanding (Schank, 1972); it allows high-speed access to the level of meaning

[14]For example, linear RT functions could result if search time increased more than linearly with target-set size, while the proportion of familiarity decisions also increased in a positively accelerated manner.

necessary for determining the class of conceptual relations that a word can enter into, and mediates the search of EKS for additional information needed to specify the "meaning" of natural language input. Even though the division between CS and EKS may be taken as conjecture, our experiments call for some such separation in order to account for the range of effects observed.

Memory Structures in EKS

The term "memory structure" has been used here to refer to collections of perceptual and conceptual codes stored in EKS. These structures represent past events and episodes as well as the full meaning of concepts in terms of their relations to other concepts. For instance, when subjects in experiments learn word lists, copies of codes representing the words are linked together to form a memory structure in EKS. Since it is likely that the ability to locate particular codes within a memory structure depends on how the structure is organized internally, the nature of these structures is a relevant issue (Herrmann & McLaughlin, 1973). It seems reasonable that the organization of EKS structures should vary with the nature of the stored information. The elements of a visual scene could be stored by linking perceptual codes and/or conceptual codes in an organization maintaining some isomorphism to the original physical display. A second form of internal organization for memory structures could be similar to Schank's (1972) conceptual dependencies. In this case, the codes underlying an event are organized on the basis of their conceptual relations. For either type of structure, the codes themselves are linked together with other codes to define the particular type of relations between other codes. The internal organization of a memory structure therefore can be thought of as a simple linking of individual codes where some of the codes define a higher-order organization of other codes. That is, objects A and B of some visual scene have codes linked by another code that defines an "above" relation between A and B if A was above B in the scene (Clark & Chase, 1972). Similarly, there is a code for the relation "actor-of" that would be linked between the actor and ACT of an event, organized on the basis of conceptual relations. When necessary, the same information may be stored in more than one memory structure (contingent on the time available). Alternately, information can be translated from one type of memory organization to another at some subsequent time; an event originally stored on the basis of physical relations (e.g., visual coding) can be analyzed for conceptual relations in the same way the original scene might have been. To the extent, however, that the information about an event stored in EKS is not a perfect copy of all the information originally available, subsequent translations of memory structures into new ones with alternative organizations may be incomplete or otherwise distorted. Therefore, the control processes for building memory structures attempt to create structures organized in a way that reflect expectations of how the information will be used at some later time. A related assumption is that the specific codes and organization used to form a memory structure affect the search and retrieval processes that operate on it; that is, there are alternative strategies that are more or less efficient, depending on the form and organization of the codes they manipulate.

Levels of Information Representation

As presented here, information codes in memory exist at two distinct levels, perceptual and conceptual. A code represents the set of primitive features or attributes that a stimulus or concept conveys; "primitive" should not be taken to mean innate in this context. Considerable research has been done on the internal coding of information (Melton & Martin, 1972), and undoubtedly the dichotomy presented in this paper is too simple to provide a detailed account of the various findings. While we do suppose that there are different perceptual codes for different sensory modalities, no distinctions have been made regarding the complexity of features within a modality. However, it is clear that there are several possible levels of analysis for any modality; for example, the evidence is that printed words produce perceptual codes that may reflect line segments, entire letters, or higher-order features like spelling patterns or vocalic center groups. A related issue is whether or not higher-order features map onto simple combinations of more basic features; if so, then different levels may be reduced to more basic ones, as we have suggested. The notion of different levels of perceptual codes adds considerable complexity to the scheme presented here, but it may prove necessary.

Fully and Partially Connected Memory Networks

The system described here differs conceptually from many other theories with regard to the overall organization of information within memory. A prevalent view is that memory is a *fully connected network* (Anderson & Bower, 1972; Rumelhart, Lindsey, & Norman, 1972). In such a network, events are stored by forming links between already existing internal nodes representing concepts. Usually, a distinction is made between type nodes and token nodes, and every token is linked to its type. In principle, it is possible to reach any node in the network from any other node by following the links from one node to the next. Our conception of LTS, in contrast, may be described as a *partially connected network*. While codes at a CS node may be viewed as types for which there are tokens present in memory structures in EKS, there are no direct links between codes in CS and in EKS. There also are no direct links between the various nodes in CS. Instead, related nodes in CS are stored "near" each other because their features tend to have similar dimension values in the CS space. Similarly, structures in EKS are not linked to one another, but similar or related events may be stored within a small neighborhood of the EKS space. The only connections in our system are those within a given CS node and within a given memory structure in EKS; thus, codes in memory form only partially connected networks. In our system, the ability to locate information in LTS depends on the ability to isolate those features of the retrieval context that index the area of memory containing the to-be-remembered structure. The success of this process depends on whether the features used for placement of a memory structure during learning are those available (or utilized) during retrieval.

A corollary to our notion of separate memory structures is the notion that the same information may be multiply represented in LTS. Whenever a particular code underlies some to-be-remembered event, a copy of that code is stored in the newly formed EKS structure. Similarly, whenever old knowledge is updated, all or part of the existing memory structure is recopied along with the new information. This view is not economical in terms of "storage space," but it may provide a more efficient basis for retrieval and modification of information already in the system because these processes do not have to deal with all the irrelevant relations associated with a given code. In a fully connected network, it is necessary to decide which and how many of the multitude of links leading away from a node are to be examined during a memory search.

It is important to emphasize that on a strictly formal basis fully connected networks and partially connected networks with directed retrieval processes may lead to equivalent predictions for a wide class of phenomena. This does not mean, however, that they are identical in a wider sense. Given a particular theoretical representation for the coding and retrieval of information, it is difficult not to opt for one or the other type of network, as we have done.

Concluding Remarks

The theoretical divisions of the memory system described in this paper offer a framework for understanding how particular variables affect recognition performance. In addition, the theory provides a basis for considering recognition in terms of processes that underlie other types of behavior; aspects of the theory thereby may be generalized to other paradigms for investigating memory and, in principle, could be extended to higher-order functions such as the understanding of language. We recognize that a direct test of the theory is not possible; however, it has proved to be a useful tool for several reasons: (a) It has permitted us to formulate and test a series of quantitative models for specific experimental tasks; (b) at an intuitive level, it seems consistent with the memory demands of more complex cognitive behaviors; and (c) it has served to identify several factors that have been shown to significantly affect memory. The theory, thus, has value as a tool for analyzing particular experiments and as a framework within which to view the broad domain of memory and cognition.

REFERENCES

Anderson, J. R., & Bower, G. H. Recognition and retrieval processes in free recall. *Psychological Review*, 1972, **79**, 97–123.

Atkinson, R. C., & Juola, J. F. Factors influencing speed and accuracy of word recognition. In S. Kornblum (Ed.), *Attention and performance IV*. New York: Academic Press, 1973.

Atkinson, R. C., & Juola, J. F. Search and decision processes in recognition memory. In R. C. Atkinson, D. H. Krantz, & P. Suppes (Eds.), *Contemporary developments in mathematical psychology*. San Francisco: W. H. Freeman & Company, 1974, in press.

Atkinson, R. C., & Shiffrin, R. M. Human memory: A proposed system and its control processes. In K. W. Spence & J. T. Spence (Eds.), *The psychology of learning and motivation: Advances in research and theory*. Vol. 2. New York: Academic Press, 1968.

Atkinson, R. C., & Shiffrin, R. M. The control of short-term memory. *Scientific American*, 1971, **225**, 82–90.

Atkinson, R. C., & Wickens, T. D. Human memory and the concept of reinforcement. In R. Glazer (Ed.), *The nature of reinforcement*. New York: Academic Press, 1971.

Briggs, G. E., & Swanson, J. M. Encoding, decoding, and central functions in human information processing. *Journal of Experimental Psychology*, 1970, **86**, 296–308.

Broadbent, D. E. Review lecture: Psychological aspects of short-term and long-term memory. *Proceedings of the Royal Society of London*, 1970, **175** B, 333–350.

Bruner, J. S., & Minturn, A. L. Perceptual identification and perceptual organization. *Journal of General Psychology*, 1955, **53**, 21–28.

Clark, H. H., & Chase, W. G. On the process of comparing sentences against pictures. *Cognitive Psychology*, 1972, **3**, 472–517.

Craik, F. I. M., & Lockhart, R. S. Levels of processing: A framework for memory research. *Journal of Verbal Learning and Verbal Behavior*, 1972, **11**, 671–684.

Fillenbaum, S., & Rapoport, A. *Structures in the subjective lexicon*. New York: Academic Press, 1971.

Herrmann, D. J., & McLaughlin, J. P. Effects of experimental and pre-experimental organization on recognition: Evidence for two storage systems in long-term memory. *Journal of Experimental Psychology*, 1973, **99**, 174–179.

Homa, D. Organization and long-term memory search. Unpublished doctoral dissertation, University of Wisconsin, 1972.

Juola, J. F. Repetition and laterality effects on recognition memory for words and pictures. *Memory & Cognition*, 1973, **1**, 183–192.

Juola, J. F., & Atkinson, R. C. Memory scanning for words vs. categories. *Journal of Verbal Learning and Verbal Behavior*, 1971, **10**, 522–527.

Juola, J. F., Fischler, I., Wood, C. T., & Atkinson, R. C. Recognition time for information stored in long-term memory. *Perception & Psychophysics*, 1971, **10**, 8–14.

Kintsch, W. Models for free recall and recognition. In D. A. Norman (Ed.), *Models of human memory*. New York: Academic Press, 1970.

Klatzky, R. L., Juola, J. F., & Atkinson, R. C. Test stimulus representation and experimental context effects in memory scanning. *Journal of Experimental Psychology*, 1971, **87**, 281–288.

Lakoff, G. HEDGES: A study in meaning criteria and the logic of fuzzy concepts. Paper presented at the Eighth Regional Meeting, Chicago Linguistics Society. Chicago: University of Chicago Linguistics Department, 1972.

Lively, B. L., & Sanford, B. J. The use of category information in a memory-search task. *Journal of Experimental Psychology*, 1972, **93**, 379–385.

Mandler, G., Pearlstone, F., & Koopmans, H. S. Effects of organization and semantic similarity on recall and recognition. *Journal of Verbal Learning and Verbal Behavior*, 1969, **8**, 410–423.

McCormack, P. D. Recognition memory: How complex a retrieval system? *Canadian Journal of Psychology*, 1972, **26**, 19–41.

Melton, A. W., & Martin, E. (Eds.), *Coding processes in human memory*. Washington: Winston, 1972.

Meyer, D. E., & Schvaneveldt, R. W. Facilitation in recognizing pairs of words: Evidence of a dependence between retrieval operations. *Journal of Experimental Psychology*, 1971, **90**, 227–234.

Mohs, R. C., Wescourt, K. T., & Atkinson, R. C. Effects of short-term memory contents on short- and long-term searches. *Memory & Cognition,* 1973, **1,** 443–448.

Murdock, B. B., Jr. A parallel processing model for scanning. *Perception & Psychophysics,* 1971, **10,** 289–291.

Naus, M. J. Memory search of categorized lists: A consideration of alternative self-terminating search strategies. Unpublished doctoral dissertation, Princeton University, 1972.

Naus, M. J., Glucksberg, S., & Ornstein, P. A. Taxonomic word categories and memory search. *Cognitive Psychology,* 1972, **3,** 643–654.

Posner, M. I. Abstraction and the process of recognition. In G. H. Bower & J. T. Spence (Eds.), *The psychology of learning and motivation: Advances in research and theory.* Vol. III. New York: Academic Press, 1969.

Posner, M. I. Coordination of internal codes. Paper presented at the 8th Carnegie Symposium on Cognitive Processes, Pittsburgh, May, 1972.

Rips, L. J., Shoben, E. J., & Smith, E. E. Semantic distance and the verification of semantic relations. *Journal of Verbal Learning and Verbal Behavior,* 1973, **12,** 1–20.

Rothstein, L. D., & Morin, R. E. The effects of size of the stimulus ensemble and the method of set size manipulation on recognition reaction time. Paper presented at the meeting of the Midwestern Psychological Association, Cleveland, May, 1972.

Rumelhart, D. E., Lindsay, P. H., & Norman, D. A. A process model for long-term memory. In E. Tulving & W. Donaldson (Eds.), *Organization of memory.* New York: Academic Press, 1972.

Schank, R. C. Conceptual dependency: A theory of natural language understanding. *Cognitive Psychology,* 1972, **3,** 552–631.

Shiffrin, R. M., & Atkinson, R. C. Storage and retrieval processes in long-term memory. *Psychological Review,* 1969, **76,** 179–193.

Sternberg, S. High-speed scanning in human memory. *Science,* 1966, **153,** 652–654.

Sternberg, S. The discovery of processing stages: Extensions of Donder's method. In W. G. Koster (Ed.), Attention and performance II. *Acta Psychologica,* 1969, **36,** 276–315. (a)

Sternberg, S. Memory scanning: Mental processes revealed by reaction-time experiments. *American Scientist,* 1969, **57,** 421–457. (b)

Sternberg, S. Decomposing mental processes with reaction-time data. Invited address presented at the meeting of the Midwestern Psychological Association, Detroit, May, 1971.

Swanson, J. M., & Briggs, G. F. Information processing as a function of speed versus accuracy. *Journal of Experimental Psychology,* 1969, **81,** 223–229.

Townsend, J. T. A note on the identifiability of parallel and serial processes. *Perception & Psychophysics,* 1971, **10,** 161–163.

Tulving, E. Episodic and semantic memory. In E. Tulving & W. Donaldson (Eds.), *Organization of memory.* New York: Academic Press, 1972.

Tulving, E., & Thomson, D. M. Encoding specificity and retrieval processes in episodic memory. *Psychological Review,* 1973, **80,** 352–373.

Underwood, B. J. Are we overloading memory? In A. W. Melton & E. Martin (Eds.), *Coding processes in human memory.* Washington: Winston, 1972.

Weaver, F. S. Retrieval processes in short-term memory. Unpublished doctoral dissertation, University of Delaware, 1972.

Wescourt, K. T., & Atkinson, R. C. Scanning for information in long- and short-term memory. *Journal of Experimental Psychology,* 1973, **98,** 95–101.

Williams, J. D. Memory ensemble selection in human information processing. *Journal of Experimental Psychology,* 1971, **88,** 231–238.

6

TRANSFORMATIONAL STUDIES OF THE INTERNAL REPRESENTATION OF THREE-DIMENSIONAL OBJECTS[1]

Jacqueline Metzler[2] and Roger N. Shepard
Stanford University

INTRODUCTION

In 1969 we initiated the first experiment in a continuing series designed to measure the times that human subjects require to respond discriminatively to spatially transformed visual objects. We are taking advantage of this opportunity to give the first full account of that initial experiment, which was only partially covered in the brief original paper (Shepard & Metzler, 1971); to report a second, corroborative and clarifying experiment that has previously been presented only orally (Metzler & Shepard, 1971); to review briefly the central findings of some still further experiments that one of us has subsequently carried out in a doctoral dissertation (Metzler, 1973); and to present a reasonably complete statement of the relevant theoretical issues, which were initially advanced by Shepard (e.g., see Shepard, in press) but which have never been fully set forth in relation specifically to the experiments in this particular series.

Our primary focus here will be on those experiments that have used objects of one particular kind (viz., abstract three-dimensional structures) as well as trans-

[1]The work reported in this paper was supported by National Science Foundation research grants GB-3197IX and GS-2283 to the second author. During this work the first author was supported by a National Institutes of Mental Health predoctoral fellowship. We are indebted to the Bell Telephone Laboratories and, particularly, to Jih-Jie Chang of those laboratories for essential assistance in the computer generation of the perspective views used in Experiments I and II. We also wish to thank Dr. J. D. Elashoff for her helpful advice concerning the statistical analyses. Finally, important programming help in connection with the statistical analyses and the computer plotting of the reaction-time distributions was provided by Phipps Arabie and Paul Goldstein.

[2]Now at the Department of Psychology, Harvard University.

formations on such objects of one particular kind (viz., single rigid rotations about some fixed axis in three-dimensional space). Other recent papers adequately cover various related experiments in which the objects to be transformed are only two-dimensional (Cooper & Shepard, 1973a, 1973b; Shepard, in press) or in which the transformations include other spatial operations—such as sequences of rotations, reflections, or foldings about different axes (Shepard, in press; Shepard & Feng, 1972).

General Nature of the Experiments

Basic paradigm. The experiments we wish to consider here have the following features in common. The subject is presented, on each trial, with a pair of perspective drawings of three-dimensional objects and is instructed to determine as rapidly as possible whether the two portrayed objects have the same three-dimensional shape (even though they may be portrayed in very different orientations), or whether they have inherently different three-dimensional shapes (and so could not be brought into mutual congruence by any rigid motion). In the first two experiments to be described here, the two perspective views are displayed simultaneously and the reaction-time clock starts with the presentation of the pair. In some more recent experiments (Metzler, 1973) that we shall also describe, however, the two views are displayed sequentially and the clock starts with the presentation of the second member of the pair. In either case, the clock is stopped as soon as the subject actuates either a right-hand switch or a left-hand switch (one of which is used to register the decision ''same shape,'' the other of which is used to register the decision ''different shape'').

The objects portrayed in the two perspective drawings are always abstract three-dimensional shapes consisting of cubical blocks attached face-to-face to form a rigid, asymmetrical arm-like structure with two free ends and two or three right-angled bends. On a random half of the presentations the two objects are identical in three-dimensional shape, though generally displayed in different orientations. On these trials the subject should actuate the switch indicating that, despite possible differences in orientation, the objects are of the same three-dimensional shape. On the other half of the presentations the two objects differ by a reflection through some plane in three-dimensional space as well, possibly, as by a rotation. Since all objects are inherently asymmetric, such objects can not be brought into congruence with each other by any rigid rotation and, hence, the subject should actuate the other switch indicating that the two objects are different in three-dimensional shape. The choice of objects that are mirror-images of each other for the ''different'' pairs was intended to ensure that the decision as to whether the two objects were the same or different was made only on the basis of global shape and not on the basis of any local features. (See Fig. 2 for illustrative examples of ''same'' and ''different'' pairs of objects.)

Factors investigated. The objective of these experiments has been to determine how the time required to make the decision as to whether the two perspective views portray objects of the same three-dimensional shape depends upon such factors as the following:

1. Whether the two objects are in fact the same or different in three-dimensional shape.

2. The angle of rotation that would have to be performed in three-dimensional space in order to bring the two objects into congruence if they are the same in three-dimensional shape (or into partial congruence if they are not).

3. Whether the axis of this rotation is or is not known by the subject in advance of the presentation.

4. Whether this axis is or is not a natural axis of the three-dimensional object itself.

5. Whether this axis is vertical, horizontal, or inclined with respect to the external frame of reference.

6. Whether this axis coincides with the line of sight (in which case the difference in orientation corresponds to a simple rigid rotation of the two-dimensional perspective drawing itself) or is orthogonal to the line of sight (in which case the difference in orientation corresponds to a much more complex nonrigid deformation of the perspective drawing).

7. Whether, for a given angular difference, such a nonrigid deformation of the perspective view would or would not pass through certain topological discontinuities or singularities in which parts of the object become completely foreshortened, disappear, or emerge into view.

8. Whether, for a given axis of rotation, the particular (clockwise or counterclockwise) direction in which the subject has been set to imagine the rotation is, for a given pair of objects, the short or the long way around the 360° circle (i.e., whether it is less than or greater than 180°).

9. Whether both perspective views are perceptually available during the entire decision process, or whether the first view is available only in memory while the subject is preparing for the presentation of the second.

10. Whether the subject must determine for himself which end of the second object corresponds to a particular end of the first object, or whether this correspondence has been explicitly indicated (by color coding).

11. The over-all complexity of the three-dimensional object (as measured in terms of the number of cubical blocks or the number of right-angled bends in the resulting arm-like structure).

12. Individual differences among subjects (including such factors as sex and handedness).

The experiments so far completed provide relatively strong evidence concerning all of these factors except the last two. In the case of these last factors, 11 and 12, the evidence is still rather weak owing to a partial confounding of factors 4 and 11, and to the relatively small and homogeneous samples of objects and subjects used in each experiment. (For the purposes of obtaining precise information concerning the several other factors, our initial strategy has been to obtain extensive data from each subject in a group of only about eight well-practiced subjects in each experiment.)

Major Theoretical Issues

Analog nature of mental transformations. The major theoretical issues to which this program of experimental research has been directed were initially advanced by Shepard (e.g., see Shepard, in press). A particularly central one, here, concerns the nature of the internal process by means of which the subject determines whether two differently oriented objects are or are not the same in intrinsic shape. Specifically, the question arises as to whether the internal process is in any sense an analog process, i.e., a *mental* process that corresponds in some way to a *physical* process of actual rotation of the one object into congruence with the other. Moreover, if there is a sense in which this internal process is indeed a mental analog of an external physical rotation, it becomes important to formulate, in as clear a way as possible, just what this sense may be.

Note in particular that, in order for a mental process to be an analog of a physical rotation, it is not required that it be neurophysiologically embodied as anything (such as a pattern of neuronal firing or as an electric field) that itself literally rotates within the subject's physical brain. In accordance with a principle of second-order isomorphism (Shepard & Chipman, 1970), the crucial requirement is that the internal representation or process correspond to the external object or its transformation by virtue of a relation that is merely one-to-one—not a relation of concrete structural resemblance.

There are two connected implications of the claim that the decision is reached by means of a mental analog of a physical rotation: One is that, whatever the nature of the neurophysiological process that goes on when the subject is comparing two differently oriented objects, that process has something important in common with the internal process that would go on if the subject were actually to perceive the one external object physically rotating into congruence with the other. The other implication is that, in the course of such a process, the internal representation passes through a certain trajectory of intermediate states each of which has a one-to-one correspondence to an intermediate stage of an external physical rotation of the object. And here, again, the one-to-one correspondence between an intermediate internal representation and an intermediate external orientation of the object is not necessarily one of structural resemblance, but only the casual, dispositional one of being especially prepared for the appearance of that external object in just that orientation at just that time (cf., Cooper & Shepard, 1973b, Experiment II).

These two implications are closely related in that the reason that a subject is especially prepared for a particular object at a particular orientation is presumably that the neural activity, whatever its nature, has at that moment much in common with the neural activity that would be caused by the external presentation of that physical object in that specific orientation. However, neither of these implica-

tions requires either that the internal representation of the object structurally resemble the external object or that the internal representation of its rotation structurally resemble its physical rotation. Either or both of these more concrete kinds
of structural isomorphism may to some extent hold, but it is not necessary that
either hold in order to speak of such a thing as mental rotation or to characterize it
as a process that, though more or less abstract, is nevertheless basically an analog
type of process.

   To speak of it as an analog type of process is, at the most fundamental level
then, to contrast it with any other type of process (such as a feature search, symbol
manipulation, verbal analysis, or other "digital computation") in which the intermediate stages of the process have no sort of one-to-one correspondence to intermediate situations in the external world. In the strictest sense, a fully analog representation of a continuous process (such as a physical rotation) should itself be
a continuous process. Hence the distinction between analog and digital computation is often drawn in terms of continuous versus discrete processes. We do not
wish to take a stand here on the neurophysiological question of whether the internal
simulation of external physical processes by the brain is, at the finest level of
analysis, basically discrete or continuous. For the present, we prefer to formulate
the hypothesis that mental rotation is an analog process in a somewhat weaker
or more general way that does not entail strict continuity. We are willing to concede that sufficiently small differences in orientation may be handled in discrete
jumps. The most essential and general implication of classifying the process of
comparing two differently oriented objects as an analog process is that, if the two
orientations are sufficiently different, *then* the comparison can be made only by
passing through some other internal states that correspond to intermediate orientations of the external object.

   Internal representation of three-dimensional objects. Among those mental
operations that may be performed in an analog manner, mental rotation has been
singled out as an example that seems particularly interesting in connection with
the problem of the internal representation of three-dimensional objects. Notice
that for most rigid spatial transformations, such as translation or dilation (uniform
expansion or contraction), there is a very simple, direct relationship between the
change in the three-dimensional object and the resulting change in a two-
dimensional perspective projection of the object—such as the retinal projection.
The same is also true of rotation in the special case in which the rotation is about
one particular axis—namely, the line of sight (or, in other words, the axis through
the point of projection). In all of these cases a rigid transformation of the external
three-dimensional object induces an essentially rigid transformation of the two-
dimensional projection.

   In the case of a rotation about any axis other than the line of sight, however, the
relationship between the change in the object and the change in its planar projection becomes much less direct. The three-dimensional object itself is still rigid
under rotation, but its two-dimensional projection is subjected to a very complex,

nonrigid deformation in which not only the metric but even the topological structure is often altered. (Portions of the projection not only shrink and deform relative to other portions, they even disappear completely and then reappear on the other side of the object.)

Clearly then, the way in which subjects deal with rotations in depth should provide information that is relevant to questions of how three-dimensional objects are internally represented. Of particular interest in this regard is the question of whether the internal representation is more akin to the two-dimensional projection of the object, which deforms in complex ways under rotation but which is at least directly available at the sensory surface, or whether it is more akin to the three-dimensional object itself, which is structurally invariant under rotation but has somehow to be indirectly constructed on the basis of the retinal projection. The answer to this question should be attainable through an examination of those pairs of perspective views that correspond to objects that differ by the same angle of rotation in three-dimensional space but that differ in different ways or to different extents in terms of their two-dimensional representations (particularly as indicated in items 6 and 7, listed earlier).

In general, as the title of this paper is intended to indicate, we believe that a study of the way an object behaves under transformation can furnish significant information about the nature of that object. In the present case, the object of interest is a mental object—namely, the internal representation of a three-dimensional structure; and the transformation is accordingly a mental transformation—namely, the internal representation of a rigid rotation of that three-dimensional structure. Despite the internal, mental nature of the transformation and of the object transformed, however, the outcome of the transformation can be objectively tested.

As in the last of the experiments to be described here, we can present a subject with a certain object and tell him that, upon its disappearance, he should imagine it rotating about a designated natural axis of the object in a specified direction. After a predetermined delay we can then present a test probe that is either that object or its mirror image, displayed in the orientation that the object should have attained by that time if it had actually been rotating during the delay (a) in the specified direction, (b) about the designated axis, and (c) at a constant rate previously estimated for that subject (specifically, a rate estimated on the basis of the time he previously required to determine the sameness or difference of two *simultaneously* presented views of that object differing by that same angle of rotation). If the subject can respond "same" or "different" accurately and with uniform rapidity when (and only when) the test probe thus appears in the particular rotated orientation appropriate for that delay—regardless of the extent of the corresponding rotation—we obtain strong evidence in support of the claim that the mental operation that the subject was carrying out during the delay was in a definite sense an internal analog of an external rotation. Moreover, we obtain support for the further claim that the internal representation upon which this mental operation was being performed incorporated considerable structural information about the external object and, further, that this structural information was preserved and appropriately transformed during this mental operation.

EXPERIMENT I

We now provide the first full description and analysis of our initial experiment on mental rotation of three-dimensional objects, which was presented only incompletely in our brief earlier report (Shepard & Metzler, 1971).

Method

Subjects. Eight adult males served as experimental subjects. Of these, six were graduate students at Stanford University and two (including one of the present authors, RNS) were faculty members. All subjects had 20:20 vision or vision corrected to 20:20. In addition, all were found able to complete 90% of the items—with less than 10% errors on the completed items—on both of two timed paper-and-pencil pretests of mental manipulation of objects in space (viz., Thurstone's Card Rotation Test and Cube Comparison Test, as modified and supplied by the Educational Testing Service). Two of the eight subjects were left handed.

Generation of the individual stimuli. The stimuli used for the experiment itself were perspective line drawings of relatively abstract and unfamiliar three-dimensional objects as viewed in different orientations in space. Each such object consisted of ten cubical blocks attached face-to-face to form a connected string of cubes with three right-angled bends and two free ends (see Fig. 2). The locations and relative directions of the three bends were chosen (a) so that each object was inherently asymmetric, i.e., so that it could not be transformed into itself by any reflection or rotation (short of 360°) in three-dimensional space; and (b) so that each object was inherently distinct from every other, i.e., so that it could not be transformed into any of the other objects by any rigid rotation in three-dimensional space. Altogether ten such distinct objects were selected for use in the experiment. These ten form two groups of five each such that (a) within either group of five no object can be transformed into any other by any rotation *or* reflection, while (b) for each object in either group there is a corresponding object in the other group that is identical to it except for a reflection through a plane in three-dimensional space. Such mirror-image pairs or "isomers" were used to construct the "different" pairs in the "same-different" tests (thus preventing discrimination on the basis of merely local features).

For each of these ten structurally distinct objects, 18 perspective views were generated corresponding to 18 equally-spaced 20° steps of rotation of the object about a vertical axis through the object in three-dimensional space. Since each object was oriented more or less at random prior to rotation, the axis of rotation in this experiment never corresponded to a natural axis of the object itself. These

10 × 18 or 180 perspective views were generated at the Bell Telephone Laboratories especially for this research by Jih-Jie Chang in accordance with specifications outlined by one of the present authors (RNS). The generation was achieved by means of special computer graphic facilities at the Bell Laboratories (including, particularly, the Stromberg-Carlson 4020 microfilm recorder) and an associated program for three-dimensional spatial transformations on two-dimensional perspective projections developed there by A. M. Noll (e.g., see Noll, 1965).

Because Noll's graphics program had not at that time incorporated the now-available computational solution to the so-called hidden-line problem (see Newman & Sproull, 1973, Chapter 14 and Appendix 6; Warnock, 1969), the objects were initially portrayed in the computer-generated pictures as completely transparent and therefore relatively susceptible to perceptual reversal (despite the somewhat stabilizing cues of perspective convergence). Such reversals could not be permitted in this experiment since the critical discrimination was to be between an object and the three-dimensional mirror image that one obtains by just such a reversal. The possibility of perceptual reversal was therefore eliminated by preparing an ink tracing of each of the perspective views to be used in the experiment on a blank sheet of paper, omitting all lines that would be invisible if the object were opaque.

In order to facilitate subsequent construction of the stimulus pairs actually to be presented to the subjects, an ink circle of fixed size was drawn around each of these revised perspective drawings, and a small tic mark was added on the outside edge of the top of the circle, to indicate the top of the vertical axis for the rotations in depth. Each of the resulting individual perspective line drawings with its enclosing circle was then photographically reduced and a number of copies were printed by a photo-offset process. The reduction was chosen so that, in the final printed copies, the circle was eight cm. in diameter while the enclosed perspective drawing of the object averaged between four and five cm. in maximum linear extent (depending upon the shape and orientation of the particular object). Changes in orientation corresponding to rotations within the two-dimensional plane of the picture itself were achieved simply by rotating the picture itself so that the tic mark was at the desired position about the circle.

Construction of the depth pairs. In order to determine how the time required to determine that two objects have the same three-dimensional shape depends upon the difference between their orientations in depth, it appeared desirable to construct, for each object, an equal number of pairs differing by each of the possible angles ranging from 0° to 180° by 20° increments about the vertical axis. At the same time, we wished to minimize the number of computer-generated perspective views that would have to be redrawn, reduced, and reproduced. Moreover, it seemed desirable to avoid certain views of each object in which the three-dimensional structure was difficult or impossible to determine visually owing to the circumstance that one arm of the object happened to be hidden behind

the rest of the object or happened to coincide more or less with the line of sight
(in which case extreme foreshortening would obscure its structure).

We found that it was possible to select a certain fixed pattern of seven of the 18
views of each object in such a way as to meet all of our requirements. This pattern
is schematically illustrated for one of the ten objects in Fig. 1. Here, the 18 perspective views corresponding to 20° steps of rotation in depth are represented by
the numerals 1 through 18 around the circle. Since each object was constructed
entirely of cubes, during a complete 360° rotation it passed through four angular
regions in which a part of the object more or less coincided with the line of sight.
These to-be-avoided "singular" orientations are indicated by the four arrows
around the perimeter of the circle. There was also a more extended range of
orientations for which one arm of the object was largely hidden from view. This
range is indicated, for the object represented in Fig. 1, by the shaded arc outside
one segment of the circle.

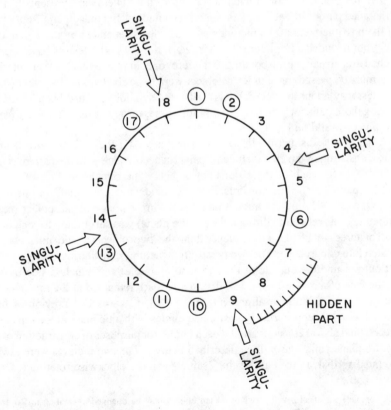

FIG. 1. Angular relations among the seven selected perspective views (circled numbers), schematically illustrated for one object (A).

For this object, the seven particular orientations labeled 1, 2, 6, 10, 11, 13, and 17 (circled in the figure) could still be chosen without encountering any of the orientations that had objectionable singularities or hidden parts. Moreover, these seven were so spaced around the circle that they could be used to construct two pairs of views at each of the equally-spaced angular separations, in 20° steps, from 0° to 180°; and to do this in such a way that (a) the two pairs at any one angular difference generally came from widely separated regions of the circle and (b) all views appeared approximately the same number of times. (The seven acceptable views selected, in accordance with the scheme illustrated in Fig. 1, for five of the ten objects—viz., those that can not be brought into congruence with each other by any rotation or reflection—may be seen on the cover of the February 19th issue of Science, in which the initial report of this work appeared (Shepard & Metzler, 1971). The corresponding views of the other five objects differ simply by a reflection of the three-dimensional objects through the picture plane.)[3]

The pairs actually constructed according to this scheme are presented, under "Included pairs" in Table 1. (As can be seen under "Excluded pairs" only three of the possible pairs of distinct views—i.e., views separated by more than 0°—were not included.) For later reference, zero, one, or two asterisks have been attached to each pair, corresponding to the zero, one, or two regions of "singularity" that must be passed through if one object were to be rotated into the other (in the shortest way about the vertical axis). Also the symbol "h" had been added following those pairs for which such a rotation passes through a region where a part of the object would be hidden.

A set of 400 distinct depth pairs was prepared. Of these, 200 were "same" pairs consisting of the 20 "included" pairs, in accordance with the pattern shown in Table 1, for each of the 10 distinct objects. The remaining 200 were "different" pairs which were constructed in the same way except that, for one of the two views, a view of the three-dimensional mirror image of the object (corresponding to its reflection through the picture plane) was substituted for one of the two pictures—with the consequence that the two objects could no longer be rotated into congruence. The two perspective pictures constituting each pair were cut out (around the outside of the surrounding circle) and attached side-by-side on the face of a 5 × 8 in. card so that the tic mark remained at the top center of each circle. To facilitate alignment, the 5 × 8 in. cards had previously been printed with two appropriately positioned circles with a tic mark at the top center of each (and also at 20° steps around each circle, for purposes of construction of the picture-plane pairs—as will be described below). The two pictures were always mounted so that, in the case of the "same" pairs, a clockwise rotation (as seen

[3]A complete set of all seven views of all ten objects may be obtained by writing to Roger N. Shepard, Department of Psychology, Stanford University, Stanford, California 94305.

TABLE 1

Construction of the 20 Pairs from the Seven Selected Views,
Illustrated for One Object (A)

Angular separation between the two views in each pair	The 20 included pairs of views		The 8 excluded pairs of views
0°	(13 − 13)	(17 − 17)	(1 − 1)(2 − 2)(6 − 6) (10 − 10) (11 − 11)
20°	(1 − 2)	(10 − 11)	
40°	(1 − 17)*	(11 − 13)	
60°	(2 − 17)*	(10 − 13)	
80°	(2 − 6)*	(6 − 10)*h	(13 − 17)*
100°	(1 − 6)*	(6 − 11)*h	
120°	(1 − 13)**	(11 − 17)**	
140°	(2 − 13)**	(10 − 17)**	(6 − 13)*h (6 − 17)**
160°	(1 − 11)**	(2 − 10)**h	
180°	(1 − 10)**	(2 − 11)**h	

Note.—The two numbers within each parenthesis correspond to the two views of the object (A) as designated in Fig. 1. The number of asterisks following a pair indicate the number of singular regions that the object must pass through in rotating from one view to the other. The letter "h" following a pair indicates that part of the object would temporarily be hidden from view if the object were to rotate from one view to the other (through the smallest possible angle).

from the top of the vertical axis) would bring the object portrayed on the left into congruence with the object on the right through the minimum angle (i.e., the short way around the 360° circle).

Construction of the picture-plane pairs. A set of 400 distinct pairs of perspective views was prepared, also, for rotations within the picture plane. Again, these consisted of 200 "same" pairs (in which, in this case, a rotation of one of the two-dimensional pictures itself would bring it into congruence with the other picture) and 200 "different" pairs (in which, as before, a picture of the inherently different three-dimensional mirror image of the object was substituted for one of the two pictures). Of the seven different perspective views prepared of each of the ten objects for the construction of the depth pairs, one particular view was selected to construct all the picture-plane pairs for that object. The views selected for five of the ten objects are shown in Fig. 5. The views selected for the other five objects (required for the construction of the "different" pairs) differ from these only by a reflection through the picture plane and, as illustrated in Fig. 9, project a similarly shaped outline in that two-dimensional plane. Except for this constraint (viz., that the views chosen for a given object and its mirror image must correspond to the same position around the circle indicated in Fig. 1), the views (shown in Fig. 5) were chosen from the seven indicated positions in such a way as to be relatively equally spaced around the 360° circle.

Although the problem of singularities and hidden parts does not arise with rotations in the picture plane, in order to achieve optimum correspondence between the picture-plane and depth conditions, the pairs of orientations for the picture-plane condition were constructed on the basis of the pattern of seven orientational positions as has already been set forth for the depth condition in Fig. 1 and Table 1. Now, however, the positions around the circle shown in Fig. 1 correspond to orientations of the perspective picture itself within its own picture plane—not to orientations of the three-dimensional object about a vertical axis, in depth (and, of course, the notations regarding singularities and hidden parts are now irrelevant).

By aligning the tic mark at the top of each picture with the appropriate mark at each 20° interval around the circles on the 5 × 8 in. stimulus cards, we ensured that the two pictures making up each picture-plane pair differed by the correct angle of rotation in the two-dimensional plane. As before, the pairs were all prepared so that, for the "same" pairs, a clockwise rotation of the left-hand picture would bring it into congruence with the right-hand picture via the smallest rotation (where, this time, the rotation is about the line of sight).

Conditions. Each subject was successively tested under each of three conditions: "depth," "picture-plane," and "mixed." The *depth condition* consisted in the presentation, in a random order, of just the 400 ("same" and "different") depth pairs. Similarly, the *picture-plane condition* consisted in the random presentation of just the 400 ("same" and "different") picture-plane pairs. The *mixed condition* was a randomly sequenced composite of all the depth and picture-plane pairs and, therefore, consisted of 800 presentations. On any one trial of any of these three conditions, the rotation was either about the vertical axis (depth pairs) or about the line of sight (picture-plane pairs), but never by a combination about both of these two axes at once. The distinguishing aspect of the mixed condition was that the axis of rotation remained unpredictable from trial to trial.

Of the six possible permutations of these three conditions, the two orders in which the mixed condition was in the middle position were omitted. The eight subjects were then assigned to the remaining four possible orders as follows: On the basis of their scores on the paper-and-pencil pretests, the highest- and lowest-scoring subjects were paired, the next-highest and next-lowest were paired, and so on, until all eight subjects were assigned to four pairs. Then each of these pairs was assigned, at random, to one of the four orders of presentation of the three conditions. At the beginning of each condition, the subject was told the nature of that condition (viz., that the rotation would be around a vertical axis, in depth; that the rotation would be in the plane of the picture; or that the rotation would switch at random between these two axes). The nature of the rotations included in that condition was further clarified for the subject by the preliminary practice or warm-up trials mentioned below.

Apparatus. The subject sat in a dimly illuminated room, looking into a simple mirror tachistoscope with a 5 × 8 in. half-silvered window at the front and a slot for a horizontally oriented 5 × 8 in. stimulus card at the back. On each trial the experimenter inserted the card with the stimulus pair selected for that trial and then closed a switch that exposed the stimulus pair to the subject's view by turning on a set of lights inside the otherwise darkened box. Simultaneously, the closing of that same switch also started a reaction-time clock calibrated in 1/100ths of a second. At the viewing distance (about 60 cm.), the perspective drawing of each object subtended a visual angle of some four to five degrees. In front of the

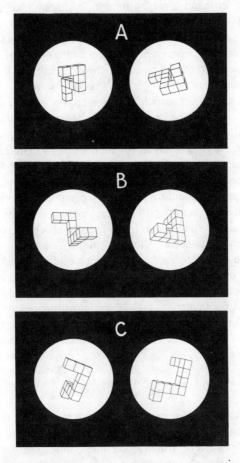

Fɪɢ. 2. Illustrative pairs of perspective views, including a pair differing by an 80° rotation in the picture plane (A), a pair differing by an 80° rotation in depth (B), and an isomeric pair differing by a reflection as well as a rotation (C).

slot for the stimulus cards was a permanently fixed black mask with two circular apertures 7.6 cm. in diameter positioned so that each of the two perspective views would appear in the center of one of the apertures, but so that the circle and tic marks used for positioning the perspective views on the card would not be visible. Figure 2 shows how a typical picture-plane "same" pair (A), a depth "same" pair (B), and a "different" pair (C) would appear when exposed to view in the tachistoscope.

As soon as he could, the subject registered his response to the exposed stimulus pair by pulling one of two spring-loaded levers comfortably positioned on the surface of the table in front of him. The right-hand lever was always used to signal "same" and the left-hand lever "different." Although large deflections were possible, the first slight deflection of either lever toward the subject actuated a microswitch that simultaneously stopped the reaction-time clock and turned off the lights inside the tachistoscope. Each lever also turned on one of two external signal lights that provided both the subject and the experimenter with feedback as to which response had been made—"same" or "different."

Procedure. Each subject participated for a total of eight to nine hours in about as many sessions, completing on the average 200 trials per session for a total of 1600 trials. Prior to the first session the subject was verbally instructed as to the nature of his task. He then received 40 practice trials to familiarize him with the stimuli and the general procedure. In addition, each subject was informed as to which of the three experimental conditions he would begin with, and of the two subsequent changes in conditions when they occurred. Before each session the subject also received ten warm-up trials representative of the type of rotation (i.e., depth, picture plane, or mixed) to follow. (The stimulus pairs presented during the practice and warm-up trials were drawn from the "excluded pairs" indicated in Table 1 and, so, did not reappear during the recorded experimental trials.)

The beginning of each trial was signaled by a warning tone followed, approximately one half second later, by the visual presentation of the pair of perspective drawings selected for that trial. The subject's instructions were to pull the appropriate lever as quickly as possible to indicate whether the two drawings represented objects of the same or different three-dimensional shape, while keeping errors to a minimum.

Results

Error rates. Although the principal dependent variable of interest in what follows is reaction time, errors were also recorded. Generally the error rates, though correlated positively with reaction times, were quite low. Over all, nearly 97% of the 12,800 recorded responses of the eight subjects were correct, with error rates ranging from 0.5% to 5.7% for individual subjects. In the ensuing graphical plots of mean reaction times, and in the reported statistical analyses, reaction times associated with incorrect responses have been excluded. However such incorrect reaction times exhibit a pattern resembling that presented for the correct responses.

Reaction time as a function of angular difference. The principal independent variable of interest is the angular difference between the portrayed orientations of the two three-dimensional objects—whether around the vertical axis, in depth, or around the line of sight, in the picture plane. Figure 3 presents the group mean reaction times, computed for "same" responses only, at each 20° interval of rotation from 0° to 180°. The data are displayed separately for the two kinds of pairs, depth and picture-plane, but have been combined over the pure and mixed conditions.

In the cases of both depth and picture-plane pairs, reaction time increases according to a remarkably linear function of angular difference in portrayed orientation, ranging from about one second at 0° (i.e., for pairs of identical perspective views) to between four and five seconds at 180°. Since the angle through which the "different" three-dimensional shapes must be rotated to achieve congruence is not strictly defined, functions like those plotted for the "same" pairs cannot be readily constructed for the "different" pairs (cf., however, the section on "recent experimental findings"). Still, the *over-all* mean reaction time for the "different" pairs was about 3.8 seconds, nearly a second longer than the over-all mean for the "same" pairs.

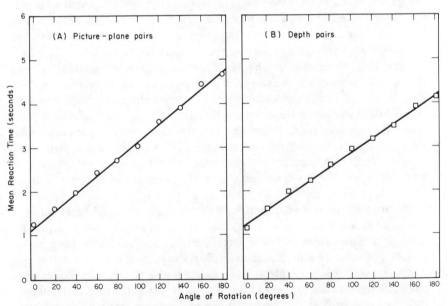

FIG. 3. Mean time to determine that two objects have the same three-dimensional shape as a function of the angular difference in their portrayed orientations, plotted separately for pairs differing by a rotation in depth (squares) and by a rotation in the picture plane (circles).

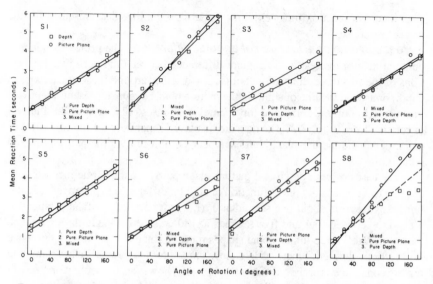

FIG. 4. Mean reaction time as a function of angular difference, plotted separately for depth and picture-plane pairs for each of the eight individual subjects.

Results for individual subjects. The data for each subject, plotted separately for "same" pairs differing either by a rotation in depth or by a rotation in the picture plane, are shown in Fig. 4. The order in which the three experimental conditions were presented to each subject is indicated in the lower right-hand corner of the corresponding graph. The mean reaction times for individual subjects increased from a value of one second at 0° to values ranging from four to six seconds at 180° of rotation, depending upon the particular individual. Note that, despite such variations in slope, the functions for each subject are also remarkably linear. Polynomial regression lines were computed separately for each subject and for the group data for each type of rotation. In all 18 cases, the data were found to have a highly significant linear component ($p < .001$) when tested against deviations from linearity. No significant quadratic or higher-order effects were found ($p > .05$, in all cases).

The one suggestion of a departure from linearity (and from equivalence of slope for the depth and picture-plane pairs) may be seen in the last two points for the depth pairs in the case of the last subject, S8 (right-most panel of the lower row in Fig. 4). Although the statistical analysis did not indicate that this seeming departure from linearity was reliable, it is at least suggestive that this one subject spontaneously reported the use of a different strategy just in the case of depth pairs differing by about 180° that permitted him to determine sameness or difference without actually carrying out the mental rotation. This strategy was based upon certain surface features of the two-dimensional perspective pictures and re-

sembled a strategy that led to bimodality in the distribution of "different" reaction times for depth pairs differing by 180° in a third experiment (see section on
"recent experimental findings"). On the basis of this conjecture, anyway, the
last two points (for 160° and 180°) were ignored in fitting the dashed line to the
data for the depth pairs for S8.

Results for depth, picture-plane, and mixed conditions. Another important finding is the relative lack of dependence of reaction time upon the kind of
rotation ("depth" versus "picture plane") required to bring the two objects into
alignment. As can be seen in Fig. 3, both functions are very similar to each other
with respect to intercept and slope; the mean response time for a given angular difference is just as large when this difference consists simply in the rigid rotation of
one of the pictures itself within its own two-dimensional plane as when it corresponds to the two-dimensionally much more complex rotation of one of the objects

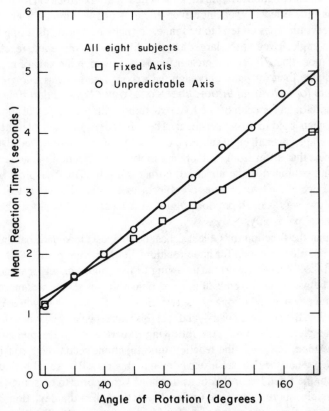

FIG. 5. Mean reaction time as a function of angular difference, plotted separately for the "pure"
conditions (in which the axis of rotation was fixed throughout any one block of trials) and for the
"mixed" condition (in which the axis of rotation varied unpredictably from trial to trial).

about its vertical axis, in depth. In fact if there is any difference, reaction times at the larger angular separations appear to be somewhat shorter for rotation in depth than for rotation in the picture plane. However, this difference is of doubtful significance; for, when subjects are individually considered (Fig. 4), the relative position of the two functions appears to be directly dependent upon the order of administration of the "pure" depth and picture-plane conditions, with but one exception. As might be expected on the assumption that there would be some general improvement with practice, the "pure" condition that was presented first yields the function having the slightly higher mean intercept and/or steeper slope.

Group mean reaction times for the "pure" blocks of trials (in which subjects knew the axis of the required rotation prior to each block) and the "mixed" blocks (in which the axis of rotation was unpredictable from trial to trial) are presented in Fig. 5. The two functions are again remarkably linear. They also have nearly the same intercepts. Not surprisingly, then, when the two perspective pictures are identical and no rotation is required, knowledge of the axis rotation for that block of trials has little effect. When, however, the axis of rotation is not known in advance, reaction times do tend to be longer for pairs of objects differing by an appreciable angle. Even at the larger angular differences, however, reaction times were no more than 20 percent greater for pairs on which the axis of rotation was unpredictable than for pairs on which the axis of rotation was known.

Results for individual three-dimensional objects. Reaction-time functions were also plotted for each of the five structurally different types of three-dimensional objects used in this experiment. These functions, as presented here in Fig. 6, are averaged over all eight subjects, over both axes of rotation, and also over the two objects that differ from each other simply by a reflection in each case. Thus the picture exhibited in the upper left corner of each of the five plots is an illustration of one of the two "isomeric" objects upon which the data in that plot were based. However, as in all previous figures, the reaction times plotted here are for the "same" pairs only.

Note that the function for Object C has the steepest slope and that the reaction times are particularly long for large rotations in the picture plane. This is consistent with the subjects' reports that, owing to the approximately symmetric relationship between the two ends of this one object, it was sometimes more difficult to determine which end of one of the two views corresponded to which end of the other view in the presented pair—and that this was especially so when the rotation was in the picture plane (cf., the following Experiment II). Despite such differences in slope, however, the reaction-time functions retain their consistent linearity even when the data are broken down in this way. The small residual departures from the fitted linear functions do, however, appear to be somewhat larger and, possibly, more systematic (in local structure) than the deviations from linearity in the plots for the individual subjects (cf., Fig. 4). The fact that these small step-like perturbations are more evident in the data for the depth pairs (plotted as small squares) suggests that they may be a reflection of purely surface

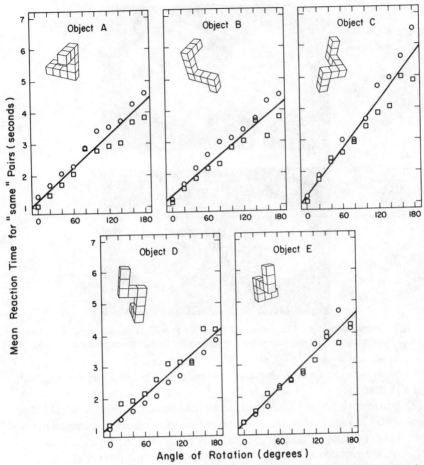

FIG. 6. Mean reaction time as a function of angular difference, plotted separately for depth pairs (squares) and picture-plane pairs (circles) for each of the five basically different types of objects. (The data in each panel are averaged over the object portrayed within that panel and the isomeric object that differs from it by a reflection.)

features that appear and disappear in the two-dimensional projection of the object as it rotates. The possible influence of a particular kind of "surface feature" will be examined more systematically in the immediately following section.

Effect of intervening singularities in the two-dimensional projections. As can be seen from Table 1, for each object there were two "included" pairs of views differing by a depth rotation of 40° and two "included" pairs differing by a depth rotation of 60°. For each of these two angular differences, moreover, such a rotation would carry the two-dimensional projection through what we have called a singularity in the case of one pair (the one followed by an asterisk in the table)

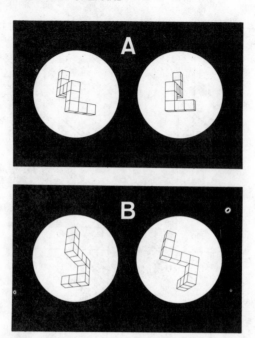

FIG. 7. Illustrative pairs in which the two objects differ by a 40° rotation in depth with (A) and without (B) crossing a topological discontinuity or "singularity" in the two-dimensional projection.

but would encounter no such singularity in the case of the other pair (the one without an asterisk).

The difference between these two cases is illustrated, for a rotational difference of 40°, in Fig. 7. Note that even though the same object is portrayed in both pairs and even though the angle of rotation is exactly the same for both pairs, the topological structure of the two-dimensional projections is preserved only in the lower pair (B). In the case of the upper pair (A), the rotation, if carried out, would pass through a singular orientation in which certain surfaces of the object coincide with the line of sight. At that point in the rotation certain of these surfaces, visible only in the left-hand picture, disappear from view while other of these surfaces, visible only in the right-hand picture, emerge into view. In the case of the lower pair (B), by contrast, exactly the same surfaces of the object remain in view in both pictures and throughout the intervening rotation.

In order to obtain evidence concerning the relative effect on reaction time of a 20° difference in extent of rotation of the three-dimensional object itself versus a topological discontinuity in the surface features of the two-dimensional projection of that object, we undertook a two-by-two analysis of the reaction times for the pairs differing by 40° or by 60° according to whether they did or did not involve an intervening singularity or "crossing." The relevant data, averaged over all subjects and all objects, are summarized in Fig. 8. Note that there was a consistent increase of about 240 msec. when the angle of rotation increased by only 20° whether or not the rotation crossed a singularity. Moreover, seven out of the eight subjects showed such an increase. The addition of one crossing of a singularity, however, produced an increase of no more than 90 msec. regardless of the extent of the rotation. And, this time, only five out of the eight subjects showed a change in this direction. Indeed, when the two factors, of rotation of the three-dimensional object and discontinuity of the two-dimensional projection, are pitted against each other (as indicated by the diagonal arrow) there was a mean increase in reaction time (of 150 msec.) as predicted by the 20° increase in angle of rotation rather than a mean decrease as might be expected from the elimination of the crossing.

These indications were supported by a three-way analysis of variance of the reaction times: angle × crossings × subjects. This analysis revealed the increase in mean reaction times as a function of angle of rotation to be significant ($F = 21.32, df = 1, 7, p < .005$). However, the effect of the number of crossings on reaction times was found to be nonsignificant ($F = 0.89, df = 1, 7, p > .10$) as was the interaction between angle of rotation and the number of crossings ($F = 0.03, df = 1, 7, p > .10$). Of course there may well be a real effect of passing through a singularity even though this test is not powerful enough to establish its existence. Indications are, however, that if such an effect exists it is in all probability quite small. On the basis of the slope of the over-all mean re-

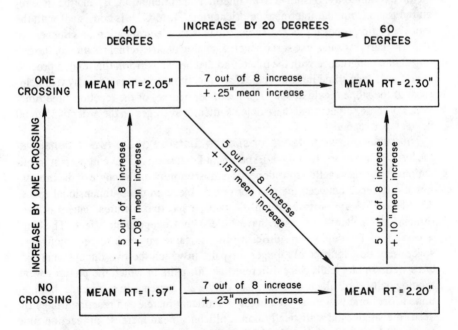

Fig. 8. Effects on reaction time of crossing one singularity in the two-dimensional projection versus a 20° increase in angle of rotation in three-dimensional space.

action time function for the "same" depth pairs (about 17.5 msec. per degree, according to Fig. 3), the mean increase in reaction time produced by the addition of one crossing (viz., about 90 msec.) is equivalent to the increase produced by a rotation in depth of only about five degrees.

Conclusions

The linearity of the reaction time functions. The first of two findings of Experiment I that we regard as especially significant is that the time required to determine that two perspective pictures portray objects of the same three-dimensional shape increases according to a strikingly linear function of the angular difference in the portrayed orientations of the two objects. Indeed this linearity is consistently found even in those subsets of the data that were obtained just (*a*) for those pairs of objects differing by a rotation in depth, or by a rotation in the picture plane (Fig. 3), (*b*) for the conditions in which the axis of rotation was constant or unpredictable from trial to trial (Fig. 5), (*c*) for each of the eight subjects individually (Fig. 4), and (*d*) for each of the five differently shaped isomeric pairs of three-dimensional objects (Fig. 6).

This linearity provides strong evidence for an additive process in which the time required to go from one orientation, A, to another orientation, C, is the sum of the time required to go from A to an intermediate orientation, B, and the time required to go from that intermediate orientation, B, to C. It is consistent with the more specific proposal that the subject makes the determination of sameness of shape by carrying out some sort of internal analog of an external rotation of the one object into congruence with the other, and that he can perform this analog process at no faster than some limiting rate. If so, this limiting rate is given by the reciprocal of the slope (again about 17.5 msec. per degree) of the reaction-time function. For these subjects and these objects, then, it averages on the order of 55 to 60 degrees per second.

The relative unimportance of surface features of the two-dimensional pictures. The second finding of Experiment I that seems to have important implications is that the reaction time depends almost entirely on the angle of the orientational difference between the two portrayed objects in three-dimensional space. The degree of similarity between the two perspective pictures, taken as two-dimensional patterns, seems to have little or no independent effect. Thus, reaction times for depth pairs differing by the same angle in three-dimensional space were not significantly longer for pairs in which the two-dimensional pictures were topologically very different than for pairs in which the pictures were topologically equivalent. (By contrast, only a 20° increase in difference in three-dimensional orientation led to a highly significant increase in reaction time.) Indeed, the small (and statistically nonsignificant) mean increase in reaction time that was observed as the result of the addition of one crossing of a singularity in the two-dimensional picture was equivalent to that produced by a rotation of no more than about five degrees in three-dimensional space (Figs. 7 and 8).

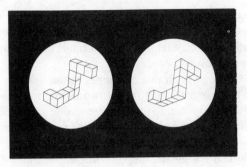

FIG. 9. Isomeric objects differing only by a reflection through the picture plane. (Notice the similarity in outlines of their two-dimensional projections.)

A further indication of the unimportance of the surface features of the two-dimensional perspective views is that the two isomeric versions of each object nearly always led to the response ''different''—even when they were oriented in such a way as to project very similarly shaped two-dimensional patterns (as shown in Fig. 9).

The most striking evidence that the surface features of the two-dimensional pictures are unimportant is to be found in the fact that the slope of the reaction-time function was just as great for pairs differing by a simple rigid rotation of one of the pictures within its own picture plane as for pairs differing by the much more complex transformation of one of the two-dimensional pictures that is induced by a rotation of the three-dimensional object in depth (Figs. 3 and 4, and Experiment II).

These results seem to be consistent with the notion that (with the possible exception of certain very special cases, such as that suggested in connection with the lower-right-most subject in Fig. 4) subjects were performing their mental operations upon internal representations that were more analogous to the three-dimensional objects portrayed in the two-dimensional pictures than to the two-dimensional pictures actually presented. The subjects themselves indicated that they interpreted the two-dimensional drawings as objects in three-dimensional space and, having done so, could as easily imagine the objects rotated about whichever axis was required.

EXPERIMENT II

The subjects in Experiment I reported that they sometimes experienced some difficulty in determining which end of one object corresponded to which end of the other object. Not surprisingly, this difficulty seemed most noticeable in the case of certain objects (particularly Object C, Fig. 6) for which the two ends resembled each other most closely—in terms of the number of blocks in each terminal arm and the relationship of each outer bend to the intervening middle bend. In addition, this difficulty seemed especially troublesome in the case of pairs differing by a rotation in the picture plane. Presumably this was because rotations in depth were always about a vertical axis and, so, (in the pure depth condition, anyway) subjects could automatically infer that the uppermost end of one object must correspond to the uppermost end of the other.

These considerations suggest that the slopes of the linear reaction-time functions plotted for Experiment I may reflect two different components of the reaction times; namely, (a) a search time needed to discover which end of one object corresponds to a given end of the other and (b) a rotation time needed to bring the corresponding ends into congruence, once they have been discovered. Indeed it seems probable that the greater slope of the reaction-time function obtained under the mixed condition (Fig. 5) was in large part a consequence of the increase in search time that resulted when the axis of rotation was not known in advance of each trial.

Now, if it is true that the search component is a larger portion of the reaction time for responses to the picture-plane pairs than for responses to the depth pairs, the possibility arises that the nearly equivalent slopes of the depth and picture-plane functions (Fig. 3) may have been fortuitous. Possibly, if the search component could be eliminated, rotations in the picture plane would turn out to be considerably faster than rotations in depth after all. Experiment II was undertaken, primarily, for the specific purpose of evaluating this possibility and, secondarily, for the more general purpose of estimating the extent to which the slopes of all the reaction-time functions obtained in Experiment I reflect such a process of search—as opposed to a process of mental rotation. The principal change from Experiment I was to minimize the need to search for corresponding ends by the simple device of attaching same-colored dots to the corresponding ends of the two objects in each stimulus pair.

Method

Subjects. The eight subjects—four males and four females—were all student at Stanford University. None had participated in the earlier Experiment I. Two of each sex were right-handed, and two were left-handed. All had 20:20 vision or vision corrected to 20:20 and were required to achieve the same criterion on two timed pre-experimental paper-and-pencil tests of spatial abilities as described in Experiment I.

Stimuli. The same perspective line drawings of three-dimensional objects used in Experiment I were again used here, with the exception of the two isomeric versions of Objects A and C (cf., Fig. 6) which were eliminated because they had seemed to lead to the most confusion and the most need for prerotational search in that experiment. The seven perspective views of each of the three remaining objects (Objects B, D, and E) and their corresponding mirror image projections permitted the construction of 480 distinct pairs in a manner similar to that described in Experiment I. Half of the 480 pairs, the "same" pairs, depicted objects of identical three-dimensional shape and differed, if at all, only by some multiple of a 20° rotation, from 0° to 180°, either about a vertical axis (for half of those pairs) or in the plane of the drawings themselves (for the other half). The remaining 240 pairs represented pairs of objects that differed by a reflection as well as a rotation (again, either about a vertical axis or in the two-dimensional plane of the drawings) and, so, constituted the "different" pairs.

On the perspective drawing of each object a circular red dot was attached beside the cube at one end of the object and a circular blue dot was attached beside the cube at the other end. These color codes were attached so that, in each pair, the two corresponding ends of the two objects were always assigned the same color. The appearance of a picture-plane "same," a depth "same," and a "different" pair as presented in this experiment is illustrated in Fig. 10, where filled

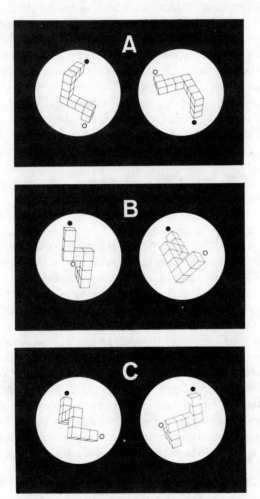

FIG. 10. Illustrative pairs differing by a 140° rotation in the picture plane (A), by a 140° rotation in depth (B), and by a reflection as well as a rotation (C). (For purposes of black-and-white reproduction the red and blue dots are represented here by filled and open circles.)

and open circles have been substituted for the red and blue dots displayed in the experiment itself. It seemed to us that such color coding would greatly reduce any time that subjects needed to determine correspondence between parts of the two objects before attempting to bring them mentally into congruence.

Procedure. Each subject participated in one practice session and three test sessions of 160 trials each. The 160 pairs presented during practice trials were a subset of the 480 constructed pairs, balanced with respect to the principal factors "same" versus "different," depth versus picture plane, and angular difference in orientation. However, these 160 pairs were blocked according to whether the rotation was in depth or in the picture plane (just as was done in the two "pure" conditions in Experiment I). Each block consisted of 80 trials, with order of presentation of the two blocks counterbalanced across all eight subjects. Prior to each block, the subject was informed as to the type of rotation by which the pairs in the trials to follow would differ. One purpose of these practice trials was to ensure that the subject understood the distinction between the two axes of rotation.

During the three test sessions, pairs of objects differing by either of the two types of rotation were randomly presented and, so, the axis of rotation remained unpredictable, as in the "mixed" condition in Experiment I. In other respects, the procedure and apparatus were as described in Experiment I.

Results

Errors. As in Experiment I, the error rates were quite low, ranging from 1.3% to 6.8% for individual subjects with an over-all mean of 3.8%. Again, the data with which we shall be principally concerned are mean reaction times after the elimination of all incorrect responses.

Over-all reaction-time results. The group results for the main part of Experiment II (in which depth and picture-plane pairs were randomly intermixed) are shown in Fig. 11. Once again, reaction times averaged over all eight subjects are plotted as a function of the angular difference in portrayed orientation, from 0° (i.e., for pairs of identical perspective views) to 180°. Although they were obtained from the same "mixed" condition, the means are plotted separately for the pairs differing by a rotation in depth (again, always about a vertical axis) and for pairs differing by a rotation simply in the picture plane. In both cases the plotted data are for the "same" pairs only since, as was pointed out in connection with Experiment I, the independent variable (the minimum angle through which one object in the pair would have to be rotated in order to achieve congruence) simply is not defined for objects of inherently different shape. As before, though, the over-all mean reaction time for the "different" pairs (about 4.6 seconds) was longer than the over-all mean reaction time for the "same" pairs (about 4.1 seconds).

The means shown here are somewhat more variable than those obtained in Experiment I owing, probably, to the smaller amount of data upon which they are based, to the correspondingly smaller total amount of practice that each sub-

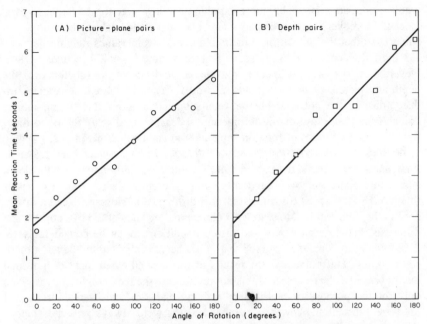

FIG. 11. Mean reaction time as a function of angular difference, plotted separately for depth and picture-plane pairs (from the principal, "mixed" condition) in Experiment II.

ject acquired during the experiment and, possibly, to differences in the populations from which the subjects in Experiment I and II were sampled. Perhaps because of the last two of these circumstances, the over-all mean reaction times in this experiment tended also to be between a half and a full second longer than those in the corresponding "mixed" condition in Experiment I.

Nevertheless, the results provide further confirmation of the principal findings of the earlier experiment. The linear increase in reaction time with angular difference is again clearly evident for both depth and picture-plane pairs, ranging from about 1.6 seconds at 0° to between 5.5 and 6.5 seconds at 180°. Polynomial regression lines computed for each type of pair separately were found in both cases to have a significant linear component ($p < .01$) when tested against deviations from linearity, whereas no quadratic or higher-order effects approached statistical significance ($p > .10$ in all cases). Moreover, the functions obtained for the two contrasting types of rotation (depth and picture-plane) are again very similar to each other with respect to intercept and slope. Indeed, the introduction of the color coding of corresponding ends of the objects seems, if anything, to have brought the two functions into even closer agreement with each other.

Results for individual subjects. Mean reaction time plots, corresponding to that shown in Fig. 11 for the whole group, are shown separately for each of the eight subjects in Fig. 12. The data for the individual subjects, like the data for the whole group, are appreciably more variable than they were for the larger Experiment I. Moreover, the slopes and intercepts vary considerably from subject to subject, so that the best-fitting functions increase from values ranging between 1.3 and 2.8 seconds at 0° to values ranging from about 4.5 to 8.7 seconds at 180°. Nevertheless the over-all linearity and the coincidence of the functions for the depth and picture-plane pairs holds up well for each individual separately. Indeed, despite the considerable between-subject variation, this within-subject coincidence is so close that it did not appear feasible to display the fitted functions for the two types of rotation separately in each panel of Fig. 12.

Results for pure versus mixed conditions. In Experiment I the reaction-time function was found to be steeper in slope for the condition in which the depth and picture-plane pairs were randomly intermixed rather than blocked by axis of rotation (Fig. 5). If, as we suggested, this difference in slope reflected a difference in the time required to search for corresponding ends of the two objects, the difference between such pure and mixed conditions might be considerably reduced when, as here, the need for search has been minimized by the addition of color coding. Unfortunately, the results of this second experiment do not lend themselves to a clear-cut test of this notion because the pure condition was given only for the purpose of preliminary training and, so, consisted of trials that (*a*) were substantially fewer in number and (*b*) were always presented *before* the mixed condition (rather than according to a counterbalanced order). Never-

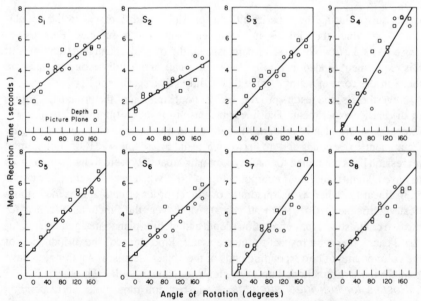

Fig. 12. Mean reaction time as a function of angular difference, plotted separately for depth and picture-plane pairs (from the "mixed" condition) for each of the eight individual subjects in Experiment II.

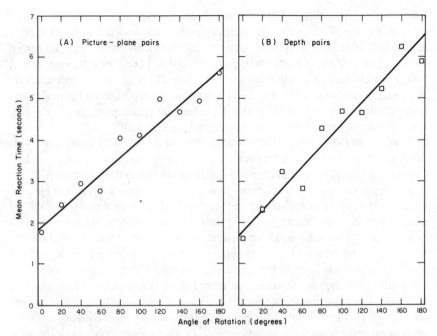

FIG. 13. Mean reaction time as a function of angular difference, plotted separately for depth and picture-plane pairs from the corresponding pure conditions administered at the beginning of Experiment II.

theless the results for these preliminary, pure trials were reasonably orderly and, so, are displayed here, in Fig. 13.

As before, these points are based on correct responses only, which ranged from 24, the maximum possible, down to only 17 correct responses per point. The appreciable variability of the points is presumably a consequence of these small sample sizes. Even so, the functions are again quite linear for both the picture-plane and the depth conditions. Moreover, although the intercepts are about 200 msec. higher than in the mixed condition which followed, the slopes are indistinguishable from those found for that mixed condition (cf., Fig. 11). Again, the confounding of conditions with order of presentation precludes the drawing of any definite conclusions. Still, the virtual identity of the slopes for the pure and mixed conditions is at least consistent with the notion that the difference in slope found in Experiment I was, as we conjectured, a reflection of the additional time required for prerotational search when the axis of rotation was not known in advance.

Conclusions

Corroboration of the conclusions of Experiment I. With an entirely new set of subjects, Experiment II has succeeded in replicating the two principal findings of Experiment I; viz., that reaction time (*a*) increases linearly with angular difference in orientation and (*b*) is relatively independent of whether this angular difference corresponds to a rotation in the picture plane or in depth. These further results thus contribute additional support for the conclusions already advanced; namely, that subjects arrive at their judgments of sameness or difference in this task (*a*) by carrying out an internal process that is a kind of analog representation of an external rotation and (*b*) by performing this process upon an internal representation that is more akin to the three-dimensional object portrayed in the perspective picture than to that two-dimensional picture itself.

Search versus mental rotation components of reaction time. The introduction of color coding in order to minimize the need to search for corresponding ends of the two objects in each pair has eliminated the former slight superiority of the depth pairs over the picture-plane pairs. This provides some objective evidence in support of the subjective impression that a larger portion of the reaction times in Experiment I was taken up with such a search process in the case of the picture-plane pairs than in the case of the depth pairs. However, this change in procedure has reduced the reaction times to the picture-plane pairs only to the level of the reaction times to the depth pairs—not to an appreciably lower level. Evidently, then, the approximate equivalence of depth and picture-plane rotations in Experiment I was not in fact fortuitous. Even more compellingly than before, then, it appears that the internal representations upon which the subjects were performing their mental operations were more analogous to objects in isotropic three-dimensional space than to their perspective projections in the special two-dimensional picture plane.

Any direct quantitative comparison between the two experiments is subject to some uncertainty owing, principally, to differences between the populations from which the two sets of subjects were sampled. Still, the fact that the reaction times in Experiment II, despite the addition of the color coding, were not appreciably shorter (and, in fact, averaged between a half to a full second longer) than in Experiment I tends to support the notion that, if the decision process can be divided into a process of searching for corresponding parts followed by a process of mentally bringing those corresponding parts into mutual congruence, then the search component was relatively small even in Experiment I. Such, any way, are the grounds for taking, as we have, the reciprocal of the empirically obtained slope of the reaction-time function as an estimate of the limiting rate of "mental rotation."

RECENT EXPERIMENTAL FINDINGS

To conclude our presentation of experimental results, we turn now to three new findings that have emerged from two further experiments on mental rotation of three-dimensional objects that one of us has recently completed (Metzler, 1973). These three new findings are concerned with how reaction time depends upon angular difference in orientation in the following three types of cases: (*a*) those in which the two objects are isomeric rather than identical, and so can be rotated only into partial congruence rather than into complete congruence; (*b*) those in which the direction in which subjects have been set to carry out a mental rotation corresponds to the long way around the 360° circle; and (*c*) those in which the presentation of the second perspective view is delayed until the required mental rotation of the first could already be completed. Although the presentation of these new findings will necessarily be quite brief here, we shall argue that these findings bear in important ways upon alternative theories of how subjects determine sameness or difference of three-dimensional shapes.

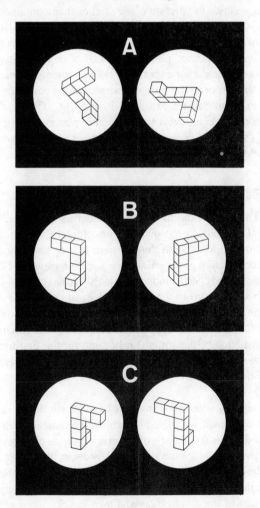

FIG. 14. Illustrative pairs in which two simplified objects differ by a 135° rotation in the picture plane (A), by a 135° rotation in depth (B), and by a reflection (C). (In the case of the depth pair (B), note that the axis of rotation is the natural axis of the object.)

The stimuli again were perspective views of differently oriented three-dimensional arm-like structures formed of cubes attached face-to-face. This time, however, a somewhat simplified set of objects was used: There were only seven (rather than ten) cubes in each object, only two (rather than three) right angled bends, and only two (rather than ten) structurally distinct objects. In the case of the depth pairs, moreover, the rotation was always about the natural axis of the object; that is, about the axis of the central and longest straight row of cubical blocks. In order to avoid undesirable singularity, this axis was always slightly inclined with respect to the picture plane, rather than contained within it (as in the case of the strictly vertical axes of depth rotation in the earlier experiments). And, finally, different depth conditions were devised in which the orientation of the projection onto the picture plane of the axis of depth rotation, in addition to being vertical (as in the earlier experiments), was sometimes either horizontal or inclined 45° to the left or to the right. Examples of the pairs of perspective views used in these experiments are exhibited in Fig. 14. The depth pair (B) illustrates a rotation about an axis that (in the picture plane) is vertical, and the "different" pair (C) shows the two structurally distinct objects to which these further experiments were confined.

Reaction Times for "Different" Pairs

Rationale. The first of the more recent experiments carried out by Metzler (1973) was similar in basic procedure to our original Experiment I. For present purposes, the most important differences were (*a*) the just-described changes in the manner of construction of the pairs of perspective views and (*b*) certain deliberate manipulations designed to induce subjects to rotate the long way around on some trials. We shall return to the consequences of the second difference in the following section. In this section we shall confine our attention to one consequence of the first difference; specifically, the consequence that (owing to the altered manner of construction of the stimuli) it became for the first time convenient to look at the reaction-time function for "different" pairs. (The reaction-time functions plotted in the previous Figs. 3–6 and 11–13 were all confined entirely to "same" pairs.)

As we have already noted, the angle through which differently shaped three-dimensional objects must be rotated to achieve congruence can not be defined. However, according to the theory of mental rotation, a subject can determine whether or not two objects are the same only by attempting to rotate one into congruence with the other. What we assume, then, is that the subject carries out a mental rotation in order to bring one part of one object into congruence with the corresponding part of the other object and *then* checks whether the other part(s) of the objects have been brought into congruence as well by this mental operation. In fact, in a questionnaire administered at the end of the experiment, all eight subjects reported that they generally attempted to bring the longer (and, except in the case of the horizontally oriented axis, uppermost) two-block arm of one object into alignment with the corresponding longer (and uppermost) two-block arm of the other object. If, after achieving this partial alignment, they determined that the shorter, one-block arms at the other (and usually lower) end of the two objects were brought thereby into coincidence as well, they could then respond "same." If, on the other hand, they discovered that, as a result of the mental transformation, the one-block arms of the two objects now pointed in opposite directions in three-dimensional space, they could infer that the opposite response, "different," was required. If this account is correct, when reaction time is plotted against the angle of rotation required to bring the two longer arms into congruence, a linearly increasing function should be obtained for the "different" pairs just as for the "same" pairs.

Results. The results of this experiment are exhibited in Fig. 15 for both the "same" pairs (A) and for the "different" pairs (B). The plot for the "same" pairs is exactly analogous to those shown earlier (in Figs. 3 and 11). The data are averaged over all eight subjects and plotted separately for depth pairs and picture-plane pairs (though, this time, the depth rotations were about natural axes of the objects, and the plotted times have been averaged over the cases in which these axes were vertical, horizontal, or inclined). Note that, despite the changes in the objects and their axes of rotation, reaction time again increases linearly with angular difference in the orientations of the two identical objects in these "same" pairs. The fact that the slope of the fitted reaction-time function is steeper in the

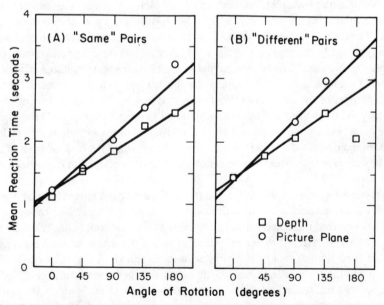

Fig. 15. Mean reaction time as a function of angle of rotation needed to achieve congruence, in the case of "same" pairs (A), or to achieve partial congruence, in the case of "different" pairs (B). (In both cases the data are plotted separately for depth and picture-plane pairs.)

case of the picture-plane pairs supports the notion that mental rotation is easier when the rotation is about a natural axis of the objects (as it was only in the case of the depth pairs). The further fact that the slopes in both cases are somewhat less than in Experiments I and II suggests that mental rotation may be faster with structurally simpler objects (i.e., in this case, objects with fewer blocks and bends).

The principal new result however is that, when the reaction times for the "different" pairs are plotted against the rotation needed to achieve *partial* congruence (in the manner described above), reaction-time functions are obtained that are generally very similar to those obtained for the "same" pairs. (Compare the B and A halves of Fig. 15.) The only discrepant point (which was not included in fitting the straight line) is the one for 180° depth pairs. The unexpectedly short mean reaction time for this one particular case was evident in the individual data for seven of the eight subjects. The reaction times for these subjects at this angular difference in orientation are bimodally distributed, with the upper mode at the reaction time predicted for 180° by the best-fitting linear function through the modes of the distributions from 0° to 135°, while the lower mode is slightly longer than the modal response time to 0° pairs which differ only by a reflection.

We conjecture that on those trials in which reaction time closely approximated the predicted value for 180° rotations of different objects, subjects were using the strategy generally employed—namely, rotating so as to bring the longer arms of the two objects into congruence, and only then assessing the relative position of the shorter arms. However, on those trials in which the modal response time approached the reaction time to pairs of objects differing by a reflection only, it seemed likely that subjects realized that the shorter arms of the two objects were already similarly oriented and so, upon discovering that the upper arms pointed in different directions, arrived at their judgment of "different" without having to carry out a rotation. Additional support for this reasoning may be found in the fact that a number of the subjects explicitly reported in a post-experimental interview that they did often use a different, nonrotational strategy in the special case of just these pairs (viz., those differing by a 180° rotation in depth as well as by a reflection). Some described it as a strategy of noting that while the bottom arms of the two objects pointed in the same direction, the top arms pointed in opposite directions.

Although the way in which the "different" pairs were generated in Experiments I and II makes it difficult to determine the angle through which the subjects may have rotated the objects into partial congruence, informal checks on the reaction times to certain "different" pairs in which this angle seemed especially well defined suggest that results similar to those shown in Fig. 15B could also be found in the earlier data. Over all, though, reaction times to "different" pairs were nearly a full second longer than reaction times to "same" pairs in the earlier Experiment I rather than only 200 to 300 msec. longer as indicated for the more recent results plotted in Fig. 15. In any case, the new results for "different" pairs, presented in section B of the figure, provide additional evidence largely consistent with the theory of mental rotation.

Reaction Times for Pairs Differing by More than 180°

Rationale. Like the corresponding earlier figures, Fig. 15 included reaction times for pairs differing by rotations only up to 180°. However, an important new feature of that same experiment was the presentation of certain other pairs under conditions designed so that, if the subjects were carrying out a mental rotation, they might go the long way around the circle. Specifically, trials were blocked by direction of rotation in such a way that, for all except a few pairs presented in the last half of a block, a particular (e.g., clockwise) rotation would carry the object on the left into the orientation of the object on the right by the shortest rotation (i.e., the rotation of no more than 180°). Then, on a few randomly inserted trials toward the end, the direction of shortest rotation was unexpectedly reversed so that, if the subjects were continuing to rotate in the same direction as before, they would end up going the long way around. In order to minimize the likelihood of their discovering that they were going the long way around on these special trials, these pairs were confined to just the next step beyond 180° which, in view of the 45° increments used in this experiment, was 225° (as opposed to 135°, if they happened to reverse direction of rotation on that trial).

These special trials could provide crucial information concerning the nature of the internal process by means of which the subjects determined sameness or difference of the two objects on each trial. For, according to the theory of mental rotation, the internal process is in a sense a simulation of an external process of rotation and, as such, has a definite trajectory and a definite direction along that trajectory. Thus, to the extent that subjects always go the long way around on these special trials, their reaction times should be even greater than at 180° and, indeed, should coincide with the linear extrapolation to 225° of the reaction-time function already obtained for angular departures from 0° to 180°. Or, to the extent that subjects sometimes go the long way around and sometimes reverse direction to take advantage of the 135° short-cut, their reaction times should be bimodally distributed with an upper mode corresponding to the linear extrapolation to 225° and a lower mode corresponding to the reaction time previously found for 135°. In contrast to this, a nonrotational theory (e.g., of feature-by-feature comparison) would seem to predict no such directional effect. The controlling variable would then be simply the absolute difference between the two pictures and, hence, the reaction time should be the same for what we have called 135° and 225° and, in both cases, should be shorter than for 180°.

Results. If the data are combined for depth and picture-plane pairs, the group mean reaction time to these special "same" pairs (which differed, the long way around, by rotations of 225°) was 2.79 sec.—very close to the 2.84 group mean reaction time to "same" pairs differing by 180°. Hence, it was not as long as predicted by extrapolation of the linear functions shown in Fig. 15. Indeed, in the case of the depth pairs, the mean reaction time for these special 225° pairs fell below the extrapolated value for five out of the eight subjects. As we have noted, however, some of the subjects may sometimes have reversed their direction for these pairs in order to go the short way around. If so, the distribution of reaction times would become bimodal with the consequence that the mean would no longer be an appropriate index of central tendency and, certainly, would not be representative of either of the two modes. Accordingly, we turn now to an examination of the distributions themselves.

In order to obtain the most stable representation of the 225° distribution, the reaction-time data were pooled from all eight subjects. Since the intercepts and, particularly, the slopes of the best-fitting reaction-time functions varied considerably from subject to subject, the data from each subject (and, indeed, for each axis of rotation used by each subject) were first linearly transformed in such a way that the linear function that then best fit the data for that subject (and for that axis of rotation) exactly coincided with the linear function that best fit the over-all group data. This normalization was performed solely on the basis of the reaction-

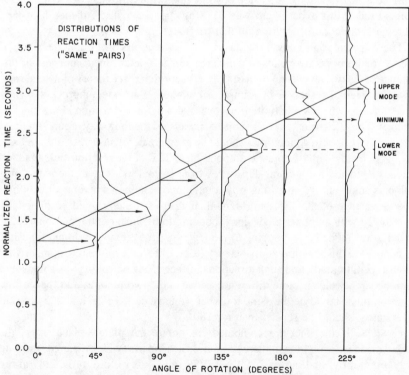

Fig. 16. Distributions of reaction time for "same" pairs at various angles of rotation. (See text for explanation of normalization of reaction times and of bimodality at 225°.)

time data for angular differences from 0° to 180° and, hence, was not biased in any way by the to-be-examined data for the special 225° pairs.

The reaction-time distributions obtained by thus combining the individually normalized distributions for each subject (and axis of rotation) are presented in Fig. 16. Notice that the combined distributions for angles from 0° through 180° are all sharply peaked, unimodal distributions and, further, that the modal reaction times increase according to a very linear function (in close agreement with the linear increase of the means already noted in Fig. 15A). The straight line in Fig. 16 represents the linear function that best fits the modal points (from 0° to 180°). It has an intercept of 1.25 seconds and a slope of about 8.3 msec. per degree. (This modal function is slightly lower than the corresponding mean function owing to the tendency of the distributions to be somewhat skewed toward the longer reaction times.)

More important, notice that the distribution for the special pairs at 225°, which did not enter in any way to the normalization of each subject's time scale, exhibits an appreciable bimodality. And, in excellent agreement with the hypothesis that on each trial a subject either rotated the long or the short way around, the two modes correspond closely to the forward and backward extrapolations of the linear function to 225° and to 135°, respectively. Indeed, whereas the mean of the distribution was close to that found for 180° (as noted above), this mean was not at all representative of the individual reaction times and, in fact, falls close to the minimum separating the two modes. (Although the individual subjects differed considerably in their tendency to go the long or the short way around, all but one of the eight subjects had more reaction times either within the time interval centered at the linearly predicted value for 225° or for 135° than within the same-sized intervening interval centered at the value for 180°.)

Reaction Times Following Delayed Presentations of the Second Stimulus

Rationale. In all of the experiments described so far, the two perspective drawings were viewed simultaneously by the subject during the entire decision process on each trial. According to the theory of mental rotation, however, it might be possible to delay the presentation of the second stimulus without affecting the over-all reaction time (from the onset of the first stimulus to the execution of the response)—provided that the subject knows both the axis and direction of the required rotation in advance. This is because the subject can then begin his mental rotation of the first stimulus as soon as it appears and, as long as the second stimulus is presented before he arrives at the orientation in which it is to be presented, he will be able to proceed to that orientation and to make the required match-mismatch comparison just as rapidly as if the second stimulus had been present all along.

In fact, if the delay of the second stimulus is made equal to the rotation time previously estimated for that angular difference when the two stimuli were presented simultaneously, the rotation would be essentially completed upon the onset of the second stimulus. Since the subject would then be in a position to make a direct template-like match of his already rotated internal representation against the externally presented second stimulus, his reaction time, when measured from the onset of that second stimulus, should now become uniformly short and relatively independent of that angular difference. This prediction is in apparent contrast to predictions from alternative, nonrotational theories which would seem to require the physical presence of the second stimulus in order for the decision process (e.g., of feature-by-feature comparison of the two pictures) to get under way.

Accordingly, in a further experiment using six of the eight subjects from the experiment just described, Metzler (1973) revised the procedure so that, following an instruction as to the axis of rotation, each trial had the following sequential structure: First one of the two perspective views was presented until the subject actuated a foot switch to signal that he would be able to maintain an adequate mental image of its shape. Thereupon that first perspective view vanished, to be immediately replaced by a uniformly colored field that, according to a predetermined random sequence, was either red or blue. The subject had previously been trained to imagine a clockwise or a counterclockwise rotation of the object (about the already specified axis) depending upon this color. Then, after a delay that was predetermined but unknown to the subject, the second perspective view appeared in place of the colored field. As before, the subject was then to actuate a right- or a left-hand switch as rapidly as possible to indicate whether the second object was the same as or different from the first.

For each subject and for each axis and angle of rotation, the delay was chosen to be identical to the mean rotation time estimated for that subject, axis, and angle from the preceding experiment (in which the views were presented simultaneously). This rotation time was estimated simply by subtracting (for that subject and axis of rotation) the previously measured reaction time for 0° from the previously measured reaction time for the angular difference on the given trial. However, one angular difference that was included (270°) exceeded any of the angular differences in the previous experiment and, so, had to be determined by linear extrapolation. The subject's reaction time was measured from the onset of the second stimulus.

The prediction of the theory of mental rotation in this situation would seem to depend upon the variability of a subject's rate of mental rotation. To the extent that a subject's rate of rotation (for a given axis) is constant and independent of the presence or absence of the corresponding external stimulus, his reaction time to the onset of the appropriately delayed second stimulus should, as we noted, be constant (i.e., independent of the angle of rotation) and short (i.e., close to the intercept of the reaction-time function for simultaneous presentation).

To the extent that a subject's rate of rotation varies from one trial or situation to the next, however, the mean time used to determine the delay on a particular trial will tend to lead to an overshoot or an undershoot, depending upon whether the subject was rotating faster or slower than average on that trial. In such cases, a further, corrective rotation would presumably have to be carried out following the presentation of the second stimulus. Since the average undershoot or overshoot will tend to be larger for larger angular differences in orientation, the reaction-time function would be expected to increase monotonically, rather than remain strictly horizontal, for subjects who had more variable rotation times as estimated from the previous experiment. For this reason, it is desirable to examine the reaction-time data separately for the two subgroups of subjects whose estimated rotation times were, respectively, least and most variable in the preceding experiment.

Results. The results, which are displayed in Fig. 17 for the "same" pairs, are in gratifying agreement with expectations based on the theory of mental rotation. The six subjects are divided, here, into the four whose reaction times in the previous experiment were relatively stable (Ss 1, 3, 4, 5, included on the left), and the two remaining subjects whose reaction times had been appreciably more variable and, in addition, whose error rates had been markedly greater in that experiment (Ss 2 and 6, included on the right). Note that, for the four subjects whose rotation rates were estimated to be relatively constant, reaction times to the second stimulus were uniformly short (generally varying only between one second and about one-and-a-half seconds), whereas, for the two more variable subjects, reaction times increased monotonically with the angle of rotation (from a little over one second to somewhat over two full seconds at 270°). Even for these two more variable subjects, however, the slope has been considerably reduced by the introduction of a delay in the presentation of the second stimulus. The product-moment correlation between the variances for individual subjects in the preceding

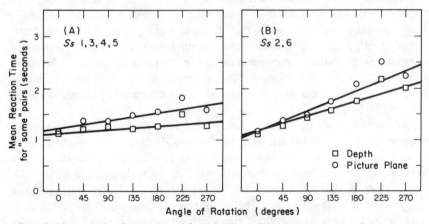

Fig. 17. Mean reaction time, measured from the onset of the delayed member of each "same" pair, plotted as a function of angle of rotation, separately, for the four subjects with relatively small variability in rotation time (A) and for the two subjects with much greater variability (B) as estimated in a previous experiment.

experiment and the slopes of the reaction-time functions for these same subjects in this experiment was .82 ($p < .05$).

The functions fitted, separately, to the data for the depth and picture-plane pairs indicate that the dependence of reaction time on angle of rotation is again quite linear and, as noted, nearly horizontal for the four most consistent subjects. The only noticeable departure of the points from the fitted linear functions is the consistently upward displacement of all four points at 225°. Even this discrepancy is interpretable however (and, for this reason, these points were not taken into account in finding the best-fitting straight line), for, as we subsequently discovered, subjects sometimes went the short (135°) way around for the 225° pairs in the preceding experiment. The consequence was that the distribution of reaction times was bimodal (Fig. 16) and the mean reaction time was spuriously reduced. Thus the delay of the second stimulus was in effect based on an average of rotation times for 225° and 135° and, generally, too short for the 225° rotation required here. Presumably, then, on most trials subjects had to continue their rotation after the somewhat premature presentation of the second stimulus and, so, yielded the longer reaction times found at 225°. The results for the "different" pairs, which are not shown here, are entirely consistent with this explanation and show, in addition, an upward discrepancy at 180° due to the similar phenomenon of bimodality for the depth pairs at that angle already mentioned in connection with Fig. 15. (See Metzler, 1973)

Effects of Certain Other Factors

Same versus different objects. A few of the dozen "factors investigated" which we listed in the introduction have not yet been evaluated in the light of the experimental results because, although they are of some interest in their own right, they do not bear in any crucial way upon the issues with which we are most centrally concerned. The factor that distinguished "same" pairs from "different" pairs, for example, does not tell us much about the structure of internal representations of three-dimensional objects or their transformations. Nevertheless, it does seem to be relevant for a more general concern with the over-all organization of the internal cognitive processes of which mental rotation may be one component.

The consistent result, in Experiments I and II as well as in the more recent experiments just discussed, has been that the over-all mean time required to determine that two views are of objects of different three-dimensional shapes is longer than the mean time required to determine that they are the same. The recent findings, shown in Fig. 15, suggest the further conclusion that this difference is independent of angle of rotation. That is, the reaction-time functions for the "different" pairs are higher than the corresponding functions for the "same" pairs primarily by virtue of their intercepts—their slopes are virtually identical. This same finding has uniformly emerged from studies that our colleagues and we have completed on the rotation of two-dimensional objects as well (see Cooper, 1973;

Cooper & Shepard, 1973b; Shepard, in press). The interpretation we favor is that subjects first test for a direct match between their (rotated) internal representation and the external stimulus. Whenever they detect a mismatch, then, they require an additional fixed amount of time to switch to the other response (cf., Clark & Chase, 1972; Cooper & Shepard, 1973b; Trabasso, Rollins, & Shaughnessy, 1971).

Inclination of (natural) axis of rotation. We have already indicated the theoretical significance of the finding that rotations about an axis orthogonal to the line of sight, despite the greater complexity of the resulting transformation of the two-dimensional picture, require no longer than rotations about the line of sight itself. With respect just to the case in which the axis is nearly orthogonal to the line of sight, the recent experiments by Metzler (1973) provide new information concerning whether the projection of that axis onto the picture plane is oriented vertically, horizontally, or at 45° (with respect to true vertical as defined by the gravitational field). Although the slopes of the reaction-time functions were found to be very similar for all three of these cases, an apparently consistent tendency toward a smaller slope was noted in the case of rotations about the axis that projected vertically (with over-all reaction-time slopes of 6.9, 7.4, and 8.2 msec. per degree for the vertical, inclined, and horizontal orientations, respectively). This is consonant with indications, e.g., from experiments by Shepard & Feng (see Shepard, in press) and by Taylor (1972), that a slightly shorter time may be needed to imagine reflections of two-dimensional objects about the vertical than about the horizontal axis. It may also be related to the generally greater salience of bilateral symmetry when the axis of the symmetry has a vertical orientation (Zusne, 1970). (For some theories as to why the vertical axis might have a unique status see, e.g., Corballis and Beale, 1970; Sutherland, 1969; Uttley, 1956.)

Complexity of objects and naturalness of rotational axis. Despite the small differences just noted among the variously inclined axes of rotation in depth, we regard it as more significant that the reaction-time slopes for all of these depth rotations were quite similar to each other and uniformly quite a bit less than the slope for rotations about the line of sight. Since the slopes of the reaction-time functions in Experiments I and II were approximately equal for rotations in depth and in the picture plane, we tentatively attribute the present shorter reaction times for rotations in depth to the new circumstance that, for the depth pairs only, the axis of rotation coincided with the natural axis of the object itself.

Another new feature of these more recent experiments is, of course, that the objects themselves were simpler (in terms of number of component cubes and number of right-angle bends). A comparison of the reaction times for these simple objects with the reaction times for the more complex objects employed in the preceding experiments is complicated in the case of depth rotations, however, by the confounding of complexity with the just-discussed factor of naturalness of rotational axis. In the case of picture-plane rotations, on the other hand, the axis of rotation (viz., the line of sight) did not coincide with a natural axis of the object in any of the experiments. Nevertheless, for the picture-plane "same" pairs the slopes were about 20 and 26 msec. per degree in Experiments I and II, respectively, but only about 8.3 msec. per degree in the subsequent experiment with simpler objects. Correspondingly, the estimated rate of mental rotation in the picture-plane was well over twice as great for the objects consisting of three fewer cubes and one less bend. Still, all of these rates are substantially slower than the rates that have been estimated for mental rotation of purely two-dimensional objects (cf., Cooper, 1973; Cooper & Shepard, 1973b; Shepard, in press).

Sex and handedness of subjects. The conclusions that we can draw concerning individual differences are extremely limited owing to the facts (*a*) that we obtained data from only eight subjects in each experiment and (*b*) that these subjects were selected from a relatively homogeneous university population to meet a minimum criterion of performance on two paper-and-pencil pretests of spatial abilities. Nevertheless, the subjects in Experiment II and again in the first of the more recent experiments by Metzler (1973) were chosen so that there were (in each experiment) four subjects of each sex and, within these, two of each handedness. Some summary statement, however tentative, may therefore be found relevant to current discussions of the influence of sex, handedness, hemispheric lateralization, and genetic makeup on the development of spatial abilities.

A substantial body of evidence now indicates that, with the possible exception of a small minority of strongly left-handed subjects, the capacity for complex mental manipulations of objects in space is normally confined primarily to the linguistically inferior right hemisphere of the brain (e.g., Gazzaniga, Bogen, & Sperry, 1965; Gibson, Filbey, & Gazzaniga, 1970; Levy, 1969; Sperry & Levy, 1970). This particular type of spatial ability shows some statistical tendency, further, to be fully developed less often in subjects with a strong family history of left-handedness. Although it is consistent with these indications that, in both of our experiments just mentioned, the slopes of the reaction-time functions were, on the average, slightly greater for the left-handed subjects (and somewhat more so in the case of the left-handed females), the magnitudes of these differences in our small sample were insignificant.

Some recent evidence has also suggested that this type of spatial ability may be bimodally distributed in the population and controlled by a sex-linked gene in such a way as to be fully present in females with a lower statistical frequency than in males (Bock & Kolakowski, 1973; Garron, 1970; Hartlage, 1970; Sperry & Levy, 1970; Stafford, 1961; Vandenberg, 1969). In both of our above-mentioned experiments, the slopes were somewhat higher on the average for the female subjects. In the more recent experiment (Metzler, 1973), the four female subjects were among the five subjects whose reaction-time functions had highest intercepts *and* steepest slopes. Moreover three of these females also had the highest error rates and most variable reaction times. (Interestingly, in this connection, two high school students, Priscilla Walker and Clare Bronowski, who tested our materials on 30 fellow students as a high school science project in La

Jolla, California, found substantially higher reaction times and error rates among their female subjects.)

Again, the small size and highly selected nature of our own sample of subjects prevents these results from being more than merely suggestive. Perhaps the only important point to be made at this stage is that, for the purposes of further study of individual differences, the type of task reported here may permit the collection of highly stable data concerning one rather pure type of spatial ability. (For one start in this direction see, e.g., Snyder, 1972.)

THEORETICAL DISCUSSION

We turn now to a fuller consideration of how certain general theoretical notions originally advanced by Shepard (see Shepard, in press; and also, Cooper & Shepard, 1973b; Shepard & Chipman, 1970; Shepard & Metzler, 1971) relate specifically to the empirical findings surveyed here. We have of course already been arguing that subjects determine the sameness or difference of shape of two differently oriented three-dimensional objects by carrying out some sort of an internal analog of a rigid rotation of one of the objects into congruence with the other in three-dimensional space. However, we have not yet given a sufficiently full explication of what we mean by an internal representation of a three-dimensional object or of its rigid rotation. Nor have we been very specific about the nature of the alternative views that we have implicitly been arguing against or about the reasons why such alternative views are difficult to reconcile with our empirical data. Finally, there remains a need to place all of this into the context of cognitive processes in general.

Some Alternative, Nonrotational Theories

Comparison of rotationally invariant structural codes. For purposes of contrast it may be useful to consider a model that seems to have some *a priori* plausibility but that is nevertheless rather different from the type that we have been advocating, and to see what kinds of difficulties such an alternative model encounters in attempting to explain our data. In order to be quite specific, let us suppose that a subject proceeds through three successive processes as follows:

First, by means of visual feature detectors or sensory analyzers of the sorts envisaged by Hubel and Wiesel (1962, 1968), Selfridge (1959), Sutherland (1969), and others, the subject detects the presence and interrelationships of the basic components of one of the two-dimensional perspective drawings—particularly, the variously oriented straight lines, the several types of vertices by which they are connected and, presumably, something of the structural relationships among these components *within the two-dimensional pattern*. Then, on the basis of some higher-level processing of these extracted features and their interrelationships, an internal representation, code, or verbal description is generated that captures the intrinsic structure of the three-dimensional object in a form that is independent of the particular orientation in which that object happens to be displayed.

Second, exactly the same two-stage process of visual analysis followed by the construction of a rotationally invariant code is carried out for the second of the two presented two-dimensional pictures. (In the case of successive presentation, of course, this second step could not begin until the presentation of the second perspective picture.)

Third and finally, the two rotationally invariant codes that have been thus independently derived are directly compared with each other, and the subject responds "same" or "different" according to whether there is or is not an exact, part-for-part match between these two separately generated codes.

It is not necessary to make any definite specification as to the form or nature of the rotationally invariant codes. As an illustration of just one possibility, we might imagine that the subject adopts the convention of always starting with the end of the object having a certain identifiable property (e.g., in Experiment I, the end with the most blocks before the first right-angled bend or, if both ends are equal in this respect, the end with the most blocks before the second such bend; or, in Experiment II, the end marked with the red dot). If, then, he always considers the first bend as, say, a right turn, he can encode the shape of the three-dimensional object adequately for Experiments I or II just in terms of whether each of the two succeeding turns is left (L), right (R), up (U), or down (D). Thus, depending upon which of the two isomeric versions is presented, the code would be either "UL" or "DL" for both Objects A and C, "DU" or "UD" for both Objects B and D, and "LD" or "LU" for Object E. (See Fig. 6.) And, in the case of the more recent experiments with objects having only two bends, the code reduces to just the two alternatives "U" and "D."

These codes need not be verbally formulated in the way that the above description suggests (and, certainly, the subjects reported that they were not consciously aware of generating any such verbal codes). The only critical features that such codes must have are (a) that they be independent of the orientation in which each object is portrayed and (b) that they be different for the two isomeric versions of each object. (The fact that the codes are the same for distinct objects—such as for Objects A and D or for Objects B and E—raises no problem since the required discrimination is always between isomeric versions and, in this case, the resulting codes do always differ.)

Objections to such a code-comparison theory. The model just outlined would account for the ability of subjects to make the kind of discrimination that they have shown themselves capable of making in our experiments. It appears to run into difficulty, however, as soon as we try to account for the time that subjects take to make these discriminations and, particularly, the linearly increasing dependence of this time upon the angular departure between the portrayed orientations of the two objects. Within the framework of the model it would be possible to allow the time needed to analyze each of the two pictures to depend to some extent upon the *absolute* orientation of the object portrayed in that picture. But, since the two pictures are analyzed independently, there could not on the average be any dependence of over-all reaction time upon the *relative* orientations of the two objects. As it stands, then, this model predicts that, when mean reaction time is plotted as a function of angular departure, the resulting function should be horizontal rather than monotonically increasing to a value that is four to five times as great at 180° as at 0°.

One could of course argue that when the two perspective views are identical, as they always are at 0°, the subject does not need to go through the "higher-order" processes of generating and comparing rotationally invariant codes. Perhaps when the two objects have essentially the same orientation, the subject can simply make a template-like match between the two-dimensional pictures themselves (or between the lower-order visual features extracted from them). At or near 0°, then, the subject would be able, in the terminology of Posner (see Posner, Boies, Eichelman, & Taylor, 1969), to make a direct "physical match" rather than the appreciably more indirect and slower type of "name match" that would be required at large angular departures. Although, with this modification, the model would predict a monotonic increase in reaction time as the difference in orientation moves away from 0°, it would have to predict that the function would level off and become essentially horizontal as soon as the orientational difference became too great to permit the direct template-like match. Certainly, even as modified, this model seems to offer no basis for explaining why the reaction-time functions should be so consistently and precisely linear.

There are other indications, too, that this model is fundamentally incorrect. One that may be worth noting is that this model predicts that subjects should have no difficulty in learning to recognize each of the two isomeric versions of one of the objects absolutely—without reference to the other version. For, if the subject derives some sort of a rotationally invariant structural description for one version (such, for example, as the code symbolized as "UL" for one version of Object A), he should have no difficulty in learning to associate one arbitrary name with that version and another arbitrary name with its mirror image (symbolized, say, by "DL"). Even after 1600 trials of Experiment I, however, subjects still reported that they could not identify any of the objects absolutely but could only determine whether two pictures were of identical objects or of mirror images by comparing them with each other. (And, of course, they claimed that in order to make this comparison they generally had first to perform a mental rotation.)

This is not at all to say that subjects could not be trained to adopt a nonrotational strategy of the sort just considered. In fact perhaps the strongest argument for the claim that most subjects do not spontaneously do so (and that subjects in our experiments, in particular, did not do so) is that, when subjects *are* induced to adopt such an alternative strategy, they apparently generate very different reaction-time functions. This is suggested, anyway, by the preliminary results (for only three subjects) from an experiment recently carried out at Stanford by Arthur

Thomas. In that experiment subjects were trained to encode each stimulus in the way we have been considering and to judge sameness or difference in terms of a match or mismatch of the generated codes. As a result, their reaction-time functions became very nearly flat. Indeed, for one subject, the reaction time at 180° was only about 150 msec. longer than at 0°, rather than some three to four full seconds longer as in our own experiments. (Surprisingly the 0°-intercept of the reaction-time function was not appreciably higher than in our experiments. But quantitative comparisons of the intercepts are hazardous owing to a number of differences in procedure and apparatus, since Thomas ran his experiment on-line, by means of a computer graphics system.)

A final observation to be made about this so-called nonrotational model is that, even when subjects adopt the sort of strategy of verbal analysis just described, they typically report the extensive occurrence, during the encoding phase, of visual imagery and, particularly, of visual and/or kinesthetic representation of transformations in space. For example, in encoding one version of Object A as "UL," they imagine themselves oriented in space in such a way that, when they move in along the appropriate terminal arm, they will encounter the first bend as a right turn. Then, after mentally negotiating that right turn, they are able to generate the "U" by noting that the next bend turns 90° upward relative to their currently imagined position; and, after executing that turn, they can generate the "L" as soon as they discover that the last turn is then to their left. Thus, although neither of the two codes generated in this way nor the subsequent comparison between them are visual or spatial in character, the process of deriving the two codes from the two visually presented pictures seems to depend upon mental analogs of motions in three-dimensional space including, apparently, a sequence of rotations. Despite the apparent feasibility of a very different strategy of verbal analysis, therefore, it remains doubtful whether it is possible for human subjects to discriminate between isomeric three-dimensional shapes, when these are presented in different orientations, without some recourse to analog operations including mental rotation. (Concerning the existence of alternative strategies for dealing with rotated structures see also the recent study by Huttenlocher and Presson, 1973— particularly p. 296.)

Objections to theories of direct feature-by-feature comparison. We have argued that any explanation based upon the notion that rotationally invariant representations extracted from each of the two pictures separately are then compared with each other can be rejected because it fails to explain the fact that reaction time continues to increase monotonically as far as 180°. However, a related possibility remains to be considered. That is the possibility that the subject compares the two presented pictures feature by feature and, without either generating a rotationally invariant code or carrying out any sort of mental rotation of either object as a whole, is able to determine in some way whether or not all of the corresponding features of the two objects achieve a suitable match. The monotonic increase in reaction time would then be explained by reference to the plausible claim that the comparison of corresponding features becomes more difficult and hence more protracted as the angular difference in portrayed orientation of the two objects increases.

Without concerning ourselves with the lack of explicit specification as to just how corresponding features are compared between the two-dimensional projections of two differently oriented three-dimensional objects, we can nevertheless note that theories of this type, too, encounter several difficulties. First, although such theories provide a basis for explaining the monotonic increase in reaction time with orientational discrepancy, they do not seem to offer a comparable basis for explaining why this increase should be so precisely linear. Nor do such theories provide a ready account for the equivalence of the slopes of the reaction-time functions for the picture-plane and depth pairs. For, in order to explain the dependence of reaction time upon angular difference, we must suppose that the features that are being compared are the features of the two-dimensional drawings, which differ more and more with angular departure, and not the features of the three-dimensional objects, which are the same regardless of orientation. But, if the comparison is between features of the two-dimensional pictures, one would expect that the comparison would take appreciably less time when these features differ by a simple rigid rotation in the picture plane than by the two-dimensionally much more complex, nonrigid deformation induced by a rotation of the object in depth. And, for similar reasons, if the features of the two-dimensional pictures are what are being compared one would expect that (relative to a fixed angle of rotation in three-dimensional space) the effect of intervening discontinuities in those features would be considerably more pronounced than was found (see Fig. 8).

Further objections to such nonrotational theories are raised by two more recent experimental findings reported by Metzler (1973) and, briefly, in the preceding experimental section. One of these is the finding that, beyond 180°, reaction time is bimodally distributed with the upper mode corresponding to the linear extrapolation of the reaction-time function to angles larger than 180° and the lower mode corresponding to the linear extrapolation of that function *backward* to a point the same distance from 180° (Fig. 16). In view of the fact that the reaction-time distributions up to 180° are sharply-peaked unimodal distributions, the particular bimodality found at 225° strongly suggests the following conclusion: Contrary to theories of feature-by-feature comparison, it is not the difference between the two pictures as such that determines reaction time. Rather, as required by a theory of mental rotation, it is the particular path or trajectory that the subject takes in passing from one picture to the other—specifically, whether he mentally rotates the long or the short way around the 360° circle.

The second additional finding that appears to pose a problem for theories of feature-by-feature comparison is this: When the presentation of the second picture is delayed until the subject should have reached that orientation by a process of mental rotation, his response to that second picture is made with a reaction time that, for most subjects, is uniformly short and independent of that orientation (Fig.

17). Indeed, this is true even for rotations beyond 180°. This, too, fits nicely with the notion that the subject starts with one picture and then mentally passes over a certain trajectory toward the second picture and, further, that comparison between the internally transforming representation and the second picture need not be made until the transformational process is completed at the end of the trajectory. This is in contrast to any theory of feature-by-feature comparison that requires that, even after the appearance of the second picture, the comparison process will take longer when the second picture is more different from the first.

We can not of course rule out the possibility that some elaboration of a theory of feature-by-feature comparison or some perhaps quite different, nonrotational theory will be shown capable of accounting for all of our empirical findings. For the present, however, the theory of mental rotation seems to us to provide the account of our findings that is at once the simplest, the most complete, and the most consonant with the introspective reports of the subjects themselves.

Analog Representation of External Objects and Their Transformations

Mental rotation as an analog process. What we wish to argue is the following: In order to prepare for the presentation of a rotated object, subjects are able to imagine that object in the rotated orientation and, so, are able to respond to it with considerable speed and accuracy when it then appears (Fig. 17). But, if the angle of rotation is at all large, subjects can only prepare for the appearance of the object in the rotated orientation by first passing through other states of preparation corresponding to an ordered sequence of intermediate orientations (see, also, Cooper & Shepard, 1973b, Experiment II).

This is in contrast to the case of the digital calculation of the coordinates for a rotated configuration of points by computer. For, in such a digital process (of matrix multiplication) the intermediate stages of the computation have no one-to-one relation to any intermediate orientation of the configuration of points and, moreover, the time required to complete the computation is essentially the same for all angles of rotation (rather than linearly increasing with angle as shown in Figs. 3, 11, and 15).

It is as if the only way the subject can represent the three-dimensional object is by means of some sort of internal model that is, at some suitably abstract level, structurally isomorphic to that object (cf., Attneave, 1973). Consequently, any intermediate stage of processing must also preserve this internal model, or the structural information about that object will no longer be available for comparison with the second stimulus. But, according to this reasoning, the structural information can be preserved only through small adjustments in the representation. Thus, in order to prepare for a large rotational displacement, there is no choice but to carry out a sequence of these small adjustments, each of which preserves the essential structure, until the desired orientation is finally achieved.

If the rotation is accomplished in a number of small steps of this sort, the question arises as to whether these small steps might not be detectable through some external indicators such, for example, as eye movements. Thanks to the interest and generosity of our colleague Dr. Norman Mackworth, we were able to use the eye camera that he has developed (Mackworth, 1967) to videotape the patterns of fixations of both an experienced and an inexperienced subject while each was making "same"–"different" judgments for some pairs selected from Experiment I. Preliminary examination of these recordings indicates that, for both subjects, fixation shifted back and forth between the two perspective views during the course of the mental rotation. However, the number of such shifts tended to be smaller in the case of the more experienced and faster subject and may in fact be too small to correspond to the number of hypothetical elementary steps constituting the mental rotation. Still, the possibility that eye movements provide useful indications of the fine-grain structure of the inner process seems to warrant further exploration.

A question has also been raised as to why we should imply that the internal process always corresponds to a rigid rotation of the entire object as a whole. In fact some subjects reported that they felt, instead, that they imagined the upper L-shaped part of one object rotated into congruence with the corresponding L-shaped part of the other object and, then, returned to carry out this same mental rotation on the lower part to see whether it was thereby brought into congruence with the corresponding lower part of the other object. Possibly other subjects may, without necessarily realizing it, have been rotating each object piece by piece rather than as a unit. Such an explanation differs from the theory of feature-by-feature comparison already discussed in that it still presupposes a mechanism of mental rotation and, so, provides an account for the linearly increasing reaction-time function. However the results of the experiment in which the presentation of the second stimulus was delayed indicate strongly that, in that experiment anyway, the objects were rotated in a unitary manner rather than piecemeal.

In summary, then, the theory of mental rotation seems to furnish the only presently available account for the principal findings of the experiments reported here; namely, (a) that the time required to complete the process increases linearly with the angle of rotation, (b) that it is bimodally distributed for angles beyond 180°—in correspondence with the subject's choice of going the short or the long way around the 360° circle, and (c) that the process can be completed in advance of the presentation of the second stimulus—provided that the subject already knows the axis and direction of the required rotation.

Representation of three-dimensional objects. But what exactly is the nature of the "internal model" that is transformed in this way? Although we can not yet say anything specific about the representation of three-dimensional objects at the neurophysiological level, our results do seem to place some significant formal or abstract constraints on the nature of the representation. Perhaps the most important of these is that the internal representation embodies important structural features of the three-dimensional object that are not manifest in the two-dimensional projection of that object on the surface of the retina, while the features peculiar to this two-dimensional projection appear to have little influence on the internal process.

This conclusion is supported by the finding that, for a given angle of rotation of the object in three-dimensional space, the reaction time is relatively independent of whether the two-dimensional projection undergoes (a) a simple, rigid rotation in its own plane, (b) a more complex, nonrigid deformation that nevertheless preserves topological structure, or (c) a still more complex, discontinuous transformation that alters even topological structure. It is also consonant with the postexperimental introspective reports of the subjects who generally claimed the following: (a) They interpreted the perspective drawings as rigid three-dimensional objects and, in an important sense, "saw" the angles corresponding to the corners of the cubes as right angles even though these angles varied widely from 90° in the two-dimensional picture plane. (b) They imagined the rotations as carried out in isotropic three-dimensional space and, in most cases, were completely unaware that the rotations differed with respect to the conservation of rigid or of topological structure in the resulting two-dimensional projection.

This is not, however, to say that the internal representation is structurally isomorphic to the three-dimensional object in itself, or that it has no unique relationship to the two-dimensional perspective view. For the three-dimensional structure of each object is inherent in that object and not in any way affected by rigid rotation. So, if the internal representations of two presented objects each encoded the intrinsic and rotationally invariant structure of its own object as such, these two representations could be compared for a match or mismatch, directly. As explained for the "comparison of rotationally invariant structural codes," above, no mental rotation would then be necessary, and reaction time would be independent of angular separation. Contrary to our experience, it would then also be easy to learn to recognize a particular object in itself, without regard to its presented orientation and without regard to any other object.

Clearly, then, the internal representation of an external object captures its three-dimensional structure—not as that structure exists in the object absolutely—but only as it appears *relative* to a particular angle of regard. Thus the internal representation shares properties with both the three-dimensional object and its two-dimensional perspective projection, without being wholly isomorphic to either. It resembles the perspective view in its incorporation of information (not contained in the object itself) concerning the relation of the object to the viewer. And it resembles the object, in that cognitive operations upon the representation are more simply related to properties specifiable in three-dimensional space than to properties peculiar to the particular two-dimensional projection. What the representation really represents, then, is the appearance, from a particular point of view, of the object in depth.

But what do we mean by "the appearance of the object in depth"—particularly in view of introspective indications that the internal representation may often be rather schematic and not purely visual? It is tempting to suppose that the internal representation is a relatively abstract scheme that, although partially isomorphic to the spatial structure of the external object, is not exclusively tied to any one modality. In part the representation resembles a "program" or "subroutine" that can be variously executed to cause the hand to reach out appropriately in depth to grasp the object (cf., Festinger, Ono, Burnham, & Bamber, 1967; Shepard, in press) as well as to generate a set of two-dimensional features for the purposes of rapid test against a retinal projection. The results of spatial transformations appear to be anticipated by means of a succession of small parametric adjustments that progressively alter the properties of the representation corresponding to the particular point of view, while leaving invariant the properties corresponding to the object's inherent structure.

Implications concerning cognitive processes generally. In the context of the general subject of human cognitive processes, the problem of a particular, apparently nonverbal process such as mental rotation of three-dimensional objects may seem rather special. However, the possibility should be considered that the long-standing preoccupation of psychologists with exclusively verbal processes in learning, memory, problem solving, and the control of behavior generally may be a reflection more of the relative accessibility of verbal processes than of the pre-eminent role that verbal processes play in human thought.

To the extent that thinking is just talking to oneself, it is relatively easy to study thinking by simply asking subjects to talk out loud—as Newell and Simon and their followers do when they develop and test simulation models on the basis of verbal protocols (Newell, 1968; Newell & Simon, 1971). Or, the notion that transfer of learning, or recall of an item, is mediated by the covert occurrence of a certain word can be tested by looking for the overt emergence of that conjectured mediator (or of its other associates) as intrusion errors, or by looking for the generalized occurrence of the correct overt response when the conjectured mediator is presented as an explicit stimulus.

Nonverbal mediating representations including mental images and mental transformations on such images, by contrast, are much more difficult to externalize. Moreover, because such mediators differ in kind (not just in degree) from overt responses, they can not, as some have proposed for subvocal speech, be theoretically treated simply as previously learned overt responses; that is, as responses that have merely retreated inward where their now covert occurrences are still governed by the original, externally reinforced habits. It is hardly surprising that, during its long submission to the strictures of extreme behaviorism, psychology found little room for even the term "mental image."

Recently, with an increasing awareness of how much has been systematically ignored and with the consequent search for new techniques for the experimental study of inner processes, work on the structure and function of mental imagery has increased dramatically. (See, e.g., Baylor, 1972; Bower, 1972; Brooks, 1967, 1968; Cooper & Shepard, 1973b; Huttenlocher, 1968; Kosslyn, 1973; Neisser, 1972; Paivio, 1970; Segal, 1971; Sheehan, 1972; Shepard & Chipman, 1970; Stromeyer & Psotka, 1970.) There has also been an increasing appreciation of the facts (a) that nontrivial thinking can go on without language—as in the non-linguistic primate (Köhler, 1925), the nonlinguistic hemisphere (Gazzaniga, Bogen, & Sperry, 1965; Sperry & Levy, 1970), the prelinguistic child (Piaget, 1961; Sinclair-de-Zwart, 1969), the linguistically impoverished aphasic (Barbizet, 1970, p. 68; Penfield & Roberts, 1959, p. 117), or the linguistically untrained deaf (Furth, 1966); but (b) that the acquisition and effective use of language depends upon an already existing semantic, referential, or "operational" system that has perceptual roots and may well consist, in part, of mental imagery (e.g., Bower, 1972; Brown, 1973; E. Clark, 1973; H. Clark, 1973; Clark, Carpenter, & Just, 1973; Greenfield, Nelson, & Saltzman, 1972; Premack, 1971; Sinclair-de-Zwart, 1969; and, particularly, Moeser & Bregman, 1972, 1973).

By definition, any "imaginable" physical operation can be tried out in a purely mental way before taking the time, making the effort, or running the risk of carrying it out in physical reality. Possibly a significant part of the planning and internal guidance of individual behavior depends upon such nonverbal, analogical thinking. This possibility is suggested, anyway, by the appreciable improvement in complex perceptual-motor skills that have been found to follow purely mental practice (Rawlings, Rawlings, Chen, & Yilk, 1972; Richardson, 1969).

Among those external operations that can be simulated internally, rigid transformations on objects in three-dimensional space would seem to be of fundamental importance. The analog operation that we are specifically considering here, viz., "mental rotation," is of course just one such type of spatial transformation. Nevertheless, even this one illustrative type seems to play a central role in tasks ranging from the relatively mundane and concrete ones of planning the arrangement of furniture in a room or fitting together the pieces of a jigsaw puzzle or mechanical device, to the relatively more intellectual and abstract ones of solving problems in geometry, engineering design, or stereochemistry.

REFERENCES

Attneave, F. How do you know? Presidential Address delivered at the annual meeting of the Western Psychological Association, Anaheim, California, April, 1973.

Barbizet, J. Human memory and its pathology. San Francisco: W. H. Freeman, 1970.

Baylor, G. W. A treatise on the mind's eye: An empirical investigation of visual mental imagery. (Doctoral dissertation, Carnegie-Mellon University) Ann Arbor, Michigan: University Microfilms, 1972. No. 72–12, 699.

Bock, R. D., & Kolakowski, D. Further evidence of sex-linked major-gene influence on human spatial visualizing ability. The American Journal of Human Genetics, 1973, 25, 1–14.

Bower, G. H. Mental imagery and associative learning. In L. Gregg (Ed.), *Cognition in learning and memory*. New York: Wiley, 1972.

Brooks, L. R. The supression of visualization by reading. *Quarterly Journal of Experimental Psychology*, 1967, **19**, 289–299.

Brooks, L. R. Spatial and verbal components of the act of recall. *Canadian Journal of Psychology*, 1968, **22**, 349–368.

Brown, R. *The first language*. Cambridge, Mass.: Harvard University Press, 1973.

Clark, E. V. What's in a word? On the child's acquisition of semantics in his first language. In T. E. Moore (Ed.), *Cognitive development and the acquisition of language*. New York: Academic Press, 1973.

Clark, H. H. Space, time, semantics and the child. In T. E. Moore (Ed.), *Cognitive development and the acquisition of language*. New York: Academic Press, 1973.

Clark, H. H., Carpenter, P. A., & Just, M. A. On the meeting of semantics and perception. In W. G. Chase (Ed.), *Visual information processing*. New York: Academic Press, 1973.

Clark, H. H., & Chase, W. G. On the process of comparing sentences against pictures. *Cognitive Psychology*, 1972, **3**, 472–517.

Cooper, L. A. Internal representation and transformation of random shapes: A chronometric analysis. Unpublished doctoral dissertation, Stanford University, 1973.

Cooper, L. A., & Shepard, R. N. The time required to prepare for a rotated stimulus. *Memory & Cognition*, 1973, **1**, 246–250. (a)

Cooper, L. A., & Shepard, R. N. Chronometric studies of the rotation of mental images. In W. G. Chase (Ed.), *Visual information processing*. New York: Academic Press, 1973. (b)

Corballis, M. C., & Beale, I. L. Bilateral symmetry and behavior. *Psychological Review*, 1970, **77**, 451–464.

Festinger, L., Ono, H., Burnham, C. A., & Bamber, D. Efference and the conscious experience of perception. *Journal of Experimental Psychology Monographs*, 1967, **74**, (4, Whole No. 637).

Furth, H. G. *Thinking without language: Psychological implications of deafness*. New York: Free Press, 1966.

Garron, D. C. Sex-linked, recessive inheritance of spatial and numerical abilities, and Turner's syndrome. *Psychological Review*, 1970, **77**, 147–152.

Gazzaniga, M. S., Bogen, J. E., & Sperry, R. W. Observations on visual perception after disconnexion of the cerebral hemispheres in man. *Brain*, 1965, **88**, 221–236.

Gibson, A. R., Filbey, R., & Gazzaniga, M. S. Hemispheric differences as reflected by reaction time. *Proceedings: Federation of American Societies for Experimental Biology*, 1970, **29**, 658. (abstract)

Greenfield, P. M., Nelson, K., & Saltzman, E. The development of rulebound strategies for manipulating seriated cups: A parallel between action and grammar. *Cognitive Psychology*, 1972, **3**, 291–310.

Hartlage, L. C. Sex-linked inheritance of spatial ability. *Perceptual and Motor Skills*, 1970, **31**, 610.

Hubel, D. H., & Wiesel, T. N. Receptive fields, binocular interaction and functional architecture in the cat's visual cortex. *Journal of Physiology*, 1962, **160**, 106–154.

Hubel, D. H., & Wiesel, T. N. Receptive fields and functional architecture of monkey striate cortex. *Journal of Physiology*, 1968, **195**, 215–243.

Huttenlocher, J. Constructing spatial images: A strategy in reasoning. *Psychological Review*, 1968, **75**, 550–560.

Huttenlocher, J., & Presson, C. C. Mental rotation and the perspective problem. *Cognitive Psychology*, 1973, **4**, 277–299.

Köhler, W. *The mentality of apes*. New York: Harcourt, Brace, 1925.

Kosslyn, S. M. Scanning visual images: Some structural implications. *Perception & Psychophysics*, 1973, **14**, 90–94.

Levy, J. Possible basis for the evolution of lateral specialization of the human brain. *Nature,* 1969, **224,** 614–615.

Mackworth, N. H. A stand-mounted eye-marker camera for line-of-sight recording. *Perception & Psychophysics,* 1967, **2,** 119–127.

Metzler, J. Cognitive analogues of the rotation of three-dimensional objects. Unpublished doctoral dissertation, Stanford University, 1973.

Metzler, J., & Shepard, R. N. Mental correlates of the rotation of three-dimensional objects. Paper presented at the annual meeting of the Western Psychological Association, San Francisco, April, 1971.

Moeser, S. D., & Bregman, A. S. The role of reference in the acquisition of a miniature artificial language. *Journal of Verbal Learning and Verbal Behavior,* 1972, **11,** 759–769.

Moeser, S. D., & Bregman, A. S. Imagery and language acquisition. *Journal of Verbal Learning and Verbal Behavior,* 1973, **12,** 91–98.

Neisser, U. Changing conceptions of imagery. In P. W. Sheehan (Ed.), *The function and nature of imagery.* New York: Academic Press, 1972.

Newell, A. On the analysis of human problem solving protocols. In J. C. Gardin & B. Jaulin (Eds.), *Calcul et formalisation dans les sciences de l'homme.* Paris: CNRC, 1968.

Newell, A., & Simon, H. A. *Human problem solving.* Englewood Cliffs, N.J.: Prentice-Hall, 1971.

Newman, W. M., & Sproull, R. F. *Principles of interactive computer graphics.* New York: McGraw-Hill, 1973.

Noll, A. M. Computer-generated three-dimensional movies. *Computers & Automation,* 1965, **14,** 20–23.

Paivio, A. *Imagery and verbal processes.* New York: Holt, Rinehart & Winston, 1970.

Penfield, W., & Roberts, L. *Speech and brain-mechanisms.* Princeton, N.J.: Princeton University Press, 1959.

Piaget, J. The language and thought of the child. In T. Shipley (Ed.), *Classics in psychology.* New York: Philosophical Library, 1961.

Posner, M. I., Boies, S. J., Eichelman, W. H., & Taylor, R. L. Retention of visual and name codes of single letters. *Journal of Experimental Psychology,* 1969, **79,** (1, Pt. 2).

Premack, D. Language in chimpanzee? *Science,* 1971, **172,** 808–822.

Rawlings, E. I., Rawlings, I. L., Chen, S. S., & Yilk, M. D. The facilitating effects of mental rehearsal in the acquisition of rotary pursuit tracking. *Psychonomic Science,* 1972, **26,** 71–73.

Richardson, A. *Mental imagery.* New York: Springer, 1969.

Segal, S. J. (Ed.) *Imagery: Current cognitive approaches.* New York: Academic Press, 1971.

Selfridge, O. G. Pandemonium: A paradigm for learning. In *The mechanisation of thought processes.* London: H. M. Stationery Office, 1959.

Sheehan, P. W. (Ed.) *The function and nature of imagery.* New York: Academic Press, 1972.

Shepard, R. N. Studies in the form, formation, and transformation of internal representations. In R. Solso (Ed.), *Information Processing and Cognition: The Loyola Symposium.* Potomac, Md.: Lawrence Erlbaum Associates, in press.

Shepard, R. N., & Chipman, S. Second-order isomorphism of internal representations: Shapes of states. *Cognitive Psychology,* 1970, **1,** 1–17.

Shepard, R. N., & Feng, C. A chronometric study of mental paper folding. *Cognitive Psychology,* 1972, **3,** 228–243.

Shepard, R. N., & Metzler, J. Mental rotation of three-dimensional objects. *Science,* 1971, **171,** 701–703.

Sinclair-de-Zwart, H. Developmental psycholinguistics. In D. Elkind & J. H. Flavell (Eds.), *Studies in cognitive development: Essays in honor of Jean Piaget.* New York: Oxford University Press, 1969.

Snyder, C. R. C. Individual differences in imagery and thought. Unpublished doctoral dissertation, University of Oregon, 1972.

Sperry, R. W., & Levy, J. Mental capacities of the disconnected minor hemisphere. Paper presented at the meeting of the American Psychological Association, Miami, September, 1970.

Stafford, R. E. Sex differences in spatial visualization as evidence of sex linked inheritance. *Perceptual and Motor Skills*, 1961, **13**, 428.

Stromeyer, C. F., & Psotka, J. The detailed texture of eidetic images. *Nature*, 1970, **225**, 346–349.

Sutherland, N. S. Shape discrimination in rat, octopus, and goldfish: A comparative study. *Journal of Comparative and Physiological Psychology*, 1969, **67**, 160–176.

Taylor, R. L. Reading spatially transformed digits. *Journal of Experimental Psychology*, 1972, **96**, 396–399.

Trabasso, T., Rollins, H., & Shaughnessy, E. Storage and verification stages in processing concepts. *Cognitive Psychology*, 1971, **2**, 239–289.

Uttley, A. M. A theory of the mechanism of learning based on the computation of conditioned probabilities. *Proceedings of the 1st International Congress on Cybernetics*, Namur, 1956, 830–856.

Vandenberg, S. G. A twin study of spatial ability. *Multivariate Behavioral Research*, 1969, **4**, 273–294.

Warnock, J. E. Hidden surface algorithm for computer generated half-tone pictures. University of Utah Technical Report TR 4–15, 1969.

Zusne, L. *Visual perception of form*. New York: Academic Press, 1970.

7
CRITIQUE OF PURE MEMORY

Frank Restle
Indiana University

This paper will be purely theoretical and is concerned not with the facts but with the concept of memory. The immediate occasion for the paper is the nature of this volume, concerned as it is both with memory and with concept formation. In recent years, studies of "long-term" memory have more and more emphasized the importance of the conceptual structure of the information, and at the same time students of concept-learning have studied how a concept-former may use his memory. This should lead to a simple theoretical amalgamation of the two fields of data, but I am afraid that this amalgamation has not occurred.

My theoretical problems have come from the extension of the concept of "memory" to encompass many cognitive processes. When we speak of a sensory buffer, of a short-term rehearsal memory, and of a long-term memory which may be divided into episodic and semantic parts, we have set up a theoretical structure capable of "handling" most of the cognitive processes from sensory through perceptual to conceptual. Furthermore, by adding a working memory this area of research has come to encompass reasoning and problem-solving as well—all this within the concept of memory (Atkinson & Shiffrin, 1968).

I do not think that the problems in applying memory theory are limited to concept formation. I feel that the problems of speech and of understanding speech, on which important progress has been made, depend upon processes very different from those offered by memory theory (Liberman, Cooper, Shankweiler, & Studdert-Kennedy, 1967). It is not easy to get grammar out of a memory system. The work I have done on serial pattern learning, as the analysis of the process proceeded to deeper and deeper levels, revealed more and more structure that subjects were using to generate their responses, and left less and less room for memory (Restle, 1970). Finally, in visual (nonverbal) perception, as in work on illusions, space perception, etc., attempts to make a major use of memory lead back to the kinds of empiricist theories of perception (Gregory, 1970) that were so successfully combated by Gestalt psychology.

This leads me to the hypothesis, which I shall put forward as a possibility, that for the concept of "memory" to be made the basis of a general theory of cognition, it must be stretched entirely beyond its natural compass. When a theory says that memory is structured, it is the *structure* that is necessary and not the memory.

LEVELS OF MEMORY

Memory theory in the past decade or so has grown with the development of concepts of various levels or kinds of memory. I should like to review them briefly, partly to ensure that we are talking about the same thing when we use certain words. Memory is usually divided into three levels: sensory buffer; short-term (STM), or primary memory; and long-term (LTM), or secondary memory. Secondary memory can usefully be divided into "episodic" and "semantic" memory (Tulving & Donaldson, 1972).

Furthermore, any level of memory has three characteristics that are logically necessary. First is coding, the question of the form the information must have to be in this sort of memory. Second is the storage or maintenance of the information. Third is the retrieval, that is, the conditions under which information can issue forth from the memory level and either go some place else in the memory or do something like initiate a response. I take these three processes to be theoretically essential in any theory of memory, because a memory cannot be said to function unless information can enter into it, stay there for a while, and be gotten out again.

If we attempt to give an analysis of memory in these terms, we arrive at a 3 × 4 table shown as Table 1. Although each of the 12 cells can be the subject of extended and detailed discussion, I have been satisfied to insert a few words in each cell merely to remind the reader of some of the basic facts or theoretical hypotheses currently in use. I must admit that I emphasize the distinction between the two kinds of long-term memory more than is commonplace in the literature, but such a distinction is very important in giving memory theory its best chance as a general theory.

All of the distinctions in Table 1 seem to me to be useful and helpful. In this sense, the development of memory theory is an undoubted gain for psychology. However, there is another theoretical problem which has never received a satisfactory answer, and which recently seems to have become more and more intractable. That is the question of the relationship between the various levels of memory.

Generally speaking, the theoretical schema for handling this problem has been to use the concept of a block diagram, and to treat each level of memory as a block, somewhat as various buffers and memory devices are used in designing a com-

TABLE 1

Modern Memory Theory

Level of memory	Coding	Storage	Retrieval
Sensory buffer (Icon or Echo)	Sensory, with low level feature extraction	Rapid Spontaneous decay	Parallel or rapid serial
STM (Primary)	Articulatory (naming), visual	Rehearsal or imagination	Parallel or rapid serial (Sternberg)
LTM episodic (Secondary)	Images, associations, time tags, list tags	Permanent (?) but access easily lost	Search sets, category systems, clustering
LTM semantic (Knowledge)	Lexicons, grammars knowledge of world, propositions	Permanent	Arousal of system generation, traversal of structure

puter system. It seems obvious that information comes from the sense organs and is immediately stored in the sensory buffer. It cannot remain long in this condition, so it is transferred to STM and is maintained there by rehearsal (as in the Atkinson-Shiffrin model). While it is in rehearsal, it may be transferred to LTM for permanent storage. This simple chain-type block diagram is shown in Fig. 1.

However, for the subject to select features when encoding information for the sensory buffer, he must know what those features are. This information about features, their definition and how to recognize them, is presumably stored in long-term store (LTS), probably in the more basic semantic store. Thus, the information must go "through" semantic LTS in order to get into the sensory buffer.

That same information is then named, identified, elaborated, simplified, or otherwise processed in getting it into STM. However, the name for the letter "A," and in fact the correspondence between the combination of features and the sound, are all to be found in long-term semantic memory. Therefore, another trip through long-term storage is required before the material can go into short-term. Once the information is safely in short-term store, it may then go into either episodic or semantic long-term memory. Perhaps the picture is not overly complicated; but when I drew it for Fig. 2, I felt somehow that all was not as simple as I had hoped. This is a revised version of Atkinson and Shiffrin (1968) obtained from R. M. Shiffrin, and a slight revision of that given by Shiffrin & Geisler (1973).

This flow chart describing movement from one memory store to another is unsatisfactory to me. You may call it a mere matter of taste, but my feeling is that

FIG. 1. Primitive flow chart connecting levels of memory.

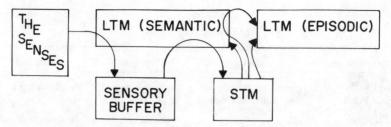

FIG. 2. Information flow chart connecting levels of memory (Mark III).

the structure is too large and complicated for the weak logic that holds it together. Therefore, I have tried to find a theoretical account of memory that preserves the gains of Table 1, and properly distinguishes the various levels of memory, but without the problem of interrelating memory stores. How is this possible?

The first stage is to divest oneself of the concept of memory stores as separate entities, and merely to consider their defining characteristics. Fundamentally, the differences among iconic memory, primary memory, secondary memory, and knowledge correspond to different degrees of organization, or as nicely put by Craik and Lockhart (1972), by different levels of processing. Whereas Craik and Lockhart emphasized perceptual processing, my remarks will parallel theirs but concentrate on the degree to which information is integrated with higher levels of existing cognitive structure, and how responses are generated. This approach may serve to complete those parts of the theory admittedly left incomplete by Craik and Lockhart, who wrote, "We have looked at memory purely from the input or encoding end; no attempt has been made to specify either how items are differentiated from one another, are grouped together and organized, or how they are retrieved from the system [p. 682]."

Information coming in from the senses, before it has been integrated into any unified meaningful structure, must first be analyzed as to various "features." Such features, when first extracted from a situation the subject does not know (like a random and unpredictable tachistoscopic presentation of an array of letters) can at most be parts of very small organizations. When the letters are recognized and named, the information is then connected into a more integrated system of rules, the articulatory–language system. Structures, once aroused, will persist for a while and therefore information in this stage of integration can be retained for a while. However, if any large volume of such information is to be held, or if retention is to be tested after a long time, then information must be integrated into larger structures—into images, scenes, stories, chains of association; into the flow of time, or into lists or other groupings. Such organizations are large and important enough to be fairly persistent but can be dropped during the course of a day or two. If information is to be permanently available, then it must become part of a highly-integrated and central information system, if possible one so complex and complete that it functions all the time.

This statement, that levels of memory correspond to degrees of organization, is itself somewhat vague, and I shall attempt to clarify it. First, however, let me show that such a concept enables us to derive, in a simple and unified way, the various properties of the levels of memory.

Since I have described the four levels of memory in terms of coding, let me show why the "storage" characteristics are what they are. First, notice that the "iconic storage" refers to information in a very early stage of analysis. Such information is isolated, being part of a very small organizational structure. These very small "tips" of the cognitive structure necessarily change all the time, for any change in the cognitive system will disrupt them. Therefore, in the event that the information is not processed to a higher level of organization, it is very rapidly lost. When the information is transferred to primary memory, this says that it is incorporated into the language (or at least the alphabet). At this level of analysis the information can be used to drive the articulatory system, and therefore the person *can* rehearse verbally. If information can go into a visual short-term memory this is because it has been incorporated into a pictorial system of some sort that identifies (but may not name) objects, and otherwise processes the information into a moderately stable system. However, these cognitive structures are especially designed to be recombined in various ways—they are too low in the organization hierarchy to be stable, they are the mere units of which more stable structures are made. Therefore, information in this level of integration is not preserved very long unless the level, itself, is temporarily frozen as in the case of simple rehearsal, (Craik and Lockhart, 1972).

The next general level of memory is secondary, or "episodic" memory. Generally speaking, this is the kind of memory studied in the verbal-learning laboratory, by free recall, paired associates, serial rote learning, etc. The basic cognitive structure is the "list" which, in well-controlled experiments, provides the subject with a poor choice of organizational possibilities. The result is that except under favorable conditions, the average subject cannot learn a list of any great length at all, and forgets rapidly. Of course, as we now know from the work of Paivio (1971), Bower (1970, 1972), Mandler (1967), and many others, the subject does not usually master the material disintegrated as it is. Instead, he finds and employs even the most unpromising organizational possibilities. He may work with images, scenes, judgments of similarity, contrast, succession, etc., which will serve to tie the materials together, or he may even use an entirely arbitrary mnemonic system like "one is a bun" or the method of locations. Obviously, information integrated into such systems is more stable than information that has merely been put into words somehow, but it is not very stable. The whole history of the theory of forgetting has shown how sensitive such information is to "interference." In my terms, interference is some task that calls upon the organizing powers of the subject and will cause him to disturb the rather delicate and insubstantial organization he has hastily erected to hold one list of materials for a few minutes. Subjects learning lists of nonsense-syllables or words must try to connect them, by using images, interactive scenes, constructing sentences that use the words, picking out simple stimulus cues, and so forth. They construct a system or a weak assembly of systems to generate the needed answers. Such a structure often has no connection with more enduring belief or cognitive systems and cannot be generated in full from any higher-order structure. Therefore, whenever the special system is terminated it cannot be regenerated, and the subject is unable to answer questions. My hypothesis is that interference, particularly retroactive interference, is any process that serves to terminate this special mnemonic activity. If the structure is very peripheral as in a short-term memory experiment, almost anything will serve to terminate it—even counting backwards. If the list has been better learned (in long-term memory) it will often be integrated with images, associative structures, etc., and these structures can be regenerated fairly well after a temporary interruption. Therefore, a truly interfering task must be similar to the original list so as to reuse and disrupt the general structures subjects use. If the material is well learned (as in "overlearning" experiments or experiments using connected, meaningful material) then it becomes part of relatively enduring and comprehensive systems, and interfering tasks must be well designed to disrupt the memories.

The last level of memory is what Tulving called "semantic memory" and what I should be inclined to call "knowledge." Here lies the lexicon with the meanings of words, the person's mastery of grammar, his understanding of relational systems like orderings, family structurings, systems of subclasses, propositions, and everything else the psychologist might want to recognize as existing in his subject's mind. This information is, in the main part, permanent because it is part of so inclusive and unified an organization that it is never disrupted. Despite the enormous volume of information in this "memory" it never seems crowded—one is never surfeited with knowledge, nor does true knowledge become inaccessible—in fact, it can be recovered with remarkable facility. If I ask "Have you ever been in Dubuque, Iowa?" most people can respond correctly within a second, and I imagine that quite a bit of that time is consumed in analyzing and interpreting the question and then deciding that the questioner, being a psychologist, very possibly does want an answer even to so silly a question.

Let me now sketch for you why retrieval is what it is in these "levels of memory." At the iconic level, the information is at a very low level of organization; if that edge of the mind is active, then the information is available; if it is not, the information is not available. The information cannot really be "generated" at all by any larger organization, so that as soon as it once disappears it is gone. While it is present, it is all present. At the level of primary memory, information has been integrated into a low-level structure, and that low-level organization can generate it. Therefore, "retrieving" the information amounts to generating it, a process studied by Sternberg (1967). Information in secondary or episodic memory is part of a relatively large and complex organization and is generated by that system. Usually, the cognitive structure is fairly complicated, so that the subject will first start by generating the "list" itself, then from that will try to get some parts of the list (what Shiffrin, 1970, calls "search sets"), or will generate categories, or may generate one item at a time through a chain of associations. The process is slow, complicated, and rather uncertain. When information is in Tulving's "semantic memory" or is knowledge, it is highly organized. Once the information is demanded, the appropriate organization is aroused, as a unit or in a rapid succession (Collins & Quillian, 1969, 1972). Retrieval from such integrated systems has little relationship to input (as shown by Bransford and Franks, 1971, and later by Potts, 1972) and can be studied either by intensive interrogation to elicit errors or by studies of reaction time.

THE NATURE OF ORGANIZATION

The main difficulty with the analysis of memory I have just given is the fact that it is built upon the shifting sands of the term "organization," which I have not defined. A cognitive organization is what controls the thoughts and acts of the person. My description of it is based on two theoretical points: (a) I must describe the element of cognition, and (b) I must show how these elements are combined to yield an organization.

The element I shall here call an "information flow." It is primarily described as a flow chart, beginning with an expectancy (which is, functionally, the entry point of the flow chart), an input which may either come from an external stimulus or from another part of the organization, and an analysis of that input. By an analysis, I mean a selection from among the myriad of possible characteristics, parts, features, properties, or cues in the input. A visual stimulus may be analyzed for redness, for its shape, for its conformity in motion to a rabbit, for its apparent distance or size, or for its inner harmony. The analysis of the input has, as its result, what might be thought of as a "description" of the input with respect to selected variables.

In an information flow, the expectancy and the analysis are really two aspects of the same process. The expectancy consists of a sort of image of a situation expected, containing specifications of some, but probably not all, possible characteristics. The analysis seeks out just the characteristics specified in the expectancy. Therefore, when the analysis has been completed, it is possible to match its product with the expectancy. If the input, as analyzed, matches the expectancy, then one result, R_1 occurs. If the input, as analyzed, is a "mismatch" with the expectancy, then another result R_2, occurs.

Thus, an information-flow branches or decides, based upon the correspondence between expectancy and the analysis of the input. A diagram of such an information flow is shown in Fig. 3.

Now the question is, what are R_1 and R_2? Generally speaking, they are information flows.

Consider a subject in free recall of a list of adjectives that are grouped by him in a rather weak categorical system: (MILKY, CRIMSON, YELLOW),

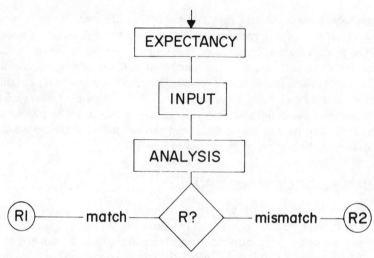

Fɪɢ. 3. Flow chart of an information flow.

((SKINNY, RIBALD), (RECKLESS, ARTLESS)). The first group is "colors or appearances," the second two groups are human characteristics. Of the human characteristic groups, one is a pair of near opposites; the other pair both end with "-LESS." A subject with this structure would enter the over-all expectancy and at once test if he had completed recalling the words, that is, if the expectancy of the total system was satisfied by the present situation. Of course, it is not, so he would have a mismatch and would drop down one level and start generating expectancies, which in this case might be either the "colors" or the "human characteristics." He at once tests to see if he has already recalled those words, and finds he has not. At this moment, both the over-all list information flow, and the human-characteristics subflow, are both active. He has not recalled the human words, and therefore his IF is not satisfied, and he must generate still lower-level expectancies. He might generate the expectancy that words end with "-LESS." Again he would test and decide he has not recalled these words, at which point he would begin to generate words ending in "-LESS," unless he actually has further structure. If he gets one he can initiate the behavior flow to report it, and then (when that report is finished) he can move back and test whether he has completed the IF of generating words ending in "-LESS." Whenever he decides he is finished with that category he terminates it, and that branch of the IF system becomes inactive. However, the higher-order IF is still active and the subject having finished a sub-part, returns to the next higher level. In this structure, he would then test whether he was done with the system of human characteristics, and would probably decide he was not. Then he would generate one of the expectancies, and he might again generate "ending in -LESS." Presumably, he would at once note that this is completed and would loop back up one stage again, repeating this until he either generated the other subcategory (a pair of opposites), or gave up and decided he was in fact finished with that general category of human characteristics.

Let us return to the subject reporting a word he recalls (ARTLESS) and is to report by typewriting. He sets up an expectancy and analysis of the finger movements, etc., that are to be controlled. However, the R_1 resulting from a match between my motor intention and input results in choosing to type the letter "A." This in turn results, when properly initiated, with a decision to use my left hand rather than right, then to work on the "home line" of the typewriter rather than above or below, and finally a choice of the little finger. At that point various muscular arrangements are made, including proper positioning of the arm and hand, and releasing the downward stroke of the key. This act also sets up an expectancy for a particular feedback of resistance, touch, and so forth, that results from a properly-executed key stroke. Therefore, a behavior flow, when it is finally initiated by a system of information flows, is not itself a simple thing but instead may be a complex structure.

It should be apparent that this information flow is a common concept in modern cognitive psychology. It has much in common with the TOTE unit, and in fact is merely something of an elaboration and generalization of that concept. However, though the information flow is not a very original concept, it is serviceable. And I propose it as the unit of cognitive organization.

The second question was, how do these units go together to make up an organization? The answer to that question is given by the statement that the two endpoints, R_1 and R_2 in Fig. 3, are both information flows, or behavior flows. If so,

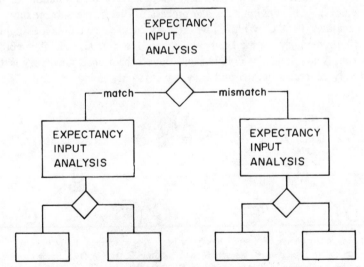

FIG. 4. Combination of information flows to make a sorting tree.

then what an information flow does is to decide between other information or behavior flows. One way of combining several information flows is into an hierarchy, a part of which is shown in Fig. 4. This, obviously, forms a simple sorting tree.

However, it is not possible to set up a functioning structure in which the system merely moves from above to below—there must be some way to get back up the tree. In fact, to be a proper description of a living cognitive or behavioral system, the flow must not start and stop arbitrarily, but instead must continue unceasingly in a loop—not a closed and rigid repetition of the same thoughts or acts, but also not a process that terminates. Only death terminates the system.

To enter an information flow and set up an expectancy is to initiate some segment of thought or behavior that may be spelled out in lower-order flows. When that segment of cognition or behavior is terminated, then control must be returned to the next higher level. How is this to be represented?

Yngve (1960), in his model of sentence production, supposed that whenever one segment of a sentence was initiated as the first of two, the other branch would also be generated and stored in memory. Then whenever the person actually uttered a word, this would terminate a branch of the tree, and he would return and take whatever was the last thing he had put into memory. This "push-down stack" memory serves as a way to keep track of which parts of the tree of behavior flows have been completed and which are to be done next. The process is indicated, in an abstract tree, in Fig. 5.

At the time Yngve's model was first put forward, it was a remarkable accomplishment. Yngve and others, especially Johnson (1965), who have used the theory have concentrated their theoretical discussions on the limitations of short-term memory. At the beginning of the process in Fig. 5, the subject starts with A and generates B and C. What Yngve's theory does is then store C, clogging up its short-term memory. However, there is no need to store C, since it can be generated from A any time. The only reason Yngve's theory needs memory is that it prematurely generates both B and C, when it is only going to use B. What it

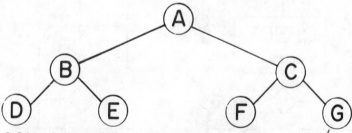

Fig. 5. Schematic picture of Yngve's theory for generating a sentence. 1. Generate A. 2. Generate B and C, store C. 3. From B, generate D and E. 4. Store E, perform D. 5. Being at a terminus, look at last thing in memory—it is E. 6. Perform E. 7. Again look in memory; last element is now C. 8. From C, generate F and G, store G, . . . , and so forth.

should have done, if it had problems in the capacity of its push-down stack was merely to generate B. When it finished at the terminus of D and E, it should have returned to A and, noting that it had finished with B, it then should have generated C.

All such a tree-traversal system needs to store is its present location. More precisely, it needs to know what branches of the tree have already been generated and which have not. It need not remember the content of those branches.

When a lower-order information flow is finished it transfers control to the flow just above it. If the lower-order flow is not finished, it is then carried out, and naturally it will then initiate a flow at a lower level. How can such a system be incorporated formally into an information-flow model?

Sometimes it may be necessary to "remember" where you are in a thought process or act, but more often the content of thought, or the external information guiding action, are sufficient cues to guide further decisions. When a particular information flow is completed, this means that the expectancy of the goal of the behavior matches the input. The requirements or conditions of the information flow are thereby satisfied, and this particular act is completed. The main decision to be made within an information flow, after the analysis of input has been compared with expectancy, is whether the act has been completed. If expectancy

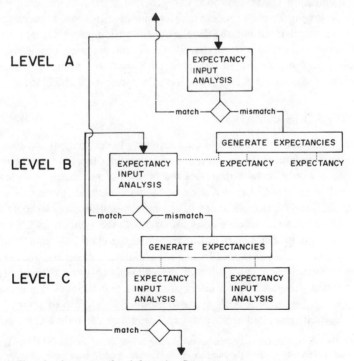

FIG. 6. Three-level segment of an information flow structure.

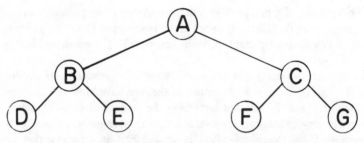

FIG. 7. Modified Yngve model of serial performance. 1. Generate A; it it unfinished. 2. Generate B; it also is unfinished. 3. Generate D. 4. Perform the behavior flow D; it is then finished. 5. Transfer control to B which is unfinished. 6. Generate E, which is then finished. 7. Return control to B, which is already finished. 8. Return control to A, unfinished. 9. Generate C, which is unfinished. 10. Generate F. The remainder of the process follows obvious steps.

and analysis agree, this generally means that the process is completed, and control is returned to the next higher level. If the analysis of the input mismatches the expectancy, then the information flow is not completed, and control must be transferred to a lower level to continue the unfinished work. Figure 6 illustrates a three-level segment of an information flow structure.[1]

The organization I have described can generate a sentence or serial pattern, generally following Yngve's process with a minor modification. Rather than storing the branches that will later be developed, the system generates a given node and then keeps a record of whether that node has or has not been completed. When it has been completed, control is transferred back up the tree to the next level. The process I propose is shown in Fig. 7, and it is to be compared with Fig. 6.

COGNITIVE ORGANIZATION

In order to mount my criticism of pure memory, I need to apply the above line of theoretical thinking in the most general way possible. Imagine that the process I described not only actually describes the process of generating a sentence or small serial pattern, but also governs a whole paragraph or conversation—that one sentence flows from a whole line of communication. In other words, that the process of generating a sentence does not start with the symbol "S" but with a higher-order system that generates this particular S rather than something else. The paragraph itself is generated by a more enduring and generalized information-flow system, one's knowledge of the subject—or more realistically, the conversation is generated by an information flow that includes one's grasp of one's own and the interlocutor's social positions. This grasp of mutual social position is itself generated from a system including the individual's position

---

[1]To some readers this diagram may seem almost as complicated as that for which I chided Professor Atkinson earlier. I merely mention the comparison, for I cannot qualify as an unbiased judge of such esthetic questions. Fig. 6 looks simple enough to *me*.

within his whole society, of which he and the partner are a subentity. A person's relationship to his society is perhaps part of his social motivational system, his system of affiliations, dominances, submissions, and so forth. This motivational system is itself part of a broader information flow, approaching a "personality." Whether this personality is or is not part of a still higher spiritual organization I shall not answer until I am equipped with appropriate experimental methods.

Realize that within this very complex structure, at least during waking hours (and perhaps with almost equal frequency and completeness during sleep) some part or other of this total personality organization is active. In fact, if it is a tree system, as diagrammed above in Fig. 7, and if various parts of the tree are marked "finished" and "unfinished," then at various times there may be nodes at many levels that are currently "unfinished" and in active process. Structures very high in the tree are probably active a large fraction of the time—in fact, one's "sense of identity" is under almost all conditions continuous—its loss is much more frequent in fiction than in real life, and is profoundly terrifying even to consider (Rokeach, 1960). I will have to delimit that statement if anyone says that when he dreams he is really someone else.

Certain kinds of semantic memory or knowledge, on the other hand, are tightly integrated into the usual on-going cognitive processes. Such information, though it can be retrieved rapidly and surely, is not actually called for very often. If I ask, "Are crows black?" you can say "Yes" quickly, even though it is possible that no one has asked you for that particular item of information in over 10 years. Why? Evidently such information is part of a system of information about common birds that is so high in the organizational tree that it is active all the time—or at least, it takes very little time to activate it from the situations that do exist at the time of questioning. I am not sure I believe this assertion, but it is a consequence of the position I am espousing here.

Now, if what I have said is true, there are not four levels of memory, but many levels. Furthermore, there are not only levels of memory, but more subtle distinctions to make. That is, common semantic information in the general area of a person's interest will show a different status from equally common semantic information in an area not used much—a nature-lover may quickly identify a "tern," a church-goer may be quicker with "pew," and a gambler with "flush." This would not mean that the information was at different levels in the over-all organization, but that different parts of essentially the same organization may usually be activated by people with different interests or personalities.

CONCLUSIONS

In this paper I have agreed with Craik and Lockhart that there are several levels of memory, but that they are not different memory stores with information being transferred from one store to another. Encoding is the process of incorporating information into a cognitive structure, and the depth of processing corresponds to the generality and size of the cognitive structure involved. Storage is the maintenance of the organization. The particular part of the organization that yields the answer may be continuously active during the period of remembering, or it may be that only a higher-order node remains active. If only a higher-order node remains active, then when a memory test is given the structure must be regenerated far enough to yield the answer. This process is usually called retrieval.

It is possible that the kinds of hierarchical trees I have used are only one example of cognitive structure, though I am inclined to accept the view that the principle of cognitive hierarchy is central to mental processing. What I have added to the conventional argument is (a) some more detail about the functional elements of cognitive structures, spelling out a "node" into an "information flow," and (b) giving somewhat more detail than usual about the tree traversal procedures intended.

One novelty of this theoretical effort, and the one that justifies the title of this chapter, is the assertion that there is no passive memory. Something is remembered only to the degree that it is part of a cognitive structure and that structure is active. If the structure S holding a given item should terminate, and if there is no higher-level structure which can generate S on demand, then that item is gone from memory. It is not stored somewhere indefinitely—it only remains accessible when it can be aroused by the structures that remain active.

Some writers think of a memory being "active" only when it is conscious and in the focus of attention. It is possible to argue, for example, that short-term memory or working memory contains those memories that are currently active. In my view, this position presents its supporters with unanswerable questions, for the very process that directs attention, that brings needed information to the mind from storage, is itself unconscious.

In my concept, at any time the subject is using a well-organized cognitive structure, there is some node active at each level from the very bottom structure shaping his responses (making phonemes, or extending muscles to reach typewriter keys) up through many intermediate levels to those nodes that are always active and constitute the highest levels of the personality. These higher-level activities are not in the focus of attention as we commonly use that term in psychology, though the person is in a somewhat more general sense aware of the direction and organization of his cognitive processes. A mathematician when writing down the letter "X" is still aware of the equation he is writing, or the line of argument or thought he is pursuing, his general strategy, and perhaps has some kind of consciousness of how this relates to his judgments of what is important. At least, his actions will show whether he feels the result he is getting is profound or trivial. A used-car salesman exudes enthusiasm and watches his customer closely, and is also aware of how long he has been talking, of apparent progress or of loss of interest, of how many cars he must sell to make a living, and so forth.

These higher-order activities, though not presented to the attention in the same form as lower-order branches and twigs, may be the most important mental events.

REFERENCES

Atkinson, R. C., & Shiffrin, R. M. Human memory: A proposed system and its control processes. In K. W. Spence & J. T. Spence (Eds.), *The psychology of learning and motivation: Advances in research and theory.* Vol. 2. New York: Academic Press, 1968.

Bower, G. H. Organizational factors in memory. *Cognitive Psychology,* 1970, **1**, 18–46.

Bower, G. H. Mental imagery and associative learning. In L. Gregg (Ed.), *Cognition in learning and memory.* New York: Wiley, 1972.

Bransford, J. D., & Franks, J. J. The abstraction of linguistic ideas. *Cognitive Psychology,* 1971, **2**, 331–350.

Collins, A. M., & Quillian, M. R. Retrieval time from semantic memory. *Journal of Verbal Learning and Verbal Behavior,* 1969, **8**, 240–247.

Collins, A. M., & Quillian, M. R. How to make a language user. In E. Tulving & W. Donaldson (Eds.), *Organization of memory.* New York: Academic Press, 1972.

Craik, F. I. M., & Lockhart, R. S. Levels of processing: A framework for memory research. *Journal of Verbal Learning and Verbal Behavior,* 1972, **11**, 671–684.

Gregory, R. L. *The intelligent eye.* London: Weidenfeld & Nicolson, 1970.

Johnson, N. F. The psychological reality of phrase structure rules. *Journal of Verbal Learning and Verbal Behavior,* 1965, **4**, 469–475.

Liberman, A. M., Cooper, F. S., Shankweiler, D. P., & Studdert-Kennedy, M. Perception of the speech code. *Psychological Review,* 1967, **74**, 431–461.

Mandler, G. Organization and memory. In K. W. Spence & J. T. Spence (Eds.), *The psychology of learning and motivation. Advances in research and theory.* Vol. 1. New York: Academic Press, 1967.

Paivio, A. *Imagery and verbal processes.* New York: Holt, Rinehart & Winston, 1971.

Potts, G. R. Information processing strategies used in the encoding of linear orderings. *Journal of Verbal Learning and Verbal Behavior,* 1972, **11**, 727–740.

Restle, F. Theory of serial pattern learning: Structural trees. *Psychological Review,* 1970, **77**, 481–495.

Rokeach, M. *The open and closed mind.* New York: Basic Books, 1960.

Shiffrin, R. M. Memory search. In D. A. Norman (Ed.), *Models of human memory.* New York: Academic Press, 1970.

Shiffrin, R. M., & Geisler, W. S. Visual recognition in a theory of information processing. In R. L. Solso (Ed.), *Contemporary issues in cognitive psychology: The Loyola symposium.* Washington: Winston, 1973.

Sternberg, S. Two operations in character-recognition: Some evidence from reaction-time measurements. *Perception & Psychophysics,* 1967, **2**, 45–53.

Tulving, E., & Donaldson, W. (Eds.) *Organization of memory.* New York: Academic Press, 1972.

Yngve, V. H. A model and a hypothesis for language structure. *Proceedings of the American Philosophical Society,* 1960, **104**, 444–466.

8
DISCUSSION: SECTION I

Following the formal presentation of an abstract of the preceding seven chapters, an informal discussion was held. This section contains the edited transcript of that discussion. The discussion members were:

Richard C. Atkinson
Stanford University

Douglas L. Hintzman
University of Oregon

James J. Jenkins
University of Minnesota

Donald H. Kausler
University of Missouri

William Macey
Loyola University of Chicago

Jacqueline Metzler
Stanford University

Frank Restle
Indiana University

Roger N. Shepard
Stanford University

Robert L. Solso
Loyola University of Chicago

SOLSO: In viewing the papers presented in this section of the symposium, I was alternately impressed with some striking similarities and some obvious differences. For example, the theme of memory must certainly be central to the *Zeit-*

219

geist of neo-cognition as each of the authors spent some time reviewing their impression of it, or using memory structure in their analysis, but the impressions are disparate.

Jenkins, in the first paper, approaches the problem of memory from the outside looking in—much as was suggested in my own paper—rather than from the standpoint of memory modelers who sometimes seem to be inside looking out. His plea is to build a theory of remembering, and I sense that his technique is similar to an archeologist trying to make visible poorly resolved stone etchings by placing onion skin over them and rubbing charcoal on the paper. The material he uses for the rubbings are verbal material and the impressions are the remembered things. His research seems to be directed at forming more powerful demonstrations of the memory etchings. In developing the things remembered, he may then have a reliable basis for inferring how they were learned, and perhaps a basis for building a model of memory.

My impression of memory is that it is composed of a loosely structured network of processed information in which associative relationships exist within the structure and possibly between structures. I feel that a more complete delineation of memory structure is premature at this time, and I choose to deal on an empirical basis with stimuli that may ultimately make visible the details of the structure and the rules related to getting in and out of it.

Kausler is even less concerned with a model of memory in his paper. He reflects the verbal-learning tradition of forging precise functional relationships between frequency of experience with verbal cues and their recognition by subjects. He is specifically concerned with expanding frequency theory to include featural components of verbal items. It seems he is abstracting the best of two theories—frequency theory and associative theory—into a comprehensive theory which allows the best of two worlds to live compatibly—indeed, even complementarily.

Hintzman, while dealing with the effects of temporally distributed verbal items, seems most comfortable with a habituation notion of the spacing effect. He used habituation theory to imply that a particular kind of internal response—that of storing a long-term memory trace of the event—is effected. Perhaps in the discussion, Hintzman will react to Kausler's notion of featural components being the recipients of frequency-of-response tags.

Atkinson, Herrman and Wescourt present the most definitive view of a memory system of all the papers. The complete system cannot be summarized easily, and the reader is encouraged to study their lucid description in Chapter 5. I was particulary gratified to learn that their memory network was not a fully-connected network but that, at least within the LTS, the EKS was conceptualized as a partially-connected network in which similar and/or related events are stored within a small neighborhood of space.

Metzler and Shepard have presented further reaction-time evidence to support their theory that some cognitive processes are analog in nature. In addition to their "classic" experiment (Shepard & Metzler, 1971) they have successfully isolated an even dozen factors which influence subjects' reaction time in making decisions on the identity of rotated three-dimensional shapes. They have gone a long way in enlightening us as to what these data really mean, and perhaps in this discussion will tell us even more.

Finally, Restle has shocked all of us by suggesting that we have stretched memory "entirely beyond its natural compass" and reminded us that, "For most theoretical purposes where structured memories have been used, it is the structure that is necessary and not the memory." If we take this notion seriously, a good many gainfully employed psychologists and an equal number of draftsmen may as well pack up their charts and follow a career in abstract art. Restle's paper on "Critique of Pure Memory" has a familiar cant to it and he, as his ancient philosophic counterpart, may be trying to rid the world of alchemists. Perhaps psychology is ready for a renaissance. He does soften his criticism at the end of his paper by acknowledging that deep down there may be such a thing as pure memory, but until he remembers it, he is going to forget it.

If I could start the discussion by looking at one aspect that is relatively common to many of these papers, the topic of memory structure, with perhaps the exception of the Metzler and Shepard paper, and arrange these in some type of continuum, I'll ask a question to open up the discussion and then many of the distinguished members of the audience will have an opportunity to ask questions.

If we take the concept of memory structure and review the papers, Metzler and Shepard avoid any mention of structure and deal with "pure cognition," which to me was reminiscent of Tolman's concept of cognition. Jenkins, on the other hand, asks that we build a theory of memory search. Kausler is functional in his research; he uses, at least in this paper, very few memory constructs. Hintzman reflects his data in light of the theories of Bower and Shiffrin. Solso developed a mini-memory structure—only large enough to encompass the inter-structural associative paradox—Atkinson, Herrman and Wescourt have developed an extensive theory of a memory model, and Restle views memory structure from the standpoint of an iconoclast. The question that I would like to ask of the group is what is the *purpose* of building memory structures? Would somebody like to react to that?

JENKINS: I can't speak for anyone else, of course, but my research group has an underlying purpose in trying to build structures that account for memory—the purpose is to understand the nature of the mind. The problem so far as the field is concerned is that every time we start out to build a structure that will do what we know people can do, we fall back to some form of the simple associative theory. We talk of items connected in a string, items located in a net, or, if we are being especially elaborate, a hierarchy of items. I believe that we ought to try models that are more sophisticated than that. Surely the mind is not limited to lists, nets, and trees.

There are many more powerful representations of the world that the mind constructs. Whether we can get those representations out of our heads and down on paper in symbolic form is another problem. See what powerful things a mathematician can do with set theory or group theory and you have some notion of the kind of power that is available in generative systems. For some particular system, a mathematician can tell you what the characteristics of the group generators must be. Then you can play psychologist and give the subject experience with the generators and see if he can generate the missing members of the group, or can recognize them when they are presented, or can identify items that "belong" as opposed to those that do not, etc. (The many exciting experiments of Bransford and Franks are of this sort. For examples see Bransford and Franks, 1971, and Franks and Bransford, 1972.)

Most of the experimentation that we do is pretty static. We expect the subject to behave like a copying machine, and if he does something different we score that as an error and try to shape him up to do our thing. The dead hand of traditional theory tells us what to do and what to look at. The surprising thing about the experiments that I talked about is that by having the subject do some simple active semantic work, he gets the remembering "for free."

Now, we mustn't expect that all remembering will come for free. If the "memory object" is a related set of, say, half a dozen items, and we give the subject information about only pairs of items ("A is to the left of D, B is to the right of A, E is to the left of C . . ."), he will not automatically construct the array by listening to the sentences. (See Barclay, 1973). We can get him to construct the array by telling him what kind of structure to build. When he does that, he will not remember the specific input sentences that he heard, but he will be able to tell us anything that is true about the arrangement of that set and he can reject anything that is false. If we ask him to remember the *sentences,* he will not be able to tell us about the "object" and, because of the interference at the sentence level, he will not be able to tell us what he heard either! This, rather importantly, tells us something about what the mind is good at and what it is poor at. It also raises the questions about the *levels* at which we see phenomena. If the "object" is the array, there is no confusion and no interference. If the "object" is each sentence, the interference is overwhelming. If the task is to construct only that set of sentences, the subject is clearly a failure.

What this says to me is that everything that you can get your head to do (building arrangements, transforming them, generating new arrangements and new transforms, etc.) can be used in remembering. It is a dangerous simplification, I believe, to talk about remembering as a storage of items in nets. It is far too easy to cheat by solving the storage and retrieval problems via *ad hoc* features and relations. If we allow ourselves to postulate the features and relations that we need every time we want them, we can explain absolutely anything. The problem is to develop a *finite* list of features and relations; or, more importantly, to characterize the mental mechanisms that let us (and our subjects) generate the features and relations appropriate to our tasks, our materials, our abilities, and the knowledge that we already have. If we can specify that machinery, then we have no special problem left in memory (as Restle has so successfully pointed out); there is only structure left.

This moves our problem back one step. It is no longer, "how is memory represented?" or, "How is knowledge represented?" It now becomes, "How shall we represent the machines of the mind that create our representations of knowledge and memory?"

SOLSO: Bill Macey, what's your impression of this?

MACEY: Off the cuff, I think that the whole idea of structure in memory is merely to describe the relationship between the different things that we have in memory. Not that I would like to throw away all operations concerning structure, but it would seem that it might be best to begin looking at memory as being a collection of features or attributes. If that is the case, we can say that items, events, occurrences, etc., may have several things in common. These commonalities would then determine the number of different dimensions that are useful to distinguish in memory. The relationships of items, or "structure," might then be determined by proximity along these different dimensions. Now, the problem I see with this approach is that it's always just a little too easy to add another floor to the structure. I think the primary difficulty we are going to have is to determine when such features actually exist or when we are just deducing them on the basis of our data.

JENKINS: Do you think that it's a finite list?

MACEY: Do I think it's finite? Let's put it this way, let's make it countably infinite!!!

SOLSO: I have a burning interest in what Frank Restle will say about memory structures after reading his paper.

RESTLE: I have some ideas on what this is all about. I recently received a paper called "Serial Learning Theory" by Edwin Martin, in which he says that he is "entirely pessimistic about the long-term utility of the nice, neat, binary constituent trees used by Johnson (1972) and Restle (1970) in analyzing sequential tasks they explicitly designed to fit such trees." The usual methods of serial learning show that if you use word lists or nonsense material, if you disorganize the task sufficiently, you are able to disorganize the subject. Then, the results of the experiments become correspondingly more complicated to understand. It may be that serial learning, as studied in the laboratory, is far more complicated than serial pattern learning, playing the piano, or speaking English.

Experimental research results in an understanding and a theory of the task the subject is working on. Atkinson's paper on rapid recognition of words in lists is a good and complete example of this process. It is also characteristic of work with artificial intelligence that researchers pick a task and then investigate the requirements of the task itself.

This means that it is important to choose an important task. I feel that we have dug ourselves into deep pits sometimes by studying a task just because it is there and has been useful at some time in the past to answer some theoretical question.

This may be true of recognition tasks, of paired associates, of concept identification, and in fact of any task we study. I think that the newer work, which consists of having a subject read or hear a paragraph and then answer sensible questions about it, the kind of work done by Bransford and Franks, by Huttenlocher, by Clark and by Potts and Scholz, meets my criterion. The task is typical of what people have to do all the time, it is important, and the material used can be highly organized rather than being a mere list. Such tasks are intrinsically more interesting than verbal-learning procedures and not necessarily more difficult for the subject.

A second point I should like to make is in support of Dr. Jenkins, that in the area of cognitive psychology there are probably no constants. As we should have learned from Noam Chomsky, we are not dealing with a physical device but with the human mind. One characteristic of a human being is that any time you observe it doing something and it finds out what you have observed, it can do the same task another way or it can switch to another task. It is an intrinsically generative system. When we try to fit human cognition into an axiom system or a fixed model we are constantly disappointed because we find that subjects can get out from under the particular model we propose.

I am not sure what to do with this difficulty. Jenkins mentioned that he wants to find out how subjects generate knowledge. This is the right question. The fearful possibility is that as soon as we answer Jenkins's question, some subject will generate a new way of generating . . .

HINTZMAN: Maybe I can react to the original question. Having been at Stanford and become familiar with a number of memory models, I think I acquired a good, healthy skepticism about them. The problem is that you can fit your model to a very specific experimental situation, and as long as you stay within that paradigm things will work out pretty well; but the model will have very little generality. (I find that I am impressed, despite my skepticism, with the way that Dick Atkinson has been able to fit data with his model). But the over-all impression I have—and this is how I interpret what the other people were saying—is that there are very few experimental findings that are really general enough to be attributed to the structure of the memory system. Most experimental outcomes probably have more to do with the structure of the task. Maybe memory theorists should only focus on those phenomena that appear in a wide variety of memory tasks.

This is why I am especially interested in the spacing effect. It is so general that there doesn't seem to be any way to get rid of it; and most importantly, it's there no matter what kind of experimental materials you use. Perhaps theorists interested in the structure of the memory mechanism, rather than the contents of the mechanism, should be trying to understand the fundamental variables that always have the same effects, no matter what the task—in particular, recency, frequency, and the spacing of repetitions. Ultimately, we may find that a structural model of memory only needs to account for effects of these basic variables. Most of the other memory phenomena that have been investigated may best be explained instead in terms of the contents of memory, the structure of the task, and the strategies subjects adopt in dealing with the task.

SOLSO: Don Kausler, in your recent book, you reviewed the concept of memory structure. Would you care to comment on the present review from this historical perspective?

KAUSLER: I wish this discussion had occurred before I finished certain chapters in the book—it would have been most helpful. The review you mentioned contrasted classical associationism and contemporary cognitive approaches to memory, especially those of information processing. Memory as an associative structure, or organization, has deep roots in verbal learning's prescientific history. It was natural for Ebbinghaus to view learning and memory in these terms. Learning a rote serial list leads to a new structure of sequential associations, however temporary that structure might be. This concept of structure is still a potent force in memory research. Later associationists added more permanent structures in the form of pre-experimental associative hierarchies that the subject brings with him into the laboratory. These structures have been useful sources of explaining mediated transfer, extra-experimental interference, and so on. Components of these hierarchies are aroused as implicit associative responses, presumably whenever words are responded to as elements of a study list. The concept of an implicit associative response has played an important role in recent extensions of memory, such as yours (Solso) and also the false-recognition phenomenon. My review was somewhat pessimistic about the concept, largely because the functional relationships based upon it haven't worked out very well. This is especially true for recognition memory. A structure based on an organization of featural components of words that are stored within some form of permanent memory seems more promising to me. The featural concept has already stimulated productive research on such neglected topics as phonemic and orthographic variables. The nature of the organization, such as binary, hierarchical, and so on, is likely to be an area of active interest for some years to come.

SOLSO: The final group we haven't heard from (and probably they are the least reliant on structured memory) are Metzler and Shepard. Do you have any reactions to our discussion?

SHEPARD: Yes, I think I disagree with the implication that we weren't as much concerned with structure and memory.

SOLSO: I am here to be enlightened on that point.

SHEPARD: I think the notion of structure is central to what Jackie and I have been saying. There may be a difference, though, in where the structure is being placed. Those other speakers who have been especially concerned with structure have been assigning it primarily to the system that is processing and storing the information (in terms of the relationship, interconnection, and flow of control among boxes representing subprocesses in a more or less rigidly fixed system). For them the question of just how the information that is processed through these boxes (typically letters or words) is structured or structurally transformed often seems to be of only secondary concern. Our principal interest, on the other hand, has focused precisely on this *representational* problem—the problem of how the information that is being processed is itself structurally represented and transformed within the system—particularly when this information is nonverbal in nature.

We argue that the ability of subjects to anticipate the appearance of a structurally complex, rotated three-dimensional object in such a way as to make a rapid and accurate response of "match" or "mismatch" (as soon as that object appears) indicates, first, that the internal representation embodies important structural information about the anticipated stimulus and, second, that the transformation that is internally applied to this representation in order to prepare for its rotated appearance embodies important structural rules about the way perspective projections behave under rigid motions of their objects.

I believe, further, that the structural phenomena with which we are dealing have important implications for the study of human memory. This becomes particularly clear in the kind of experiment that Jackie has done in her thesis. I mean the experiment in which a delay was interposed between the offset of the first stimulus and the onset of the second. Notice that the internal process that intervened between the two presentations in this experiment was not a passively fading memory trace of the first stimulus but a process of active and systematic transformation. I want therefore to reinforce Jim Jenkins' earlier remarks on the active nature of human cognition. Along with him, I would suggest that much research on memory fails to appreciate the dynamic, goal-directed nature of thought by treating man as little more than a passive repository of satic words and pictures.

Another aspect of our work that appears to distinguish it from that of many of the speakers here is its emphasis upon *nonverbal* internal representation. It's not that verbal processes are unimportant. It's only that nonverbal processes, though much less studied, may be just as important. Of course, verbal representations are essential in communication. But their implicit occurrence during private thought may often amount to a merely habitual, epiphenomenal concomitant of that thought—they need not constitute its underlying dynamism or essence.

My own feeling has been that, in large part, thinking by humans (and probably by other higher animals as well) is basically analogical in nature. When the situation in which we find ourselves is, as it usually is, in some way incomplete or tantalizing, or else threatening or painful, we imagine a situation that represents a completion or satisfaction, or else a removal of the threat or pain. We then try out various possible transformations, mentally, in order to determine which one is likely to succeed in converting the existing state of the external world into the more desired state. (As Solso has already suggested, this viewpoint represents something of a recurrence of some of Tolman's old ideas concerning the role in behavior of "cognitive maps," "expectancies," and the like). Examples range from the most simple and largely unconscious servomechanical acts, such as picking up a pencil, to highly skilled or intellectual efforts, such as mentally rehearsing a complex high dive or designing a high-energy particle accelerator. It strikes me that such tasks depend heavily upon subtle or complex spatial components, and, hence, are governed by processes that are largely analog in character. Indeed, translation into the digital form of purely verbal communication often turns out to be almost impossible.

As we mention in our paper, it is easy to see why verbal mediational processes have come to be studied so much: Internal representations are so much more readily externalized when they are letters, numbers, or words than when they are images, schemata, or spatial transformations. Our recent results encourage us to hope, though, that new experimental techniques will enable us to gain significant structural information about such nonverbal internal representations, their transformations, and their role in human cognition generally.

SOLSO: Are there audience questions . . . Dr. Loftus:

LOFTUS: I don't exactly have a question, but I would like to say something about structure. That is, if you are going to have a theory about retrieval, it seems to me that you have to have something to retrieve from. One of the main reasons that I and other people postulate structures is to have some place from which information can be retrieved. One problem with a theory that postulates structure and also postulates a retrieval scheme is that it is hard to keep them apart. If you find experimental support for the theory, then you have supported the structure and the retrieval scheme; if your experiment doesn't "come out," then you don't know where you have gone wrong.

And I also wanted to say something to Jim Jenkins . . . he said something like "strings, networks, hierarchies . . . there must be a better representation," and what I want to say about that is the following: If I asked you over for dinner and I made some beef stroganoff, and you said to me, "There must be a better beef stroganoff," I would say, "When you find it, I'll come over to your house for dinner!"

JENKINS: There are two "standard" lectures that I give to my graduate students. With your kind permission, I would like to give them here since one is relevant to Loftus's question, and the other relates to the earlier discussion of "simplicity."

Lecture I—the reason that the Gestalt psychologists didn't take over academic psychology in the United States wasn't because the Gestalt psychologists were not right. As a matter of fact, it was clear in some sense that they *were* right. Everyone knows that they had demonstrations that no one could account for . . . demonstrations clearly outside the scope of the prevailing theories. The reason the Gestalters didn't win was that they never got past the phase of demonstrations. Everyone looked at the demonstrations and said, "Wow!" and then they went back to their laboratories and did the same things that they had always done. Why? Because those were the things that they knew how to do, that related to the theories that were extant, and that fit the prevailing "paradigms." The Gestalt psychologists never came up with a theory—they never delivered the new beef stroganoff. They gave tasks, sniffs, and views, but they never gave the recipe.

I agree with Dr. Loftus. Unless we deliver the recipe (or the new family of recipes), all the current struggle and confrontation isn't going to mean a thing. Clearly, we have an enormous job to do to "deliver it." We don't have it yet to deliver. We must still find the better set of models or metaphors.

I was just looking at Restle's note pad and I saw Frank writing down other metaphors. Consider "holograms" for example. The hologram is a radically different metaphor for memory from our traditional strings and nets. Holograms are so different they are frightening. We don't know the parallels for the required amplitudes, frequencies, and angles. But the physicist can perform miraculous "retrieval" feats that are startling with stacks of holograms. If we have a piece of one of the holograms that is in the stack, and we shine a light through it and through the stack, the original total image glows—a physical instance of redintegration that the functionalists used to talk about. How about that?

The point is that there are a lot of exciting candidates for new metaphors or models that we must examine. The "clarion call" of the present is not to *a* new model but to a call to look for better models.

Lecture II—this lecture is on *simplicity* and *faith*. Everybody (and most especially experimentalists) argues that we should begin with simple things and work up to complicated things. A favorite form of argument is, "if we can't understand a simple thing like this, we have no chance at all of understanding . . ." I always illustrate this to my students by saying, "That's exactly right. So if we are going to study locomotion, we should begin with something really easy, like how does one ride a unicycle? Then when we have that licked, we will move up to the bicycle. When we figure that out, we can try to understand the tricycle. Finally, we may get to something as complicated as the wagon!"

Well, of course, you will object that that is an incorrect analysis. The simplicity of operation is not measured by counting the number of wheels. In fact, it is the inverse. The moral, of course, is: "*Simplicity is not always what it appears to be.*"

This brings in the related question of faith in our favorite procedure. I am sure that it is a procedure that every experimenter believes in. The faith is that if you can take some small area and make a model that works well under that constrained condition, then you can ease up on the constraints and take in more and more of the world. Start small and include more and more as you go along.

I would like to believe that this view is correct and that this is the way science ought to work, but I don't think there is much reason to believe that it is true. (Both Restle and Shepard have made this point.) It may well be that the "natural phenomena" (the things we are wired to do because we are the kinds of creatures that we are) even though they appear global and complicated, need to be tackled on their own level. This may be the only level at which we can cut nature "at the seams." It may be only at the apparently complex level that we can find out what truly "simple" means. When we force behavior into the restricted set of actions we usually look at in the lab, we may make the human being behave like a very odd kind of machine. We may then fall victim to our own creation and say that we must delay attacking complicated behavior while we work harder in trying to understand the unnatural thing that we have created. So we devote years to it and wind up writing a theory of the experiment rather than a theory of man.

It seems to me that there is a middle course that all rational men will admit is best. (You can see that the end of the lecture is coming.) We ought to study natural phenomena as much as we can. If we must build a theory of the task anyway, let us take a task that we care about—like, how do people perceive objects in space and recognize those objects when they see them from other points of view? That is a pretty good problem. Whether you are alive or dead may depend on your ability to handle problems like that. Once you have taken a problem that you care about, a very important interaction may take place between the world and the laboratory. I think it is a powerful corrective to have the world intrude on the laboratory as well as the laboratory on the world. It keeps the work focused or centered. My favorite example is the research on speech perception. The speech perception problem turned out to be an excellent problem for a number of reasons—it is something special that only humans can do; it is a very important thing for people to do; the experimenter can readily judge when he is making progress, etc. The progress that has been made on understanding speech perception has been very impressive over the last 25 years. Interestingly enough, the progress did not come from the traditional work on psychoacoustics on pure tones. Even yet, no one knows how to bridge the gap between the two fields. Two relatively independent disciplines are building up; one in speech perception, and the other in psychoacoustics. For our purposes it is important to note that you don't understand speech perception by doing more and more psychoacoustics; you get there by tackling speech perception itself.

THEIOS: Hearing today's discussion about what should or should not be the structure of memory has made me think about the history of science, especially the history of physical science. I cannot help but think of the analysis that Thomas S. Kuhn has given, that at any moment in time what a group of scientists think is going on in the universe is really a figment of their imagination. They build up a series of structures that will cover the data in which they are interested, but in a few years others will come up with theories or structures that are even more wild than those. It seems to me that our fate is going to be just that, but at a much more accelerated rate due to the current information explosion. I for one cannot keep up with the proliferation of different ways that people represent theories these days, especially the theories about memory. And I am very alarmed about this. Given the limited amount of time we have, the choice of what memory theorists to read and study is not a trivial decision. One of the greatest questions facing us is, "Is not there anything more to the memory system than just the way a few scientists would have you think about it?"

SOLSO: With that puzzle, we will close the discussion.

REFERENCES

Barclay, J. R. The role or comprehension in remembering sentences. *Cognitive Psychology,* 1973, **4**, 229–254.

Bransford, J. D., & Franks, J. J. The abstraction of linguistic ideas. *Cognitive Psychology,* 1971, **2**, 331–350.

Franks, J. J., & Bransford, J. D. The acquisition of abstract ideas. *Journal of Verbal Learning and Verbal Behavior,* 1972, **11**, 311–355.

Johnson, N. F. Organization and the concept of a memory code. In A. W. Melton & E. Martin (Eds.) *Coding processes in human memory.* Washington: Winston, 1972.

Restle, F. Theory of serial pattern learning: Structural trees. *Psychological Review,* 1970, **77**, 481–495.

Shepard, R. N., & Metzler, J. Mental rotation of three-dimenional objects. *Science,* 1971, **171**, 701–702.

SECTION II

9
AN INFERENCE MODEL FOR CONCEPTUAL RULE LEARNING[1]

L. E. Bourne, Jr.
University of Colorado

A variety of cognitive events and processes characterize the performance of human beings as they attempt to solve conceptual problems. Many of us have been engaged, in recent years, in an attempt to identify and to isolate some of the most important of these processes for examination in the laboratory. In this paper I wish to summarize one line of research which has developed from this approach. My purpose will be to develop a specific model of performance in one kind of conceptual task, the rule-learning problem. The route to that goal will be a bit circuitous for, to place this model in proper context, a number of general matters must be addressed. Thus we shall consider some definitions, some matters of methodology, and some global theoretical issues, all before coming to grips with concrete questions about rule learning.

PRELIMINARY ISSUES

Definition of a Concept

Our assumption is that most concepts, real or imaginary, can be defined in terms of a listing of relevant or criterial stimulus attributes and some rule-form relationship among them. The concepts of central concern to us are categorical, nominal, or class concepts. We assume that any such concept, C, can be described in general form as follows: $C = R (x, y, \ldots)$, where $(x, y, \ldots)$

[1]This research was undertaken within the Institute for the Study of Intellectual Behavior and is publication no. 36 of the Institute. The work was supported by a research grant, MH 14314, and a Research Scientist Award 1-K5-MH-37497, both from the National Institute of Mental Health, and by GB-34077X from the National Science Foundation. The author wishes to thank Peder Johnson and Rita Yaroush for their critical comments on earlier versions of this manuscript.

are the relevant attributes of the concept, C, and R is some relationship among attributes. Such a concept divides the universe of objects, events, processes, and states of affairs into two categories—positive instances, that is, stimuli which are consistent with the concept description, and negative instances, that is, stimuli which are inconsistent with the concept description. It is assumed that this general descriptive form applies to many concepts in the real world, no matter how concrete or abstract. The concept of a *red triangle* can be described as a *conjunction (R)* of *redness (x)* and *triangularity (y)*. The concept of a *strike* in baseball (slightly simplified) is a *disjunction (R)* of *pitched ball passing through an imaginary rectangle above home plate (x)* and *pitched ball swung at and missed (y)*.

Conceptual Tasks

There is an infinite variety of conceptual problems one might give a human being to solve. Our research program has been limited basically to two, which are predicated on the utility of the foregoing definition of concepts. We give tasks suggestive names. In an *attribute identification* problem, we tell S what the relationship among relevant attributes is, leaving him the task of figuring out which of several variable attributes of the stimuli is or are relevant to the unknown concept. In *rule learning,* we list the relevant attributes beforehand for S, leaving him the task of determining the correct relationship among those attributes for a complete concept description. Diagrammatically,

Attribute identification: $C \equiv R\,(\underline{?},\underline{?},\ldots)$
Rule learning: $C \equiv ?\,(x, y, \ldots)$.

In attribute identification, the relationship is given and the relevant attributes are unknowns. In rule learning, the attributes are the givens and the relationship is an unknown.

Specifics of a Rule Learning Problem

Instructions. In a rule learning experiment, the session begins with a set of instructions delivered by E to S. These instructions are nondeceptive. The E tells S all he needs to know to solve the problem, short of the solution itself or a strategy which will produce it. The general nature of a class concept is outlined. Stimulus dimensions and values within dimensions are listed for S's reference throughout the problem. The S is told about the kind of responses he is required to make and the kind of feedback he can expect to get about the correctness of those responses. In most of the studies to be discussed, S will make a category response to each stimulus, naming it either a positive or a negative instance. He will be told immediately thereafter whether his response is correct or not.

Next, an illustrative concept is given and E demonstrates how a series of stimuli might be categorized according to the concept. The S is asked to do the same thing on his own. When both S and E are confident about the general nature of the task, the experimental problem begins. Because these are rule-learning problems, E names the two relevant attributes and lists them for S's reference throughout the problem. The S is told that he must find a relationship between the two given relevant attributes which will allow him to classify, without error, all stimuli subsequently presented to him.

Nature of the rule. For a variety of reasons, most rule-learning research has been structured on a set of relationships derived from propositional logic or set theory. We shall consider only binary relationships, which combine two attributes to specify a class. An example would be a familiar conjunctive relationship, "and." The concept in question consists of all stimuli that exhibit both attribute x and y, say, for example, both *redness* and *squareness*. There are 16 binary relationships in the complete calculus. They are not entirely unique, however, and we have shown elsewhere (Haygood & Bourne, 1965) that the calculus is well represented by what we have called the four primary bidimensional rules. These rules are described in Table 1. They are, in summary, the conjunctive "and," the inclusive disjunctive "and/or," the conditional "if, then," and the biconditional "if and only if." The positive and negative categories formed by applying each of these rules to the relevant attributes, redness and squareness, are shown, for illustrative purposes, in Fig. 1.

The task. In a rule-learning problem, S will be required to learn a particular way, such as one of those illustrated in Fig. 1, of partitioning some well-known stimulus population. We begin by presenting a stimulus that S must categorize as positive or negative. The S's response is followed by informative feedback and a short intertrial interval during which he has a chance to think about things. Then, a new stimulus is presented. Again S must respond, and again he receives feedback. This series continues until S can classify a series of stimuli without error and/or can verbalize the rule or concept.

TABLE 1

Primary Bidimensional Rules Describing Binary Partitions
of a Population of Geometric Designs

Name	Symbolic description[a]	Verbal description
Conjunctive (Cj)	R ∩ S	All patterns which are red and square are examples
Inclusive disjunctive (Dj)	R ∪ S	All patterns which are red or square or both are examples
Conditional (Cd)	R → S $[\bar{R} ∪ S]$	If a pattern is red then it must be square to be an example
Biconditional (Bd)	R ↔ S $[(R ∩ S) ∪ (\bar{R} ∩ \bar{S})]$	Red patterns are examples if and only if they are square

[a]R and S stand for red and square (relevant attributes), respectively. Symbolic descriptions using only three basic operations, ∩, ∪, and negation, are given in brackets.

ILLUSTRATIVE PARTITIONS

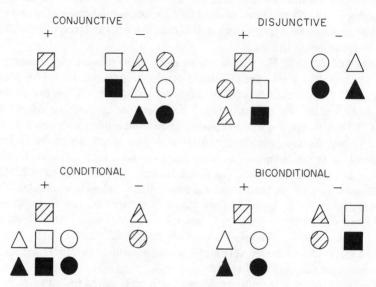

FIG. 1. Illustrations of the binary partitions generated by the four primary rules when redness (cross hatching) and squareness are the two relevant attributes.

PROCESSES IN CONCEPTUAL PROBLEM SOLVING

What does S do to solve a rule-learning problem? In recent years it has become abundantly clear that S's problem-solving behavior is best characterized by a system of operations or principles. I'd call it a rule system if it were not for the confusion engendered by using that term in reference to both a relationship among physical stimulus attributes and behavioral processes. The specifics of these operations are not entirely obvious. Still, we do have a skeleton outline of what is going on and have developed, from that outline, a rudimentary model that gives us the general details of some aspects of S's activity.

In our view, S's operations can be distinguished and categorized along qualitative, substantive dimensions. They have reference to various components or processes in behavior, that is, to the different processes S performs on information in the course of deciding how to perform. In this discussion, I commonly use the concepts of an information-processing system, for they cover handily most of the operations we know about. It should be borne in mind, however, that we think of these operations as descriptions of what S is doing, i.e., his behavior, rather than a description of some physical computing machine. Reference to Fig. 2, which is an intentionally harmless representation of the interplay of the processes involved, will help in following this discussion.

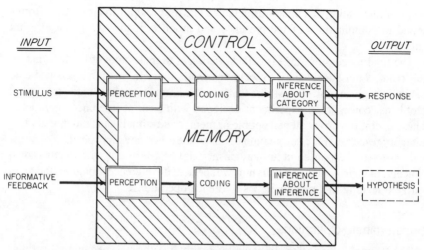

FIG. 2. Idealized representation of some of the processes involved in conceptual problem solving. Front-line operations, viz., perception, coding, and inference, are carried out against a background of memory, i.e., knowledge and skill, and control. Representation shows how these processes operate on the two sources of solution-relevant information available to S on any trial of a problem, the stimulus and informative feedback after S's response.

Frontline Operations

On each trial, a stimulus is presented and S must decide how to respond to it. The initial stage of information processing is *perceptual*. At the outset of most problems, S must perceive all attributes of the stimulus exactly. Failure to register certain attributes (for example, seeing a single large red square as "one red square") or inaccurate perception of one or more attributes (seeing the same stimulus as "one medium-sized red square") will, in general, affect performance adversely. If the problem involves rule learning, then, in principle, S need only attend to and therefore perceive the values of a stimulus on dimensions which contain the two given relevant attributes. Still, the same consideration holds in this case for a smaller number of stimulus attributes.

Secondly, perceived information passes through a *coding* stage. We see this stage as distinct and independent of perception. In rule-learning problems, we envision three primary coding possibilities, differing in terms of their efficiency in this type of task. The first is really the null case; the stimulus-as-perceived is merely passed along to the next stage of processing. Another possibility is to introduce a gate (Posner, 1964) into the flow of perceived information, eliminating the values taken by any stimulus on irrelevant dimensions. Thus, S codes the stimulus-as-perceived in terms of its two values on the given two relevant dimensions. The third coding possibility represents the highest level of coding relevant to rule-learning problems. In this case, the stimulus-as-perceived is coded in terms of its location in a binary truth table. The four rows of the truth table correspond to combinations of the presence and absence of the two given relevant attributes.

The final processing stage is called *inference*, to make note of the fact that, at this point, S must decide how to act upon the stimulus information made available to him on a given trial. We assume that an adult S, no matter how naive to concept problems, comes to an experiment equipped with a set of inference operations. These operations cover all perceptible or memorized stimuli and lead directly to a category response, i.e., designation of one or the other category, positive or negative instance. Response output may or may not be consistent with the unknown concept, of course, and when it is not, we speak of an inference violation, the main variable leading to a change in S's inference operations.

Superordinate Operations

The flow of information, initiated by a stimulus, through perceptual, coding, and inference operations is affected by two higher-order systems. The first is *memory* (or knowledge). Conceptual tasks are so designed that, by definition, no stimulus ever provides sufficient information for S to solve the problem. He must see and integrate information from two or more stimuli. We shall not dwell on types of memory, for relatively little is known about the uniqueness of their contributions in concept formation, and they have been considered in detail elsewhere (e.g., Norman, 1969). Here, we need only note that because the two or more stimuli required to solve a problem are spread out over a series of trials of several minutes duration, S *must* make use of information commited to a relatively long-term storage system.

One fact about the function of memory in concept problems is quite clear and central to the characterization of concept learning employed in this paper. The content of memory is both factual and propositional. The S retains both specific (detailed) information about the events of preceding trials, such as previously-seen stimuli and associated feedback or previously-tested hypotheses, and more general, operative, or propositional information, such as stimulus codes and inference principles. The distinction intended here is akin, though probably not identical, to Tulving's (1972) analysis of memory into episodic and semantic types. We assume that coding, inference, and possibly other operations, as well as the events of preceding trials, have a place in S's permanent memory, coming forward to a working mode on the appearance of a triggering stimulus.

The second superordinate system is what Atkinson and Schiffrin (1968) have called *control* processes. There is some set of operations to determine S's attention to particular facets of a given stimulus, which of several coding routines and inference procedures he applies, and other similar decisions. At this stage of our thinking, however, we have nothing unique or nontrivial to say about how these processes relate to perceptual-coding-inference operations in a concept task.

Recall that S's category response on any trial is followed immediately by informative feedback. Thus, S quickly learns whether his perception-coding-inference sequence led him to make a correct or an incorrect response. Feedback represents the second source of information available to S within any trial. Like the stimulus pattern that S had to categorize, feedback passes through a perception-coding-inference sequence which is in part a function of what S remembers about preceding events. We think of the inference process, at this stage, acting on itself. The processing of feedback may yield, among other possibilities, a change of existing inference operations, some uncertainty about existing inference operations, or an elaboration of existing inference operations, if feedback is negative and an inference is violated; or, confirmation and lessened uncertainty about existing inference operations, if feedback is positive. We shall have more to say about these possibilities later.

Comments

As noted earlier, the details of these processes are largely unknown. It remains for precise experimental techniques to be developed, which will isolate and allow Es to examine each one unaffected by other informational operations. Research is going on in a number of areas with the expressed purpose of detailing coding, inferential, memorial, and other processes not unlike those said to be involved in concept problems. But, while concept problems suffer the disadvantage of complexly combining several processes in ways which are difficult to sort out, they have what is perhaps the more important compensating advantage of providing an experimental context which is closer to the way these processes work in the everyday affairs of human beings. This is the main reason I continue to work with complex tasks, rather than using a more direct approach to informational processes through simpler perceptual (e.g., Sperling, 1963), memorial (e.g., Atkinson & Schiffrin, 1968), decision-making (e.g., Hawkins & Shigley, 1972), or related tasks.

I have succumbed to one simplifying assumption, however. As a first approximation, I argue that the various operational systems outlined in the foregoing schema are independent. Each system or process proceeds on the basis of information provided by the just preceding stage, with no complex interactional relations between stages. This assumption is not unique and appears to work reasonably well in other contexts (Sternberg, 1969). There are at least two senses in which this independence assumption is important in an analysis of concept learning, one of which is especially critical to the present discussion. First, independence of stages or operations means that variables affecting one stage of processing or set of operations, say, inference, will have no effect, or a substantively different effect, on any other stage. A complete theory would, of course, contain explicit statements about the unique effects of significant conditions on components of behavior. We use this implication of state independence as a basis for the model of rule learning described later in this chapter.

Second, and less important for present purposes, is the implication that informational stages are temporally additive. As presently developed, the stages are grossly conceived, with perhaps a number of substages within each one. We expect, once more is known about the details of the substages, to be able to use Donders' subtractive reaction-time technique to identify the real-time characteristics of these stages, in Sternberg's (1969) sense, and to test the assumption of additivity.

INTERPRETATIONS OF RULE DIFFICULTY

One of the most stable findings of research in rule learning is that the primary bidimensional conceptual rules (conjunctive, disjunctive, conditional, and biconditional) differ significantly in difficulty in sorting tasks. There are data to suggest that a similar ordering holds for speeded classification and deductive reasoning problems. This phenomenon has been relatively resistant to orthodox interpretation. Earlier, I (Bourne, 1970) considered the following four theoretical possibilities and found each of them lacking. First, if S solves a rule-learning problem by associating each unique stimulus with a response category, then all rules should be equal in difficulty. Since all rules assign the same number of stimulus patterns to the same number of response categories (see Fig. 1), all rules should require the same number of trials to learn. The fact that the pattern of assignments is different from rule to rule has no apparent place in this theory. But rules do differ in difficulty for the naive S and, therefore, this theory is clearly inadequate. It may be noted, however, that such a theory, surprisingly, may have more to say about the performance of sophisticated Ss who have mastered the rule system. Sophisticated Ss can, in fact, solve any new rule-learning problem in the same number of trials (a theoretical minimum), regardless of differing configurations of stimulus assignments. More on that later.

A second interpretation, arising out of the early work of Smoke (1933), Hovland (1952), and Bruner, Goodnow, and Austin (1956), claims that Ss focus on instances of the positive category, attempt to formulate a definition or hypothesis that describes those instances, and assign all others to the negative category by default. In such a theory, intuitively, rule difficulty should depend on the number of stimuli in the positive category. The stimulus population most commonly used in rule learning experiments is defined by three values on each dimension. For this population, conjunctions (1:8) should be easiest, followed by disjunctions and biconditionals (5:4, equivalent in difficulty), with conditionals (7:2) most difficult (the ratio of positive to negative instances are in parentheses; see Fig. 1).

There is recent evidence to suggest that Ss sometimes focus on the smaller, more homogeneous category of stimuli, positive or negative (Bourne & Guy, 1968). If this is true in rule-learning problems, then rule difficulty may not

TABLE 2

Predicted and Actual Rule Difficulty

Theory	Prediction
S-R	Cj = Dj = Cd = Bd
Positive category focus	Cj < Dj = Bd < Cd
Homogeneous category focus	Cj < Cd < Dj = Bd
Neisser and Weene	Cj = Dj = Cd < Bd
Obtained	Cj < Dj < Cd < Bd

depend upon the size of the positive category, but rather upon the size of the positive or negative category, *whichever is smaller*. In our data, this interpretation would predict the following order of rule difficulty: conjunction, conditional, and disjunction-biconditional (equivalent), inconsistent once again with the empirical order of difficulty.

Finally, we examined a model by Neisser and Weene (1962) in which the main parameter is the structural complexity of the symbolic description of each rule (see Table 1). In this theory, the details of which we shall omit, conjunctions, disjunctions, and conditionals should not differ, for each of them can be reduced to an expression using a single logical operator. The biconditional, in contrast, can only be expressed as a disjunction of conjunctions, two logical operators, making this rule, theoretically, more difficult than the other three.

As shown in Table 2, the predictions of all four theories are at odds with the data.

A MODEL BASED ON INFERENCE OPERATIONS

How then are we to understand the phenomenon of rule difficulty? Is it merely a curious, but inexplicable, empirical result? Or is there some hidden psychological significance that the foregoing theories have failed to capture? We are convinced that rule differences are psychologically meaningful and interpretable within the appropriate theoretical idiom. We propose that the necessary structure is provided by a theory based on assumptions (and some empirical evidence) about operations S will perform on information provided by the task. It seems to us, intuitively, that the rule as a variable is more likely to interact with S's inference system than it is with any other independent set of operations, such as coding or memory. We will argue that S comes to rule-learning problems with a preconceived set of inference operations. These inferences cover all possible stimuli and thereby determine all of S's initial category reponses. We see the problem of rule difficulty reducing to a matter of inference violations—i.e., in how many and in what ways does a particular trial outcome conflict with S's existing inference operations? What is required to correct the violation, change S's operations, or both, to be consistent with given trial outcomes?

A couple of preliminary remarks are in order. First, our thinking in this matter was largely initiated and guided by some theoretical work published by Sawyer and Johnson (1970) and later refined by Sawyer (1972). Sawyer and Johnson have presented an account of the relative difficulty of the four primary bidimensional rules based on assumptions about S's pre-existing response tendencies and stimulus generalization processes. While this model fits most existing data with reasonable accuracy, it seemed to us that its formulation was overly restrictive. It is not clear, for example, how the model might apply to rules other than the four primary ones. What will be presented here, then, can in some sense be seen as a revised and extended model, based on Sawyer-Johnson ideas but with greater interpretive ability and a wider range of possible theoretical tests.

Second, the model is largely about inference processes. It prescribes a certain set of operations that S is assumed to execute, given a stimulus and the usual preliminary information about S's task. To be complete as a theory, postulates about memorial, perceptual, coding, and other processes obviously have to be added. We'll have more to say about that later. For the time being, we think of the model as a component in a larger system, and as such, describing what some Ss will do with a combination of perceived and memorized information in the context of a rule-learning problem.

Assumptions

In a rule-learning problem S must learn to categorize stimuli from four different classes, defined in terms of the presence (T) and absence (F) of two relevant attributes. We assume that the performance of naive Ss is governed by the following inference operations: (A) All stimuli perceived to exhibit both given relevant attributes (using truth table notation, we shall call them TT stimuli) are positive. (B) All stimuli perceived to exhibit neither of the given relevant attributes (FF stimuli) are negative. (C) All stimuli perceived to contain one but not both relevant attributes (TF and FT stimuli) are placed in the category to which FF instances are assigned. By inference B, FF instances are negative; therefore, TF and FT instances will, by inference C, be assigned to the negative category. If, however, in the course of a rule-learning problem, S encounters some number of violations of inference B sufficient to replace it with B'—FF instances are positive—then, by inference C, FT and TF instances will similarly be assigned to the positive category. (D) TT and FF instances belong in different response categories. Initially, by inference A, TT instances will be assigned to the positive category and, by inference B, FFs to the negative category. If, in the course of a rule-learning problem, S encounters some number of violations of either A or B sufficient to replace it with its complement (A' or B'), then, by D, he will replace them both.

The primary rationale for these inference operations is an assumption, first explicitly stated by Bruner et al. (1956), that the predominant extra-laboratory experience of adults in Western culture is with conjunctive categories, defined on the basis of the joint presence or joint absence of some number of relevant stimulus attributes. In effect, these inference operations formalize a conjunctive hypothesis. They are explicit enough, however, to establish certain expectations about what S will do when his initial conjunctive hypothesis encounters difficulty in the course of a rule-learning problem.

The model prescribes a set of operations on information contained in any stimulus, which generate specifiable response output. In principle, these processes would be quantifiable. In fact, however, because we have no explicit theory at this time, it is unclear which of several possible quantification schemes one might use. As a simple, first approximation, we propose the following. Violation of any of the foregoing inference operations results in some increment in difficulty. Because the naive S deals with the individual, uncoded stimulus patterns or attribute combinations, we assume that the increment in difficulty is equivalent to the number of unique stimuli which must be assigned to a response category inconsistent with a given inference.

Examples

To see how this reasoning works, consider first a conjunctive problem. Because TT stimuli are positive, FFs are negative, TFs and FTs are assigned in a way consistent with FFs, and there is no necessity to combine TTs and FFs in the same category, the difficulty value of a conjunction is 0. The conjunctive concept is entirely consistent with S's pre-experimental expectations, and he should make none or at most a few errors on that type of problem. Consider the disjunction. TTs are positive and FFs are negative. TFs and FTs, however, are assigned to the positive category, inconsistent with the assignment of FFs and with inference C. In a stimulus population defined by two values on each of the two relevant dimensions, there is one stimulus corresponding to each truth-table class. The difficulty of the disjunctive problem, therefore, would be 2, corresponding to the two unique stimulus patterns, one TF and one FT, whose assignment conflicts with S's inference operations. In the problems used in most rule-learning experiments, there are typically three values per relevant dimension, thereby giving the disjunctive a difficulty value of 4, corresponding to the 2 TF and the 2 FT stimuli, whose assignment violates existing inference operations.

Next consider the conditional rule, where TTs, FTs, and FFs are positive and TFs are negative. In this case 4 plus 2, or 6 unique stimulus patterns, are in violation of inferences B and C. Moreover, TT and FF instances must be placed into the same (positive) category, contrary to inference D, which magnifies the difficulty of the problem, say, arbitrarily, by a factor of 2. Accordingly, the difficulty value for conditional problems is 12. Similar reasoning applied to biconditional problems yields a difficulty value of 16.

Recall that the system which these rules represent consists of 16 possibilities, four of which are complements of the primary bidimensional rules. In Table 3, we present an analysis of both primaries and complements.

TABLE 3

Four Primary Bidimensional Rules, Their Complements, and
Predicted Difficulty Value, in Truth-Table Form

Rules and dimensions	Difficulty Values		Truth-table classes			
	2-value dimensions	3-value dimensions	TT	TF	FT	FF
Primary rules:						
Conjunctive	0	0	+	−	−	−
Disjunctive	2	4	+	+*	+*	−
Conditional	4	12	+	−*	+	+*
Biconditional	6	16	+	−*	−*	+*
Two-value dimension			RS	RTr	GS	GTr
Three-value dimension			RS	RTr, RC	GS, BS	GTr, GC, BTr, BC
Complementary rules:						
Alternative denial (AD)	2	5	−*	+	+	+*
Joint denial (JD)	4	9	−*	−*	−*	+*
Exclusive (Ex)	4	6	−*	+*	−	−
Exclusive disjunctive (ED)	6	10	−*	+*	+*	−

Note.—Names of rules are arbitrary, though intended to be descriptive. Asterisks denote stimulus classes which the theory predicts will be relatively difficult for S to handle when the indicated rule applies. The following abbreviations are used: R—red, G—green, B—blue, S—square, Tr—triangle, C—circle.

We do not anticipate the numerical values obtained by an arbitrary calculational process like the one described here to correspond exactly with the quantitative data one obtains in a rule-learning experiment. Still, if this kind of reasoning is in any sense correct, the predicted order of rule difficulty ought to correspond with the empirical order. On this reasoning, then, we expect the following order of rule difficulty: conjunctive, disjunctive, alternative denial, exclusive, joint denial, exclusive disjunctive, conditional, and biconditional.

The predicted order of rule difficulty is not intuitively obvious and, as we have seen, there are a variety of alternative possibilities. With respect to the difficulty of complementary rules, perhaps the most straightforward expectation is based on the fact that complements are the mirror images of primary rules. All stimuli assigned to the negative category of a primary rule are positive instances of its complement. In a sense, the labels "positive" and "negative," are arbitrary. If S treats them in that way, then the order of complements ought to be exactly the same as the order of primaries. That is, a primary ought to be essentially equivalent to its complement in difficulty. In the inference model, however, positive- and negative-category labels make a fundamental difference.

Experiment I

Harriet Salatas performed the obvious experiment to test the difficulty order predicted from the inference model. Each of 8 groups of college students was asked to solve one rule-learning problem. Groups differed in terms of the unknown rule for which they had to solve. Details of the experimental paradigm were essentially those described earlier in this paper. Subjects learned to sort geometrical patterns presented one at a time, according to an E-defined concept. The solution criterion was 10 correct category responses in a row, plus an adequate verbalization of the concept by S.

Table 4 presents the mean trials and mean errors to solution for each of the 8 rules. There are several ways in which we might examine these data. Note first that there are significant rule differences. The rules tend to fall into clusters with conjunction and disjunction significantly easier than exclusion, alternative denial, exclusive disjunction, and joint denial, which in turn are significantly easier than conditional and biconditional. The order of rule difficulty is predicted accurately by the inference model, except for the exclusive–alternative-denial and the joint-denial–exclusive-disjunction reversals within the second cluster, neither of which differences is statistically significant. The alignment is consistent with predictions by a statistical test of ordered hypotheses.

But the model does better than predicting ordinal relationships. While the details of our calculational scheme were partly arbitrary, there is some reasonable correspondence between the scale of rule difficulty and actual performance, as is shown if Fig. 3.

Encouraged by the results of the foregoing analysis, we attempted some more precise tests of the assumptions of the model. Table 5 shows the distribution of

TABLE 4

Mean Trials and Errors for the Eight Bidimensional Rules
(Experiment I)

Rules	Mean trials	Mean errors	Obtained order	Predicted order
Primary:				
Conjunctive	6.92	2.67	1	1
Disjunctive	8.83	3.33	2	2
Conditional	60.58	23.08	7	7
Biconditional	66.42	27.25	8	8
Complementary:				
Alternative denial	35.00	13.75	4	3
Joint denial	49.17	21.42	6	5
Exclusive	32.50	12.67	3	4
Exclusive disjunctive	40.33	18.17	5	6

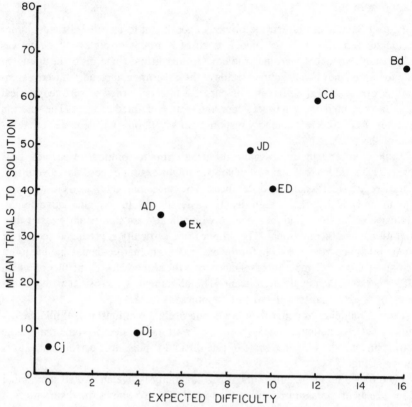

FIG. 3. Relationship between predicted and obtained problem difficulty, Experiment I.

errors across stimulus classes, defined by the bidimensional truth table, within each rule. Those classes which are predicted, on the basis of our model, to be especially difficult within each rule are distinguished by asterisks. The difficulty patterns revealed in the data correspond reasonably well with expectations from the theory. Statistical comparisons of "difficult" versus "easy" classes were made where possible within each rule. All differences were in the predicted direction and were statistically significant except in two cases. Next, we compared performance levels for rules which violated an assumed inference operation versus rules which did not. The results of this analysis are presented in Table 6. They confirm, without exception, the following assertions of the theory. (A) Subjects have more difficulty with TT instances when they are assigned to the negative in contrast to the positive category. (B) Subjects have more difficulty with FF instances when they are assigned to the positive, in contrast to the negative category. (C) Subjects have more trouble with TF and FT instances when their assignment is different from, as opposed to the same as, FF instances. (D) Subjects have more

TABLE 5

Error Distributions Across Truth-Table Categories
for the Eight Rules

Rules	TT	TF	FT	FF
Primary:				
Conjunctive	.33	1.08	.92	.33
Disjunctive	.42	1.25*	.67*	1.00
Conditional[a]	1.25	7.50*	2.42	8.92*
Biconditional[a]	1.75	8.08*	6.08*	11.33*
Complementary:				
Alternative denial	5.58*	2.83	2.67	2.67*
Joint denial	4.92*	6.50*	3.50*	6.50*
Exclusive[a]	5.17*	3.25*	2.58*	1.67
Exclusive disjunctive[a]	5.33*	4.25*	5.17*	3.42

Note.—Asterisks denote stimulus classes which the theory predicts will be relatively difficult for S to handle when the indicated rule applies.

[a]In this rule, classes predicted to be more difficult produce significantly ($p < .05$) more errors than classes predicted to be easier.

difficulty with rules which require that TT and FF instances be combined in the same category. Arbitrarily, we assumed that the difficulty factor introduced by combining TT and FF instances into the same category has a doubling effect. While it may be fortuitous, the means upon which comparison (D), above, was made differ approximately by a factor of 2.

Experiment II

As a part of his Master's thesis experiment at Colorado, Paul Neumann collected data which reproduce certain essential features of Experiment I. We should note that Neumann used a different stimulus population and provided Ss with pretraining designed to have facilitative effects on rule learning. Thus, the fact that Neumann's mean scores are not identical to those of Experiment I is not surpris-

TABLE 6

Mean Errors in Particular Truth-Table Stimulus Classes When Assumptions of the Model
Are or Are Not Violated

Assumption	Violated	Not violated	F	p
TTs are +	21.00	3.75	34.20	.001
FFs are −	29.42	6.42	60.80	.001
TFs with FFs	5.14	1.96	4.64	.025
FTs with FFs	15.42	8.58	5.37	.025
TTs and FFs separate:				
TT and FF classes only	38.83	21.75	33.55	.001
All classes	78.17	41.17	157.36	.001

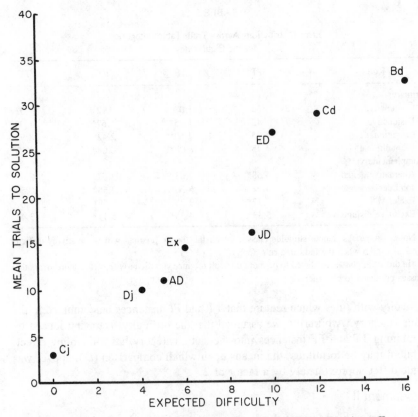

FIG. 4. Relationship between predicted and obtained problem difficulty, Experiment II.

ing. What is important is the ordering of rules in mean trials to problem solution. Figure 4 is a scatter plot of obtained values and those predicted by the inference model.

If anything, the fit between the model's predictions and Neumann's data is even closer than that in Experiment I.

Experiment III

One assumption about which the foregoing data are unclear has to do with the relationship between problem difficulty and the number of stimulus-to-response category assignments which conflict with existing inference operations. In the stimulus population used, each relevant dimension had three values. There are, therefore, nine unique combinations of values from the two relevant dimensions. Across the classes of the truth table, these nine combinations distribute themselves in a 1:2:2:4 ratio for TT, TF, FT and FF stimuli, respectively. Thus, when TF stimuli must be assigned to a conflicting response category, we assume that 2 units of difficulty are thus engendered. When the FF class is assigned to a conflicting category, 4 units of difficulty are generated.

This assumption appears to fit the empirical results of the preceding experiment. A more powerful test of the assumption, however, would require experimental variation in the intradimensional variability of the stimulus population. Suppose, for example, stimulus dimensions had two rather than three values. Then, the distribution of stimuli across truth-table classes would be 1:1:1:1. Suppose the stimuli had four values per dimension; the distribution would be 1:3:3:9. These distributions lead to different orders of rule difficulty from those predicted in Experiment I. Therefore, both the generality of the model and the assumed importance of number of stimuli per truth-table class within the model can be tested by varying intradimensional variability.

While we have no parametric investigation to report, we do have some data which lend additional support to these ideas. These data come from a simplified version of Experiment I, conducted by Barbara Scherer, in which each S learned one of four rules, either conditional, biconditional, exclusive, or exclusive disjunctive, with a stimulus population generated by four binary dimensions. These four rules were chosen to represent two levels of predicted difficulty in this stimulus production. As can be see in Table 3, when there are two values per dimension, performance should be equivalent for the biconditional and the exclusive disjunctive, and for the conditional and the exclusive. It is well to keep in mind that performance on these four rules varied markedly when the stimulus population had three values per dimension.

The results of this comparison are shown in Table 7. There is a significant overall difference among rules. The effect is almost entirely attributable, however, to the

TABLE 7

Performance on Four Rules when the Stimulus Population has
Binary Dimensions, Experiment III

Rule	Conditional	Exclusive	Biconditional	Exclusive disjunctive
Mean trials	24.11	22.27	32.56	35.90
Mean errors	9.62	8.81	13.77	15.23
Predicted difficulty	4	4	6	6

difference between the conditional–exclusive set and the biconditional–exclusive-disjunctive set. There was no significant difference between conditional and exclusive or between biconditional and exclusive-disjunctive rules. Results of Experiments I and III are compared in Fig. 5.

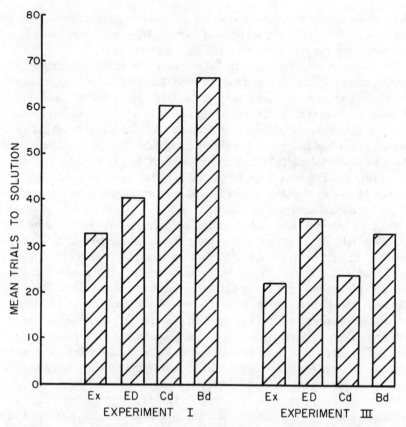

FIG. 5. Comparison of performance on four different rules when stimulus dimensions have three (Experiment I) and two (Experiment III) values.

Other Tests

There are other ways to examine the model empirically. An approach suggested by Sawyer and Johnson (1970), and which we plan to pursue immediately, involves pretraining S in ways which should either enhance or change the inference operations that he brings to experimental situations. If we give S pretraining, for example, consistent with the inference that TTs are positive or FFs are negative, we would expect, in a subsequent rule-learning problem that involves the violation of either of these inferences, that S would have a more difficult time than would another S given comparable control pretraining. Conversely, there is the possibility of weakening an inference operation through pretraining. Suppose, for example, we pretrained S to place FFs in the positive category or to assign TFs and FFs differentially. In this case, we would expect improved performance in a subsequent problem based on a rule which violates this inference. These and other tests should, we think, help us to determine the limiting conditions of the model.

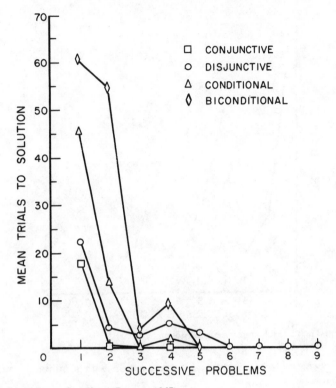

FIG. 6. Intrarule transfer effects (Bourne, 1967).

Changes in Inference Operations

But we know one limiting condition already. Order of rule difficulty is not static or invariant. It can be changed, especially by giving experience with the rule-learning paradigm. The most important processes of change are intra- and inter-rule transfer. Subjects improve to the point of errorless performance over a series of problems, all based on the same rule but differing in relevant attributes. The kind of data we typically get are shown in Fig. 6, which were taken from an experiment in which independent groups of Ss practiced a series of problems based on one of the four primary bidimensional rules (Bourne, 1967). Moreover, performance improves over a series of problems in which both rule and attributes change from one problem to the next. Performance in this paradigm never becomes errorless, because it takes exposure to some minimal number of stimuli before the unknown rule can be determined. But, rule differences disappear. After a sufficient number of problems, most Ss are able to solve for any unknown rule in the same minimal number of trials. Data from an experiment illustrating both intra- and interrule transfer effects are shown in Fig. 7. In this experiment, after 12 problems, three based on each of the four primary bidimensional rules,

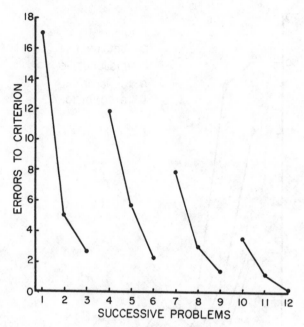

FIG. 7. Intra- and interrule transfer effects (Bourne, 1970).

83% of Ss were able to identify an unknown rule with a minimal amount of information.

Thus, with multiple rule-learning experience, the order of rule difficulty changes. Whereas there are marked differences among rules for the naive S, differences are nonexistent for the sophisticated S. This is essentially the phenomenon alluded to earlier. A trained logician would have little or no trouble with the rules used to define nominal concepts in these problems. If he were to apply his knowledge of formal logic successfully, he could solve for any of the rules we used in the same number of trials.

The process of change in rule difficulty over problems (though not necessarily within Ss) is gradual. As far as we can tell from available data, the order of rule difficulty observed for the naive S is preserved throughout the various stages of practice until S achieved full competence within the system of conceptual rules. In Fig. 8 we show the data of Ss at the outset, half-way through, and after solving 12 problems of a multiple rule-learning experiment. As can be seen, on the average, rule order is the same at all points within the sequence, despite massive changes in the level of performance. After 12 problems, nearly all differences have removed, althouth 17% of Ss still made more than the theoretically minimal number of errors.

Revisions in the theory. Obviously, the theory about inference operations, given above, is not entirely viable for the sophisticated S. Still, we think the gen-

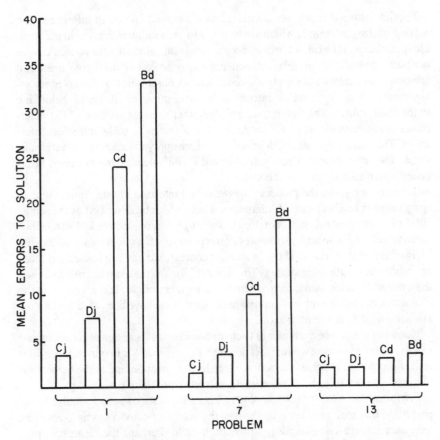

FIG. 8. Relative rule difficulty at various stages of *S* sophistication. Order of difficulty remains stable across massive training and transfer effects.

eral idea of an inference system to characterize *S*'s problem-solving behavior is useful. The evidence suggests clearly that *S*'s inferences change with problem-solving experience within a given conceptual system. While the evidence is not definitive, we propose two processes of change. First, inferences tend toward openendedness. Instead of predetermining the assignment of particular stimuli to response categories, the operations of a sohpisticated *S* allow the stimulus itself to determine its own assignment. Thus, instead of inference operation *A*—all stimuli with both given relevant attributes are positive—the sophisticated *S* operates with inference *A**—the category assignment of the first instance with both relevant attributes determines the assignment for all stimuli with both relevant attributes. Similar operations *B**, *C** and *D** apply to stimuli with the first but not the second relevant attribute, the second but not the first relevant attribute, and neither relevant attribute, respectively.

Implicit within this new set of operations is a second change in inference. The naive S utilizes inferences which apply either to each unique stimulus in the stimulus population, if he cannot or does not gate irrelevant attributes, or to each unique attribute combination on relevant dimensions, if he can or does gate irrelevant attributes. In contrast, the sophisticated S lets his observation of the category assignment of a single stimulus determine the assignment of all stimuli belonging to the same subset. The first instance with neither relevant attribute (FFs) determines the assignment of all FF instances. The S comes to make intraclass inferences. The naive S operates with inferences which apply uniquely to each stimulus input. The sophisticated S recognizes stimulus equivalences and develops inferences which take them into account.

Thus, in our view, the processes of intra- and interrule transfer reflect underlying changes in S's system of inferences. Transfer can be described as the acquisition of a more general set of operations, covering both conjunctive and all nonconjunctive cases. These new procedures correspond to what a logician would call a bidimensional truth table. Thus, in another context, we have characterized these operations as a truth-table strategy (Bourne, 1970). We make no claim that S uses the truth table in the same, formal sense as a logician might. It is merely that the characteristics of his problem-solving behavior that we have been able to examine are consistent with the truth table.

Knowing where one exemplar of each truth-table class is assigned is tantamount to solving for any unknown rule. As noted earlier, 83% of S's in our multiple rule-learning experiment achieve a performance level corresponding to the theoretical minimal number of trials (4) needed to solve the problem.

Evidence for a truth-table strategy. There are other data, too detailed to report fully, that are consistent with the idea that a sophisticated S learns to adopt an inference scheme corresponding to the truth table. Perhaps the clearest is provided by several experiments in which Ss have been given pretraining of truth tables. Invariably, the effect is to reduce the difficulty of subsequent rule-learning problems, in the direction of equalizing performance across a variety of rules. Results of one experiment of this sort (Dodd, Kinsman, Klipp, & Bourne, 1971) are shown in Fig. 9. A second example reverses the procedure. Subjects are first

TABLE 8

Mean Trials to Last Error on a Truth-Table Sorting Problem
After Practice with Varying Numbers of Rules (Bourne, 1969)

Number of rules	Trials
0	23.96
1	14.59
2	16.31
3	9.04
4	5.58

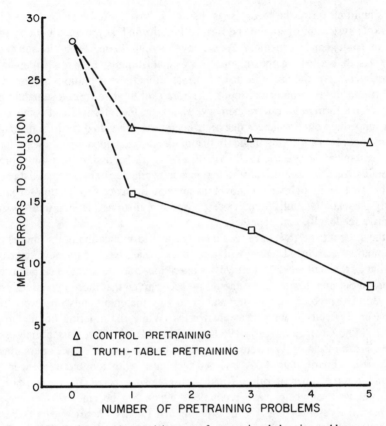

FIG. 9. Effects of truth-table pretraining on performance in rule-learning problems.

given a series of problems based on a variety of rules to solve and are subsequently tested for their knowledge of truth tables. In one experiment, the tests required S to sort stimulus patterns into four unlabelled bins, the bins (unknown to S) corresponding to the four truth-table classes. The results of this test, taken by Ss before and after solving 12 rule-learning problems, are shown in Table 8.

SUMMARY AND CONCLUSIONS

This paper has presented a general theoretical orientation toward the behavior of human adult Ss solving conceptual problems. It is a position toward which we have gradually drifted over the last three or four years. No single experiment has been completely convincing to us. Still, we think now that the weight of the evidence suggests that such a characterization is the best account of what we now know.

In simplified form, the theory says that S's behavior can be characterized in terms of a system of operations performed on information provided both by the problem context and by memory. As we have seen, these operations are substantively classifiable. Along one dimension, we can distinguish between perceptual, coding, and inferential operations. To the extent that these operations are not implicit within the environmental input, they are said to arise from a semantic or propositional form of long-term memory. That is, as the informational content of one's immediate circumstances demand, operations are called forth from long-term memory into a working mode. In that mode, they act upon input in ways that can at least in part be specified and formalized. We further assume that some form of memory for task-specific information is also available. Experimental data are far from clear, although we do know that some Ss evidence recollection for previously-presented stimuli, stimulus-response combinations (as signified by informative feedback), and hypotheses.

In the present paper, we have seen a fairly specific application of this model to one empirical question. Dealing with this concrete case has had the advantage of allowing us to detail what we believe S's operations are and to make certain predictions about how performance should proceed, given that those operations are followed. The problem in question had to do with the empirically observed difference in difficulty among conceptual rules. While the ordering of rules has been well known since the early 1960s, an accurate and self-consistent interpretation has been lacking. We were able to show how a set of inference operations, which arise primarily out of S's assumed familiarity with conjunctive concepts, accounts for the order of rule difficulty observed for naive Ss. Furthermore, the model was shown to make predictions which can be, and in some cases have been, successfully checked in experiments. Finally, there appears to be a way to make the model consistent not only with the behavior of naive Ss but also with the performance of highly sophisticated and well-trained individuals, if we allow for a simple set of assumptions about the manner in which inference operations change in the face of consistent and repeated violations.

Clearly, there is more work to be done toward developing this loose schema into a bona fide theory of concept learning. Among the conceptual problems which must be examined is the specification of perceptual and coding operations relevant to rule learning. There is a need to be more explicit about changes in inference (and other) operations. What, for example, is the weight of a single violation toward a change of operation? Are the effects all-or-none or gradual? A more detailed consideration of learning processes is required. This analysis will presumably lead us to a rationale for the presently arbitrary conversion of theoretical problem difficulty into performance measures such as trials to solution. A related and as yet unresolved problem has to do with the assumed hierarchical arrangement of control processes, memory, and specific informational operations. The principles of this relationship and the possibilities for change are, as yet, unspecified.

Finally, a clearer representation of the distinction between attribute identification and rule-learning processes needs to be developed. In the application emphasized in the present paper, we spoke exclusively about rule-learning problems, wherein the focal, relevant attributes of the stimuli are known to S at the outset. The inferential operations assumed to be used by S were all predicated upon the fact that attributes were given. In the attribute-identification task, where relevant attributes are unknown to S, different inferential operations are required to solve the problem. An extension of the theory to attribute identification depends on complete representation of these operations.

On the empirical side, a different set of questions remains to be answered. To illustrate, given our assumptions, S's initial inference operations must change to accommodate solutions or concepts generated by nonconjunctive rules. Does the "change" or learning parameter differ with type of inference or type of violation, or does each violation have an essentially equivalent effect? Further, does the change in S's inference system as he becomes more sophisticated entail any consequent changes in coding? One might argue that inferences based on truth-table classes, a system which appears to be characteristic of the sophisticated S, should lead to changes in the way S codes the stimulus population. That is, given the two relevant attributes x and y at the outset of a problem, S may immediately redefine the stimulus population, passing along each stimulus for inference in xy, x–not-y, not-x–y, or not-x– not-y form. Examination of S's recollection for nonrelevant (not-x and not-y) values along relevant stimulus dimensions, or his tendency to generalize a learned concept to stimuli which contain new values on a given relevant dimension, may help to provide some leverage on the question of coding changes. Other empirical questions involve possible developmental changes in S's inference system. Children of a young enough age should be relatively unencumbered by prior familiarization with conjunctions of attributes. Their inference system may be such as to produce less of a difference among conceptual rules than those observed for adults (King, 1966). Finally, we would like to examine the generality of S's inference system. Is it specific to the stimulus features which have characterized the population used in training problems or does that system, as the model would presently suggest, ignore stimulus features and generalize over an infinite range of stimulus variation?

REFERENCES

Atkinson, R. C., & Schiffrin, R. M. Human memory: A proposed system and its control processes. In K. W. Spence & J. T. Spence (Eds.), *The psychology of learning and motivation.* Vol. 2. New York: Academic Press, 1968.

Bourne, L. E., Jr. Learning and utilization of conceptual rules. In B. Kleinmuntz (Ed.), *Concepts and the structure of memory.* New York: Wiley, 1967.

Bourne, L. E., Jr. Development of conceptual skills: Some preliminary findings. Technical Report No. 81, Wisconsin Research and Development Center, 1969.

Bourne, L. E., Jr. Knowing and using concepts. *Psychologiccal Review,* 1970, **77,** 546–556.

Bourne, L. E., Jr., & Guy, D. E. Learning conceptual rules: II. The role of positive and negative instances. *Journal of Experimental Psychology,* 1968, **77**, 488–494.

Bruner, J. S., Goodnow, J. J., & Austin, G. A. *A study of thinking.* New York: Wiley, 1956.

Dodd, D. H., Kinsman, R. A., Klipp, R. D., & Bourne, L. E., Jr. Effects of logic pretraining on conceptual rule learning. *Journal of Experimental Psychology,* 1971, **88**, 119–122.

Haygood, R. C., & Bourne, L. E., Jr. Attribute- and rule-learning aspects of conceptual behavior. *Psychological Review,* 1965, **72**, 175–195.

Hawkins, H. L., & Shigley, R. H. Irrelevant information and processing mode in speeded discrimination. *Journal of Experimental Psychology,* 1972, **96**, 389–395.

Hovland, C. I. A "communication analysis" of concept learning. *Psychological Review,* 1952, **59**, 461–472.

King, W. L. Learning and utilization of conjunctive and disjunctive rules: A developmental study. *Journal of Experimental Psychology,* 1966, **4**, 217–231.

Neisser, U., & Weene, P. Hierarchies in concept attainment. *Journal of Experimental Psychology,* 1962, **64**, 644–645.

Norman, D. A. *Memory and attention.* New York: Wiley, 1969.

Posner, M. I. Information reduction in the analysis of sequential tasks. *Psychological Review,* 1964, **74**, 491–504.

Sawyer, C. R. A concept learning model. Unpublished doctoral dissertation, University of New Mexico, 1972.

Sawyer, C. R., & Johnson, P. J. A conceptual rule learning model. Paper presented at the meeting of the Rocky Mountain Psychological Association, Santa Fe, May, 1970.

Smoke, K. L. Negative instances in concept learning. *Journal of Experimental Psychology,* 1933, **16**, 583–588.

Sperling, G. A model for visual memory tasks. *Human Factors,* 1963, **5**, 19–31.

Sternberg, S. Memory scanning: Mental processes revealed by reaction time experiments. *American Scientist,* 1969, **57**, 421–457.

Tulving, E. Episodic and semantic memory. In E. Tulving, & W. Donaldson (Eds.), *Organization of memory.* New York: Academic Press, 1972.

10
HOW DO PEOPLE DISCOVER CONCEPTS?

Roger L. Dominowski
University of Illinois at Chicago Circle[1]

I assume that obtaining a reasonable answer to the question posed above is the objective of research on concept identification. It seems clear that researchers in this field are interested in more than the "simple facts," i.e., that variable X affects efficiency, even though such knowledge allows some prediction and control. Rather, they seek to understand and describe the process of concept identification. Previous research has contributed much information about the factors which influence the difficulty of conceptual tasks, and there has been vigorous theoretical activity as well. I believe that a survey of the field gives the distinct impression that this is a healthy research area in which good work is done and progress is being made. However, I also believe that a closer look reveals some important, nagging problems that have not been resolved and perhaps not even carefully addressed. In this paper, I will discuss some of these problems as they relate to the development of an adequate account of conceptual behavior.

THE SCOPE OF THEORIES OF CONCEPTUAL BEHAVIOR

The initial question needs some redefinition—it is necessary to indicate what kinds of people, what kinds of concepts, and what kinds of situations are under consideration. My present concern is with the conceptual behavior of normal adults (note that "behavior" is used here in its fullest sense; see Bourne, Ekstrand, & Dominowski, 1971). While recognizing the existence of a variety of concepts, such as probabilistic concepts, relational concepts, quantitative concepts, and

[1]This paper was completed while the author was a research fellow at the University of Aberdeen, Scotland. Appreciation is expressed to Rosalind Heaton and John Elliott for their help in collecting data.

linguistic concepts, I will restrict the discussion to those deterministic class concepts which have received the greatest attention. As was stated quite clearly by Haygood and Bourne (1965), a class concept is defined in terms of both relevant attributes and a rule applied to those attributes to determine category membership. Although one might question the accuracy of some of their labels for the rules, and while the system they used for bidimensional concepts gets messy when more than two relevant attributes are involved, their essential point stands—one must consider both the attributes selected as relevant and the way in which they are used to determine category membership. There are very good reasons for our being concerned with a domain of class concepts which includes, at the very least, unidimensional concepts, conjunctive concepts, and disjunctive concepts (some feel that other rules are better described as different kinds of disjunctions).

Haygood and Bourne (1965) also pointed out that because class concepts involve attributes and rules, we can give S three different tasks, depending on what is known and unknown about the target concept: attribute identification (rule known), rule learning (relevant attributes known), or complete learning (both aspects unknown). The behavioral domain we seek to understand can thus be reasonably defined to include at least three kinds of concepts and three tasks (although all combinations of concept and task are not necessarily viable).

The variety of conceptual tasks is increased through procedural changes. Even granting that the essence of our method is to require S to discover a concept on the basis of information contained in a number of stimulus presentations distributed over time, there are a number of procedural variations which demand attention. These include whether S or E has control over the stimulus series (selection vs. reception), the extent to which stimuli shown previously remain available for inspection, and whether or not S is required to categorize each stimulus when it is first encountered. Since researchers appear to have lost interest in having Ss work with near-tachistoscopic presentation and 2-second intertrial intervals, I will ignore temporal variations and assume that sufficient time is typically allowed. To the procedural variations, one can add two more definitional features: the type of stimulus dimension (binary, trinary, etc.) and the number of irrelevant dimensions (for a fixed target concept). Additional variations can be listed, but these strike me as most salient.

This description illustrates the scope of our task. Even accepting certain constraints as to type of concept, type of S, and fundamental procedure, and even minimizing procedural variations to a reasonable number (e.g., previous stimuli are either available or not), it is the case that in studying the discovery of class concepts we are dealing with perhaps 600 situations (Table 1). In one sense, this "space" might be handled without fundamental difficulty. That is, I can almost imagine having Ss identify concepts in all of these situations, e.g., from attribute identification of a unidimensional concept, binary dimensions, one irrelevant dimension, selection, no prior stimuli available, no categorization required, through complete learning of a disjunctive concept, trinary dimensions, eight irrelevant dimensions, reception, all prior stimuli available, and categorization required. The result would be "the grand data matrix," i.e., the mean number of trials to some common criterion for each situation. Such an effort would be the epitome of crass empiricism, but I believe that it is apparent that, if we limit ourselves to assessing the over-all efficiency of Ss' performance, the result would provide a kind of over-all picture.

TABLE 1

The Behavioral Domain of Class Concepts: An Estimate

Concepts (Unidimensional, Conjunctive, Disjunctive)	×
Type of Dimension (Binary vs. Trinary)	×
Number of Irrelevant Dimensions (1, 2, 4, or 8)	×
Task (Attribute Identification, Rule Learning, Complete Learning)	×
Sequence Control (Selection vs. Reception)	×
Categorization Procedure (Required or not)	×
Stimulus Availability (Available or not)	= 576 Situations

However, if we are interested in understanding and describing the process of concept identification, we then encounter a most difficult problem. In answering the question "How do people discover concepts?" how many different answers would we need? I have no idea other than that the magic number is undoubtedly not one. Obviously, the number of process descriptions we will accept as distinguishable will depend on what level of detail we decide is appropriate for such an account. It seems a truism that a good account is one which is detailed enough not to be trivial and general enough to apply to a reasonable number of situations. If the number of such accounts is not too large, and particularly if some order can be imposed upon them, then some theoretical achievement would be attained. I know of no *a priori* criteria which indicate when the right balance of detail and generality has been reached, but I do believe that this is an issue worth our concern, now, in the context of our own research.

Consider how the behavioral domain of "people discovering class concepts" might be subdivided. The little evidence available suggests that complete learning might be more than the simple sum of attribute identification and rule learning (e.g., Haygood & Bourne, 1965). For the present, let us set complete learning aside, either on the grounds that it might be fairly well understood on the basis of its components or that its analysis is better left for the future. There is evidence in the literature indicating that rule learning is different in important respects from attribute identification. Some variables have different effects on the two tasks (e.g., Bourne & Guy, 1968), and the highly-efficient "truth-table" strategy described by Bourne (1970) does not seem directly applicable to attribute identification. Let me further hazard the guess that the kinds of procedural variations listed earlier might be relatively unimportant for rule learning. In contrast, these variations do seem important for attribute identification; let us concentrate on this task.

Limiting attention to attribute identification means that we are still faced with up to 100 situations when procedural variations are taken into account. Let me indicate why these variations might be theoretically important. Theories of attribute identification have been proposed, and they regularly take the form of proposing that Ss are following a particular strategy. In considering the question of how many strategies might be involved, I find myself in increasing sympathy with the general remarks of Bruner, Goodnow, and Austin (1965). They proposed that the reasonable objectives of a concept-identification strategy are to maximize the information gained from each stimulus presentation, to insure that the concept will be attained with certainty, to minimize errors on the way to solution, and to minimize cognitive strain. These objectives can be in conflict with each other, with the most relevant conflict indicated by the notion that an information-maximizing strategy might involve so much cognitive strain that Ss will not use it. "Cognitive strain" seems to be a vague and thus unpalatable term, but one that we probably all intuitively understand. Cognitive strain refers in a more subjective fashion to the stress placed on the "central information-processing capacity" discussed by Posner (e.g., 1965) or to what Newell and Simon (1972) refer to as the difficulties encountered by a problem solver due to the limited capacity of short-term memory. It seems a quite plausible notion that Ss' concept-identification strategies might vary with the cognitive strain imposed by the task.

The need for a change in process description need not depend on a change in cognitive strain. For example, consider selection versus reception paradigms. It is not clear that these paradigms differ in cognitive strain; comparisons of relative efficiency under the two procedures lead to no simple conclusion (Bourne & Dominowski, 1972). However, the literature indicates that what is of interest with the selection paradigm is substantially different from that which researchers using the reception paradigm seek to describe. Much effort has been expended in attempts to describe how Ss choose stimuli in the selection paradigm; by definition, this part of the theoretical account is irrelevant to the reception paradigm. A similar idea applies to the question of whether or not Ss are required to categorize each stimulus. When this is required, a number of issues arise, e.g., whether Ss' categorizations are predictable from their hypotheses (Schwartz, 1966), or if an S testing several hypotheses responds on the basis of majority rule or on the basis of a working hypothesis selected from those under consideration (Levine, 1970). When categorization is not required, these are irrelevant issues. Whether or not procedural variations in stimulus control or response requirements involve changes in cognitive strain, these variations will result in theoretical changes because there are different things to be accounted for. Let me suggest that it might be worth contemplating whether the way S selects stimuli or chooses responses is a major or minor theoretical issue.

With respect to the other variations mentioned, the idea of changes in cognitive strain is quite plausible. The difficulty of attribute identification is affected by the type of concept (e.g., Bourne & Guy, 1968; Laughlin, 1968; Neisser & Weene, 1962), binary versus trinary stimulus dimensions (Haygood, Harbert, & Omler, 1970), the number of irrelevant dimensions (e.g., Dominowski, 1969; Walker & Bourne, 1961), and the availability of previous stimuli (e.g., Bourne, Goldstein, & Link, 1964). A difference in difficulty can occur when Ss are all following the same basic strategy, with different levels of efficiency, but we should be alert to the possibility that a change in approach is involved. A few suggestions along this line have been made. Taplin (1972) has argued that while it might be plausible for S to test several hypotheses simultaneously when attempting to identify a simple concept applied to stimuli with few attributes, the limitations of short-term memory and information processing make it highly unlikely that such a strategy would be followed when a more complex concept or more stimulus dimensions are involved. Similarly, Denny (1969) has suggested that Ss might use different strategies for different target concepts when prior stimuli are unavailable but employ an alternative, common strategy when a record of prior stimuli is provided.

Let me narrow the focus of attention still further. For the moment, let us concede that theoretical accounts for the selection paradigm must, at least in part, be different from those for the reception paradigm. I will concentrate on the reception paradigm because it has been the subject of considerable theoretical work. I have deliberately taken a long path to the focus on attribute identification under the reception paradigm because I believe it is important to recognize that the behavior observed in such situations represents only a fraction of what can reasonably be called "discovering class concepts." Sufficient information exists for us to get some idea of how well we understand conceptual behavior under this restricted set of conditions, and the analysis might provide guidelines for future theoretical development.

Theories of Attribute Identification

Over the past decade, there has been little development of theories based on associative learning principles, and I will not consider this approach. Clearly, the associative approach has been replaced by the view of Ss as active information-processors, i.e., testing hypotheses, drawing inferences, etc. Before listing proposals, it will be helpful to specify the usage of the term "hypothesis," which unfortunately carries several meanings in the literature. To designate a possible solution or a "guess" at the solution, I will use the term "H"; to say that S tests an H is to say he tests a possible answer. The H-testing approach has been contrasted with an attribute-centered approach (Bruner et al., 1956; Eifermann, 1965; Taplin & Jeeves, 1972; Wetherick, 1969). According to an attribute-centered approach, S at any time carries a list of attributes which he will test for relevance to the solution. The important point is that S is trying to determine what should be included in his solution, rather than adopting and testing an H which is a possible solution. The attribute list will be designated by "AH". The term "hypothesis" itself will be used as a general description; in the discussion to follow a hypothesis could be an H, AH, or some other idea the subject is entertaining about the solution.

For the reception paradigm, four rather formal theoretical proposals have been made. Their capsule versions are as follows:

1. One-H Model: S adopts an H and classifies stimuli in accordance with it, keeping that H if correct but adopting a new H if wrong (e.g., Bower & Trabasso, 1964). The model has gone through a number of revisions related to the manner in which S selects a new H after an error. Bruner et al.'s (1956) "partist strategy" can be seen as one version of this model.

2. H-Sample Model: S adopts an initial sample of Hs (n > 1), categorizing either on the basis of majority rule or according to one of these Hs used as a working H, in either case evaluating all Hs in the sample on both correct and error trials, with a new sample drawn if all Hs in the present sample prove incorrect (Levine, 1970; Trabasso & Bower, 1968). Bruner et al.'s "simultaneous scanning" represents the extreme version of this model, in which the "sample" consists of all possible Hs.

3. Wholist strategy: S adopts as an initial AH the set of all attributes of the first positive instance (for unidimensional and conjunctive concepts). Irrelevant attributes are then eliminated by keeping only those attributes common to AH and subsequent positive instances, with negative instances ignored (Bruner et al., 1956; see also Haygood et al., 1970).

4. Category search: S searches for an attribute or set of attributes which appears in all positive instances but in no negative instances (Hunt, Marin, & Stone, 1966). This is an incomplete description of the model, which has been extended to disjunctive concepts and leads to their solution by parts.

In addition to these formal proposals, researchers typically draw inferences about processes on the basis of the effects of experimental manipulations. I wish to add two such notions to the list because they imply strategies different from those already mentioned.

5. S initially tries to remember everything, subsequently switching to an H-testing strategy (Bourne & O'Banion, 1969).

6. S compares successive stimuli in the sequence to determine the relevance and irrelevance of attributes (Anderson & Guthrie, 1966; Dominowski, 1969).

If the listing is stopped at this point, there are six different process accounts to be considered, all of which are applicable to attribute identification under the reception paradigm. These proposals vary in completeness and have unequal levels of support; roughly, the amount of support probably decreases from the beginning to the end of the list. However, each proposal has some empirical support, and, to my knowledge, it has not been demonstrated that the data used to establish a proposal are inconsistent with it. What are we to make of this state of affairs? One possibility is that one of these proposals is largely correct and the others are wrong.

This seems very unlikely, but it is worth considering an implication of this conclusion. If it were true, it would mean that the data used to support at least some proposals are not sufficiently sensitive to allow a choice among models. While I doubt that there is a "winner," the implication that we rely on insensitive data has much merit. Gregg and Simon (1967) provided a demonstration that apparently "fine-grained" analyses based on measures such as number of errors to solution are insensitive to rather drastic changes in process assumptions. More will be said about this later.

Consider an alternative conclusion, that all of these proposals (or almost all, if you prefer) are correct, but for different variations of the reception–attribute-identification task. This would certainly complicate matters but cannot be dismissed, primarily because of the lack of evidence. Different proposals tend to be supported by different kinds of data. Comparisons among models are rare. There have been comparisons of different versions of the one-H model, and the fact that latencies decrease after the trial of the last error has been interpreted as favoring an H-sample model over a one-H model (Levine, 1969, 1970), but it seems more common to interpret a result only in terms of one model consistent with it. It is difficult to rule out the conclusion of different models for different situations. For example, H-testing models have been extensively investigated only with unidimensional concepts, although Nahinsky (1970) has proposed an H-sample theory for conjunctive concepts. The wholist strategy was proposed in the context of conjunctive concepts. Category search requires the availability of a large number of stimuli; it is doubtful that Ss' memory would allow this strategy to be used when previous stimuli are removed, but the model is plausible for situations in which an "external memory" is provided.

While the idea that different models are correct for different versions of the reception task has some merit, it is no panacea. To an extent, it does seem that different models have been proposed for what appears to be the same version of the reception task. To maintain the idea that there is really no conflict would mean that we must consider even more variations than have already been listed. This leads to the unappetizing suspicion that we will need many models indeed. However unappealing this thought might be, I wish to argue that our theoretical task is much more complicated than is implied by the alternative of "different models for different versions of the task."

Consider the possibility that all models might be simultaneously correct and wrong. What this refers to is the idea that, for a given version of attribute identification under the reception paradigm, one will find a variety of strategies being used over a group of Ss. The discussion of this argument is closely intertwined with the question of what sorts of data are collected.

METHODS OF DATA COLLECTION

If an investigator limits his observations to gross measures of efficiency, such as trials or errors to solution, two things follow. First, the connection between data and any inference about processes is likely to be indirect. Second, there is likely to be no reasonable alternative to the assumption that all Ss were following the same basic strategy. While a given distribution of, e.g., trials to solution, might allow a choice among two or more formal models, it does not rule out an account based on a multiplicity of strategies. The fundamental problem is that, given that S has required a certain number of trials to reach criterion and has made a certain number of errors, there remain a number of ways in which S might have approached the problem (see also Gregg & Simon, 1967).

If one accepts the argument that drawing inferences about Ss' processes will at least be made easier by examining additional data, there remains the question of what data to examine. One possibility is to analyze response sequences, which has been tried in attempting to describe Ss' selection strategies (e.g., Bruner et al., 1956; Byers, 1963; Giambra, 1971; Laughlin, 1965, 1968). The success attained in describing selection strategies should represent a high estimate of the success likely in analyzing Ss' response sequences in the reception paradigm because, in the strictest sense, the choice of one of 64 or 81 stimuli is much more informative than the choice of one or two category responses. In recent years, attempts to infer strategies on the basis of stimulus choices have been strongly criticized (Eifermann, 1965; Taplin & Jeeves, 1972; Wetherick, 1969). The critics argue that one cannot infer S's strategy solely on the basis of his choices. The problem in miniature can be illustrated as follows: S, having been shown as an initial positive instance of a conjunctive concept a stimulus which is *one, large, unfilled, red circle,* selects a stimulus which is *one, small, unfilled, red circle.* Has S chosen this stimulus to find out if size is relevant, to test the H "red circles," or "red unfilled figures," or both, or what? The argument is that one needs to know not only which stimulus is selected, but why it was chosen.

Another attempt to gain process information has been to ask Ss for hypotheses as they proceed through the task. Indeed, Levine's theoretical development has been based largely on the analysis of Ss' Hs, obtained through his blank-trials procedure or simply by asking for them (Karpf & Levine, 1971). There are two interpretive difficulties associated with analyzing Ss' hypotheses. First, it has been shown that, at least under some circumstances, Ss required to hypothesize after each trial solve the problem more efficiently than "control" Ss (Byers & Davidson, 1967; Dominowski, 1973). The most appealing explanation is that requiring Ss to hypothesize forces them to process information differently. If the difference is in type of information processing rather than simply in efficiency of carrying out common processes, then the process model based on Ss' hypothesizing will not apply to behavior under the control condition.

A second and related problem concerns the extent to which the investigator, in obtaining Ss' hypotheses, effectively instructs them to follow an H-testing approach. If S is carefully informed of the stimulus dimensions, the type of concept, and the number of relevant dimensions, and is instructed or indirectly encouraged to make his hypotheses of the appropriate form (= possible answers), it is possible that such instructions will make him into an H-tester. Alternatively, his protocol will give this impression whether or not he was proceeding in this fashion. It is possible to require hypotheses but to be somewhat nondirective about the form they should take. The results of requiring hypotheses have varied considerably, suggestively as a function of the directiveness of the instructions, although the studies also differ in terms of type of concept, number of dimensions, and sophistication of Ss. With a simple, unidimensional concept, Levine (1966, 1969, 1970) has found that virtually all of his well-practiced Ss show one H per trial. It should be noted that Levine (1969, 1970) has argued that the single H exhibited by S is really only a working H selected from a sample of Hs that S is considering, which can be taken as indicating a limitation of his method of obtaining hypotheses. (For a different criticism of the blank-trials technique, see Levison & Restle, 1973). When hypotheses are required of "naive" Ss who are not told what form their hypotheses should take, it has been found that hypotheses involving varying numbers of attributes are offered by different Ss (Bruner et al., 1956; Bourne, 1963, 1965; Dominowski, 1973; Siegel, 1969). This observation has been made primarily with conjunctive concepts, although it has also occurred with unidimensional and disjunctive concepts. The impression is strong that if we look for it, we will find a variety of strategies in use.

I have reached the opinion that, if our goal is to understand how Ss discover concepts, it is worth trying to give them ample opportunity to "tell us" how they do it. In the remainder of this paper, I will describe some recent attempts to obtain information about the solution process by the use of techniques such as requiring hypotheses, post-task reports, and thinking aloud. The studies do not hang together neatly as a series; although all involve attribute identification under the reception paradigm, the tasks differ in other respects. Some of these techniques involve, at least operationally, a change in the task from a "control" condition. Thus, the data need to be considered in light of the possibility that "task + investigative probing" yields conceptual behavior importantly different from that involved in "task only," a point to which I'll return later. The data give some idea of the kinds of information each technique makes available, as well as suggesting issues requiring theoretical attention.

EXPERIMENT 1. HYPOTHESES: HOW MANY AND HOW SURE?

These data were collected as part of an experiment conducted by Norman Wetherick and myself. In the experiment, each S was given two attribute-identification tasks; the present data come from the first task which was the same for all Ss (the main interest of the experiment was in various second tasks, which will not be discussed). The Ss were required to identify a unidimensional concept under the following procedural constraints: Ss offered hypotheses, did not have to categorize stimuli, and had available a complete record of previous trials. The data provide information regarding how Ss attempt to solve the problem under such conditions. In addition, evidence was gathered concerning the confidence Ss had in their hypotheses, which might be of theoretical importance. Taplin (1972) raised this issue in a specific context. He noted that the fact that latencies decrease after the trial of the last error has been interpreted as indicating that S starts his errorless run with several Hs (using what happens to be the correct H to categorize), with the decrease in latency over trials reflecting the elimination of incorrect Hs from S's sample (Levine, 1969; 1970). Taplin argued that the same function would occur if S held only one H but gained confidence in it. His point may be considered more generally: Is it the case that S simply holds or doesn't hold an H, as assumed by formal H theories, or do Ss consider Hs with varying degrees of confidence? The present study provides relevant data.

The 32 Ss were university students who were paid for their participation, and each was seen individually. Each stimulus consisted of a row of four boxes labeled A, B, C, and D, in each of which there could be a numeral 1, 2, or 3; thus, there were 81 possible stimuli. The Ss were carefully instructed that all positive stimuli would have a particular numeral in a particular box, that this would occur with no negative stimuli, and that their task was to figure out what this attribute was. The instructions encouraged H testing, indicating that the first trial would leave only four possible answers and that, by paying attention to further trials, S would be able to figure out which one characteristic was necessary for a stimulus to be positive. Categorization of stimuli was not required, and Ss were told that they could propose hypotheses (Hs) after each trial. Each S was told that, while E would like to know what S was considering, S was not obliged to offer an H after every trial; S was also informed that he could offer more than one H if he so wished. For every H that S offered, he was asked to indicate his confidence in it, on a scale ranging from 1 (considering it a possibility) to 5 (certain it is the answer). It was further explained that, when S offered an H with confidence 5, E would indicate whether it was right or wrong and, if right, the task would be over.

The stimulus sequence was so constructed that, logically, there were 4 tenable Hs after trial 1; 3, after trial 3; 2, after trial 4; and 1, after trial 8. On each trial S was shown a stimulus and its category, and then he offered his Hs (if any); trials were S-paced. The S had a complete record of previous trials but no record of his Hs. A maximum of 24 trials was given. After the task, each S was asked, "How did you go about solving the problem?"

Results and Discussion

As might be expected, this task was quite easy. Of the 32 Ss, 18 solved it in exactly 8 trials, 10 solved it in less than 8 trials, and 4 required "unnecessary" trials. The behavior of the 10 Ss who solved "too soon" was interesting; to be understood, it must be noted that after trial 4 there were two tenable Hs, B1 (the solution) and D3 (proved wrong on trial 8). One S, knowing after trial 4 that one of these two was correct, simply guessed B1 (with confidence 5) on trial 5 to see which was the answer; three Ss concentrated on B1 to the exclusion of other Hs for, as one of them said, no real reason. Five Ss offered D3 with confidence 5 after trial 4 or 5, believing it to be the answer, offering B1 as their answer only after being told that D3 was wrong; one S reversed this process, offering B1 (confidence 5), indicating that only later did she realize that the answer could have been D3 (at that time). Thus, nine of these ten Ss, all of whom "solved" in fewer trials than Ss processing the trial information perfectly, erred in processing information, being sure they knew the answer (whether B1 or D3) before the evidence warranted such confidence.

Of the 32 Ss, only 5 consistently offered one H per trial; the remaining 27 gave at least some evidence of multiple H testing, 9 showing the logically perfect reduction in the number of Hs under consideration allowed by the stimulus sequence (4-3-2-1). Based on post-task reports and H records, 7 Ss appeared to use only positive instances in solving the problem, while 25 tried to use both positive and negative instances (not all successfully). A total of 348 Hs was offered by all Ss, of which 32 (9.4%) were inconsistent with the information available at the time they were offered. Proposing a tenable H as the answer "too soon" was not counted as an error in this analysis; errors took the form of considering an H which had been shown to be wrong, or overtly eliminating an H which was still tenable (e.g., stating "B1 is out" on trial 3). It should be noted that 17 Ss made no overt errors; thus, the 32 errors were contributed by 15 Ss who made an average of 2.1 errors each (range $= 1-6$). Eighteen errors were inconsistent with the current trial; of these, 14 occurred after presentation of a negative instance. Of the 14 errors consistent with the current trial, 11 were inconsistent with the information contained in an earlier negative instance. Thus, of the 32 errors, 25 involved failures to correctly process information contained in negative instances (21 consisting of offering an H which had been proved wrong by a negative instance).

These data indicate considerable variation in problem solving among the Ss. It seems possible to distinguish at least four subgroups. There were five Ss who apparently tested one H at a time, all of whom said they tried to use both positive and negative instances; four of these Ss "solved too soon," and three made at least one overt error prior to solution, all errors involving negative instances. There were seven Ss who considered multiple Hs, used only positive instances, and who all made at least one overt error prior to solution, the errors with one exception involving negative instances. There were fifteen Ss who considered multiple Hs, used both types of instances, and made no overt errors; however, this group could be subdivided into nine logically perfect "simultaneous scanners" and six Ss who were not quite so neat, two of whom "solved too soon." Finally, there were five Ss who considered multiple Hs and tried to use both types of instances, all of whom made at least one overt error (errors being equally likely to involve positive or negative instances), three of whom "solved too soon."

It is a matter of conjecture whether or not the same strategies would be observed if prior stimuli were not available. Some changes would seem likely. For example, a number of Ss implied that, rather than formulating Hs and then checking them against the next trial, they tended more to search the display on each trial to see what possibilities existed, saying things like "I looked to see what the positives had in common and then checked to see if any of these were in the negatives." It is doubtful that Ss could attempt to do this if they had to remember prior stimuli. At the very least, the present data suggest that no single description would be adequate for all or even most Ss in the group.

Consider now the question of Ss' confidence in their Hs. All but two of the Ss offered the correct H at a lower level of confidence prior to submitting it as an answer (confidence = 5). An analysis of presolution changes in confidence was performed on data provided by 30 Ss who gave Hs on two or more trials prior to solution. The datum per trial was the mean confidence for the Hs offered. The number of trials varied over Ss both because Ss had differing numbers of presolution trials and because some Ss did not offer Hs on all trials. As a point of information, seven Ss gave their first Hs on trial 3, while nine did so on trial 4. Of the 30 Ss, 9 showed no change in confidence over presolution trials, whereas 21 showed an increase; 15 of these exhibited a consistent increase with no reversals, while the remaining 6 showed a general increase but with some fluctuation.

Two factors which could contribute to an increase in confidence over trials are (a) a reduction in the number of Hs under consideration and (b) the fact that an H considered later in the presolution phase is likely to have been correct for more trials than an H considered earlier. To gain some idea of the influence of these factors, the following analyses were conducted. For trials 4 through 7 of the stimulus sequence, there were two tenable Hs (B1 and D3). Sixteen Ss held just these two Hs during these trials, thus there was no change in the number of Hs under consideration but there was, for these 2 Hs, an increase in the number of trials consistent with them. Over these trials, 5 of the 16 Ss showed an increase in confidence in these Hs while 11 showed no change. Thus, an increase in "number of reinforcements" was associated with increasing confidence for a minority of these Ss. Thirteen Ss showed, at some time during the presolution phase, the following H pattern: On trial n, S offered k Hs, and on trial $n + 1$, S offered all but 1 of these same Hs. Of the 13 Ss, 7 showed an increase in confidence in the Hs which they kept, while 6 showed no change. While the present data indicate that, for a majority of Ss, Hs were considered with greater confidence over trials prior to solution, it can only be tentatively suggested that both a reduction in the number of Hs and an increase in the number of confirmations for an H might serve to increase confidence. One difficulty faced in separating these factors is that, if Ss behave sensibly (as was generally true in the present case), a reduction in the number of Hs will be confounded with an increase in the number of confirmations for those Hs remaining. The present data do suggest that a theory assuming that Ss simply either have or do not have an H is at least incomplete.

EXPERIMENT II. RECEPTION STRATEGIES FOR SIMPLE AND CONJUNCTIVE CONCEPTS

The second set of data comes from a study in which the basic task conformed to the "standard reception paradigm" in which prior stimuli are not available and S is required to categorize each stimulus when presented. The design consisted of the combination of three types of concept (unidimensional, conjunctive, and disjunctive) with three working conditions (control, hypothesis required, and free responses). I will not discuss the data concerning the disjunctive concept other than to note that Ss used a considerable variety of approaches which were often "erratic" and sometimes incomprehensible (see also Bruner et al., 1956). I will concentrate on the unidimensional and conjunctive concepts, which have received greater theoretical attention and for which the data are more readily interpreted.

The data come from 54 introductory psychology students who were fulfilling a course requirement; each received only one task, and 9 Ss were assigned to each combination of concept and working condition. The stimuli were cartoon-type drawings of men varying in the following ways: tall or short, fat or thin, having mustache or beard, smoking a cigar or pipe, wearing a hat (derby) or beret, and bowtie or necktie. The stimulus population thus consisted of 64 stimuli; slides were prepared for use in the experiment. For each concept, a sequence of 12 stimuli was constructed such that the first stimulus was a positive instance, the concept could logically be identified after trial 6, and there were equal numbers of positive and negative instances.

Each S was seen individually and was thoroughly instructed regarding the stimulus dimensions, the type of concept, the number of relevant dimensions, and the procedure to be followed. On each trial, a stimulus was projected in front of S, who pressed one of two buttons labeled "yes" and "no" which resulted in the illumination of one of two lights labeled "right" and "wrong". Trials were S-paced, and S was given a card listing the stimulus dimensions and their values, which could be consulted during the task. It was emphasized that if S could discover the concept, he would be able to categorize stimuli without error. Upon completion of the twelfth trial, each S was asked what he thought was the answer and how he had gone about trying to identify the concept. This part of the procedure applied to all Ss and summarizes the control condition.

In the hypothesis-required condition, it was explained that, since we wished to know something of what Ss were doing during the task, they should complete a hypothesis slip after each trial. These slips contained the stimulus values in pairs (e.g., tall-short, fat-thin, etc.), and Ss were asked to check those characteristics they were considering. It was emphasized that they were free to do the task in whatever manner they preferred, that all we asked was that they indicate on the slips what they were considering. Each time Ss completed a hypothesis slip they placed it face down on the table and thus had no record of their hypotheses.

In the free-response condition, Ss were told that, since we wished to know what they were doing, they should after each trial write on a slip of paper what they had learned from that trial. It was emphasized that they could do the task in whatever way they chose and that all that we requested was that they indicate on each slip what information they had obtained from that trial. When completed, each slip was placed face down on the table and thus was not available for S's inspection.

Results and Discussion

Since the task was stopped after 12 trials, a number of Ss failed to solve it, especially with the conjunctive concept. Of the 27 Ss given a unidimensional concept, 19 found the solution, 7 each in the control and hypothesis-required conditions, and 5 in the free-response group. The greater difficulty of the conjunctive concept is indicated by the fact that only 7 of 27 Ss found the solution, 1 in the control condition and 3 each in the other two groups. Other than indicating a clear difference between concepts, these data are too insensitive for other comparisons.

The data of particular interest concern the methods which Ss followed. Post-task reports were used to identify Ss' strategies. Let me emphasize that Ss were simply asked how they did the task and were not pressed to provide details or to explain their remarks. Nonetheless, post-task reports were sufficiently informative to allow classification in terms of over-all approach. Where supplementary information was available, it was generally consistent with Ss' reports. However, this statement must be interpreted cautiously. That is, for control Ss, there was typically no useful supplementary information against which to evaluate their reports. For some Ss, one could "see" in their categorizations what they said they had done, but in many cases the pattern of responses was sufficiently ambiguous to be "consistent" with any of a variety of methods. The most useful information came from the hypothesis-required condition, and it frequently agreed nicely with S's report and was regularly in general agreement with the report. To a lesser extent, the same was true of what was gained from the free-response condition; the difficulty here was that a fair amount of what Ss wrote was uninformative (e.g., describing the stimulus) and thus not very useful. In sum, Ss typically described the method they used with some conviction and clarity, and supplementary information sometimes clearly corroborated their reports and never really contradicted them.

TABLE 2

Number of Subjects Reporting Various Strategies

Type of strategy	Type of Concept	
	Unidimensional	Conjunctive
One H at a time	11	16
Several Hs at a time	5	0
Remember all attributes of 1st stimulus and eliminate	5	5
Remember all attributes of 1st stimulus and only compare positives to eliminate	0	2
Changed strategy during task	4	2
Other	2	2

The data in Table 2 are combined over working conditions, among which it is difficult to argue for important differences, due in part to the small number of Ss under each condition for a given type of concept. The most noticeable differences were that no Ss in the control condition reported testing several Hs at a time (unidimensional concept) or changing their strategy during the task, but the frequencies of such reports were small in general.

In Table 2 it can be seen that the most popular strategy was "one H at a time." Among Ss reporting this strategy, the most common report was a simple statement to the effect that they had tested one H at a time and changed when they had to (made an error). Only a minority of these Ss volunteered additional information. With respect to memory, Ss' statements varied from "didn't pay attention to other attributes when testing a hypothesis" to "tried to use the 'failure trial' in picking a new hypothesis" to "tried to be consistent with all previous trials." For the conjunctive concept, H-testers reported a variety of methods for forming a new H, of which the following are exemplary: "Picked a pair of attributes and tested; when wrong, dropped them both." "Picked a pair, etc.; when wrong, dropped one attribute and added a new one randomly." "Picked, etc..; when wrong, dropped one attribute and replaced it; if wrong again, tried the previously dropped attribute with the one that had replaced it." "Thought *short* (e.g.) was one attribute and tried pairing different attributes with it." In addition, it is perhaps worth mentioning that a few Ss exhibited the tenacious adherence to a hypothesis that apparently dismayed Wason (1960) in another context—in this case, adopting an H early in the task and keeping it, despite errors, on the belief that "one can't really expect to be right all the time," or "the feedback lights weren't working properly because they kept telling me I was wrong," or, unfortunately in two cases, "the experimenter was tricking them or had changed his answer."

It is of some interest that no S given a conjunctive concept tried to test several Hs at a time, a finding consistent with Taplin's (1972) argument that such a strategy is unlikely in any but the simplest situations because of the demands it places on short-term memory. Of the five Ss reporting this strategy for the unidimensional concept, three indicated that they had difficulty keeping track of what they were doing. Similar difficulties beset those who changed strategies, all but one of whom began by trying to remember all attributes of the first stimulus and eliminate, but they became confused and changed to testing one H at a time.

The strategy of remembering all of the attributes of the first stimulus (which was a positive instance), and then eliminating, was followed by a minority of Ss for both types of concepts. With the conjunctive concepts, this is clearly an attribute-testing approach as opposed to an H-testing approach. However, it is not apparent that any distinction can be made between these two approaches for a unidimensional concept, for which attributes are Hs. Thus it might be sensible, for the unidimensional concept, to place together those Ss who eliminated attributes from the list of all attributes present in the first instance with Ss who tested several Hs at a time, considering their only difference to be in the number of Hs under consideration. However, it might be argued that an S who selects some attributes (Hs?) will have some commitment to his selection and will desire to be correct in categorizing, whereas the S who takes all attributes will not care whether he is right or wrong, seeking only to discover which attributes to eliminate on the basis of E's categorization. Whether such a distinction is worth attempting is debatable. What can be reported is that, for the unidimensional concept, the five Ss who eliminated from a list of all initial attributes had no difficulty with the task, all finding the solution by trial 6. This can be contrasted with the difficulty reported by some of those testing several Hs at a time, all of whom solved the problem, but later (1 S on trial 9, the other 4 after trial 12). Of course, the differences between these two groups in strategy and efficiency might be explained solely in terms of differences in short-term memory (central information-processing capacity).

As in Experiment I, Ss' reports indicate a variety of strategies in use. For the unidimensional concept, no strategy achieved a majority. A one-H model could claim a majority for the conjunctive concept, but even among this subgroup, Ss' additional remarks imply differences in what Ss tried to remember and how they selected new Hs after errors.

The data regarding Ss' inferences on individual trials provide additional information about the solution process. Within H theory, considerable attention has been directed toward the differential influence of correct and error trials on the solution process. According to one-H theory, S keeps his H when correct and adopts a new H when wrong. According to H-sample theory, on each trial S keeps consistent Hs and drops inconsistent ones. Of course, Ss do not always (not all Ss do?) follow these principles (e.g., Milward & Spoehr, 1973; Taplin, 1972). Other research, emphasizing the difference in effectiveness of positive and negative instances (see Bourne & Dominowski, 1972), can be taken as indicating that one must consider more than whether or not an H is confirmed or infirmed on a trial.

Bruner et al. (1956) found that, with a conjunctive concept, Ss were most likely to handle correctly a positive confirming trial and least likely to handle correctly a negative infirming trial. Their results indicated that whether S's H was right or wrong, and whether the instance was positive or negative, were both important. Similar analyses were conducted using the present data. One analysis was based solely on those trials for which S had shown only one H immediately prior to the trial and only one H after the trial. Less than a third of the total trials could be used for this analysis; as might be expected, the data came primarily from the hypothesis-re quired condition, less often from the free-response condition, and only rarely from the control condition (when S, after the task, stated explicitly that he had tested, e.g., "beret" until trial 4, then switched to "tall," etc.).

Given that S has a single H, he can encounter four types of contingency: positive confirming, positive infirming, negative confirming, and negative infirming. For confirming trials, "correct handling" was defined as keeping that H (as in Bruner et al., 1956). For infirming trials, correct handling was defined as switching to a new H consistent with the current trial (which is less stringent than Bruner et al.'s criterion). The results of this analysis are shown in Table 3.

TABLE 3

Number of Contingencies and Percent Handled Correctly

Contingency	Unidimensional	Conjunctive
Positive Confirming	54% (n = 24)	94% (n = 33)
Positive Infirming	57% (n = 14)	57% (n = 14)
Negative Confirming	76% (n = 21)	82% (n = 39)
Negative Infirming	33% (n = 21)	7% (n = 15)

In Table 3 it is apparent that correct handling is affected both by the type of instance presented and by the relationship between S's H and the trial information. The relative difficulty of the different contingencies for the conjunctive concept is consistent with the findings of Bruner et al. (1956). Two further comments seem in order. First, the percentage of positive confirming contingencies handled correctly with the unidimensional concept seems surprisingly low. The low percentage stems from the fact that, on those trials, shifting to a different H consistent with the current trial occurred almost as often as keeping the H which S held prior to the trial. Making this kind of change might not be the most appropriate behavior, but it is not a "terrible" error, nor does it seem particularly surprising if it occurs on an early trial when locally-consistent Hs are likely to be fairly equally viable or if Ss are only tentatively trying out Hs (see Experiment I). Second, since negative infirming contingencies were handled so poorly, one does wonder what Ss did. Of the 28 errors made on these trials, 6 consisted of keeping the infirmed H while 22 involved choosing a new H inconsistent with the current trial. This suggests a tendency to treat a negative instance like a positive instance (by adopting an H present on a negative instance), a tendency which was shown by some Ss in Experiment I and which has been reported by Denny and Benjafeld (1969) and Wetherick (1966).

One of the difficulties with a contingency analysis is that it requires Ss to have only one H before and after a trial, which, in the present case, severely restricted the amount of useable data. Furthermore, it is not obvious that it is necessary to describe a trial in relationship to S's prior H. It seems reasonable that some Ss enter and leave a trial with a single H, some might entertain different numbers of Hs before and after a trial, and some might enter a trial with no particular H but leave it with one or more. One can ask for all of these Ss what are their chances of making inferences consistent with a trial as a function of the type of trial, positive vs. negative × correct vs. error (note that for an S categorizing on the basis of a single H, confirming vs. infirming = correct vs. error). Such an analysis was performed on the present data, which allowed more of the data to be used. For a trial to be included in this analysis, for the unidimensional concept, S had to indicate one or more Hs (attributes) after that trial. For the conjunctive concept, only trials on which S checked two attributes (in the hypothesis-required condition), or otherwise clearly indicated his H, were used (trials on which Ss checked 3 or more attributes were not used because these cannot be scored unambiguously). When S gave more than one H, each was tabulated separately. Thus, the analysis was addressed to the question, "Of the Hs considered after each type of trial, what percentage were consistent with the information on that trial?" The data are given in Table 4.

The over-all impression given by this local consistency analysis is similar to that obtained from the contingency analysis (of course, the trials used in the contingency analysis also contributed to the data in Table 4). In the present case, there is a stronger suggestion of a difference between concepts, with Hs considered after all but positive correct trials being less likely to be locally

TABLE 4

Number of Hypotheses Offered and Percent Locally
Consistent After Different Types of Trials

Type of Trial	Type of concept	
	Unidimensional	Conjunctive
Positive correct	96% (n = 120)	98% (n = 51)
Positive incorrect	83% (n = .52)	62% (n = 34)
Negative correct	83% (n = 81)	65% (n = 48)
Negative incorrect	51% (n = 55)	36% (n = 25)

consistent when seeking a conjunctive concept. Both analyses indicate that negative instances and error trials are more likely to be followed by faulty inferences. Although this finding agrees with the results obtained by Bruner et al. (1956) and seems worth pursuing, such analyses must be interpreted with great caution. It must be kept in mind that, in the present case, only trials on which Ss offered Hs were used, and that, even if all Ss were forced to give Hs on all trials, all Ss will not equally experience the different types of trials, and only some Ss make inferential errors. It seems likely that Ss who make poorer use of information will be more likely to encounter error trials, which would mean that the data for such trials overrepresent these Ss. It would be clearly inappropriate to assume that the various types of trials are encountered by chance or that there is for all Ss a fixed probability of making an erroneous inference.

One last bit of information from this experiment is the observation that, of the 20 Ss who failed to identify the correct conjunctive concept after 12 trials, 11 offered answers that were "half-right," i.e., contained one of the two relevant attributes. By comparison, only 18 of the 59 theoretically possible incorrect answers contain one correct attribute. This suggests that some Ss might discover one relevant attribute without attaining the complete solution. Several pairs of successive trials in the stimulus sequence allowed such an inference to be made. Such knowledge would enable S to avoid categorization errors on certain negative instances, i.e., having learned that "short" is one relevant attribute, S would not make errors on large stimuli whatever their other attributes. Although this idea is quite speculative, it is consistent with the observation that on trials 6–12 (after sufficient information to solve had been given), 14 Ss made fewer errors on negative instances than on positive instances, while the reverse was true of only 3, with 10 Ss showing no difference (including those who made no errors on these trials).

At this point, let me comment briefly on the techniques used in these studies. If one merely has Ss categorize, it seems clear to me that inferences about processes are quite tenuous, and certain kinds of information (like that in Tables 3 and 4) are unavailable. Of the two trial-by-trial techniques, requesting hypotheses yielded more useful information than having Ss "write what they've learned from a trial." I recall, upon reading Laughlin's (Laughlin, 1968; Laughlin & Doherty, 1967) reports that allowing Ss to use pencil and paper had no effect on efficiency, wondering if perhaps they did not know what to write. Having now tried a similar technique, I hold this view with greater conviction, at least for some Ss. Asking Ss, after the task, how they had tried to solve the problem was a technique that yielded largely intelligible reports which characterized Ss' approaches to some extent. Of course, even a combination of post-task reports and trial-by-trial hypotheses leaves gaps in our information. It seems that the sort of question to which we might want more of an answer is of the type, "On the trial 6, what was S doing after learning that he'd made an error?" If S offers a hypothesis, it gives only a hint of an answer, and it seems doubtful that S could give much of an answer if the question were put to him after the task. Therefore, I decided to try a technique which Newell and Simon (1972) have used with considerable success for other tasks, namely, having Ss think aloud.

EXPERIMENT III. CONCEPT IDENTIFICATION WHILE THINKING ALOUD

For this exploratory study, the reception paradigm was used, with S required to discover the two attributes of a conjunctive concept. The stimuli were geometric forms drawn on index cards and varying in the following ways: circle or triangle, red or black, large or small, 1 or 2 figures, filled or open, and on the left or right side of the card. A stimulus sequence was constructed such that the first stimulus was a positive instance, the concept could logically be identified after trial 6, and there were equal numbers of positive and negative instances. The sequence contained 24 stimuli, and the information provided by the first six trials was roughly repeated by each successive block of six trials.

The Ss were five nonstudent women of approximately college age who were paid for their participation. Each S was seen individually, and sessions were tape recorded. The S was carefully instructed regarding the stimulus dimensions and the type of concept to be discovered, by the use of examples. It was emphasized that, if S could figure out which two stimulus features had been chosen to define membership in the positive category, she would be able to categorize stimuli without error. It was explained that the task would proceed at S's pace: on each trial, E presented a card, waited for S to categorize it, gave the correct response, and waited for S to indicate that she was ready for the next trial. Only the current card was available to S on any trial.

With respect to thinking aloud, Ss received the following instructions. They were told that the general idea was to do all (as much as possible) of their thinking aloud. They were asked to say aloud what they were looking at when a card was presented. It was pointed out that, since S would have some sort of reason for choosing one of the two categories for a card, she should state that reason. It was emphasized that the nature of the reason made no difference —whether it was a guess, to try out an idea, because she felt she knew the answer, because she just felt like saying "yes," or whatever—that the important thing was to say what the reason was. Similarly, Ss were asked to do aloud any thinking they engaged in after E told them the correct response for a card. Finally, they were told that, if it appeared that they were thinking silently, E would ask what they were thinking. When the task was over, an informal interview was held with each S.

Results and Discussion

The tape recordings were transcribed (by the writer) into typewritten protocols, two of which are given at the end of this paper. For four of the five Ss, the protocols contain an abundance of information, which can be seen by examining the two protocols included with this paper. The fifth S proceeded through the task at a very rapid rate, and her protocol seems somewhat sparse. Virtually every trial consisted of the following sequence of events: Upon presentation of a stimulus, she, without hesitation, described it (typically naming about 4 attributes) and categorized it. Then E asked for her reason, which she gave without hesitation. Upon being told the correct response, she was ready for the next trial. After the task, this S indicated that she had done nearly all of her thinking aloud, which seems doubtful but, given the small amount of "blank" time which elapsed, somewhat plausible.

Let me provide some general information about the method. After the task, Ss were asked how much of their thinking they had done aloud, i.e., how much was on the tape. Three felt they had done all or nearly all their thinking aloud. Another indicated that she had probably made some mistakes—what she had said was not exactly what she had thought in one or two instances. Asked to explain what sort of difference there had been, S said she didn't know, that she would have to listen to the tape and look at the cards again in order to tell. The fifth S's immediate response was "about 50%." Asked what had been left out, she explained that she'd had to think and then say it—that she hadn't told about the thinking she'd done when saying what she had just previously thought. In response to another question, she indicated that she felt that very little of her problem-related thinking was left out. Thus it can be seen that, in Ss' opinions, the protocols are rather complete and accurate records of how they did the task.

From an examination of the protocols and the experience of observing Ss, the following comments can be made. For three Ss, perception of the stimulus was so automatic that they almost never described what they were looking at. It was frequently necessary to ask S her reason for a categorization, although three Ss gave them without prompting on the vast majority of trials, and all Ss seemed to find it easy to respond to a request for a reason. It is also worth noting that, through hesitations, pauses, and the content of their reasons, it is rather easy to discern changes in Ss' confidence in their categorizations. Further, Ss' reasons for categorizations and the thinking aloud they did after learning the correct response provide considerable information about what they were able to remember as they proceeded through the task.

After the task, Ss were also asked if they felt they had done the task differently from the way they would do it if the procedure consisted simply of presenting stimuli and having them categorize. One believed that thinking aloud made no difference at all, while two felt that the technique had resulted in their thinking more carefully about the problem. Another felt that thinking aloud made the task more difficult because of the need to think of what one had thought and then say it. The fifth believed that she had done the task differently but, in response to questioning, indicated that she had no idea what the difference might have been. There is in these comments little indication that thinking aloud yielded very atypical thinking for these Ss, although the suggestion that thinking aloud resulted in more careful information processing seems plausible (such an effect would seem rather desirable). In terms of efficiency, the Ss' performance does not appear unusual, the trial of the last error for the five Ss being trials 12, 14, 17, 9, and 15.

The technique yielded the following observations. All five Ss gave evidence that they tried to remember the first stimulus (a positive instance) and use it as a basis for comparison. Thus, four Ss noted the similarity of the second stimulus to the first (five common attributes) and said it too was positive (it was negative). After this experience, they then attended to differences between the current stimulus and the first, categorizing stimuli as negative for several trials and making errors on positive instances on trials 4 and 5. Subject 4 showed a different approach in that, on several trials, she indicated that her response didn't matter since she only wanted to determine, on the basis of E's feedback, whether a particular dimension was relevant or not (see, for example, her last "error" on trial 9).

Having seen several positive instances, Ss gave evidence of trying to remember stimuli in the positive category, rather a mixture of commonalities and memory for individual stimuli. There are frequent references, in giving reasons for categorizations, of the sort "because all those which have belonged have been . . .". In addition, several Ss used a partial exclusion approach, learning that certain stimulus types are negative while having no firm idea of what defined the positive category, as in "No, because large figures are out." This was most apparent for Ss 1 and 3 who, after the first six trials, made errors only on positive instances. There are indications that Ss had difficulty remembering their earlier decisions, e.g., getting part of the answer on one trial, then getting the other part on a later trial but forgetting the earlier inference. Subject 2 gives an interesting example of memory failure on trials 7–10, tentatively formulating the correct answer and then forgetting it.

The protocols do not indicate that Ss were adhering to a strategy of forming a bidimensional H and testing it, although Ss 1 and 2 give evidence of hypothesis testing on some trials. Subject 4 provides the best example of an attribute-testing approach. In general, Ss exhibited considerable searching and tentative decision-making, attempting to use the current trial and what they could remember to determine what might be involved in the answer, with attention directed primarily to positive instances. While Ss had reasons for their categorizations, and these were seldom guesses, their reasons could rarely be simply described as Hs. Their reasons were to some extent developed after inspection of the current stimulus and, over trials, represented rather disconnected and partial ideas.

CONCLUDING REMARKS

Let me briefly summarize some of the issues raised by these studies. The data suggest that theoretical attention be given to the topic of Ss' confidence in their decisions and to the influence of positive and negative, correct and error trials on the solution process. With respect to memory, the thinking-aloud protocols suggest tendencies to remember (a) the first stimulus, (b) characteristics of positive instances, and (c) "isolated" stimulus features associated with negative instances, as well as pointing to difficulties which Ss encounter in remembering their earlier decisions. However, the most salient finding is that in all the studies, Ss were not homogeneous in terms of solution processes. Among a group of Ss given the same problem, a variety of strategies would be followed, a kind of finding which has been reported with considerable frequency (e.g., Bourne, 1963, 1965; Bruner et al., 1956; Dominowski, 1973; Eifermann, 1965; Milward & Spoehr, 1973; Nahinsky, 1968; Schwartz, 1966; Siegel, 1969; Wetherick, 1969).

These issues perhaps cannot be considered separate from an examination of the techniques used to obtain data. As one proceeds from categorizations through trial-by-trial hypotheses and post-task reports to thinking aloud, the information gets richer but also more complicated and difficult to handle theoretically. These techniques involve another issue as well. A possible objection to having Ss hypothesize or think aloud is that doing so results in Ss doing the task differently (compared to a "control" condition). It seems almost inevitable that making such changes in the task will in some way affect S's approach to the task, although I believe it is useful to distinguish between techniques which appear to encourage S to use some particular method and those which, as suggested for thinking aloud, result in Ss working more carefully. However, whether the likely effects of such techniques warrant an objection to their use is another matter. In a general attempt to understand conceptual behavior, is a situation in which Ss offer hypotheses, or think aloud, or whatever, to be included in what we seek to understand? I see no *a priori* reason for their exclusion. We could decide that our goal is to account for data coming exclusively from situations in which S is only shown stimuli and required to categorize, but this does not seem an appealing goal. Even with this restriction, one could still interview Ss after the task, which the present results suggest would be sufficient to demonstrate nonhomogeneity among Ss.

Formal theories of concept identification have taken the form of proposing strategies which Ss are assumed to follow in solving the problem. The present results and others cited indicate that a variety of strategies will be exhibited over a group of Ss, as well as implying that strategies will change with certain task alterations. This state of affairs not only casts doubt on any theory assuming a common strategy for all Ss but also raises the question of whether this kind of theory is useful.

It might be possible to engage in what Wetherick (1970) calls Type II psychology, which means developing theoretical accounts which apply only to grouped data, with no claim made that the statements apply to individuals (the contrast with Type I psychology is obvious). Thus, it is conceivable that a theory could be developed in terms of probabilities—of testing one H at a time, of testing several Hs, of being locally consistent, of ignoring negative instances, etc. Differences among Ss would be "ignored," and the probabilities could be adjusted for different situations. Such an attempt might soon become unwieldy, and the outcome is not very appealing.

An alternative would be to deal with subgroups of Ss who are rather homogeneous. If the subgroups are appropriately formed, then a description of the strategy for the subgroup could reasonably apply to each of the individual members. The manner of forming subgroups, the number formed, and the accuracy of the theoretical accounts would depend on the level of detail which is chosen as appropriate. While this approach would have certain advantages, it would still lead to a multiplicity of descriptions over subgroups and task variations.

As a final comment, let me suggest that perhaps the attempt to describe strategies is not the most useful direction to follow. Trying to develop an account of some detail of how Ss do a particular task would seem to be valuable only if, on some basis, that particular task is important. Stated conversely, if we agree that there are a number of concept-identification situations worthy of consideration, and if we agree that strategies will change over subgroups of Ss and with the situation, it is then unclear that much effort should be expended in attempting to develop a detailed account of any particular strategy. Perhaps we would make greater progress by directing our attention more to those characteristics of thinking which will influence conceptual behavior, dealing with aspects of behavior "smaller" than strategies. For example, regardless of strategy, Ss will encounter positive and negative instances on correct and error trials.

How do we account for the fact that incorrect inferences are more common for some types of trials and for some *S*s? The answer to such a question seems likely to be relevant to conceptual behavior in a considerable variety of situations. Although the question "How do people discover concepts?" seems to imply a strategy description as an answer, this may not be the best way to interpret the question.

PROTOCOLS OF SUBJECTS WORKING ALOUD

Note.—Each trial begins with a description of the stimulus shown to the subject. The subject's speech is in ordinary type, while the experimenter's speech is in capital letters. With a few exceptions, the subject's indication at the end of a trial that she was ready for the next one is not indicated. The following symbols are used in the protocols:

CORR = ———— = Experimenter's indication of the correct response.

? = An inquiry by the experimenter, either a request for the reason for a categorization or, when the subject paused, an inquiry as to what the subject was thinking.

— = A hesitation in the subject's speech.

. . = A pause in the subject's speech (. . . . = a longer pause).

Subject 2

1. TWO SMALL BLACK OPEN TRIANGLES ON THE LEFT. . . I'll say yes it does belong—it's a pure guess because it's the first one. CORR = YES. . .? I'm just trying to memorize what it looks like.

2. TWO LARGE BLACK OPEN TRIANGLES ON THE LEFT. Second one's got two triangles as well, and they're on the left side so I would say it does belong. CORR = NO. . .? . . . . Don't know . . . must be . . small . . before they belong and these are large, so . .

3. ONE SMALL RED FILLED TRIANGLE ON THE RIGHT. That's a small red triangle on the right side. Since it's a small one I would say it does belong, cuz the second one didn't. CORR = NO. Em, it must be . . black triangles which belong—small black triangles.

4. TWO SMALL RED OPEN CIRCLES ON THE LEFT. . . No, that doesn't belong. ? Because I'm looking for small black triangles and these are two small red circles. CORR = YES. Oh. Well it must be something to do with the left side because . . this one and the first card both have two symbols on the left.

5.   ONE SMALL RED OPEN CIRCLE ON THE LEFT. That's only one symbol
on the left side so I'll say it—it doesn't belong. CORR = YES. It does.
So that's small—one or two small symbols on the left side—I'm looking
for.

6.   ONE SMALL RED FILLED CIRCLE ON THE LEFT. . . . .? I'm thinking
about—it's not—it is a small symbol on the left side but the others were
open and this one's filled in, so I'd say no it doesn't belong. CORR =
NO. Eh, I'm thinking I've maybe got it now—a bit better—cuz I can recognize
them.

7.   TWO SMALL BLACK OPEN TRIANGLES ON THE RIGHT. These are
two small symbols on the right side so I'll say they don't belong.
CORR = YES. Oh . . it must be two small symbols on either side—that
I'm looking for—two small open symbols—or one small open symbol.

8.   TWO LARGE BLACK OPEN TRIANGLES ON THE RIGHT. I'd say
this doesn't belong because the symbols are large whereas all the rest
were small. CORR = NO. Em . . so it must be two or one small open
symbols.

9.   TWO SMALL RED OPEN TRIANGLES ON THE RIGHT. Eh, yes that
does belong because it's two small red triangles on the right side.
CORR = YES. Em, I think I must have got it by now.

10.   TWO SMALL BLACK FILLED CIRCLES ON THE LEFT. Yes that does
belong because there are two small red circles-black circles on the left
side. CORR = NO. . . . .? I'm trying to think where I've gone wrong
. . must be, um . . red only –no . . . . um . . . . um . . . red on the
left side and black—no . . . . . . I don't know—I'll try another one.

11.   TWO SMALL BLACK FILLED TRIANGLES ON THE LEFT. . . Eh
. .? Two small black triangles on the left side . . I would say it doesn't
belong because they're black and all the rest have been red—the last one
was black and it didn't belong, so I'll say this one doesn't belong either.
CORR = NO. So, um, must be something to do with black filled-in symbols
do not belong whereas red ones and black outlines do . .

12.   ONE SMALL RED OPEN CIRCLE ON THE RIGHT. This one does belong.
? Because it's a small red circle on the right-side—an unfilled one.
CORR = YES. Eh, I think I understand about the red circles and so on–I'm
not too sure about the black filled-in ones.

13.   ONE SMALL RED OPEN TRIANGLE ON THE LEFT. This one does
belong—it's a small red open triangle on the left side which seems quite
in common with the rest. CORR = YES.

14. ONE SMALL RED FILLED TRIANGLE ON THE LEFT. I think this one might belong although I'm not quite sure about filled-in ones yet–but it's a small filled red triangle on the left side—yes. CORR = NO. Oh, um–don't think I'll ever get this. Well, filled-in ones must all be no . . um, especially if they're on the left side, no?

15. ONE LARGE BLACK OPEN CIRCLE ON THE RIGHT. I would say that one doesn't belong because it's a large circle and all the other symbols have been small. CORR = NO. I think that sort of proves that large ones are completely out–ok.

16. ONE SMALL BLACK OPEN TRIANGLE ON THE RIGHT. I would say this one–does belong–it's a small black open triangle on the right side–um, and that seems to run through the whole lot–that have been right. CORR = YES. I'm not thinking anything now. Ready for another–I don't think I've solved it yet.

17. ONE SMALL BLACK OPEN CIRCLE ON THE RIGHT. I'll say that one does belong–once more it's a small black open circle on the right side, and I think we've had a card like that before. CORR = YES. . . . . Next.

18. ONE SMALL BLACK FILLED CIRCLE ON THE RIGHT. I would say this one doesn't belong–it's a small filled black circle on the right side–if I remember correctly, filled ones didn't belong. CORR = NO. I seem to be getting somewhere–I don't think there are any left now (indicating cards). THERE ARE SOME.

19. TWO SMALL RED OPEN TRIANGLES ON THE LEFT. That one does belong–two small red triangles on the left side–*open* triangles–I think I've seen that one before as well. CORR = YES.

20. TWO SMALL RED FILLED TRIANGLES ON THE LEFT. These are two small red triangles on the left side, filled in . . I'll say they don't belong. ? Because . . filled-in ones don't belong . . although they must be small–small open symbols, either one or two, on the right side or the left . . CORR = NO.

21. TWO SMALL RED OPEN CIRCLES ON THE LEFT. These are two small red–small black circles on the left side–eh, open so I'd say that they do belong. CORR = YES. Yeh, I think I've got it–maybe I haven't but it seems to be one or two small symbols which must not be filled in.

22. ONE LARGE BLACK OPEN TRIANGLE ON THE LEFT. No, that one doesn't belong. ? It's a large triangle and so far all large triangles haven't belonged. CORR = NO. Good.

23. ONE LARGE RED OPEN TRIANGLE ON THE LEFT. This is a large red open triangle on the left side, and since it's a large one I would say it doesn't belong. CORR = NO.

24. ONE SMALL BLACK OPEN TRIANGLE ON THE LEFT. Eh, this is a small black triangle on the left side–an open one, so it does belong. ? Because it's . . small–open–black–doesn't matter if it's black or red but . . anything that belongs must be small–and–open, and either one or two, on the left or right. CORR = YES.

Subject 4

1. TWO SMALL BLACK OPEN TRIANGLES ON THE LEFT. Two small black triangles, on the left . . they're open. I'm going to say that that's not in your category because . . . if I say it is and you say it isn't that doesn't give me much of a clue. YOUR RESPONSE IS NO? I'm saying no. CORR = YES. . . ? I'm now trying to work out what possibilities that means–and of course I'm trying to memorize this card. So, two on left black triangles, small unfilled.

2. TWO LARGE BLACK OPEN TRIANGLES ON THE LEFT. . . . That's very similar–the only difference is that the triangles are big; so—if this is not in your category then you can eliminate bigness as your–as one of the features–so it doesn't really matter what I say for this. Let us say it is not. CORR = NO. That eliminates large ones from your category.

3. ONE SMALL RED FILLED TRIANGLE ON THE RIGHT. . . . ? I'm looking at a small red triangle on the right, eh, it's filled. Now, I can't see that this will give me any information because the only thing it has in common with the first one, which is included, is that it's–oh–a small triangle–that's two features, isn't it. Um, I'll say it's not in. CORR = NO. Uhuh.

4. TWO SMALL RED OPEN CIRCLES ON THE LEFT. Small triangle and it's not–um . . two small red circles, unfilled on the left side of the card. Um . . I'll say they are in your category. ? Well, I'm just wondering whether they are similar to the first card in that they are two small objects on the left –the difference is in color and shape. This'll give me–you know . . CORR = YES. I'd say that if both this one and the first one are in your category I think the–what have they got in common–on the left, unfilled, two . . . . and small. Um, that's not a lot of help.

5. ONE SMALL RED OPEN CIRCLE ON THE LEFT. One small red circle unfilled on the left . . I would say that is not in your category. ? I've decided that previous–must be purely guesswork–that there are two objects in your category. CORR = YES. Oh! Aha–now I'm trying to put all the facts together. Well, there are three which have been in your category so far;

I'm trying to calculate the things which the three have in common. Um, it's no longer necessarily–uh–but they are on the left, they are small and they are open . . but they can be either color, either shape, or there can be 1 or 2 of them—ok.

6. ONE SMALL RED FILLED CIRCLE ON THE LEFT. . . . . This is a small red filled circle on the left and, . . um, no–what have we got so far–um, its bound to be on the left so from that point of view it's in your category. It's–this one is filled whereas so far the ones you've had on the left have been open. So let's find out whether the filling makes any difference–I say yes, this is in. ? I'm trying to get more information about whether filling or openness makes any difference. CORR = NO. Aha, so that confirms that an unfilled–I mean a filled shape is not in your category–I think I'd already said that . .

7. TWO SMALL BLACK OPEN TRIANGLES ON THE RIGHT. This is two small black triangles on the right-open, and I think I have established that anything on the right is not in your category, so I say no. CORR = YES. . . Oh dear . . so it must be coincidence that the ones you said yes to before were on left . . so how far have we got. I think the figures have to be small . . and they have to be open. I think perhaps that is all we've established . . cuz circles and triangles, ones and twos, left or right all seem to fit.

8. TWO LARGE BLACK OPEN TRIANGLES ON THE RIGHT. Well, this is two large open black triangles on the right, I will say these are not in your category because they are large and the others were small. CORR = NO. Right! Well, I think that definitely eliminates large shapes . .

9. TWO SMALL RED OPEN TRIANGLES ON THE RIGHT. Two small red triangles on the right–open, um–now then . . I don't think that color makes any–oh wait!–we've got to establish whether color makes any difference . . um . . I would say that these are not in your category. ? Well, two cards ago we had this same thing in black which were included–well, again it doesn't really matter whether I say yes or no because you're going to tell me whether I'm right or wrong and I just want to know whether color is a factor, if it's involved or not. YOU SAY NO? My response is no. CORR = YES. I see–so the color doesn't make any difference. So, still the only thing that I know is that they must be small . . or must they be small and open–let's try that next time.

10. TWO SMALL BLACK FILLED CIRCLES ON THE LEFT. These are two small filled black circles on the left, and to test my hypothesis that your category is small open figures, I'm going to say that these are not in your category. CORR = NO. Uhuh–well, let's try another to see if my theory is supported.

11. TWO SMALL BLACK FILLED TRIANGLES ON THE LEFT. These are again two small black triangles, filled on the left, and—I think I'll just go on testing my hypothesis and say that these, because they are filled, are not in your category. CORR = NO. Uhuh. I think I'll try this until I'm proved wrong.

12. ONE SMALL RED OPEN CIRCLE ON THE RIGHT. Um, this is a single small red circle, open on the right, and since it is small and open, I shall say that it is yes–it is in your category. CORR = YES. Uhuh.

13. ONE SMALL RED OPEN TRIANGLE ON THE LEFT. . . A small red triangle open on the left–is in your category. ? Because it's not filled in and it's not large–I think these are two things which you've defined. CORR = YES.

14. ONE SMALL RED FILLED TRIANGLE ON THE LEFT. I think you've defined the concept on these two and therefore anything which is filled and anything which is large is not included, and therefore this one, which is a small red filled triangle on the left, is not in your category. CORR = NO. Right, well–I haven't been proved wrong yet. I don't know that this is a very scientific way of doing it.

15. ONE LARGE BLACK OPEN CIRCLE ON THE RIGHT. Ah, now this is a large black circle on the right, open but since it is large it is not in your category. CORR = NO. Uhuh.

REFERENCES

Anderson, R. C., & Guthrie, J. T. Effects of some sequential manipulations of relevant and irrelevant stimulus dimensions on concept learning. *Journal of Experimental Psychology,* 1966, **72**, 501–504.

Bourne, L. E., Jr. Factors affecting strategies used in problems of concept-formation. *American Journal of Psychology,* 1963, **76**, 229–238.

Bourne, L. E., Jr. Hypotheses and hypothesis shifts in classification learning. *Journal of General Psychology,* 1965, **72**, 251–261.

Bourne, L. E., Jr. Knowing and using concepts. *Psychological Review,* 1970, **77**, 546–556.

Bourne, L. E., Jr., & Dominowski, R. L. Thinking. *Annual Review of Psychology,* 1972, **24**, 105–130.

Bourne, L. E., Jr., Ekstrand, B. R., & Dominowski, R. L. *The Psychology of thinking.* Englewood Cliffs, N.J.: Prentice-Hall, 1971.

Bourne, L. E., Jr., Goldstein, S., & Link, W. E. Concept learning as a function of availability of previously presented information. *Journal of Experimental Psychology,* 1964, **67**, 439–448.

Bourne, L. E., Jr. & Guy, D. E. Learning conceptual rules: II. The role of positive and negative instances. *Journal of Experimental Psychology,* 1968, **77**, 488–494.

Bourne, L. E., Jr., & O'Banion, K. Memory for individual events in concept identification. *Psychonomic Science,* 1969, **16**, 101–102.

Bower, G., & Trabasso, T., Concept identification. In R. C. Atkinson (Ed.), *Studies in mathematical psychology.* Stanford: Stanford University Press, 1964.

Bruner, J. S., Goodnow, J. J., & Austin, G. A. *A study of thinking.* New York: Wiley, 1956.

Byers, J. L. Strategies and learning set in concept attainment. *Psychological Reports,* 1963, **12**, 623–634.

Byers, J. L., & Davidson, R. E. The role of hypothesizing in concept attainment. *Journal of Verbal Learning and Verbal Behavior,* 1967, **6**, 595–600.

Denny, N. R. Memory load and concept-rule difficulty. *Journal of Verbal Learning and Verbal Behavior,* 1969, **8**, 202–205.

Denny, J. P., & Benjafeld, J. G. Concept identification strategies used for positive and negative instances. *Psychonomic Science,* 1969, **14**, 277–278.

Dominowski, R. L. Concept attainment as a function of instance contiguity and number of irrelevant dimensions. *Journal of Experimental Psychology,* 1969, **82**, 573–574.

Dominowski, R. L. Required hypothesizing and the identification of unidimensional, conjunctive, and disjunctive concepts. *Journal of Experimental Psychology,* 1973, **100**, 387–394.

Eifermann, R. R. Response patterns and strategies in the dynamics of concept attainment behavior. *British Journal of Psychology,* 1965, **56**, 217–222.

Giambra, L. M. Selection strategies for eight concept rules with exemplar and non-exemplar start cards: A within-subjects replication. *Journal of Experimental Psychology,* 1971, **87**, 143–145.

Gregg, L. W., & Simon, H. A. Process models and stochastic theories of concept identification. *Journal of Mathematical Psychology,* 1967, **4**, 246–276.

Haygood, R. C., & Bourne, L. E., Jr. Attribute- and rule-learning aspects of conceptual behavior. *Psychological Review,* 1965, **72**, 175–195.

Haygood, R. C., Harbert, R. L., & Omler, J. A. Intradimensional variability and concept identification. *Journal of Experimental Psychology,* 1970, **83**, 216–219.

Hunt, E. B., Martin, J., & Stone, P. J. *Experiments in induction.* New York: Academic Press, 1966.

Karpf, D., & Levine, M. Blank trials and introtacts in discrimination learning. *Journal of Experimental Psychology,* 1971, **90**, 51–55.

Laughlin, P. R. Selection strategies in concept attainment as a function of number of persons and stimulus display. *Journal of Experimental Psychology,* 1965, **70**, 323–327.

Laughlin, P. R. Focusing strategy for eight concept rules. *Journal of Experimental Psychology,* 1968, **77**, 661–669.

Laughlin, P. R., & Doherty, M. A. Discussion versus memory in cooperative group concept attainment. *Journal of Educational Psychology,* 1967, **58**, 123–128.

Levine, M. Hypothesis behavior by humans during discrimination learning. *Journal of Experimental Psychology,* 1966, **71**, 331–338.

Levine, M. The latency-choice discrepancy in concept learning. *Journal of Experimental Psychology,* 1969, **82**, 1–3.

Levine, M. Human discrimination learning: The subset-sampling assumption. *Psychological Bulletin,* 1970, **74**, 397–404.

Levison, M. J., & Restle, F. Effects of blank-trial probes on concept-identification problems with redundant relevant cue solutions. *Journal of Experimental Psychology,* 1973, **98**, 368–374.

Milward, R. B., & Spoehr, K. T. The direct measurement of hypothesis-sampling strategies. *Cognitive Psychology,* 1973, **4**, 1–38.

Nahinsky, I. D. A test of axioms of all-or-none concept identification models. *Journal of Verbal Learning and Verbal Behavior,* 1968, **7**, 593–601.

Nahinsky, I. D. A hypothesis sampling model for conjunctive concept identification. *Journal of Mathematical Psychology,* 1970, **7**, 293–316.

Neisser, U., & Weene, P. Hierarchies in concept attainment *Journal of Experimental Psychology,* 1962, **64**, 640–645.

Newell, A., & Simon, H. A. *Human problem solving.* Englewood Cliffs, N.J.: Prentice-Hall, 1972.

Posner, M. I. Memory and thought in human intellectual performance. *British Journal of Psychology,* 1965, **56**, 197–215.

Schwartz, S. H. Trial-by-trial analysis of processes in simple and disjunctive concept-attainment tasks. *Journal of Experimental Psychology,* 1966, **72**, 456–465.

Siegel, L. S. Concept attainment as a function of amount and form of information. *Journal of Experimental Psychology,* 1969, **81**, 464–468.

Taplin, J. E. Evaluation of hypotheses in concept identification. Program on Concept Learning Report No. 20, University of Colorado, 1972.

Taplin, J. E., & Jeeves, M. A. Strategies in concept learning. Program on Concept Learning Report No. 19, University of Colorado, 1972.

Trabasso, T., & Bower, G. *Attention in learning.* New York: Wiley, 1968.

Walker, C. M., & Bourne, L. E., Jr. Concept identification as a function of amounts of relevant and irrelevant information. *American Journal of Psychology,* 1961, **74**, 410–417.

Wason, P. C. On the failure to eliminate hypotheses in a conceptual task. *Quarterly Journal of Experimental Psychology,* 1960, **12**, 129–140.

Wetherick, N. E. The inferential basis of concept attainment. *British Journal of Psychology,* 1966, **57**, 61–69.

Wetherick, N. E. Bruner's concept of strategy: An experiment and a critique. *Journal of General Psychology,* 1969, **81**, 53–58.

Wetherick, N. E. On the object of study in psychology. *International Journal of Psychology,* 1970, **5**, 149–155.

11

A TRANSFER HYPOTHESIS, WHEREBY LEARNING-TO-LEARN, EINSTELLUNG, THE PREE, REVERSAL-NONREVERSAL SHIFTS, AND OTHER CURIOSITIES ARE ELUCIDATED

Marvin Levine
State University of New York at Stony Brook

INTRODUCTION

For the past decade Hypothesis (H) theory has largely been confined to the behavior of adult humans during complex concept-identification problems. More specifically, the theory has emphasized the dynamics of H testing within a given problem. This paper contains an expanded application of the theory, an expansion which may be characterized in two ways. (a) The focus will be not upon within-problem dynamics, but upon changes occurring from problem to problem during a series (at least two) of problems. In a word, *transfer* will be the concern of this theoretical development. (b) A variety of phenomena, all from studies with adult humans, will be treated. These include learning-to-learn, Einstellung, the partial reinforcement extinction effect (PREE), and reversal-nonreversal shift effects.

The argument will be made that a relatively simple transfer process is important for elucidating the various above-mentioned phenomena. This proposed process, labeled the Transfer Hypothesis, will furthermore be shown to be a straightforward supplement to existing statements of H theory. Before presenting this hypothesis, therefore, it will be useful to review a bit of conventional H theory.

There is a basic assumption which all H theorists hold: During a problem S considers some universe of Hs from which he samples Hs to test. From the standpoint of the present topic, the critical phrase within that assumption is the "universe of Hs." This construct, appearing within the basic assumption, is at the very foundation of H theory. Figure 1 portrays and elaborates upon that construct. The figure contains a pictorial model of the H universe, subdivided into a variety of domains. In the standard concept-identification task, the S, instructed merely to say "alpha" or "beta" to a series of typical, four-dimensional, compact-geometric stimuli, may guess that the solution will be simple (e.g., "red forms are 'alpha,' green forms are 'beta' "). That is, he might sample from the domain of simple Hs (domain A, Fig. 1). Or, he might think that the solution has a conjunctive form (e.g., "forms both large and red are 'alpha'; anything else is 'beta' "), sampling, that is, from the domain of conjunctive Hs (domain B). He might think it is some other logical rule (domain C). He might think the solution is some sequence (e.g., "it goes, 'alpha,' 'alpha,' 'beta,' repeatedly"). Note that the domain of sequences (D) is open-ended, reflecting the fact that there are an infinite number of sequence Hs. Finally, a "miscellaneous" domain (E) is included, to cover idiosyncratic Hs (e.g., "If E scratches his head, say 'alpha'; otherwise, say 'beta'," or " 'Alpha' is called 'correct' only if I respond quickly."). In short, Fig. 1 portrays a universe of Hs subdivided into some representative domains of Hs. These domains are to be thought of as H sets within which S is restricting his sampling. At the start of some problem the S may think "It will be some sequence solution." He would then be thought of as sampling within the domain of sequence Hs.

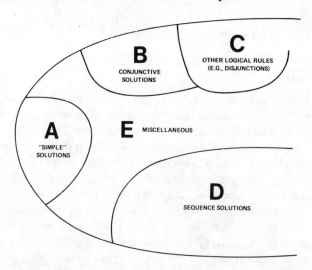

FIG. 1 A schematic representation of the H universe, showing some of the possible domains.

It can be acknowledged at the outset that this conception is severely oversimplified. No attempt has yet been made to define the term "domain." A discussion of the concept will be presented at the closing of this essay. For a tentative working definition, we may take as domains those sets of Hs that have relatively simple category labels. Thus, the S may think the solution will be "simple," "a complicated sequence," "unrelated to the pictures," "has something to do with the colors," etc. Each of these thoughts or states of the S would specify a different H set in which he was searching for the solution.

Another way in which Fig. 1 is oversimplified concerns the relation between domains. First, the domains are presented as mutually exclusive, but this is only for clarity. Domains can overlap. In simultaneous-discrimination tasks, Hs of position are typically included in the set of "simple Hs." But the H "choose left-side all the time" is also in the domain of left-right sequence solutions. Second, domains can be nested within each other. For example, the S may assume that the solution will be some logical rule relating the stimulus components. This is a higher-order domain containing, in Fig. 1, the A, B, and C domains. Or, the S may think that "It's a simple solution based upon the colors." This is a domain containing two Hs (red = alpha, green = beta, or green = alpha, red = beta) nested within the domain of simple Hs. Figure 1 should be read, then, as a simplified schema of the H universe. The refinements should be noted, but they will rarely be necessary to the subsequent argument.

Instructions and Pretraining

The Transfer Hypothesis (when finally presented) will be clearer if seen in the context of the pretraining procedures employed in contemporary research. One type of pretraining, which had been widely used in earlier concept-identification research (and is still used in some experiments today), entails minimal instructions. The S is told merely that he will see cards, that he is to make one of two responses (e.g., "say 'alpha' or 'beta' to each card"), that he will then be told "right" or "wrong," and that he is to be "right" as often as possible. This procedure, which will be referred to as Minimal Pretraining, instructs S only in the mechanics of the task.

When first exploring techniques to probe for Hs, I saw that it would be valuable, if not necessary, to know the domain from which S was sampling. To put this another way, if S could try anything in the universe, it would be virtually impossible to detect his H from response sequences of moderate length. I, therefore, decided to restrict S's sampling in advance to the domain of simple Hs. The assumption (subsequently called the Composition Assumption—Levine, 1969) that S was sampling from this domain could, I hoped, be fulfilled by extensive pretraining. For this pretraining, S was presented with a series of problems, each of which had a different simple solution. These problems were reasonably long, affording S the opportunity to solve them. Furthermore, when S did not solve the problem, E announced the solution. Thus, there were these two modes whereby S could experience the solution: by having a long run of correct responses, or by hearing E state the solution. I assumed that these two experiences were roughy equivalent in communicating to S a sample solution. This procedure—preliminary problems with the solution experienced at the end of each—will be referred to as Extended Pretraining.

Just what did Extended Pretraining accomplish? My intuition was that the successive problems were changing S from one who might sample any place in the universe to one who sampled only from the domain of simple Hs. We were in effect saying, "Look here. The solutions are not complex sequences. They are not conjunctives, etc. They are *simple*." Furthermore, I felt that the primary information packet was the solution-knowledge, gained either by solving the problem directly or from E's statement at the end of the problem. This, then, was my interpretation of pretraining, that the experience of the series of solutions caused S to ignore all but the critical domain. Performance during subsequent experimental problems, incidentally, confirmed this interpretation. Virtually all the Hs from all Ss were of the "simple" type (Levine, 1966).

THE TRANSFER HYPOTHESIS

The Pretraining just described presumes some sort of transfer from early problems to later problems. The critical features inherent in this transfer may be stipulated formally as follows:

The Transfer Hypothesis

When S receives a series of problems, he infers from the first n solutions the domain within the universe from which the $n + 1^{st}$ solution will be taken. He will start the $n + 1^{st}$ problem by sampling Hs from this domain.

This hypothesis merely sounds like an articulation of my feelings about pretraining. We will see, however, that it has general significance. Let us first acknowledge some difficulties with this hypothesis. We already mentioned, in connection with the universe-schema, that the concept of "domain" is not rigorously defined. A new concept introduced within the hypothesis is that S makes an inference. We will generally assume that the S who receives minimal instructions (i.e., at the outset of the very first problem—pretraining or otherwise) will sample from the entire universe and that successive solutions will cause a narrowing with greater and greater precision toward the domain from which E selects the solutions. Thus, if E presents a series of problems with simple (or sequential, or conjunctive, etc.) solutions, S will soon start looking for simple (or sequential, or conjunctive, etc.) solutions. Since all the phenomena discussed below deal with grouped data, the precise process within an individual S needn't be delineated at this time. Thus inferences may proceed in step-wise fashion (i.e., be made suddenly) or be gradual; they may lead to the identical domain from which E has, in fact, selected solutions, or to a somewhat larger or smaller domain. Strong assumptions about these details need not be made here.

On the positive side, the Transfer Hypothesis is not a disembodied statement. It is part of a well-established theory (see Trabasso & Bower, 1968; Levine, 1974) delineating within-problem learning. It is based, as we have seen, upon the fundamental notion within that theory that S samples from a universe of Hs. Furthermore, the hypothesis generalizes in a straightforward way the assumptions within the theory about the effects of feedback. Just as right-wrong feedback at the end of each trial permits S to eliminate incorrect Hs and to narrow down to the correct H, so feedback about the solution to each problem permits S to eliminate incorrect domains and to narrow down to the correct domain.

One final qualification: The Transfer Hypothesis and the general cognitive machinery will be applied to experiments in which the college student has been the subject. Application is, for the present, intended only for the behavior of this S. Experiments similar to some of those discussed below have also been performed with animals. I am ignoring these experiments, no matter what their results. For example, learning-to-learn by the college student will be considered. That a monkey does or does not show a similar result is, for now, irrelevant.

APPLICATIONS

Learning-set

Problem-to-problem improvement in the concept-identification experiment has been demonstrated by Paul Fingerman (1972) in my laboratory, and by a number of other investigators (e.g., Grant & Cost, 1954; Wickens & Millward, 1971). Typically, in these experiments the S is given minimal instructions. In Fingerman's experiment, for example, S was seated before the stimulus window, was told that pictures would appear in the window, that he should choose one of the two pictures, that he would be told "correct" or "wrong" for each response, and that he was to be "correct" as often as possible. Nothing was said about the stimulus dimensions, the stimulus values, or the possible solutions to these problems. No pretraining was presented.

Certain procedural details of the learning-to-learn experiments make it extremely likely that S will experience the solution to each problem. He receives a large number of trials in which to discover the solution, and he must manifest a long criterion run before the problem is ended. Fingerman, who employed a fixed number of trials per problem, announced the solution to all Ss at the end of each problem. In each of the three experiments mentioned above, the solutions always came from the domain of simple solutions. With each successive problem, therefore, S is experiencing solutions from the simple domain. The Transfer Hypothesis asserts that S is more and more likely with each successive problem to sample only from the simple domain. It follows that the group of Ss, because they are going from sampling in the universe at large to sampling in a limited domain, should solve the problems faster and faster—and, as is well known, they do.[1]

There is another implication from the Transfer Hypothesis that relates to this

[1]A subsidiary assumption is needed: The smaller the set in which the S searches, the faster the S will locate the solution (given, of course, that the set contains the solution). This, in effect, says that it is easier to find the marble hidden in one of the eight boxes than in one of eighty boxes. It is so obvious that it was not stated as part of the formal treatment. Nevertheless, there is evidence for this assumption. The larger the number of irrelevant dimensions, the longer it takes Ss to solve (Archer, Bourne, & Brown, 1955). Also, if Ss are told the form (the logical rule) of the solution, they solve faster than if they are not told the form (Haygood & Bourne, 1965).

topic. If we probed for S's H at the outset of each problem, we should find that these Hs more and more come from the simple set. Fingerman probed for the initial H. In each problem immediately after the first feedback trial, a series of six blank trials was inserted. From this it was possible to determine whether or not the S was employing a simple H. This probe was followed by the remainder of the problem, i.e., the remaining feedback trials in the problem. According to the Transfer Hypothesis, the S's H on the early problems and, therefore, his response patterns, should be of all varieties. As the problems proceed, however, the patterns denoting simple Hs should appear more frequently. Figure 2 shows the proportion of Ss on each problem who show a simple H. It is seen that initially about half of the patterns are simple Hs and that this increases toward an asymptote of about ninety percent. The initial Hs more and more come from the domain of simple Hs, which, again, is stipulated by the Transfer Hypothesis.

The technique of probing for the initial H may also be used to investigate the character of S's inference about the domain. The result in Fig. 2 might occur either because S merely repeats experienced solutions or because S is searching within the domain of simple solutions. The latter would occur if S infers that the solutions are keyed to the attributes of the stimuli in the window. According to this interpretation there should be an increase in the frequency of simple Hs even for attributes which had not yet served as the solution. Fingerman, Taddonio, and I performed the following experiment.

A series of problems were presented with blank-trial probes at the outset of each. The stimuli were constructed from four dimensions. Solutions, however, came from only three of these. Color, for example, never contributed a solution. We then looked at the series of initial Hs to see how often a color H appeared. In three replications, Hs from the excluded dimension increased in frequency over the first few problems. The Ss, therefore, were not merely repeating experienced solutions, but were more and more sampling from the domain of simple Hs.

One might conclude that the Transfer Hypothesis definitively accounts for the phenomena of learning-to-learn. This conclusion, however, is a bit strong, even for the basic experiment. The hypothesis describes a necessary and important process, but there are undoubtedly other processes. For example, once the S has narrowed down to the correct domain, he can still improve his strategy (see Gholson, Levine, & Phillips, 1972) for dealing with the Hs within that domain. The Transfer Hypothesis, then, describes an important transfer process, but not necessarily the only process. In general, for all the phenomena discussed below, the hypothesis will elucidate, rather than explain.

Einstellung

Consider the following experiment. The S sees a card with the letters A and B on it. Following the tradition of the simultaneous-discrimination task the A (or B) may be on the left (or right) side of the card. The S sees a deck of cards consisting of these two configurations randomly interspersed. He is required at each card to

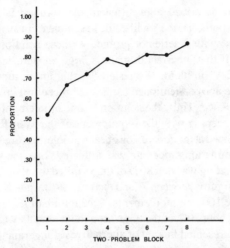

FIG. 2 The proportion of Ss showing a simple H at each block of two problems (sets of 6 blank trials presented after the initial feedback trial on each problem served as the H probes).

say one of the two letters, and he is then told "correct" or "wrong." The solution to this task will be for S to say "A" on every trial. This task is usually learned by college students in two or three trials. Nevertheless, one can derive from H theory conditions under which these Ss will fail to learn. These ideas have been detailed in a previous article (Levine, 1971) and will only be summarized here. The topic requires a supplementary assumption. This assumption is not an ad hoc formulation to deal specifically with Einstellung, but is a generalization from an earlier experiment. This earlier experiment compared the performance of Ss who failed to solve a concept-identification problem to the performance when virtually the identical problem was constructed so as to be insoluble (E said "right" and "wrong" based upon a dimension which was hidden from S). The Ss who failed to solve the normal, soluble problem behaved in a manner that perfectly matched the performance during the insoluble problem. It is as though the failing S has temporarily forgotten (or otherwise obliterated) the relevant dimension. The corresponding theoretical notion is that S fails to solve a normal, soluble problem because the solution H is not in his domain. The supplementary assumption referred to above is the converse of this, that S will learn nothing about the solution if that H is not in the domain from which he is sampling. In the previous paper I proposed that such an S could eventually solve this problem if he first exhausts this incorrect domain and then, searching for other possibilities, shifts to a new domain. If this new domain contains the solution H, then S will be able to solve the problem. Suppose, however, that the initial incorrect domain is so large that S is not able to exhaust it. Then he should never find the solution H. He will not, that is, solve the problem no matter how simple it is.

The Transfer Hypothesis specifies how we may produce an S who never solves the trivial problem described above (where the solution is to choose "A"). According to the hypothesis, the S will come to sample from an incorrect domain if he is first presented with a series of problems whose solutions come from that incorrect domain. If that incorrect domain is large enough, then S should never solve the "say 'A' " problem. We tested out this implication by giving S six problems (using the above-mentioned cards and procedure) in which the solution was a position sequence. Thus, the solution to one problem might be of the form LLRLRLRRR. In keeping with the requirement of the Transfer Hypothesis, the solution was announced at the conclusion of each problem. After six such problems, the standard discrimination procedure was followed, i.e., the solution was "say 'A' ". The basic finding was that 80% of the Ss failed to solve this problem in 100 trials. Despite contiguity between A and "correct," despite the repetition of the pairing, and despite 100 "reinforcements," the failure of learning was complete: These Ss say "A" about 50% of the time throughout, and they fail to recognize the solution when it is presented in a set of alternatives (Fingerman & Levine, 1974). Thus, according to the Transfer Hypothesis, when in the Einstellung language we say the S is "set wrong," we mean that he is sampling from the wrong set of solutions.

According to the present analysis, learning-set and Einstellung are complementary aspects of the same process. In both experiments S receives n similar problems whose function, according to the Transfer Hypothesis, is to cause S to sample from a particular domain. In the learning-set experiment the $n + 1^{st}$ problem comes from the same domain; in Einstellung, the $n + 1^{st}$ problem comes from a new domain.

The Partial-Reinforcement Extinction Effect

The PREE goes back to an experiment by Humphreys (1939) in which one of two events can occur and S makes one of two responses, predicting one of the two events. In a contemporary form of the experiment, S predicts which of two lights will come on by pushing one of two corresponding buttons. The S receives a long series of prediction trials under one of two conditions: In the 100% condition, the same light flashes at every trial; in the 50% condition, the two lights come on randomly from trial to trial. In conditioning terms (circa the 1930s), the 100% condition yields a response which is strongly conditioned and, therefore, difficult to extinguish, whereas the 50% group has a response which is only moderately conditioned and which should, therefore, be relatively easy to extinguish.

Extinction is begun for both groups by presenting on every trial the light that, for the 100% group, had never appeared during conditioning. Contrary to the prediction from the simplistic conditioning theory, the 100% group extinguishes faster, i.e., consistently makes the correct prediction-response in phase 2 in fewer trials. An alternative and popular explanation is the Discrimination Hypothesis. According to this, the 100% group extinguishes faster because they receive a clear signal that the situation has changed, i.e., the continual appearance of one light is suddenly replaced by the continual appearance of the other light. The 50% group, on the other hand, lacks a comparable clear signal. This signal facilitates the change in behavior by the 100% group. It is, incidentally, possible to make the two groups more similar with respect to such a signal. At the end of phase 1, Ss in both groups may be told, "This ends the first problem. We will now start a new problem."

From the framework of H theory the 100% group should extinguish faster than the 50% group, even if both groups receive this "new problem" signal. The reason is straightforward. Before it is elaborated, however, a subtle shift in the view of this experiment should be noted. The S is traditionally thought of as receiving one *experience,* divided into two phases, conditioning and extinction. I would propose, rather, that S be viewed as having two *problems.* Thus, from this latter view, there is nothing qualitatively different about the two phases. They are simply two problems with two different solutions. According to the Transfer Hypothesis, then, Ss in the 100% group have just experienced a problem with an extremely simple solution. It is plausible to expect some number of Ss to infer that the E is presenting "baby problems" to them. At the start of problem (or phase) 2, they, therefore, tend to look within the domain of easy solutions. The 50% group, on the other hand, has no basis for a similar conclusion. Their experience with problem 1 was that the solution was not obvious. Simple solutions hadn't worked. Thus, at the outset of problem 2, there would be some tendency for these Ss to be searching for solutions which are quite complex, or which come from some obscure domain. According to the Transfer Hypothesis, therefore, even with a special signal that a change in the situation is occurring, the 50% group should "extinguish" more slowly than the 100% group.

This experiment, where E announces at the end of phase 1 that a new problem is about to begin, has not yet been done. I present it simply as an implication from the Transfer Hypothesis. There is, however, another implication which has been checked out in two experiments. If, as just suggested, the second part of the procedure is thought of not as extinction, but as a new problem, then any new problem, if it is relatively simple, should be learned faster by the 100% group.

One experiment using a new solution, rather than extinction in phase 2, comes from my laboratory. The S was instructed to choose between two identical squares on the right or left of a card and was told "right" or "wrong" for his choice. In addition to the two positions, another dimension, letter, was employed: Within each square was the letter A or B. The letters varied randomly from side to side on each trial. Two groups were run: One group received a nonreversal shift, i.e., choice of the left side was correct for problem 1, and choice of the letter "A" was correct for problem 2. The other group received random feedback as problem 1, followed by letter "A" correct.[2] The random group required (significantly) twice as many trials as the 100% group to learn the second problem. Thus, the impairment produced by random feedback is not a phenomenon of extinction but of new learning. According to the Transfer Hypothesis, problem 1 provided the 100% group with a

---

[2]Counterbalancing over the various nonreversal shifts was employed. The random group was matched with the 100% group for the phase 2 solutions.

better example of a typical solution than was provided to the random group. The Ss in the 100% group are directed to a small and appropriate domain.

This conclusion is further supported by another variant of the Humphreys experiment. Meyers, Driessen, and Halpern (1972), who also interpret the PREE in hypothesis-theory terms, ran two groups of 15 Ss each, varying in problem-1 treatment. One group (100%) received a simple single-alternation (LR) problem; the second group (50%) received random outcomes.[3] Phase (or problem) 2 was not extinction, but a new problem: For all Ss the LLR pattern was correct. Two results are pertinent: (*a*) Whereas all the Ss in the single-alternation group learned the LLR pattern, 11 of the Ss in the 50% group failed to learn the LLR pattern in 90 trials. Thus, even though phase 2 is now unambiguously new learning, Ss who had first learned a simple sequence (LR) learned a new simple sequence (LLR) faster than Ss who previously had an infinitely complex sequence. That the experience with the first solution has directed the S to search the set of simple sequence solutions is borne out by the next result. (*b*) A third group was run that received the LLR pattern as the initial task. The single-alternation Ss learned the LLR pattern faster than these Ss. The latter required more than twice the number of trials. The S for whom LLR is an initial problem starts out facing a universe of Hs; the S who receives this problem after single-alternation tends to start within the subdomain of simple sequence solutions.

Reversal-Nonreversal Shifts

These experiments are also traditionally regarded as two-phase procedures. Two groups, after minimal instructions, receive a multidimensional (ideally, a two-dimensional) simple discrimination problem as phase 1. When S reaches some clear criterion (e.g., 10 errorless trials) he is automatically shifted to a new problem. For the *Reversal-Shift Group*, the new solution is the reverse of the phase 1 solution; for the *Nonreversal-Shift Group*, the new solution comes from a previously irrelevant dimension. When the Ss are adult humans, a reliable finding (with one regular exception to be noted below) is that the Reversal-Shift Group learns the new problem faster than the Nonreversal-Shift Group.

What has the Transfer Hypothesis to say about this result? Again, we will assume that the procedure consists of two problems and that the first problem provides S with a sample solution. Furthermore, we will continue to assume that sample solutions permit S to eliminate wrong or unlikely domains and to reduce the size of the universe to a section, some fraction of the starting universe. We initially suggested that for a rough approximation one could assume that all the Hs within that working domain were of equal strength, i.e., were equally likely to be sampled. For the topics above, that approximation was adequate. For the present topic, how-

---

[3]The description is schematized. Meyers et al. (1972) used a different form of the binary task, had Ss make confidence judgments, and employed a special "random" sequence for the 50% group. The essentials of the experiment are, however, properly represented.

ever, it will be necessary to refine that approximation. Instead, we will suggest that the domain of simple Hs is divided into subdomains, each containing the Hs associated with a dimension. Thus, a four-dimensioned problem may provide the basis for eight simple Hs. It will be assumed, however, that these are paired according to the dimensions. Within this domain of simple Hs, therefore, there would be four subdomains. There is a tendency, furthermore, for Ss to sample Hs within a subdomain before exploring other subdomains. Thus, within the domain of simple Hs not all Hs have equal probability. The probability of sampling Hs within a dimension is greater than across dimensions.

The foregoing may be summarized with two assertions: (a) Dimensions tend to produce a grouping, or subdomain, of related Hs, and (b) when one simple H is salient for S, he is likely to test Hs within the corresponding subdomain. These assertions sound like a crude bending of the theory to the new topic. They would be outrageously *ad hoc* were it not for independent supporting evidence. This evidence is in two forms, negative and positive.

Negative evidence for the assertion that dimension-related Hs tend to cohere comes from Levine, Miller, and Steinmeyer (1967). The H was probed for at each trial within a problem. The authors wished to test the implication from H theory that the solution H (e.g., "large") would not appear prior to the last error. Not only was the solution H absent, but the other H ("small") on the same dimension was also absent. It was as though the entire dimension was overlooked during the precriterion phase of the problem.

The positive evidence was presented by Andrews, Levinthal, and Fishbein (1969) and was replicated by Gumer and Levine (1971). These authors probed for the H before and immediately after the first feedback trial. When E said "wrong" at this trial the second H tended to come from the same dimension as the first. If, for example, the H at the outset of the problem was "black," then the next H was "white" more than half the time (chance, in both studies, was .25). It is clear, then, that Hs within dimensions cohere for Ss and that this coherence can influence the sequence in which S tests Hs.

Application of this refined conception to the Reversal-Nonreversal Experiment is straightforward. The S receives minimal instructions. The first problem provides a solution example (e.g., "large") to S.[4] At the start of the next problem, which is signalled by "wrongs" after a long string of "rights," "small" will be sampled with higher probability than Hs in the other domains. Thus, a Reversal Shift is learned faster than a Nonreversal Shift.

Since this result is nicely explained by neoconditioning ideas, one wonders whether it was worth invoking the Transfer Hypothesis and complicating the domain conception just to treat this same result. There is, however, another set of

---

[4]Note that typically in this research Ss who fail to attain criterion on problem 1 are dismissed from the experiment. This procedure is followed even though the results are traditionally related to conditioning theory. The dynamics specified by conditioning theory should operate whether S reaches criterion or not, i.e., the solution experience is of no special importance within that theory.

results more readily handled by the Transfer Hypothesis. Suppose, instead of minimal instructions one gives elaborate instructions about the stimulus dimensions and about the solutions. A few such experiments (Erickson, 1971; Johnson, Fishkin, & Bourne, 1966; Neumann, 1972) have been performed in which E tells S that the solutions will be simple, and *enumerates the possible solutions*. According to the foregoing theory, E is providing S with sample solutions. These should direct S's search for solutions within the domain of simple Hs. Furthermore, for these Ss, after problem 1 the various Hs should have more nearly equal sampling probabilities than they do for Ss who have experienced only a single solution. For the extensively instructed Ss, therefore, the various solutions should tend to be equally easy. That is the standard finding. The Reversal-Shift Ss lose their advantage.

DISCUSSION

H theory has long held, as an approximation to the learning process, that S is in one of two states: the precriterion state, when he samples only incorrect hypotheses, and the criterion state, when he holds only the solution H. The Transfer Hypothesis supplements this by stressing that the solution experienced during the criterion state determines transfer. This view contrasts with that of the various conditioning and neoconditioning theories. For these, the cumulative trial-by-trial reinforcement effects are the important dynamics determining both intraproblem learning and transfer. According to the Transfer Hypothesis, Ss who proceed through a problem (thereby experiencing the repeated trial-by-trial contingencies) but who do not manifest the criterion run, should show very different transfer effects from those who do so manifest it. The definitive test of this implication has not yet been made. Hints that it is correct, however, come from two sources.

Grant and Berg (1948) presented a series of six card-sorting concept problems to several groups, two of which are of interest here. For one group, each problem ended after a criterion run of 10 successively correct trials; for the other group, only a 3-trial criterion run was required. Interproblem performance improved for the 10-trial group but not for the 3-trial group. The former Ss are experiencing the solutions and thereby inferring the correct domain. The latter do not have this advantage.[5]

A second hint comes from an unpublished variant of the Humphreys experiment in which one group received a simple alternation problem for the first phase.[6] A few of these Ss failed to learn this alternation rule. During the "extinction" phase, in which only one of the two responses was always correct, these Ss performed like Ss who had previously received random feedback. The implication again is that not the consistent trial-by-trial feedback contingencies but the solution experience dictates the transfer.

[5]Grant and Berg's (1948) precedure is not in perfect accord with present purposes. Problem type (i.e., solution) was confounded with problem sequence, and solutions were shifted without any announcement or other break in procedure.

[6]F. Irwin, personal communication.

A concomitant of this emphasis upon the solution experience is the question of how the solution is conveyed to S. Three modes were mentioned. (a) The S may discover the solution, as revealed by a criterion run of reasonable length. (b) The E may announce the solution after some number of trials. There are no data on the relative effectiveness of these two methods upon subsequent transfer performance. My impression, from experience with both methods during pretraining, is that they are roughly equivalent. (c) The E may present instructions, i.e., before any problems are presented, E may announce the various solutions. That this has some effect is suggested in the discussion above of Reversal-Nonreversal Shift problems. D. M. Johnson (1972) has also noted comparable effects: "Telling a college student . . . the relevant attributes in a concept problem or the class of words that are solutions to anagrams reduces the solution time drastically. One sentence of instructions might be equated with twenty minutes of practice [p. 162f]." Johnson proceeds to criticize theories of human learning for neglecting these instruction effects. The Transfer Hypothesis points to one function of the instructions. They provide solution experiences (or examples) to the S, leading him, thereby, to sample from a restricted domain. Within concept learning, extensive instructions have included recitation of the individual solutions. Johnson's examples suggest that simply stating the name of the domain might be adequate. There are no systematic data on the effectiveness of such procedures within the field of concept learning. My own experience, however, suggests that verbal instructions abstractly presented, i.e., before an actual problem is given, are less effective than the other two modes.

The Transfer Hypothesis, then, not only points up an important process common to a variety of research topics, but interrelates instructions, pretraining, and criterion attainment. Along with these virtues two residual problems should be noted. First, no attempt has yet been made to define the term "domain." A tempting definition is that it is a class of Hs which tend to be similar. Thus, all Hs in the simple domain are similar by virtue of being based upon cues which are in the stimulus window and which have the same logical relationship to those cues (and to the correct response); sequence Hs are similar to each other in specifying relations among the responses, relations which are repeated in periodic fashion. The term "similarity" has the connotation of more or less, so that one may associate sampling probabilities with the Hs according to their similarity to solutions which S has already experienced. For example, if the solution to the first 4-D concept problem is "large," for the next problem Hs about size may be most probable, with Hs about other simple Hs less probable, and Hs about sequences still less probable. Or, if the solution to the first problem is a simple sequence, then for the next problem other simple sequences may be most probable, with complex sequences less probable, etc.

The chief difficulty with the use of "similarity" to specify domains is that it is not sufficient. As Wertheimer (1923) noted, similarity is only one basis by which elements become grouped. Another rule is "proximity." We have, for example, constructed 8-D stimuli from two clusters of 4-D stimuli: a geometric 4-D stimulus surrounded by a border whose attributes contributed the other 4-Ds. My impression is that Ss would investigate first the Hs associated with the border cues, then those associated with the inner-figure cues (or vice versa). Thus, because the cues divide into two clusters, the Hs tend to divide into two subdomains.[7] There could similarly be grouping by temporal proximity. Imagine a task with eight quite different possible solutions. On Monday the S receives four of these. On Tuesday he receives the other four. On Wednesday, after a problem or two S may realize that E is using "Monday's solutions" again. Thus, the eight Hs will have become grouped into two sets of four because of relative temporal contiguity within each set.

Any relationship which contributes toward the grouping of elements should contribute toward the establishment of H domains. This seems to suggest that our knowledge of transfer will ultimately depend upon perceptual grouping rules. This may indeed be true—ultimately. For the present, however, it appears to be adequate to characterize domains as sets of Hs for which there exist simple verbal labels ("Monday's solutions," "sequence solutions," etc.). This was the assumption made above, an assumption which with little awkwardness served us well.

A second problem with the Transfer Hypothesis is its restrictedness. It deals primarily with S's mode of definition of the appropriate domain. This, clearly, is not the only process important in transfer. In learning-to-learn, for example, Ss may improve, not only by discovering the proper domain, but by learning to search efficiently within that domain for the solution. In the PREE the 100% group is undoubtedly helped by the presence of a signal of a new problem (the shift from one outcome event to the other). Furthermore, S's experience with the sequence of solutions over a series of problems may influence the probability distribution of the Hs within a given domain. In particular, the S may become sensitive to the sequential regularities within the solution series. The most general conclusion, then, is that H theory provides a plausible framework for viewing transfer. The applications described above demonstrate its plausibility.

REFERENCES

Andrews, O. E., Levinthal, C. F., & Fishbein, H. D. The organization of hypothesis testing behavior in concept identification tasks. *American Journal of Psychology*, 1969, **82**, 523–530.

Archer, E. J., Bourne, L. E., Jr., & Brown, G. G. Concept identification as a function of irrelevant information and instructions. *Journal of Experimental Psychology*, 1955, **49**, 153–164.

Erickson, J. R. Problem shifts and hypothesis behavior in concept identification. *American Journal of Psychology*, 1971, **84**, 100–111.

Fingerman, P. How subjects select hypotheses to test. Unpublished manuscript. SUNY at Stony Brook, 1972.

[7]Employing a different type of 8-D stimulus, Nelson (1971) has demonstrated the effects of spatial proximity upon H sampling.

Fingerman, P., & Levine, M. Nonlearning: The completeness of the blindness. *Journal of Experimental Psychology*, 1974, in press.

Gholson, B., Levine, M., & Phillips, S. Hypotheses, strategies, and stereotypes in discrimination learning. *Journal of Experimental Child Psychology*, 1972, **13**, 423–446.

Grant, D. A., & Berg, E. A. A behavioral analysis of degree of reinforcement and ease of shifting to new responses in a Weigl-type card-sorting problem. *Journal of Experimental Psychology*, 1948, **38**, 404–411.

Grant, D. A., & Cost, J. R. Continuities and discontinuities in conceptual behavior in a card-sorting problem. *Journal of General Psychology*, 1954, **50**, 237–244.

Gumer, E., & Levine, M. The missing dimension in concept learning: Dimensionality or local consistency? *Journal of Experimental Psychology*, 1971, **90**, 39–44.

Haygood, R. C., & Bourne, L. E., Jr. Attribute- and rule-learning aspects of conceptual behavior. *Psychological Review*, 1965, **72**, 175–195.

Humphreys, L. G. Acquisition and extinction of verbal expectation in a situation analogous to conditioning. *Journal of Experimental Psychology*, 1939, **25**, 294–301.

Johnson, D. M. *A systematic introduction to the psychology of thinking.* New York: Harper & Row, 1972.

Johnson, P. J., Fishkin, A., & Bourne, L. E., Jr. Effects of procedural variables upon reversal and interdimensional shift performance: II. *Psychonomic Science*, 1966, **4**, 69–70.

Levine, M. Hypothesis behavior by humans during discrimination learning. *Journal of Experimental Psychology*, 1966, **71**, 331–338.

Levine, M. Neo-noncontinuity theory. In G. H. Bower & J. T. Spence (Eds.), *The psychology of learning and motivation.* Vol. 3. New York: Academic Press, 1969.

Levine, M. Hypothesis theory and nonlearning despite ideal S–R reinforcement contingencies. *Psychological Review*, 1971, **78**, 130–140.

Levine, M. *Hypothesis testing: A cognitive theory of learning.* Potomac, Md.: Lawrence Erlbaum Associates, 1974, in press.

Levine, M., Miller, P., & Steinmeyer, C. H. The none-to-all theorem of human discrimination learning. *Journal of Experimental Psychology*, 1967, **73**, 568–573.

Meyers, L. S., Driessen, E., & Halpern, J. Transfer following regular and irregular sequences of events in a guessing situation. *Journal of Experimental Psychology*, 1972, **92**, 182–190.

Nelson, J. Perceptual influences in concept identification. Unpublished doctoral dissertation, SUNY at Stony Brook, 1971.

Neumann, P. G. Transfer effects of simple and detailed instructions in the presence and absence of pretraining in reversal and nonreversal shifts. *Psychological Science*, 1972, **29**, 233–237.

Trabasso, T., & Bower, G. H. *Attention in learning.* New York: Wiley, 1968.

Wertheimer, M. Untersuchungen zur lehre von der gestalt, II. *Psychologische Forschung*, 1923, **4**, 301–350. Cited in D. C. Beardslee & M. Wertheimer (Eds.), *Readings in Perception.* Princeton, N.J.: Van Nostrand, 1958. Pp. 115–135.

Wickens, T. D., & Millward, R. B. Attribute elimination strategies for concept identification with practiced subjects. *Journal of Mathematical Psychology*, 1971, **8**, 453–480.

12

A SET ANALYSIS THEORY OF BEHAVIOR IN FORMAL SYLLOGISTIC REASONING TASKS

James R. Erickson
Ohio State University

The dictionary on my book shelf defines the word "reasoning" as the drawing of inferences, thinking with a view to a conclusion believed to be valid. Similarly, a logic book defines reasoning as the kind of mental activity in which an individual is trying to arrive at a conclusion on the basis of reasons. We speak of "reasoning out a problem" or "reasoning with someone." Simply stated, reasoning is the kind of thinking we do when we want to be correct about something—when we wish to come to a valid conclusion on the basis of a given set of facts or arguments —or premises.

Philosophers have been writing about the art of reasoning for a long time, since Aristotle presented his theory of the syllogism, which provided a method of testing the validity of argument-connections in certain simple forms of arguments. Through the years the field of logic has become the branch of philosophy which concerns itself with reasoning, concentrating in the analysis and critique of argument connections. Logic is the science of the *form* of an argument, without respect to its content.

In a very real sense, then, logic provides us with a normative model for reasoning behavior, in the same sense that Bayes' theorem provides us with a normative model for decision making in certain contexts. The field of logic tells us how we ought to reason in certain situations, but of course it may or may not have much to say about the way in which people actually reason in these situations.

The average college student doesn't seem to be very "logical." That is, there exist a number of very simple situations in which the typical subject doesn't behave the way a logician would say he ought to behave. In a recent book, Wason and Johnson-Laird (1972) have examined a number of these situations. What I want to do in this article is to examine one of these situations in some detail, first stating the "logic" of the situation, then examining the literature and noting how subjects perform in the situation. Finally, I will try to provide an analysis of the situation which will account for this behavior.

The situation I have in mind is the Aristotelian syllogism, one of the oldest reasoning tasks in existence. As you may recall, an Aristotelian syllogism is a logical form in exactly three sentences, two premises and a conclusion. Some examples are shown in Table 1. In each case, the predicate of the conclusion is labeled P, and the subject of the conclusion is labeled S. The major premise of a syllogism links the predicate of the conclusion P, with a middle term, labeled M. The minor premise of a syllogism links the subject of the conclusion, S, with the middle term, M.

Exactly four sentence types are allowed in a syllogism. These have a standard terminology in the literature of logic and are illustrated in Table 1. An A sentence is a universal affirmative sentence "All S are P." An E sentence is a universal negative sentence "No S are P." An I sentence is a particular affirmative sentence "Some S are P," and an O sentence is a particular negative sentence "Some S are not P."[1]

The *mood* of a syllogism is a shorthand notation giving the sentence types used

TABLE 1

Examples of Standard Terms Used to Describe Syllogisms

Example of a Syllogism			
Major Premise	All M are P		All churchgoers are honest
Minor Premise	All S are M		All politicians are churchgoers
Conclusion	All S are P		All politicians are honest

Possible sentence types that can be used in a syllogism

A	All S are P	All psychologists are wise	
E	No S are P	No poor research is published	
I	Some S are P	Some elected officials are truthful	
O	Some S are not P	Some professors are not rich	

Possible syllogistic figures

Figure 1 (Forward Chain)	Figure 2 (Stimulus Equivalence)	Figure 3 (Response Equivalence)	Figure 4 (Backward Chain)
M–P	P–M	M–P	P–M
S–M	S–M	M–S	M–S
S–P	S–P	S–P	S–P

[1]A and I are the first two vowels in the Latin word "affirmo" (to affirm), and E and O are the first two vowels in the Latin word "nego" (to deny). The first vowel in each word is the universal, and the second is the particular.

in the syllogism; thus a syllogism may be labeled AAA, or EAO, etc., giving the sentence types of the major and minor premises, and the conclusion.

One more bit of notation is necessary—that is the *figure* or *form* of the syllogism. While the conclusion of a syllogism is necessarily in the order S-P, the order of terms in the two premises can vary. For example, either M or P can be the subject or the predicate of the major premise. The way in which the major and minor premises are arranged defines the figure of the syllogism. The four possible figures are given in Table 1. In logic texts these are usually labeled Figs. 1–4. However, since these correspond exactly to the four standard mediation paradigms from verbal learning, (Frase, 1968; Jenkins, 1963; Pezzoli & Frase, 1968) they will be referred to here as forward chaining (Fig. 1), stimulus equivalence (Fig. 2), response equivalence (Fig. 3) and backward chaining (Fig. 4) syllogisms.

Since each premise and the conclusion may be one of 4 sentence types, and there are 4 different syllogistic figures, there exists a total of 256 possible syllogisms. Of these 24 are logical, 6 within each figure. By a logical syllogism, I mean one in which the conclusion follows *necessarily* from the two premises. One usually spends some time in a logic course learning how to identify these 24 logical syllogisms—perhaps by learning such rules as "the middle term must be distributed at least once" or "no valid conclusion can be drawn from two negative premises."

RESEARCH ON SYLLOGISTIC REASONING

When college-student subjects are presented with syllogistic arguments in the laboratory, they don't seem to do particularly well. They are quite willing to accept a variety of syllogistic arguments as valid when they are not. This has been a source of interest to a number of psychologists for many years, as different explanations for this behavior have been proposed and tested. One of the earliest explanations was called the *atmosphere effect*. Woodworth and Sells (1935) and Sells (1936) performed a series of experiments on Aristotelian reasoning tasks and proposed a number of principles relating to the *mood* of the syllogism to account for their data. The general idea behind these principles is that people are "seduced" by the atmosphere created by the premises into accepting a conclusion which is in agreement with this atmosphere. Begg and Denny (1969) have recently restated Woodworth and Sells' arguments in two basic principles: (*a*) Whenever at least one premises is negative, the most frequently accepted conclusion will be negative; otherwise, it will be affirmative. (*b*) Whenever at least one premise is particular, the most frequently accepted conclusion will be particular; otherwise, it will be universal. For example, if the premises are "No M are P," and "Some S are M," the most frequently accepted conclusion would be "Some S are not P," which happens to be a valid conclusion.

The atmosphere effect explains syllogistic reasoning in terms of a response set toward a particular kind of response. As such it attempts to explain behavior in reasoning tasks in terms of "a-logical" principles.

Another explanation of behavior in a syllogism judging task was offered by Chapman and Chapman (1959). They were willing to assume that their subjects used logical reasoning processes but made errors in interpreting and in combining premises. The mistakes in interpretation they discuss involve illicit conversion of premises, as converting a premise such as "All S are M" to "All M are S," which is not necessarily true—all dogs are animals, but all animals are not dogs. Chapman and Chapman argued that many so-called atmosphere errors could be accounted for by assuming that subjects reasoned validly, but with illicitly converted premises. Another error they discussed was probabilistic reasoning, an error of interpreting the combined premises. Probabilistic reasoning occurs when subjects call a conclusion which could be correct, but is not necessarily correct, valid.

Henle (1962) is another researcher who has argued that subjects basically reason correctly, but may refuse to accept or may misinterpret the premises given to them, and so appear to reason incorrectly. In a recent article, Ceraso and Provitera (1971) have investigated effects of various ways in which premises can be interpreted. They note that A, I, and O sentences are ambiguous in terms of specifying the set relations between the terms in the sentence and found that specifying these set relationships more clearly significantly reduced errors in syllogistic judgments.

AN ANALYSIS OF SYLLOGISTIC REASONING

What I would like to do in this paper is to elaborate on some of these ideas, particularly those of Ceraso and Provitera, and formulate a preliminary theory of the way subjects deal with syllogistic inference. The theory assumes that syllogistic inference is a complex process with at least three stages. The first stage involves interpreting the premises, the second stage involves combining the premises after interpretation, and the third stage involves choosing a verbal label (an A, E, I, or O sentence) to describe the interpretation. At each stage, there is an opportunity for either partial or complete analysis, and the basic assumption of the theory is that it is partial analysis that leads to syllogistic errors. Syllogistic errors involve drawing an illogical conclusion or judging that a given conclusion is valid when in fact it is not.

Let us examine one syllogism and follow a hypothetical subject through the process of responding. Table 2 gives a pair of premises. The major premise states "All P are M," and the minor premise states "All M are S." What conclusion can be drawn from these premises?

According to the proposed theory, the subject's first task is to interpret the premises. I assume that he does this in a manner analogous to forming Venn diagrams. Table 2 shows that there are two possible set relations which can describe

TABLE 2

Analysis of Problem of Drawing a Conclusion
From Premises in a Syllogism

Task: Draw a conclusion from premises (or state that no conclusion is logical)

All P are M	Major Premise
All M are S	Minor Premise
? ? ?	Conclusion

Stage I: Interpretation of premises

Possible Interpretations

	1	2
All P are M	(P) M)	or (PM)
	3	4
All M are S	(M) S)	or (MS)

Stage II: Combination of interpreted premises

Possible Combinations

1 and 3	1 and 4	2 and 3	2 and 4
((P) M) S)	(P (MS))	((PM) S)	(PMS)

Stage III: Labeling of set relation of S to P

Possible Labels

1 and 3	1 and 4
Some S are P	Some S are P
or	or
Some S are not P	Some S are not P

2 and 3	2 and 4
Some S are P	All S are P
or	or
Some S are not P	Some S are P

Logical Conclusion: Some S are P

---

each premise. "All P are M" can either mean that P is a subset of M or that P and M are identical.[2]

The subject's next task is to combine the premises. Again, I assume that this is done in a manner which can be modeled as the combination of Venn diagrams. Table 2 shows that there are 4 ways of forming a combination of the premises. Finally, the set relation of S to P implied by the combination must be interpreted verbally in an A, E, I, or O sentence whose subject is S and whose predicate is P. Stage 3 in Table 2 shows the possible statements. The only sentence common to all possible combinations of set relations is "Some S are P," which is the logical conclusion.

[2]Note that given the first interpretation, that P is a subset of M, conversion of the premise to "All M are P" would be illicit, but that given the second interpretation, conversion would be licit.

At this point we note that the word "some" does not mean the same thing in logic as it does in ordinary language—in logic "some" means "at least one, and possibly all"; it does *not* mean "some, but not all." Thus a statement like "some dogs are animals" is perfectly all right in logic, even though a stronger statement could be made.

As can be seen, drawing the proper conclusion demands the processing of a lot of information, even in this relatively simple syllogism. As we noted, the logical conclusion to the premises given in Table 2 is "Some S are P." The majority of subjects respond "*All* S are P" when asked to choose a logical conclusion to these premises. Why do they do this?

According to the atmosphere effect, they are seduced by the universal atmosphere of the premises. According to Chapman and Chapman, they might reason correctly after illicitly converting one or more of the premises (if both premises are converted to "All M are P" and "All S are M," the conclusion "All S are P" does follow logically). However, according to the interpretation given here, subjects respond as they do because they do not process all of the information. In other words, they perform an incomplete analysis in at least one of the three stages. For example, if most subjects interpret "All P are M" and "All M are S" as indicating set identity relations, using interpretations 2 and 4 in stage 2 of Table 2, the conclusion "All S are P" follows logically from this interpretation. The subject's illogical conclusion follows naturally, given this incomplete analysis of the premises.

Table 3 shows the possible set relations that can be used to describe each of the four possible sentence types. A sentence of the type "All A are B" can be described by two different set relations. An E sentence, "No A are B" is unambiguous; only one set relation describes this sentence. An I sentence can be described by no less than four of the possible set relations, and an O sentence can be described by three different set relations. Similarly, by scanning the *columns* of the table it can easily be seen that two different sentences can be used to label each of the possible set relationships.

The proposed theory states that the average subject does not consider all of the possible set relations when interpreting a premise at Stage I; neither does he con-

TABLE 3

Possible Set Relations Implied by Syllogistic Sentences

	Set Relations of A to B				
	Subset	Superset	Identity	Overlap	Exclusion
	(A) B	(B) A	A B	A(B	A B
A - All A are B	X		X		
E - No A are B					X
I - Some A are B	X	X	X	X	
O - Some A are not B		X		X	X

sider each of the possible sentences when labeling a set relation at Stage III. Instead, for example, he selects one (or more) of the Stage I interpretations for further processing. In a general version of the theory, each of the Xs in Table 3 would be replaced by two parameters—first, the probability that a given set relation is used to interpret the sentence, and second, the probability that a given sentence is used to label the set relation. I will have more to say about this later.

I have performed preliminary investigations of the general theory just outlined and will report results from two of its special cases, or models. Both of these models seem promising but are almost certainly not correct, or at least not complete. However, as will be seen, comparison of predictions from these models with data from syllogistic reasoning experiments indicates rather clearly directions for improving the models. Before presenting these data, let me spell out the theory (and its models) in more detail.

The theory, which will be called the Set Analysis Theory of Syllogistic Reasoning, assumes that people perform syllogistic reasoning tasks according to the general three stage process outlined above. Specification of the exact way in which this three stage analysis is performed provides a family of models, or special cases of the theory. Both of the models discussed here assume partial analysis at various points in the three-stage process.

Stages 1 and 3 are common to the two models being considered and will be discussed first. It is assumed that during Stage 1, each premise is interpreted in terms of one of the possible set relations. Table 3 shows the possible set relations which could be used, but the theory assumes that the average subject does not consider all possible set relations. The set relations that are considered are circled in Table 3. Thus, I assume that the subject interprets the statement "Some A are B" as either indicating that A is a superset of B (Some animals are dogs) or as indicating that Sets A and B overlap (some swimmers are birds). One of these relations is chosen (with a probability to be estimated from the data) as the interpretation of the premise. This probability is a free parameter, presumably influenced by the subject's biases in the case of context-free material, or by the semantic content of the statement in the case of verbal material.

At Stage 3, the subject has combined the two premises and must choose a verbal statement to interpret the combination. In Table 3, the circles indicate the statements that the theory assumes are chosen. Thus a subject is assumed to report the set relation "A is a subset of B," as "All A are B." Two of the set relations are quite ambiguous; for example, set overlap could be reported as either "Some A are B" or "Some A are not B"; either would be adequate. It is assumed that the subject chooses the statement which agrees with the premises. Thus, if there is one more negative premise, he would choose to say "Some A are not B," but if the premises are positive, he would choose to say "Some A are B."

These models could be criticized at this point for building in an atmosphere effect, via the verbal labeling process at Stage 3. In a sense this is correct. However, as the atmosphere effect is usually discussed, it provides a general set for responding—a non-analytic influence. In the present models, the subject is assumed to go through an analytic reasoning process (although an incomplete one) but must provide verbal output from this process to label an ambiguous relationship. Presumably, he could report accurately the set relation he infers but instead is forced to make an ambiguous A, E, I, or O statement, and the context of the premises helps him to choose one of these labels.

The two models considered here differ in what they say about processing during Stage 2—during which the two premises are combined to provide a set relation between the subject and predicate of the conclusion. The first model assumes that the subject randomly chooses one of the possible combinations of the premises as he has interpreted them in Stage 1. Sometimes there is only one possible combination, but often there is more than one. Model 1 assumes that he randomly chooses one of these. In Model 1 it is assumed that all combinations are equally likely. This is almost certainly incorrect—subjects surely have biases about how sets are combined. Model 1 will be called the Random Combination Model.

Model 2 assumes that the subject makes a complete analysis of the premises as he has interpreted them. In other words, when there is more than one possible way in which the set relations of the interpreted premises could be combined, Model 2 assumes that the subject examines all of them, then selects for the conclusion a verbal statement which fits all of these combinations. If two or more of the combinations provide conflicting information (such as one of them implying that "All A are C" and another implying that "No A are C") the subject would report that no conclusion logically follows from the premises. Model 2 will be called the Complete Combination Model.

To clarify the difference between the Random Combination Model and the Complete Combination Model, consider the interpreted premises shown in Table 4. The major premise has been interpreted (as it must be) as indicating set exclusion, and the minor premise has been interpreted as indicating that M is a subset of S. As shown, there are three possible combinations of these set relations. The Random Combination Model assumes that only one combination is formed by the subject, and it is assumed that all combinations are equally likely. Depending on which combination is chosen, one of three set relations between S and P are implied, and during Stage 3, the subject chooses a verbal label with S as the subject and P as the predicate, perhaps using the ones shown in Table 4. The superset and overlap relations have been labeled "Some S are not P" because of the negative premise.

The Complete Combination Model, on the other hand, assumes that all possible combinations of the interpreted premises are examined. If there is a verbal label which can be used for all possible relationships between S and P, it is chosen; if there is no label which describes all relationships, the response would be that no logical conclusion can be drawn. In the example, "Some S are not P" would be chosen with probability equal to one.

TABLE 4

Example of Stage 2 and 3 Analyses from Two Models

| Major Premise | No M are P |
| Minor Premise | All M are S |

Stage I: Interpretation
    Major Premise   (M) (P)

    Minor Premise   ((M) S)

Stage II: Possible Combinations

((M)(P) S)

Random Combination Model
    One combination chosen with $p = \frac{1}{3}$
    Resulting in one of the following, each with $p = \frac{1}{3}$

Stage III:

    Some S are not P   Some S are not P   No S are P

    The verbal responses
        "No S are P" has $p = \frac{1}{3}$
        "Some S are not P" has $p = \frac{2}{3}$

    Complete Combination Model
        All three combinations analyzed

Stage III: The only common response possible is "Some S are not P," which would be chosen with
    $p = 1$

APPLICATIONS OF MODELS OF SYLLOGISTIC REASONING DATA

In order to examine the potential usefulness of the two models, their predictions were compared with data collected in our laboratory by Brian Zax (briefly described in Erickson, 1972). In this study, groups of subjects were given a "logic test." The logic test consisted of a series of syllogisms with missing terms. The subject's task was to fill in the missing term from a list provided to him. In different sections of the test, subjects were asked to supply the missing conclusion which followed from a pair of premises, or to supply a missing premise which would make the entire syllogism logical. Only the missing-conclusion data will be examined here. In all syllogisms, the letters A, B, and C were used, A and C being the subject and predicate of the conclusion, respectively, and B being the middle term. One major difference between these data and those reported in other studies is that all 24 logical syllogisms were used. Most experimenters have presented data only from syllogisms that have no logical conclusion, probably because there are so many more of them than syllogisms from which a conclusion can logically be drawn. At any rate, most studies in this area have concentrated on the errors subjects make in drawing illogical conclusions from syllogisms that are not valid arguments, and there are almost no data in the literature on the extent to which subjects draw correct conclusions when they exist.

Two forms of the test were used, so that any one subject only worked on half of the syllogisms with missing conclusions, and so that within each form, no syllogism appeared with both a missing major and a missing minor premise. Both forms of the test had items with a missing conclusion as the first section.

Instructional conditions were also varied. One group of subjects was given instructions on how to use Venn diagrams in interpreting statements and shown several examples illustrating their use. A second group was given, hopefully in understandable form, formal rules for deciding whether a syllogistic argument was valid—rules like "no conclusion is possible from two negative premises," "the middle term must be distributed at least once," etc. These subjects could refer to the list of rules at any time, and of course the Venn group was urged to sketch out Venn diagrams whenever they needed to. A third group of subjects was given what we considered to be the minimal instruction necessary to do the task—definition of a syllogism, and directions to the effect that the conclusion must necessarily follow from the premise in order for the syllogism to be valid. Several examples were given to illustrate the point.

Some summary data from this study are given in Table 5. The data show two things. First, subjects did fairly well at finding a logical conclusion when one existed. One additional breakdown of the missing-conclusion data is of some interest. The over-all probability of a correct conclusion from forward chaining syllogisms was .79; for the stimulus equivalence syllogisms, .76; and for response equivalence syllogisms, .59. The backward chaining syllogisms were the most difficult, with only a .49 probability of a correct conclusion. There results parallel those from verbal mediation studies.

TABLE 5

Summary Data Missing-Term Test:
Probability of Correct Responses

| Term missing | Instructions | | | Mean |
	Venn diagram	Formal rules	Minimal	
Major premise	.335	.330	.296	.320
Minor premise	.469	.467	.464	.467
Conclusion	.652	.666	.608	.642
Mean	.501	.505	.469	.491

When the missing term was one of the two premises, the subjects performed poorly, especially when the major premise had to be filled in. Examination of popular error responses for these items reveals a strong tendency to select a premise which is similar to the other term—picking a premise with "some" in it if the other items contained a "some," and picking a negative premise if the given terms were negative.

One somewhat surprising result was the lack of instructional effects in this study. Showing subjects how to use Venn diagrams, or giving them formal rules, just didn't help much. While there are a variety of reasons why this result might occur, it is a fortunate one for the present situation, since it is possible to argue that subjects approach a syllogism judgment task in a fairly consistent way no matter what kind of simple instructions are given.[3] At any rate, the data from all three instructional groups were similar enough so that they have been combined for the present analysis.

Before we turn to the data from individual syllogisms, it is necessary to consider the problem of parameter estimation—estimation of the probabilities of various interpretations of the premises during Stage 1, and estimation of the probabilities of various verbal labels given to possible set relations during Stage 3. No serious effort has been made to estimate these parameters, since what I ultimately want to do is to obtain empirical estimates of the probabilities from subjects asked to perform these interpretations in carefully controlled experiments. Parameters were roughly estimated to approximate the data from two or three of the syllogisms used (syllogisms 2, 3, and 5 in Table 8); then these probabilities were used to predict performance in other syllogisms. Thus, the fits of the models to the data should not be examined too critically in terms of quantitative agreement, since no effort was made to maximize this agreement. What should be looked at is qualitative agreement—the agreement of the models and the data in terms of the most likely conclusions to the various premise pairs.

Table 6 shows the assumed probabilities of various set relations being used to interpret premises. It has been assumed that there is a bias to interpret the premise "All A are B" as indicating an identity relation, and a bias to interpret "Some A are B" in terms of set overlap. As will also be noted, it has been assumed that subjects interpret the premise "Some A are not B" exclusively in terms of an overlap relation. The major factor in filling in these probabilities was a desire for simplicity. Thus, probabilities were placed in a given cell only if the data indicated that this was absolutely necessary. Let me stress that I have absolutely no faith that the numbers in Table 6 are correct. They have been used only to see if reasonable parameter values could account for qualitative aspects of syllogistic judgment data.

---

[3]Additional research has shown that when subjects are run one at a time rather than in groups, and when instructions are more thorough, subjects given Venn diagram instructions perform best, and those given minimal instructions perform worst, with rule instructions intermediate.

TABLE 6

Assumed Probability That Set Relation is Used as
Description of Statement

Premise	(AB)	(A) B	(B) A	A(B)	(A) (B)
All A are B	.75	.25	0	0	0
No A are B	0	0	0	0	1
Some A are B	0	0	.25	.75	0
Some A are not B	0	0	0	1	0

TABLE 7

Assumed Probability That Statement Will Be Used to
Describe Set Relations

Set relation	All A are B	No A are B	Some A are B	Some A are not B
(A B)	1	0	0	0
(A) B	1	0	0	0
(B) A	0	0	1/.10*	0/.90*
A(B)	0	0	1/.10*	0/.90*
(A)(B)	0	1	0	0

Note.—Asterisks denote statements having two probabilities, where the statement made depends on whether the context is positive or negative.

Table 7 gives the assumed probabilities that subjects interpret various possible set relations in terms of sentences having "A" as the subject and "B" as the predicate. Again, simplicity was the overriding factor. Note that when the premises are both positive, it is assumed that subjects always interpret overlap or superset relations as "Some A are B," but when one or more premises are negative, it is assumed that there is a strong probability that they will be interpreted as "Some A are not B." However, in the latter case, there is a small assumed probability that subjects interpret these ambiguous relations positively, even in the presence of negative premises. There is a plethora of data showing that subjects prefer to avoid negatives when possible and have trouble handling them.

In fitting the models, the probabilities given above were used, and standard rules of probability provided the predictions from the two models. It should also be noted that independence was assumed. In other words, it was assumed that the two premises were independently interpreted in terms of set relations. This is undoubtedly an oversimplification. It seems reasonable to assume, for example, that after having interpreted one premise of the form "All A are B" as indicating an identity relation, the probability of another such premise being similarly interpreted would be increased, but this has not been done here.

Table 8 gives data from the several pairs of premises used in the logic-test experiment conducted by Zax. All premise pairs used in this experiment have one

TABLE 8

Observed and Predicted Probabilities of Choosing Possible Conclusions
to Premise Pairs Where a Valid Conclusion Exists

Syllogism name	Premises	Conclusions[a]		Observed	Complete combination	Random combination
1	All B are C	(A) All A are C (X)		.910	1	1
	All A are B	(E) No A are C		.015	0	0
		(I) Some A are C (X)		.045	0	0
		(O) Some A are not C		.015	0	0
2	All B are C	A		.612	.75	.78
	All B are A	E		.030	0	0
		I	(X)	.328	.25	.22
		O		.015	0	0
3	All C are B	A		.580	.56	.56
	All B are A	E		.014	0	0
		I	(X)	.261	.44	.44
		O		.029	0	0
4	All B are C	A		.060	.25	.34
	Some B are A	E		.000	0	0
		I	(X)	.806	.75	.66
		O		.090	0	0
5	All B are C	A		.058	0	.12
	Some A are B	E		.014	0	0
		I	(X)	.870	1	.88
		O		.058	0	0
6	All C are B	A		.030	0	0
and	No A are B	E	(X)	.817	1	1
7	All C are B	I		.052	0	0
	No B are A	O	(X)	.052	0	0
8	All C are B	A		.000	0	0
	Some A are not B	E		.029	0	.08
		I		.188	.10	.09
		O	(X)	.768	.90	.82
9	Some C are B	A		.045	.19	.21
	All B are A	E		.045	0	0
		I	(X)	.761	.81	.79
		O		.119	0	0
10	Some B are C	A		.014	0	0
	All B are A	E		.000	0	0
		I	(X)	.899	1	1
		O		.043	0	0

[a] An (X) denotes a valid conclusion.

(Table 8 continued on page 318)

TABLE 8 (cont'd)

Syllogism name	Premises	Conclusions[a]		Observed	Complete combination	Random combination
11	No B are C	A		.022	0	0
and	Some A are B	E		.432	0	.33
12	No C are B	I		.097	.10	.07
	Some A are B	O	(X)	.440	.90	.60
13	No B are C	A		.008	0	0
and	Some B are A	E		.396	.25	.50
14	No C are B	I		.127	.08	.05
	Some B are A	O	(X)	.448	.68	.45
15	No C are B	A		.022	0	0
and	All A are B	E	(X)	.797	1	1
16	No B are C	I		.050	0	0
	All A are B	O	(X)	.087	0	0
17	No B are C	A		.036	0	0
and	All B are A	E		.602	.75	.83
18	No C are B	I		.072	.02	.02
	All B are A	O	(X)	.224	.22	.15
19	Some B are not C	A		.014	0	0
	All B are A	E		.058	0	0
		I		.130	.10	.10
		O		.783	.90	.90

[a] An (X) denotes a valid conclusion.

or more valid conclusions; these are indicated with an X in the conclusion column. The table requires careful study in order to absorb it in any detail, but a quick scan provides some of the important information. First, in every case but one, both models predict the most popular response, although in the cases of syllogisms 11, 12, 13, and 14 the quantitative fits are only fair. Second, both models, but especially the random combination model, predict *all* popular responses. In other words, almost every place in the observed data column where there is an appreciable probability ($> .05$), the models predict some appreciable probability.[4] It should be noted, however, that the models sometimes predict responses that the subjects did not make. For example, in syllogism number 4, both models predict that "All A are C" should be a fairly popular response, but subjects rarely chose this alternative.

The qualitative agreement between the models and the data seems very good. As noted previously, the quantitative fit should not be examined too critically,

[4]The main exceptions occur when the most popular response is an I sentence; a few subjects chose O sentences. The fits of the models could obviously be improved by allowing a small probability of an O sentence to overlap and to superset relations in Table 7 when the premises are positive.

since no effort was made to maximize this; however, it is hard to ignore the reasonably good quantitative agreement that does exist. As a rough index, correlations were calculated between observed and predicted probabilities. The correlation between observed and predicted probabilities for the complete combination model was .84; for the random combination model, it was .97. With the set of parameters used, the random combination model did better. This is easy to see in Table 8; in many cases, the complete combination model predicts behavior which is too extreme—too good. The best example of this is in syllogisms 11 and 12. The complete combination model predicts that almost all subjects will choose the correct conclusion "Some A are not C," but many subjects chose to respond "No A are C." The random combination model does a much better job of accounting for the data from these syllogisms. These syllogisms (and 13 and 14) are interesting for another reason. The atmosphere effect would predict that subjects would choose to respond "Some A are not B," since one premise is negative, and the other is particular. That the models do not simply have the atmosphere effect built in is clear from these syllogisms.

Predictions from the models were next compared with data reported by Ceraso and Provitera (1971). In their experiment, subjects chose responses to what Ceraso and Provitera called "traditional" premise pairs and to "modified" premise pairs. The traditional premises were of the type we have been examining: A, E, I, and O statements. The modified premises specified set relations more precisely. Thus instead of saying "All A are B," a modified premise might state "All A are B, but there are some B which are not A." Some of the syllogisms used had valid conclusions with both kinds of premises; some had valid conclusions with the modified, but not the traditional premises; and others had no valid conclusion with either type of premise. One other fact about this study requires that the models be modified slightly. The conclusions reported by the subjects seem to have been different from standard conclusions. Ceraso and Provitera report data only for conclusions of the forms "All A are B," "Some A are B," "No A are B," or "Can't say." The last answer was to be used when none of the other conclusions followed logically from the given premises. In Stage 3 of the models, the responses "Some A are B" and "Some A are not B" were considered equivalent, because of the form in which Ceraso and Provitera reported their data. In fitting the models to these data, the parameter values specified in Tables 6 and 7 were used with the modification mentioned above. Thus, again, the quantitative fits cannot be taken too seriously; the qualitative fits are the most important.

Table 9 shows the observed data, and predictions from the two models, for both the traditional and modified premises. The correct response is indicated by an X in the "observed" columns. For syllogisms that have a logical conclusion, the models performed very well; for syllogisms not having logical conclusions, they did not do as well. The subjects performed better on the modified syllogisms, and the models predict that they will do so as there is less room for uncertainty during Stage 1 when the premises are interpreted. Correlations between model predictions and observed proportions for the traditional premises were .89 and .85 for the

TABLE 9

Observed and Predicted Probabilities of Choosing Possible Conclusions
to Premise Pairs. (Data from Ceraso and Provitera, 1971)

Syllogism number	Premises Traditional	Premises Modified	Conclusions	Traditional Observed	Compl comb	Rand comb	Modified Observed	Compl comb	Rand comb
1	All A are B	(AB)	All	.775(X)	1	1	.925(X)	1	1
	All B are C	(BC)	Some	.05	0	0	.05	0	0
			None	0	0	0	0	0	0
			Can't Say	.175	0	0	.025	0	0
2	All A are B	(AB)	All	.85(X)	1	1	1(X)	1	1
	All B are C	(B C)	Some	.025	0	0	0	0	0
			None	0	0	0	0	0	0
			Can't Say	.125	0	0	0	0	0
3	All A are B	(AB)	All	.475	.75	.78	0	0	0
	All C are B	(C B)	Some	.300	.19	.21	.925(X)	1	1
			None	0	0	.01	.025	0	0
			Can't Say	.225(X)	.06	0	.05	0	0
4	All A are B	(AB)	All	.075	0	.09	0	0	0
	Some B are C	(B C)	Some	.75	.75	.84	.975(X)	1	1
			None	.025	0	.08	0	0	0
			Can't Say	.15(X)	.25	0	.025	0	0
5	All A are B	(AB)	All	0	0	0	.025	0	0
	No B are C	(B) (C)	Some	0	0	0	0	0	0
			None	.95(X)	1.0	1	.95(X)	1	1
			Can't Say	.05	0	0	.025	0	0
6	All A are B	(A B)	All	.975(X)	1	1	.925(X)	1	1
	All B are C	(B C)	Some	.025	0	0	.05	0	0
			None	0	0	0	0	0	0
			Can't Say	0	0	0	.025	0	0
7	All A are B	(A B)	All	.375	.75	.78	.15	0	.40
	All C are B	(C B)	Some	.15	.19	.21	.325	0	.40
			None	.025	0	.01	.075	0	.20
			Can't Say	.45(X)	.06	0	.45(X)	1	0
8	All A are B	(A B)	All	0	0	.09	0	0	.33
	Some B are C	(B C)	Some	.525	.75	.84	.225	0	.33
			None	.125	.25	.08	.15	0	.33
			Can't Say	.35(X)	0	0	.625(X)	1	0

TABLE 9 (cont'd)

Syllogism number	Premises Traditional	Modified	Conclusions	Traditional Observed	Compl comb	Rand comb	Modified Observed	Compl comb	Rand comb
9	All A are B	(A) B)	All	0	0	0	0	0	0
	No B are C	(B) (C)	Some	0	0	0	.025	0	0
			None	.95(X)	1	1	.925(X)	1	1
			Can't Say	.05	0	0	.05	0	0
10	All B are A	(B A)	All	.60	.75	.77	.175	0	.33
	All B are C	(B C)	Some	.025(X)	.25	.23	.675(X)	1	.60
			None	0	0	0	.025	0	.07
			Can't Say	.375	0	0	.125	0	0
11	All B are A	(B A)	All	.075	0	0	.05	0	0
	Some B are C	(B)(C)	Some	.85(X)	1	1	.825(X)	1	1
			None	0	0	0	0	0	0
			Can't Say	.075	0	0	.125	0	0
12	Some A are B	(A)(B)	All	0	0	.22	0	0	.40
	Some B are C	(B)(C)	Some	.400	.25	.59	.175	0	.40
			None	.125	0	.18	.10	0	.20
			Can't Say	.475(X)	.75	0	.725(X)	1	0
13	No A are B	(A) (B)	All	.05	0	.40	.025	0	.40
	No A are C	(B) (C)	Some	.10	0	.40	.15	0	.40
			None	.35	0	.20	.30	0	.20
			Can't Say	.50(X)	1	0	.525(X)	1	0

Note.—Correct responses are marked (X).

complete comparison and random comparison models, respectively. For the modified premises, the correlations were .94 for the complete comparison model and .82 for the random comparison model.

Despite these reasonably high correlations (recall that no parameters were estimated) neither model is completely satisfactory. However, directions for improving the models are clear. The random combination model, you will recall, assumes that during Stage 2 the subject selects one of the possible ways in which the two premises, interpreted in terms of set relations, can be combined. Thus, some combination is always chosen, and it is interpreted during Stage 3, using one of the allowable verbal responses. The random combination model always predicts that one of the possible responses will be chosen and *never* predicts that the subject will make the response "can't say." Syllogism number 13 from Table 9 illustrates this point nicely. Given the premises "No A are B" and "No B are

C,'' the set relationship between A and C is completely ambiguous. It could be any of the five possible relationships shown earlier. Since two of these can be interpreted as "All A are C," two can be interpreted as "Some A are C," and one as "No A are C," the random combination model makes the predictions shown (.40, .40, and .20) and predicts that the subject will never say "can't say." Obviously, this is incorrect; subjects have a strong tendency to response either "No A are C" or "can't say." They almost *never* respond "All A are C."

The complete combination model, on the other hand, predicts that performance will be better than it is. Again, syllogism 13 illustrates this point. At Stage 2, the complete combination model would assume that the five possible set relations between A and C are examined and the conflicting interpretations noted. The subject would then always report "can't say." Obviously this too is incorrect.

If the subject analyzes only one combination of premises, he will never report "can't say" to a syllogism having no logical conclusion. If he analyzes all possible combinations of the interpreted premises, he will say "can't say" too often (in terms of the data). These are parameter-free statements—they are true for any set of parameters that can be filled in Tables 6 and 7. Obviously, some compromise is needed. The data suggest that more than one combination is often analyzed but that all possible combinations are not. What is needed are data showing exactly how subjects *do* combine set relations. Such data do not exist, to my knowledge, so what follows is somewhat speculative, but data bearing on these speculations should not be difficult to collect.

A MODEL FOR INVALID SYLLOGISMS

Examination of the fits of Models I and II to the Ceraso and Provitera data for syllogisms having no valid conclusions indicates that they are too simple. Two things are clear from the data in Table 9. First, when subjects are faced with premises having incompatible combinations, there is some probability less than one that they will notice this. Second, all possible combinations of premises are not equally likely. Subjects obviously have biases in the way in which the premises are combined. One compromise model, Model III, will be considered here in order to demonstrate that the general theory can account for the data.

Model III is frankly a rather descriptive model incorporating these biases in an attempt to account for the data in Table 9. For each pair of premises (interpreted as set relations) where conflicting combinations are possible, probabilities of various reasonable combinations were assumed. It should be stressed that the main purpose in doing this was to demonstrate that the general theory is capable of accounting for these data, not to argue for the particular probabilities used here.

Table 10 illustrates the combination rules used during Stage II of the compromise model, Model III. There are 6 pairs of set relations which have contradictory combinations. In pair 1, sets A and B are disjoint, and so are sets B and C. It was assumed that there is a probability of .50 that subjects will notice that this means

TABLE 10

Combinations of Set Relations from Invalid Syllogisms and Assumed
Probabilities that each Combination is Used
Model III Analysis,

	Pairs of set relations	Combinations	Probability of use of combinations
1	Ⓐ Ⓑ Ⓒ Ⓑ	(?)	.50
		Ⓐ Ⓑ Ⓒ	.40
		Ⓑ A C	.10
2	(Ⓐ B) (Ⓒ B)	(?)	.50
		(A C B)	.25
		(A C B)	.25
3	(A B) (C B)	(?)	.50
		A B / C	.20
		A B C	.10
4	(Ⓐ B) (C B)	(?)	.60
		(A B) / C	.25
		(A B C)	.15
5	Ⓐ Ⓑ (Ⓑ C)	(?)	.50
		(Ⓑ C Ⓐ)	.25
		(Ⓑ C Ⓐ)	.25
6	Ⓐ Ⓑ B C	(?)	.40
		B C Ⓐ	.30
		B C A	.30

that the set relationship between A and C is completely ambiguous and report that
no logical conclusion exists. It was assumed that there is a probability of .40 that
subjects will assume that all three sets are disjoint and that, therefore, "No A are
C." Similarly, .10 was assigned as the probability that subjects will assume that
there is some overlap between sets A and C—presumably because they have in
common the fact that neither has anything to do with B. These probabilities were
chosen to approximate the data from syllogism 13 in Table 9. Obviously, the syllo-
gism-13 data could be matched exactly with appropriately chosen probabilities,
but there seems little point in doing so. The other probabilities in Table 10 were

similarly chosen, using "reasonableness" of selected set combinations, and of probabilities assigned to them, as basic guidelines. Obviously, there is a need for research in which subjects are asked to form combinations of the six pairs of set relations in Table 10 (along with others used in syllogisms that have a valid conclusion) in order to determine whether the assumed combinations and probabilities in Table 10 still seem reasonable in the light of real data.

The results of this effort are shown in Table 11, which gives predictions from Model III for all syllogisms used by Ceraso and Provitera where there was no valid conclusion. As can be seen, Model III is able to provide an adequate account of the

TABLE 11

Observed[a] and Predicted Probabilities from Model III of Choosing
Conclusions to Invalid Premise Pairs

Syllogism number	Conclusions	Traditional		Modified	
		Observed	Model III	Observed	Model III
3	All	.475	.76		
	Some	.300	.20		
	None	0	0		
	Can't Say	.225	.04		
4	All	.075	.01		
	Some	.750	.81		
	None	.025	.03		
	Can't Say	.150	.15		
7	All	.375	.76	.15	.25
	Some	.150	.20	.325	.25
	None	.025	0	.075	0
	Can't Say	.450	.04	.450	.50
8	All	0	.01	0	0
	Some	.525	.81	.225	.25
	None	.125	.03	.150	.15
	Can't Say	.350	.15	.625	.60
12	All	0	.06	0	0
	Some	.400	.19	.175	.20
	None	.125	.14	.100	.10
	Can't Say	.475	.61	.725	.70
13	All	.050	0	.025	0
	Some	.100	.10	.150	.10
	None	.350	.40	.300	.40
	Can't Say	.500	.50	.525	.50

[a]Data on observed probabilities from Ceraso and Provitera (1971).

data. The only case where the qualitative agreement is not good is traditional syllogism 3 (and the identical item, traditional syllogism 7). The fit here could have been improved, too, by choosing different parameters than those shown in Table 6 for "All A are B" sentences.

In order to examine the generality of the conclusions reached thus far regarding the predictive power of Models I, II, and III, they were fit to one more set of data, the data of Chapman and Chapman (1959). In that study, subjects were asked to choose one of the four types of responses (A, E, I, or O) or to respond "Can't say" to a series of syllogisms. The Chapmans report data only for syllogisms that do not have a logical conclusion. Of the 52 syllogisms given to their subjects, 42 had no logical conclusion.

The data from this study are summarized in Table 12. Since the data from various syllogistic figures having the same mood were so similar, they have been averaged across syllogistic figures, and only summary data are reported. Predictions from the models have also been averaged across syllogistic figures within a given mood. The parameter values in Tables 6, 7, and 10 were used.

TABLE 12

Observed[a] and Predicted Probabilities of Choosing Possible
Conclusions to Premise Pairs

Number	Premises	Models and observed (OBS)	Conclusions				
			A	E	I	O	Can't say
1	AA	OBS	.81	.05	.04	.01	.09
		Compl	.75	0	.19	0	.06
		Rand	.78	.01	.21	0	0
		Model III	.76	0	.20	0	.04
2	AE	OBS	.02	.83	.02	.05	.08
		Comp	0	.75	0	0	.25
		Rand	.08	.83	.01	.08	0
		Model III	0	.81	0	.06	.13
3	AI	OBS	.05	.05	.76	.06	.07
	or	Comp	0	0	.78	0	.22
		Rand	.15	.07	.78	0	0
	IA	Model III	.01	.03	.83	0	.13
4	AO	OBS	.01	.05	.11	.71	.12
	or	Comp	0	0	.09	.82	.08
	OA	Rand	.07	.03	.09	.84	0
		Model III	0	.04	.08	.73	.15

[a] Observed data from Chapman and Chapman (1959); the correct response is always "Can't say."

(*Table 12 continued on page 326*)

TABLE 12 (*cont'd*)

Number	Premises	Models and observed (OBS)	Conclusions				
			A	E	I	O	Can't say
5	IE	OBS	.02	.56	.06	.18	.19
		Comp	0	.12	0	0	.88
		Rand	.29	.42	.02	.26	0
		Model III	0	.48	.02	.20	.30
6	II	OBS	.02	.04	.65	.08	.21
		Comp	.06	0	.19	0	.75
		Rand	.41	.15	.44	0	0
		Model III	.06	.09	.35	0	.50
7 ·	IO	OBS	.01	.06	.12	.55	.25
	or	Comp	0	0	.02	.15	.83
	OI	Rand	.40	.19	.04	.36	0
		Model III	0	.10	.03	.28	.59
8	EE	OBS	.02	.54	.04	.05	.35
		Comp	0	0	0	0	1
		Rand	.40	.20	.04	.36	0
		Model III	0	.40	.01	.09	.50
9	EO	OBS	.03	.31	.08	.24	.34
	or	Comp	0	0	0	0	1
	OE	Rand	.16	.33	.05	.45	0
		Model III	0	.30	.03	.27	.40
10	OO	OBS	0	.07	.11	.52	.30
		Comp	0	0	0	0	1
		Rand	.40	.20	.04	.36	0
		Model III	0	.10	.02	.18	.70

The results are similar to those reported previously. Models I and II do not predict well for syllogisms where there is no logical conclusion, particularly those with negative premises. The correlations between observed data and predicted proportions were .57 for Model II, the complete combination model, and .69 for Model I, the random combination model. These models fail in the same manner as they did with the Ceraso and Provitera invalid syllogisms. The random combination model never predicts a "Can't say" response, and the complete combination model predicts this response too often. This is very obvious in syllogistic moods 5–10. Model III, on the other hand, performs well and is able to account reasonably well for the qualitative aspects of the data. The quantitative fits of Model III also are satisfactory, especially since no parameters were estimated for these data; the same ones were used as had been used in previous examples. The correlation between Model III predictions and observed probabilities was .86.

DISCUSSION

What conclusions can be drawn from these analyses? A general theory was proposed which assumes that subjects draw a conclusion from a pair of syllogisms according to a three stage process. The first stage involves interpretation of a (possibly ambiguous) verbal premise in terms of one of the possible set relations implied by the premise. The second stage involves combining the set relations which have been inferred from the premises in order to determine the set relationship between the terms in the conclusion. The third stage involves interpreting this new relationship in a verbal statement, as required by the experimenter.

Three models or special cases of the theory were examined, which assumed different methods of combining premises during Stage 2. Model I, the random combination model, assumes that one of the possible combinations is selected and interpreted during Stage 3. Model II, the complete combination model, assumes that all possible combinations of the set relations inferred during Stage 1 are examined, and that during Stage 3 a response is chosen which agrees with all of the possible combinations; if no such response exists, the response is that no valid conclusion exists. Model III, a compromise model, assumes that subjects do not examine all possible combinations but choose a particular combination or combinations according to certain biases. If there are combinations leading to conflicting conclusions, this is noticed with some probability.

Both Models I and II were able to predict subject's choices of conclusions in syllogisms where a valid conclusion was possible.[5] In general, both models predict almost all popular responses, with the random combination model doing a slightly better job. Although quantitative prediction was not the focus of the analysis, since the parameters of the model were not estimated in any formal way, the quantitative agreement seemed satisfactory, too, with high correlations between predicted and obtained response proportions.

However, when data were examined from syllogisms that have no valid conclusion, Models I and II were not able to make satisfactory predictions, particularly when the premises were negative (E and O statements). The random combination model is not able to account for cases where the subject responds that no valid conclusion exists—it always chooses a conclusion. The complete combination model, on the other hand, predicts that subjects will say that no valid conclusion exists much more often than they do.

Model III, on the other hand, a much more general model than Models I and II, *was* able to account for these data. Further development of the general theory is certainly warranted. Data from tasks where subjects are asked to interpret syllogistic premises as set relations, and data from tasks where subjects are asked to form combinations of set relations, would be particularly useful in testing some of

---

[5]Model III can also account for these data. Although the fits of Model III to data from syllogisms with a logical conclusion were not presented here, Model III will always fit at least as well as the better fitting of Models I or II.

the assumptions of the general theory and in guiding future choices of special cases, or models, of the theory for various specific reasoning tasks.

Let me say a little bit about some other aspects of this kind of analysis of syllogistic reasoning tasks. The studies reported here all used abstract material, letters in the case of the studies of Zax and of Chapman and Chapman, and statements about blocks of various shapes and colors in the study of Ceraso and Provitera. With such material, the premises are much more likely to be ambiguous in terms of set relations than with more familiar material drawn from a world in which the set relations are well known. It has been known since at least 1928 that people respond differently to abstract syllogisms than they do to syllogisms in which the material is familiar (Wilkins, 1928). The theory seems potentially able to account for these effects. The data of Ceraso and Provitera show that when set relations are specified more clearly in the premises, subjects perform much better than when they are ambiguous, and the theory was able to account for these data fairly well. One would expect that effects of different kinds of materials would be localized in Stage I of the theory, since it is at that stage that the premises are interpreted. This should be testable in suitable experiments.

In the studies analyzed here the subject either formed his own conclusion or chose a conclusion from a list given to him. This is, of course, not the only type of syllogistic judgment task. For example, in other experimental situations, subjects have been asked to give a rating as to whether or not a particular conclusion follows from a given pair of premises (Sells, 1936). The theory seems potentially able to account for this kind of situation also. Particular response demands seem likely to be localized in Stage 3 of the theory. However, they could also have an influence in Stage 2. For example, one possibility is that when a conclusion is given to the subject, he interprets it, too, in terms of a set relation. Then he could compare this interpretation with the one or more combinations of premises which are possible, and make his judgment as to whether or not the conclusion follows from the premises. On the other hand, one could form a model stating that the relationship implied by the interpreted conclusion influences the way in which premises are combined during Stage 2. Again, these possibilities seem to be testable. Since many of the syllogisms met in "real life" are apt to be of this nature— following someone's arguments, for example—it seems important to develop models for this kind of task within the general theory that has been proposed.

I believe that the set analysis theory provides a useful framework for thinking about syllogistic reasoning tasks, and that it points to a number of fruitful areas in which research is needed. In particular, it points to the need for more careful manipulation and control of set relationships in such reasoning studies. Such research should provide us with much more precise knowledge about how subjects try to handle one type of reasoning task and may point the way to similar analyses of other related tasks.

REFERENCES

Begg, I., & Denny, J. P. Empirical reconsideration of atmosphere and conversion interpretations of syllogistic reasoning errors. *Journal of Experimental Psychology,* 1969, **81**, 351–354.

Ceraso, J., & Provitera, A. Sources of error in syllogistic reasoning. *Cognitive Psychology,* 1971, **2**, 400–410.

Chapman, L. J., & Chapman, J. P. Atmosphere effect re-examined. *Journal of Experimental Psychology,* 1959, **58**, 220–226.

Erickson, J. R. Memory search in formal syllogistic reasoning. Paper presented at the meeting of the Midwestern Psychological Association, Cleveland, May, 1972.

Frase, L. T. Associative factors in syllogistic reasoning. *Journal of Experimental Psychology,* 1968, **76**, 407–412.

Henle, M. On the relation between logic and thinking. *Psychological Review,* 1962, **69**, 366–378.

Jenkins, J. J. Mediated associations: Paradigms and situations. In C. N. Cofer & B. S Musgrave (Eds.), *Verbal behavior and learning.* New York: McGraw-Hill, 1963.

Pezzoli, J. A., & Frase, L. T. Mediated facilitation of syllogistic reasoning. *Journal of Experimental Psychology,* 1968, **78**, 228–232.

Sells, S. B. The atmosphere effect: An experimental study of reasoning. *Archives of Psychology,* 1936, No. 200.

Wason, P. C., & Johnson-Laird, P. N. *Psychology of reasoning: Structure and content.* Cambridge, Mass.: Harvard University Press, 1972.

Wilkins, M. C. The effect of changed material on ability to do formal syllogistic reasoning. *Archives of Psychology,* 1928, No. 102.

Woodworth, R. S., & Sells, S. B. An atmosphere effect in formal syllogistic reasoning. *Journal of Experimental Psychology,* 1935, **18**, 451–460.

13

THE ORIGINS OF
LANGUAGE COMPREHENSION[1]

Janellen Huttenlocher
Teachers College, Columbia University

This paper is concerned with a neglected but central aspect of language development, namely, the development of comprehension in the child. While the investigation of language development has advanced rapidly in the last decade, it has been far more concerned with children's speech production than with their understanding of what is said to them. There exist no in-depth investigations of the emergence of comprehension during the period before and while the child learns to talk. Rather, what study there has been of comprehension in children, as in adults, has involved discrete experimental studies. For the most part, such investigations have been concerned with the comprehension of particular grammatical distinctions; for example, with the ability to choose between pictures representing "The cup is falling" versus "The cup has fallen," "The truck is pushing the car" versus "The car is pushing the truck," "The mother's baby" versus "The baby's mother," etc.

I will present below pilot data for a few subjects from a longitudinal investigation of the development of receptive language. The data concern the very first stages in systematic response to word sounds in three children during the age period from approximately 10–18 months. The gist of the findings thus far is the following:

[1]The preparation of this paper and the collection of the pilot data reported here were supported in part by Career Development Award 5-K-HD-21,979, and in part by Research Grant HD 03215, both from the National Institutes of Health. The issues considered in the section *The Linguistic Code in Relation to Events* are taken up in greater detail in two theoretical papers written in collaboration with E. Tory Higgins. I want to thank Lois Bloom for our many discussions about language development, Rosalind Charney for her editorial assistance, and Deborah Burke, E. Tory Higgins, and Clark Presson for their comments on the paper. Most of all, I want to thank the mothers of Craig, Kristen, Thomas, and Wendy for their cooperation.

that receptive language is considerably in advance of productive language; that there is not a simple relation between the child's systematic response to the words he hears and his production of words; that there is a progression in the type of response the child makes to words in the period before he speaks; and that the child's systematic response to speech may prove valuable in supplementing the information one can obtain about the infant's knowledge of objects and events from his linguistic output or from his behavior in Piaget-type tasks.

The Neglect of Comprehension in Studies of Language Development

Traditionally, investigators of normal language development have failed to distinguish sharply between receptive and productive language. For the most part, insofar as the issue was raised at all, the relation between the two was not seen as an interesting one. As the common sense view might have it, one must be able to understand in order to be able to talk, and the relation between the two no doubt involves a simple lag. The lack of explicitly separate consideration of receptive and productive language development was reinforced by the theoretical bias which motivated the detailed studies of syntactic development carried out in the 1960s. The vantage point that guided these studies was that the acquisition of language reflects a separate, specifically linguistic competence. Since that competence was taken to underlie both comprehension and production, there was no reason to consider these two processes separately. The focus on the acquisition of the linguistic code itself in studies of language development led to a concern with production; the corpus of the child's utterances was examined in an attempt to find what syntactic rules guided their utterances.

One cannot easily deal with comprehension within a framework that focuses only on the code itself. To have understood a sentence implies that the listener has obtained a knowledge of the state of affairs described in a sentence. These states of affairs include information about the world of objects and events, etc. Thus the study of comprehension cannot progress far without explicit recognition that the linguistic code is mapped onto people's mental representations of their experiences. At present, the focus of interest in children's language and in psycholinguistics generally has shifted in a manner consistent with progress in the study of comprehension. Even investigators who are primarily concerned with the acquisition of the linguistic code itself now explicitly recognize that that code is mapped onto a cognitive domain. This is because they have found considerable evidence that the child's productive language development is closely related to his mastery of certain conceptual relations which he encodes in his syntax (Bloom, 1970; Bowerman, 1973; Slobin, 1973).

Increasingly, comprehension and production are being examined separately. Thus Friedlander (1970) argues that "To focus investigation only on the emergence of expressive functions, or to wait two years or more until the baby can use his own speech to offer what is at best highly restricted evidence of what he comprehends, is to neglect what may be one of the most important stages of developmental organization in all the child's growth [p. 20]." Susan Meadow has gathered data on receptive vs. productive vocabulary which are discussed below. Bloom, Higgins, and Hood (1973) are beginning to examine Bloom's production data to determine the extent to which the content of adult speech plays a role in children's utterances. Not only is comprehension becoming recognized as a separate source of information about language development, but some investigators even raise the question of whether comprehension necessarily precedes production. It has been proposed that for certain aspects of language development the reverse may hold; that is, the child may produce syntactic structures that, at least under certain conditions of testing, he cannot comprehend (Chapman & Miller, 1973). We consider this argument in a later section of this paper.

Although a broad consensus has developed that the important questions about language development concern the relation of the linguistic code to the mental representation of events, many of the implications of this position remain to be worked out. We will briefly consider here those issues that will be critical to our later discussion. First, let us explicitly examine the minimal type of cognitive *structure* one must postulate to account for people's ability to deal with simple descriptions of objects and events. We will only consider words for "perceptual" categories here (e.g., dog, whistle), because these are the words to which infants respond. While the relation between word and meaning is comparable for other types of words (justice, worship) the analysis of meaning is obviously quite different. Second, let us briefly consider the *processes* involved in the comprehension and production of linguistic messages as these may relate to the early stages in the development of language.

The Linguistic Code in Relation to Events

With respect to the structure necessary to account for people's ability to use language in relation to perceptible objects and events, let me summarize the argument made in Huttenlocher and Higgins (1972). The argument deals with the following questions: What is involved in a person being able to name an object or in knowing, when presented with a particular word, the object or object class it specifies? Second, what is involved in a person being able to formulate a description of a relation between two objects, or in knowing, when presented a description, what relation between objects or object classes it specifies?

First, let us consider object names. In order to know the name of an object, a person must have stored information about how a particular object or class of objects looks. We refer to that stored information as an *object-schema*. He must be able to recognize an object he sees as being the particular object or an instance of the object class. In addition, he must have stored information about the sound of a particular word. We refer to that stored information as a *sound-schema*. He must be able to recognize an incoming word as an instance of that word-sound class. Finally, he must have stored a *mapping of the sound-schema onto the object-schema,* to know when the word is appropriately applied.

The same issues arise with respect to the descriptions of perceptible relations between objects (e.g., the relation "above" considered by Huttenlocher and Higgins, 1972). First, the person must have stored a particular type of perceptual relation between objects (in this case verticality) which we call a *perceptual-relation-schema.* He must also be able to recognize the vertical array involving the pair of objects as belonging to the category of vertical relations. In addition, he must have stored an ordered relation among words in a sentence, which we call a *syntactic-schema.* He must be able to recognize an incoming sentence as an instance of that syntactic-schema. Finally, he must have stored a *mapping of the ordered relation among words onto the ordered relation among objects.*

Finally, let us consider words for perceptible actions. The actions we are concerned with here are those that the children carry out in response to particular words: whistling, making a blowing sound, sitting down or standing up when asked, and making pattycake and peek-a-boo on command. These actions may be carried out either by a person himself or by other people. Thus in order to know the name for such actions, a person must have stored information about their appearance, or how it feels to carry them out, or both. In this sense, the mental representation of such actions is more complex than that for objects. We refer to the stored information about perceptible actions of this sort as *action-schemas.* It is not always clear, however, whether these small children can recognize the acts which they themselves carry out when they see them carried out by others. (That is, the recognition of these acts in others is not easily tested through comprehension tasks, as discussed below.) In any case, the general issue of how particular movements or acts are cognitively represented is poorly understood at present. Animal psychologists tend to treat actions, even complex actions, as "responses" which are conditioned to stimuli, e.g., "sit down" as a stimulus which is wired up to the motor plan of sitting down. Such an analysis bypasses the issue of whether to attribute to the person (or animal) who carries out such an act a conceptualization of that act. If the child "simply responds" to a verbal stimulus, one need not postulate an action-schema. We do refer to an action-schema in the case of an adult who both recognizes and carries out particular types of acts and who gives evidence that he can imagine them without actually carrying them out. With respect to his understanding of a word like "whistle" or "sit down," he has stored a *mapping of a word-schema onto an action-schema.*

With respect to both receptive and productive language, one wants to distinguish between two types of processes: those related to the linguistic code itself (that is, the sound-schemas of words and syntactic-schemas) and those related to the mapping of that linguistic code onto meaning. The discussion of receptive language below concerns comprehension, where the link between word-sound and meaning is involved, rather than simple word recognition which involves only the categorization of incoming speech sounds as being members of particular sound-schemas. Similarly, the discussion of productive language concerns encoding, where the link from meaning (initiated by an encounter with objects and events) to word-sounds is involved, not simply the making of word-sounds *per se*.

One simple difference between receptive and productive language is that the first involves *recognition* of words and *recall* of the objects, acts, and relations for which they stand, whereas the latter involves *recognition* of objects, acts, and relations and *recall* of the words that stand for them. This constitutes an important asymmetry between receptive and productive language; words only have significance in man's life insofar as they are mapped onto his nonlinguistic experience, whereas the objects and events are significant in themselves. Thus while the only function of words is to give rise to their meanings, events are chiefly experienced for their own properties.

Let us examine more closely the asymmetry between receptive and productive language, specifically with respect to words that designate perceptible objects, properties, and acts. As we have said, such words are mapped onto stored information about these percepts. Given a familiar word, retrieval of meaning may well be obligatory or automatic[2] except when interfering events occur during the retrieval process. The link from a particular perceptual experience to a particular word is almost certainly less direct. First of all, during many of one's encounters with events, there may be no verbal encoding, not even "implicit" encoding. One continually sees trees, houses, and cars, as well as people going about their ordinary activities, and despite the claims of some psychologists, there is little reason to believe that people assign words to all such experiences, even for those experiences that readily allow for verbal description. In any case, particular perceptible events certainly are not automatically named by particular words, since countless different things may be said about any single event. Indeed, the most common utterances pertaining to particular events probably are not descriptions of the events themselves, but rather comments on those events.

Finally, in comprehension, words and syntax are used by the listener to form mental representations of states of affairs. In some cases the message leads the listener to retrieve information he had stored earlier. The most important function of linguistic messages, however, is to provide the listener with *new* information which he did not have until he decoded the message. This function rests on people's ability to represent states of affairs that they have not directly encountered. The listener makes use of the meanings of individual lexical items and of the relational meanings encoded by the syntax to create such mental representations; the mental processes involved are only dimly understood at present.

In speaking, on the other hand, a person begins with a mental representation of some state of affairs. The mature articulate speaker has many options in describing a particular state of affairs he has encountered. The contents of his utterances

---

[2]In the sense of automatic used by Posner and Warren (1972).

reflect various judgments as to what information is needed by his listener, as well as a choice of particular lexical items and syntactic forms. The ability to formulate effective messages is clearly a complex skill. (See, for example, Glucksberg, Krauss, and Higgins, in press.) Many issues concerning the communication process in adults and older children have no counterpart in the consideration of the relation between receptive and productive language in the very young child. What *will* concern us in the discussion below is whether the nature of the mental representations of events which form the basis for encoding language differ from those involved in decoding language.

Context and Comprehension: Evaluating Receptive Language

The very fact that language encodes information about events leads to difficulties in investigating comprehension. As we noted above, the events described in an utterance may already be known to the listener; indeed, the events being described may even be occurring at the time the utterance is made. Thus in the ordinary contexts of discourse, it may be difficult or impossible to determine the extent to which the listener must decode the linguistic message itself in order to make available to himself the information encoded in that message.

Particularly for very small children, much of the language the mother uses is redundant with respect to context. Mommy makes dinner and says "Mommy is cooking." Johnny pulls off his shoes and Mommy says "Johnny is taking off his shoes." At a still earlier stage, the baby gazes at a light and Mommy says "light," or he hugs his dog and Mommy says the dog's name. Surely such pairings of linguistic messages with objects and events is critical in order for the child to learn how the code is used in relation to events. In the usual conversations between mother and child, however, the child rarely needs to rely on the linguistic message itself to react appropriately to something that is said. Indeed, the mother's utterances may even be guided by what she guesses the child is about to do.

Let us consider how one can evaluate whether a listener knows an object name. To be confident that the listener actually pairs a particular word with a particular object or object-class, one must first of all make sure that the testing situation involves a range of possible choices in addition to the target object. This is not all; even if there are many objects to choose among, the child might choose correctly simply because he has a preference for the particular object that has been named. Thus if one says "Where is the ball?" and the child selects it, one cannot be certain that he pairs the word "ball" with the object *ball*, until one makes sure that he does not select the ball when he is asked "Where is the table?" or "Where is the apple?"

The same issues arise in evaluating sentence comprehension. First of all, there is the question of whether the listener understands each of the individual lexical items. Second, there is the question of whether the listener understands the relational meanings encoded in the syntax. Clearly there are many cases in which one can interpret a sentence without considering relational aspects of sentence meaning. For example, the nature of the individual lexical terms may themselves alone specify the direction of a transitive relation, as in "The man drank the coffee." In other cases, even though the described relation is not inherently irreversible, it may be habitually so, as in "The cup is on the saucer." Even in cases where the relation described in a sentence is clearly reversible, the extralinguistic context may determine which item is to be moved. Consider a context where only one of two described items can be moved. For example, "The doll goes on top of the bunny" occurs in a context where there is a ladder with a bunny fixed on one shelf and a doll standing alongside, or "The truck is pushing the car" occurs in a context where a toy car is fixed onto a toy road while a toy truck stands alongside. These tasks are easier when the mobile item is described as the grammatical subject, as in the examples above, rather than as the grammatical object (Huttenlocher & Strauss, 1968; Huttenlocher, Eisenberg, & Strauss, 1968). Thus the actual roles of items in the situation create predispositions in regard to which object should function in which grammatical role.

Even when the mobile item is the grammatical subject and the fixed item is the grammatical object, there remain possible variations in context. That is, there may or may not be more than one mobile item, e.g., a ball as well as a doll. If there is more than one mobile item, the listener must attend to the subject term. There may or may not be free shelves both above and below the fixed bunny. If there are, the listener must attend to the relational term. Finally, there may or may not be a second ladder with another fixed item (e.g., a ladder with a block, as well as a ladder with a bunny). When there is more than one fixed item, the listener must attend to the object term. In contexts that do not suggest in which role each item serves in the transitive relation, for example, where both items initially stand alongside the ladder, syntactic cues are needed to determine which item goes "on top of" the other. Such variations in the extralinguistic context in which particular sentences may occur have been investigated in a series of experiments (Huttenlocher & Strauss, 1968; Huttenlocher et al., 1968; Huttenlocher & Weiner, 1971; Huttenlocher & Presson, 1973).

Even if the investigator makes available various reponse options, appropriate response to a sentence does not necessarily imply comprehension. Consider, for example, that several times in succession the child correctly places a block on top of a cup in response to the sentence "The block goes on top of the cup," and that it was possible for the block to go underneath as well. One still cannot be certain that the child understands "on top of." Children frequently exhibit behavioral preferences, and in a particular situation they may tend to put one particular item on top of, rather than under, another. To establish the child's comprehension one must make sure that the child does not put the block on top when the sentence is "The block goes under the cup" and "The block goes next to the cup" as well. Behavioral preferences may be due to differences in the motor difficulty of the alternatives, e.g., it may be harder to balance the cup on top, or to perceptual factors, e.g., the block may look better on top.

Issues concerning children's possible perceptual and behavioral preferences pose challenging problems in the design and interpretation of experiments on comprehension. Consider, for example, certain experiments that have been interpreted as showing that the child at first attributes the same meaning to certain relational terms which are actually oppositional in meaning, e.g., "same" and "different," and "more" and "less" (Donaldson & Wales, 1970). Children picked an object that was similar to, rather than different from, a target object regardless of whether they were asked for one that was "the same" or one that was "different." Similarly, they picked the larger of two arrays regardless of whether they were asked for the one that had "more" or the one that had "less." (The findings with "more" and "less" are empirically reliable; they have recently been replicated by Palermo, 1973, with added controls.) However, the interpretation of the findings as indicating that the child knows the meaning of "more" and assigns that same meaning to "less" is doubtful for all the reasons outlined above. This issue is critical, since some authors base various broad theoretical positions on this interpretation of the findings. Thus Clark (1973) takes these data as part of the basis for a theory of the acquisition of word meanings, which we will examine in the discussion section.

THE PRESENT STUDY

During the last year I have been following four children in their homes, with the goal of tracing, as far as possible, their comprehension of what is said to them and the knowledge of objects and events that underlies their comprehension of linguistic messages. In order to investigate the emergence of systematic responses to speech sounds, I began when the children were very young. Three of them were between 10 and 11 months when I first saw them, and the remaining child was 13 months. Each child has been seen every few weeks over a period of six months. The testing on each visit lasted for as long as it was possible to keep the child's attention, or until all the testing was completed.

To study comprehension is not as straightforward as studying production. At the start, each child understood little of what was said. The words to which he responded might be idiosyncratic to his family. One could not easily determine these early systematic responses to word-sounds by selecting a random sample of English words, even the most frequent ones. I attempted to determine what words or expressions they seemed to respond to systematically. To do this requires a middleman, who is habitually with the baby and can thus notice which words he seems to "understand." The mothers gave their impressions of the baby's comprehension of words or phrases. After obtaining information that the baby seemed to understand a particular word or phrase, I tested him contrastively in order to make sure that the response did not reflect mere perceptual bias, that it was made only to the particular lexical item in question, that no accompanying extralinguistic cues were given, etc.

There are some obvious weaknesses in this approach. First, there may be pairings between word-sounds and events that are familiar to the baby, but that one *cannot test* for. Indeed, among the few words these babies produced themselves, there was a high proportion of just such words. For example, I don't know how to test whether the child knows that "hi" is said as people arrive and "bye-bye" as they leave. The most easily testable words are nouns that name the various objects and object classes in the child's environment. Words for perceptible actions are easily testable when the action is one the child can carry out himself. However, it is not easy to test words for actions that the child might know as an observer but that he cannot carry out himself. Suppose, for example, that the child knows that Mommy's activities at the stove can be called "cooking"; I have not tested for this sort of knowledge. The same can be said for words like "pretty," "nice," and "bad." Secondly, *the mother may be unaware* of certain of the baby's systematic responses to speech sounds. Indeed, those pairings of which she is aware may favor certain classes of words over others. Insofar as the investigator follows the mother's lead, these could be missed. To correct to some extent for this possible source of bias, I have periodically tested for various common words for objects and acts that the mother had not noted. With respect to multiword expressions, I have not depended on the mother at all but have simply included familiar lexical items in various syntactic expressions.

Overall Aspects of the Children's Behavior

Certain overall features of the children's behavior should be noted; first, the general issue of the baby's attentiveness to speech and the maintenance of attention during a session, and, second, the types of responses by which the babies demonstrated their comprehension.

Attention. A striking fact about all of the children was their apparent disregard of ongoing conversation. Such inattention to conversation has been noted by Shipley, Smith, and Gleitman (1969), and informally by other observers as well. The phenomenon is quite remarkable and suggests that at least in the early stages of language development the child obtains little information from ongoing speech unless that speech is specifically directed to him. Indeed, it was difficult to get the child's attention at all. The way I did this was to call the child's name in a loud sing-song manner, until he or she made eye contact with me. Then I could proceed to ask "Where is the bottle?" or whatever. That request also had to be said in a distinct and sing-song manner or the child looked away and did not respond. I can only say this informally because I did not systematically vary my intonation so as to test the limits of the child's responsivity. Our related research with somewhat older children suggests that intonation may play a role not only in capturing children's attention, but may also serve as an aid in the short-term retention of ordered sequences of items (Huttenlocher & Burke, 1973; Burke and Huttenlocher, 1973).

The other feature of direction-giving which I noted informally, but which we are now examining systematically, was a tendency to repeat directions to the child. Mothers frequently said "Where is your bottle? Where is your bottle?" and I found myself doing the same thing. A very noticeable feature of children's responses in some cases was an arrest of ongoing activity accompanied by a look of concentration, almost of perplexity. For me, and quite obviously for the mothers, this facial expression creates a strong impulse to repeat what one has just said. It is not yet clear to me whether such repetition actually serves a function for the child in retrieving information about meaning.

For all of the children, it became difficult or impossible to get their attention after a period of time. They simply stopped making eye contact and one could not direct a request to them. This type of alteration in attention during a sequence of interactions has been noted by Stern (1973). He found that babies make eye contact repeatedly with mothers during an interactional sequence, that they gradually become more excited, and finally they avert their gaze. The children I have followed seem to get worn out. Responding to speech, one gets the feeling, is hard work, and when they are unwilling to do any more work they will no longer make eye contact.

Responses to Words. Before I began observing these children I was concerned that their responses to words might be uninterpretable, or that I would only occasionally be able to elicit responses; in short, that I would be uncertain as to whether or not they knew certain words. I was surprised by how easy it was to elicit unambiguously interpretable responses. There were two characteristic responses to noun words: picking up and showing an item, or directing gaze towards the item. The response to words for actions was to carry out the designated action.

The children were (and still are) variable in their motor abilities. Only one of them walks, and he did so at the time I first saw him at 13 months. The others only crawl, and two of them could not even do that at the time I first saw them. The children who could not move could only indicate their familiarity with an object by directing their gaze towards that object when it was named, unless it was within reach. The only child who walked easily did not typically indicate knowledge of words through a gaze; he rather went out and got the objects.

Given that a child's attention has been gained, the response to a request was frequently prompt and unequivocal. In these cases, responses were generally correct. With respect to gaze, as long as a set of objects was suitably separated spatially, the child's response was completely obvious. He would turn his head, stop abruptly upon encountering the target object, and stare at it for an easily discernible period of time. With respect to getting objects, the children picked them up and showed them. There were few mistakes, and these typically occurred with long latency, although until we systematically examine filmed records, there is no precise measure of this.

It is not obvious how best to present the data from the three children who do show receptive language, since these data consist of a series of vignettes where the child's comprehension is tested. I cannot present all of the interactions that occurred.

Rather, I will present certain highlights that show some of the interesting aspects of the development of their receptive language. In general, I will not make any consistent attempt to describe the many interactions in which it became obvious that the child was relying on extralinguistic cues, tone of voice, etc., or where a response could not be reliably obtained on several occasions. It must be emphasized that these are not unique or isolated incidents, but rather the most salient examples from a considerably larger body of data. By way of organization, I will present these vignettes chronologically.

In order to orient the reader to an important feature of the data, let me point out briefly a major finding which will be discussed at the end of the paper. The largest category of words was object names. There were three different conditions under which children demonstrated familiarity with object names, and these appear to have been ordered chronologically. At first, children looked around them until they found the object named. Next, they would take a direct route to an object that was out of view. At first, such behavior seemed restricted to objects that occupied fixed positions, like the bathtub, or cookies kept in a particular kitchen cabinet. Finally, the two most advanced children would take a direct route to an object that not only was out of view but that occupied only a temporary position. I will argue below that these different types of behavior in seeking objects in response to their names may reflect different stages in the child's ability to represent information about objects.

Selections from the Protocols

Wendy (born January 28, 1972)

10 months, 13 days. At the time of my first visit Wendy used four words. Two of them had occurred for the first time only a few days before I saw her. They are "hi" and "see." Both of these words have continued to be used, off and on again, until the present. "Hi" is initially used in her crib when someone comes into the room. Since then, it has been used in the same context of a person appearing, but in places other than the crib. "See" is almost always used when she holds up an object, or sometimes when she is gazing at it. (Now, six months later, it is still used in the same way and continues to occur with high frequency.) At this initial visit, "Mommy" is used in the context of wanting to be picked up when Wendy is in her high-chair or playpen. "Daddy" is used when his footsteps are heard outside her room, and when the garage door opens in the evening and she is in the kitchen with her mother.

Wendy's mother believes she understands the words "bye-bye," "peek-a-boo," "bangbang," "cookie," "pretzel," and "no." Wendy demonstrates her comprehension as follows: During the session Mommy leaves the room. Wendy watches Mommy while she stands up, walks to the side of the room, turns and talks to me for a moment, then says, looking at Wendy, "Bye-bye, Mommy is going bye-bye." Wendy raises her right hand immediately and opens and shuts it very precisely several times in the bye-bye motion. Also at the end of the session, I have my coat on and have been standing talking to Mommy for some time. She turns to Wendy and says, "Say goodbye." Wendy does the exact same thing she did to Mommy earlier, this time making eye contact with me.

Wendy is equally successful in responding to the two other action words. During the session Mommy puts on the floor near Wendy a diaper, a cookie, a pretzel, and a stainless steel mixing bowl with a spoon in it. A bunny book, milk truck with bottles, and her bottle have already been put there. She says to Wendy, "Make peek-a-boo." Wendy promptly picks up the diaper, puts it over her face, and peeks out smiling. Through the session I say the same thing three other times with the same prompt response. A little later Wendy again has many things around. Now, however, the diaper is not in view. I say "Make peek-a-boo." She looks around, sees no diaper, and looks puzzled. Then with a smile she picks up the bowl and hides, peeking around the side and breaking into laughter as she does so.

At another point in the session, Mommy moves the bowl in front of Wendy and says "Make bangbang," which Wendy does for a time with the spoon. A little later, her bowl and most everything else *except* the spoon are in front of her. I say "Make bangbang." Wendy stops, looks at the bowl, looks around, then takes her hand and very deliberately bangs it against the side of the bowl.

Wendy also demonstrates her knowledge of at least one object word—cookie. During the session, Mommy asks Wendy, "Where is the cookie?" She looks around, picks it up, takes a bite, and puts it down. A little later Wendy is drinking from her bottle. I say "Where is the cookie?" She looks among all the things, then takes one hand off her bottle and fishes up the cookie with the other, holding it up to show me and then putting it down again.

Wendy does not seem to know "no," however. During the session, Wendy is playing with the Pat-the-Bunny book. She has ripped out the book-within-a-book which is glued to one of the pages and is putting paper into her mouth. Mommy says "no" and Wendy stops. As Wendy starts to eat the paper again, I ask Mommy to say "yes" in the same tone. This stops her as well. In fact, we try "yes" a second time and again it works.

Finally, I ask "Where is Mommy?" Three times there is no response. Recall that Mommy reports that Wendy says "Mommy." We will trace this word through later sessions.

What do these responses indicate? Wendy apparently knows at least three different acts which she has linked to words. They are represented in terms which allow flexibility of execution. She knows at least one object word—cookie—which is used in reference to a class of objects rather than to only one individual object.

10 months, 23 days. Wendy has become much harder to work with because she has learned to get into a crawling position. By this time she has acquired at least two proper names as well as two new object names which may or may not have reference to a *class* of objects. Several times during this session I ask her "Where is Mommy?" Each time she sharply turns her gaze to Mommy. Wendy's brother

Danny is home for vacation and watching TV down the hall. I ask her "Where is Danny?" three times, and each time she stares down the hall.

Wendy has a blanket, bottle, and boat. Mommy thinks she knows the boat. It's new and she plays with it a lot. I test each of these words four times and although she always responds correctly to "blanket" and "bottle," she never responds at all to "boat."

11 months. Wendy says "Mama" three times when her Mommy leaves the room for a few minutes. Further, when I say "Good-bye Wendy," she says "bye-bye" (for the first time ever, according to her mother).

At this session we see the first instance of loss of systematic response to words. The bowl and spoon are here, and Wendy is asked eight different times to "make bangbang." She looks puzzled the first few times. One time she even has the spoon in her hand with the bowl nearby. On later requests she no longer stops and looks puzzled, but rather acts as if nothing has been said. Peek-a-boo, however, is played successfully. She also responds consistently (four times) when asked "Where is Mommy?" There are several episodes where Mommy asks Wendy to "kiss the doll" and "show your teeth" which she thinks Wendy knows. There is no evidence of this. If her attention is caught, she looks puzzled. She still knows "blanket." On one occasion she plays peek-a-boo with it on request; it is the only piece of cloth present.

11 months, 11 days. Today there is another instance of loss. I ask Wendy "Where is Mommy?" She looks totally blank. This question is repeated several times with the same response and, indeed, to the present time, more than three months later, she gives no evidence of familiarity with the word "Mommy," nor does she say it any longer.

Wendy has also learned "ball" and reliably shows both wooden bottles and her milk bottle as "bottles." Which bottle she shows seems to depend upon which is easier to find.

1 year, 14 days. By this time Wendy has learned "Pat-the-Bunny book" and "teddy bear," later reduced to just "bear." Neither of these words is later lost, but sometimes there is a long hesitation, and occasionally a degree of ambiguity of response which had not occurred when they were first tested. For example, when asked for the teddy bear, she looks over all the toys, *including* the teddy bear, several times before she finally and triumphantly picks it up to show it. This type of hesitation may be contrasted with the following type of case: When completely surrounded by toys and drinking her bottle, I ask "Where is the ball?" Twice she puts down the bottle, picks up the ball to show it, then puts it back down and picks up the bottle again. The third time she just raises her bottle slightly rather than again doing the same. This last example is typical of requests that follow one another closely in time. In such cases, lack of response seems to result from boredom, and no visual search occurs.

1 year, 30 days. Wendy has begun to pick up a small china dog when asked

"Where is the dog?" In conversing with Wendy's mother, I find she expresses the belief that Wendy knows real dogs and stuffed dogs as well as the china dog and that, further, she knows dog pictures. We proceed to test this by using several stuffed animals, which belong to Wendy's older brother and which she has never played with. Of these animals, there are three stuffed teddy bears and two stuffed dogs. (Wendy is still at the stage of looking all around to find an instance of a word.) During the period of testing she is in several different positions in the room. When there are both dogs and teddies in view, she is asked for dogs twice and for bears three times. Each time she produces the correct type of animal. We test her with two animal books, however, and when asked for "dog" she is just as likely to point to deer pictures or to raccoon pictures as to dog pictures. Wendy does not discriminate among different animal pictures, only among different toy animals and, according to her mother, among different real animals.

1 year, 1 month, 6 days. Wendy will now get to her knees and wiggle rhythmically when asked to "dance." She is also able to point out her "hair" when asked to do so. However, she often looks confused and will tentatively touch another body part, her teeth, en route. Wendy's mother asks her for her teeth repeatedly and is sure she knows them, even though I never see evidence for this during this period of time. By 1 year, 1 month, and 20 days, she also points to her teeth and to her belly button. On the first day belly-button pointing occurred spontaneously several times and thus seemed less convincing as a response to the word than other responses. However, since then Wendy's pride in showing her belly button has diminished, yet her constant response to "Where is your belly button?" has remained.

Here Wendy first gives evidence of behavior I believe requires postulation of a more complex mental process than that involved in randomly searching around for an object when it is named. Let me explain. We are down in the very large playroom which has a six- by four-foot barrier jutting out into the room and separating an area with toys and furniture from an area, leading to another room, where there is a fish tank with fish. I ask Wendy "Where are the fish?" while she is playing. She goes all the way over to the fish, a trip of some 15 feet, although she can only see the fish at the very end of her trip. She does this reliably whenever she is asked.

1 year, 2 months, 3 days. Now, there occurs even more of a shift from her earlier search behavior. When asked "Where is the x," Wendy has now begun to give evidence of retaining information about the current transitory position of an object after she has stopped looking at it. The first such instance occurred when she was asked "Where is the dog?" some three or four minutes after she has turned her back on it, and she turned directly to it without random search.

A more startling example occurs a week later when I ask "Where is your blanket?" when the blanket has not been in view for approximately 10 minutes. Earlier Wendy was cranky and Mommy gave her the blanket. Then she put it on the couch out of Wendy's sight. Various activities have intervened. The blanket is very important to Wendy. Since she was asked for the blanket while on the other side of the room and immediately went for it on the couch, one can only conclude that she retained the information as to its position during the entire period.

1 year, 2 months, 10 days. Wendy has learned to stand up but has not yet learned to get herself back down to sitting position. She consistently responds to "stand up" by doing so. She becomes quite desperate after she has stood up for awhile, and for several days she would cry until Mommy put her down. Mommy would say "sit down" to her at these times. She reports herself to have been shocked to hear Wendy say "sit down." Wendy says it twice during my visit. It is enunciated very clearly.

1 year, 2 months, 17 days. Wendy has learned to sit down by herself. She does so on command. She no longer says "sit down," and has not ever sat herself down until the present time.

It should be noted that at this time the only frequent word in Wendy's productive vocabulary is "see." The only nouns she uses are "bear" and "fish," and these may be proper names in the sense that they apply to only one particular object. They are used very rarely. Indeed, I have only heard "fish," not "bear," and that only twice. "See," on the other hand, I have heard countless times.

Wendy does not at present, at 17 months of age, give any evidence of comprehension of relational meaning based on syntax, nor indeed of any comprehension of more than one word at a time. It is interesting to note that she seemed in no sense prepared to understand possessives as do both Craig and Kristen. First of all, she does not know the word "Mommy," nor does she know my name. Thus it would be difficult to communicate possessives of the sort understood by the other two children. Secondly, although she points to her own hair and teeth on command, she gives no evidence of interest in corresponding parts of other people.

Craig (born October 3, 1971)

1 year, 2 months, 2 days. Craig's parents are convinced that, although he only uses one word, "di," he understands a great deal of what is said to him. It is easy to demonstrate that Craig knows his dog's name. If you say to him "Where is Candy?" he looks all around the room, runs over to the dog, and hugs him. He does this three times during my first visit. Furthermore, he twice looks over at Candy and says "di." His mother said he often said "di" (apparently his name for Candy). He recently calls other animals, including ducks, "di." However, every other test of comprehension that I attempt with Craig fails to reveal any evidence that he understands other words. For example, his mother is certain that he knows the word "bottle." We put his bottle, a ball, a stuffed animal, and a teething ring on the coffee table near Craig. His mother says "Where is your bottle?" Craig looks over the array, and after the request is repeated, picks up his ball and throws it. Among several other commands tested unsuccessfully, his mother is also certain that he knows to wave when told "wave bye-bye." We try this with no success, even when I stand up and put on my coat. Finally, when I stand outside a glass door and am moving out of sight, he waves, but no command has been made at that time.

As I noted above, all verbal contacts with children involved first getting their attention and making eye contact. For Craig, if one gets his attention and he does not understand what is said to him, there is a characteristic response. He becomes very active and starts running around, making a characteristic noise and usually looking back at the speaker several times.

1 year, 2 months, 9 days. There was no change in Craig on my second visit. Again Craig did not respond appropriately to the various words that his mother was sure he understood. For example, she was certain he understood "apple" because he responds appropriately to "Give Julie the apple." When we put an apple alongside his bottle and spatula he picked up the apple when I said "Where is the apple?" A succession of tests assures me that he does not distinguish among the various objects by virtue of the words used. Rather, he behaves randomly with a greater overall chance of picking the apple over other objects. His mother is still sure that he knows "bottle," so I test this when the bottle is in clear view on the floor just after he has been looking at it. However, the request "Where is the bottle?" brings only the usual increased activity level. He runs around and around the bottle in the course of several minutes and repeated requests. Indeed, he finally trips over the bottle, at which time he begins to drink from it. I will not continue the recital of the various words we test.

1 year, 2 months, 13 days. On my third visit, the situation has changed with respect to the discrimination of objects by name. We put on the table a cookie, an apple, and Craig's bottle. I ask "Where is the apple?" and Craig picks it up and shows it to me. While he is still holding it, I ask him "Where is the bottle?" He puts down the apple, picks up the bottle, shows it to me, and begins to drink. While he is drinking, I ask "Where is the cookie?" He carefully puts down the bottle and holds up the cookie to show, putting it down then to take back his bottle. We repeat this set of requests several times each. The words Craig has learned are just the words his mother believed he knew earlier. Perhaps Mommy paired these words with their referents more frequently than with other objects because of her expectation that he knew these words. On the other hand, her belief that he knew these words may have been based on the importance of these objects to him, and it may have been their importance in his life that was critical to his learning words for them. We also try the more complex "Give Candy a cookie," to which Craig picks up the cookie and wanders off with it. One should note that, at this time, Craig could not, apparently, process a command of this form. Other cases of this sort occurred as well during this period, where he would either attend to the item he was to get, or to the intended recipient, but not to both.

1 year, 3 months. This session Craig demonstrates, for the first time, the ability to indicate comprehension when the referent cannot be seen by merely looking around. (Recall that Wendy first gave evidence of this at approximately 14 months.) I am in the living room with Craig when he sees his mother go up the stairs that lead out of the room. Some minutes later I ask "Where is Mommy?" to which Craig runs across the room and starts up the stairs, stops, looks back at me, and then continues up the stairs making a characteristic "comment" noise, "rehuhuh." I ask the same question about five minutes later when Craig is far from the spot and get the same response. Further, when we are sitting in the kitchen, his mother

asks, "Do you want a cookie?" to which Craig goes over to the cookie drawer and tries to open it.

I will not make reference to repeated testing for object names, which is carried out for Craig because, contrary to Wendy, he never to my knowledge forgot a word after he learned it. The one exception is my name, which he did sometimes forget, as we will see below.

1 year, 3 months, 15 days. Craig can now follow the command "sit down" and has added a second word to his productive vocabulary, "uh-uh." To give an appropriate interpretation to these acquisitions, one must be told that Craig is, as his mother puts it, "quite wild" during this period, and his mother, quite pregnant, is no doubt less able to run after him than she might otherwise have been. Thus the family has repeatedly been saying "no," "uh-uh," and "sit down" to him during this time. His usage of "uh-uh" is equivalent to saying no to a request that he understands. Throughout this and succeeding periods, Craig never says "uh-uh" to a message that he has not already shown he can respond appropriately to. In addition, we never hear him say "uh-uh" to "Where's the x," although he might walk away. He only says "uh-uh" to "Do you want x?" in which case he never follows up the request by getting the item in question. At this time, he also begins to play "patty cake" and "peek-a-boo" (with his hands) upon request. He also gives evidence of remembering the permanent locations of various objects. When asked for a cookie while in the living room, he will go to the kitchen and return with cookies.

1 year, 4 months, 2 days. Craig shows two significant gains. First, he follows commands involving three differentiable elements. The first time this increase occurs is when I notice that Craig will follow a command of the form "Show the x to Mommy" vs. "to Jane" vs. "to Candy" vs. "to Julie." Within a week he also differentiates "give" from "show" so that by 16 months he can follow the command "Give Jane the cookie" vs. "Show Jane the cookie." I test this capacity many times, contrasting each of the three critical elements.

The other big gain during the period around 16 months is an awareness of not just the permanent objects in his environment but of the current and temporary state of affairs as it exists outside his immediate view. As described above, he has one month earlier demonstrated a memory for where his mother has disappeared, but that is the only indication up to this time of short-term preservation of information. Furthermore, the stairs that his mother climbed could have served as a visible "signal" for his mother's location, thus not necessitating preservation of an image completely independent of Craig's present environment. Now, however, several unambiguous examples of preservation of short-term information about object location occur. One will suffice here to make the point. During this visit there is a pile of cookies on the living room floor which Craig has apparently spilled. We spend the latter part of the visit in the kitchen, where his mother says to him, "Do you want a cookie?" He goes out of the kitchen and returns somewhat later, carrying the entire stack of cookies.

He has also learned several new words during this period, including "wash cloth," "pen," and "hair." With respect to hair, he will run his hand through his hair or point to it depending on whether one says "Brush your hair" or "Where is your hair?"

1 year, 5 months, 3 days. Craig first demonstrates comprehension of a possessive form along with a precise discrimination of objects in the following limited context. He has a two-week-old baby sister by this time and, for the first time that I know of, there are items of the same type and thus of the same name that clearly belong either to him or to the baby, and which it is important for him to discriminate between. One such object class is diapers; the other, and more important, is bottles. The two classes of diapers, all disposable diapers, can be distinguished by the places where the boxes are kept and by the type of box. The bottles could be distinguished by the colors of their respective rims—black for the baby and white for Craig. When asked for "your bottle" Craig will get his bottle and hold it up to show. When asked for "the baby's bottle," he will hold *it* up to show. I test him several times on each request, always with success. The request for "baby's diaper" is met successfully by Craig taking me into the baby's room and pulling out diapers from her diaper box at the end of the crib. There is some question of whether Craig knows "baby's bottle" as a single name for a particular class of objects, black-rimmed bottles, or whether he knows that baby or other person names can combine with object names to indicate possession. The appearance together of the two contrast pairs, with respect to diapers and bottles, suggests that this is really combinatorial. More on this later.

Craig's ability to retain information from a verbal command over a long period also becomes more marked. For example, while sitting with Craig in his room, his mother asks him "Where is the duck?" He disappears, and a few minutes later I can hear the toilet seat being banged in the bathroom. His mother says that the duck generally refers to his potty seat which is attached to the toilet. The noise continues for some time. A little later Craig returns carrying a large inflated rubber duck which he holds up to show—which surprises his mother. It was also in the bathroom, being a water toy sometimes used in the tub.

By this time Craig has also learned some additional words such as "telephone," and certain names like "Jolly Jalopy," while his only productive speech is still "uh-uh" and "di." During the visit, Craig also says "Mama" twice in imitation: Mommy says "Give Mommy the piggy bank." He apparently does not know what the piggy bank is. His mother asks him many times because for this, as for many other words, she believes he knows it. When she says this, however, he just says "Mama."

1 year, 5 months, 30 days. On my next visit I try out commands that have three contrasting terms of the form Give (show) Mommy (me) the baby's (your) bottle. I have the two bottles standing on the high chair in the kitchen. Each time, before a request is made, Craig is put in the living room where he can see neither the bottles nor the two people to whom he was to show or deliver them. Each of the eight

possible commands is given twice over a short period of time and is always correctly carried out.

<u>1 year, 6 months, 16 days</u>. Craig has learned "nose" in addition to "hair" and his mother thinks he knows "eye," "ear," and "mouth," as well, but he repeatedly points to his open mouth when asked for his ear or for his eye. I ask "Where is your diaper?" and he shows me the one he has on, as he does for "shoe." This response to diaper contrasts with that to "Get (bring) a diaper," in which case Craig will go to his room to get a diaper.

It is interesting to note what Craig does *not* pick up by way of frequently used lexical items as well as by what he *does*. Craig's mother frequently uses the following words: "kitchen," "living room," and "den." In addition she repeatedly refers to the "refrigerator." In the dozens of occurrences of "kitchen"—"Go to the kitchen," "Where is the kitchen," "It is in the kitchen"—Craig never demonstrates the slightest understanding of the word. In the case of "den," Craig might be eagerly seeking his coat or his sister, but if his mother says the location is the "den," he looks totally blank. Recall that we know that Craig has an excellent memory for where various items are kept in all of these rooms, but he seems unable to learn the names for these locations. Indeed, on one visit when I enter the den, Craig's mother says "Take Jane to the living-room. Where's the living-room?" Craig looks confused but apparently knows he is to go somewhere. He leads me through the den to the bathroom and into the shower room rather than upstairs to where all the familiar rooms which contrasted with "den," namely, "living-room," "kitchen," or "bedrooms," are located. The same is true for "refrigerator." Craig's mother repeatedly refers to the refrigerator, asking where it is, asking Craig to wash it, and asking him to get an apple from it. If she asks him for an apple and he determines that there is none on the table or counter, he will run straight to the refrigerator, open it, and try to open the opaque drawer where the apples are kept. However, even though in my visits the word refrigerator is used paired with this activity repeatedly, he never gives evidence of learning it. The refrigerator is very large, and, from Craig's perspective, I suppose it seems almost as big as a room.

<u>1 year, 7 months, 16 days</u>. A full month elapses before I am able to test Craig again because he contracts chicken pox and then lengthy flu. I try to test him during the period when he is ill (at 18 months and 23 days) but he only cries. The few responses to grammatical expressions during that period suggest that the apparent treatment of "baby" as a possessor of objects may not have been the reflection of any general ability to treat people as possessors: When I finally get his attention and ask him "Where is your shoe?" he points to his shoe. But when I ask "Where is Mommy's shoe?" he again points to his own shoe. When I say it again with stress, and no doubt indicate from my tone that he is in error, he gets off his mother's lap, comes over, and touches *my* shoe.

At the end of his sickness, Craig shows two skills. The first is a clear-cut ability to treat the other people around, namely Mommy and myself, as possessors. The second is an ability to treat "baby" not only as an object to be shown to people, and as a possessor of bottles and diapers, but also as a recipient of various items.

Craig responds correctly to the following directions: "Show me your hair (nose, shoe)," "Show me Mommy's hair (nose, shoe)," "Show me Jane's hair (nose, shoe)." Actually, with respect to the last of these, I say "Show me my hair (nose, shoe)." However, Mommy immediately repeats each of these commands transformed as above. I don't know whether Craig would have responded to the other directions or not. Each of these nine directions is given three times during the course of the session.

With respect to baby as recipient, Craig responds correctly to "Give the baby the pencil" and "Show (give) the baby the bottle" (there was only one bottle, the baby's, to show). Each of these directions is given twice. Previously, only Mommy, Jane, Candy, and Julie have been understood as recipients.

Finally, as we sit in the kitchen, Mommy says, "Get Jane's coat." Craig immediately leaves the kitchen and returns with my jacket which has been lying on a bench in the entry. What is interesting about this is that Craig has many times gotten his coat (hat, boots, etc.) to show Jane, but never before my coat. Nor have any cues to my departure been given. This shows a still more general mastery of the possessive, as well as a rather amazing (to me) memory for the temporary positions of various items which one would not believe to be of central importance to Craig personally.

Kristen (born March 30, 1972)

10 months, 24 days. When I first see Kristen she responds systematically to "Mommy" and to "Cantebury" (her cat). Wherever in the room either of them are located, if she is asked for one of them, she will look around, until her gaze becomes arrested when the appropriate object is found.

1 year. At this time, the family acquires a furry-looking mongrel puppy of roughly the same size as the cat, so it becomes possible to test whether or not "Cantebury" might be an object-class word which would be applied to other pets as well. I visit the day after the dog is acquired. We test Kristen by placing the cat at one end of the room and the dog at the other end. When asked "Where's Cantebury?", Kristen looks around, at and past the dog, and her gaze is arrested on Cantebury. We test her four times and always obtain this same response. It is not clear, however, whether the word is a proper name or whether it is a class name which would be applied to other *cats*.

At this time, she also knows "Pink Bunny" and will pick out this stuffed animal from the others.

1 year, 1 month, 14 days. At this time, Kristen first exhibits the ability to locate a named object that occupies a permanent position, and that is out of view. When asked either "Where is the mirror?" or "Do you want to look in the mirror?", she will crawl from any position in her parents' bedroom into the closet where the mirror is kept along the rear wall and look into it. Recall that comparable behavior of seeking out by a direct path an object that is out of view and that has a fixed place

in space occurred between 14–15 months in Craig and Wendy. This response does not seem to depend upon where in the bedroom Kristen was located, or whether she is facing towards or away from the closet, or on whether she is near or far from the closet. In any case, she goes directly to the mirror.

Until the present time, I have been unable to demonstrate that, in response to a request, Kristen has an ability to locate an object in a temporary position. She looks around for objects, never looks straight to an object that is out of immediate view, even if she has been looking at it shortly before. Kristen also demonstrates a memory for where her mother has disappeared on being asked "Where's Mommy?" approximately 3 minutes after her mother has disappeared.

Kristen now knows the names of several stuffed animals. We test for six different animals in two different sets of three (they were in very different parts of the house) and she is always successful. She can also carry out two different acts on command: one is "whistle," to which she makes a whistling sound; and the second is "make a wind," to which she makes a blowing humming sound which is clearly different from the whistle in the entire way in which she holds her mouth and moves it.

Another test of interest at this same time is the following: Kristen's mother reports that she has been having trouble keeping her from eating the cat's food, which is in a bowl on the floor. She comments that, while Kristen likes Cheerios, which are similar in size and texture to the cat food, she believes Kristen can discriminate between the two. We evolve the following problem for Kristen: Mommy puts on the floor a mixture of Cheerios and cat pellets (which can be differentiated in that the latter are a darker brown and somewhat star-shaped, whereas Cheerios are round with a hole in the middle). When Mommy says "What is for Kristen?" she picks up a Cheerio and eats it. She does this four times in succession. Then I ask "What is for Cantebury?" She picks up a cat pellet, shows it to me, and lays it back down. We ask two more Cheerios questions and then I repeat my earlier request, to which Kristen again picks up a cat pellet to show. This behavior by Kristen seems to indicate some understanding of possession. What Kristen responds to is not the name of the objects, but who they belong to. Given the present constraints of vocabulary, I do not know how to test for understanding of syntax with respect to the possessive form.

1 year, 2 months, 1 day. Kristen pointed to her own nose in response to "Where is your nose?" and crawled across the room to put her finger on her mother's nose when asked "Where is Mommy's nose?" She did the same with respect to "shoe." Her mother was genuinely surprised, having been totally unaware that Kristen could do anything of this sort. Indeed, she was even surprised that Kristen knew "nose" as an object to be pointed at. The only use of nose, she reports, has been as part of a game where she says "Let's rub noses," and Kristen comes up to do so. This is also a further indication that Kristen has learned the possessive, at least with respect to "your shoe/nose" vs. "Mommy's shoe/nose."

Kristen produces no words.

<u>Thomas</u> (born January 14, 1972)

<u>10 months, 14 days.</u> At this time Thomas's parents say that he knows the name of his dog, "Cora." He says "cwa" to her and has done so since approximately 8 months of age. We test him several times during this session, as he sits on his mother's lap and the dog lies in various positions in the room. Each time he is asked "Where is Cora?" he looks all around the room until he sees her, and then his gaze becomes arrested on her.

I have seen Thomas nine times until approximately 17 months of age. He has retained his familiarity with "Cora" and will always look around until he finds her. He has never exhibited any familiarity with any other word since that time, nor has he shown any willingness to pursue Cora into some other room or to indicate in any other clearly observable way that he remembered her current position. At several of my visits, Thomas's parents state that they think he now knows "Mommy" or "Daddy" or "Michele" (his sister). I test him by placing these people at widely discrepant points in the living room or den. Despite repeated testing, there is no indication that he has become familiar with these object names. Thomas is very shy and frequently clings to his mother during a session. Therefore, I would wonder whether he might know other words but be unwilling to respond except for "Cora." While Thomas clings to his mother, making no response to "Where is Mommy?" or "Where is Daddy?" I say "Where is Cora?" and he looks, while clinging, until he finds her each time.

RELATED STUDIES

As indicated in the introduction, there is little systematic data on receptive language, and thus there is also little data on the relation of receptive to productive language. An exception involves two unpublished studies, one by Seligman (Seligman, Seligman, & Weber, 1971), who tested the vocabularies of two children 20 and 24 months of age with respect to nouns, and the other a study by a graduate student of Seligman's at the University of Pennsylvania, Meadow (1972). The two children in the Seligman study produced approximately as many nouns as they understood. Meadow extended the vocabulary test to include verbs and prepositions in addition to nouns. Her study involved a cross-sectional examination of six children 21 to 26 months of age and a longitudinal study of one of them. She did not try to make an exhaustive accounting of the children's vocabularies, but instead sampled their vocabularies by means of a standard set of frequent words. She used a list of the 70 nouns previously used by Seligman, plus 30 verbs and 10 prepositions. The nouns fell into nine categories: body parts, parts of the house, articles of clothing, animals, letters, shapes, foods, vehicles, and miscellaneous household articles. These nouns all named objects for which it was possible to obtain a representative toy. There were three types of verbs, intransitives (e.g., jump, dance, stand), transitives (e.g., touch, point to, eat), and transitive pairs like "push and pull" and "open and close." For verbs, either the child was to carry out the act named, or a doll or toy animal was to be made to carry out that act.

Three of the six children she tested had receptive noun vocabularies that were several times in excess of their productive noun vocabularies. Their receptive-to-productive ratios were 7.6:1, 4.4:1, and 3.1:1. These children had essentially no productive verbs. The other three children produced almost as many nouns as they understood; that is, their receptive-to-productive noun ratio was almost 1:1. While these three children produced some verbs, their ratio of receptive to productive verbs was much higher than for nouns (approximately 3:1 for two of them and 2:1 for the other). The one child Meadow traced longitudinally went from a noun ratio of 5:1 to one of 1:1 between 20 and 26 months. When the noun ratio was 2:1, the child began to demonstrate a knowledge of verbs, initially with a 9:1 ratio, which at last testing was 3.9:1.

Meadow's data thus supplement the data from Craig, Wendy, and Kristen. Her data indicate that for at least some children who are somewhat older than these three, there is also a discrepancy between receptive and productive vocabulary. Further, Meadow's data suggest that this discrepancy for nouns may disappear sometime around two years of age. Presumably the discrepancy for verbs follows the same course, but somewhat later.

In a recent study of sentence comprehension, Wetstone and Friedlander (1973) reported that children whose own speech consists of single words are unaffected by the order of words in a command. Commands were, for example, "Where's the truck" or "Give the ball to Mommy." The behavior of these children was unchanged if the word order was scrambled, as in "Truck the where is" or "Mommy the give ball to." There was some fall off in performance with scrambled order for "fluent children," whose MLU was 3.73. These authors suggest that children who do not yet have productive control of syntax extract only lexical and not syntactic information from a sentence; thus they are not bothered by scrambled word order. However, all of the sentences used by these authors could only be interpreted in one way, regardless of word order. Indeed in certain cases (e.g. "Where is the truck?") the child only needs to identify the word "truck" since, as we have seen above, holding up an object is a very natural response for children in any case. For their more complex sentences like "Put the marble in the truck" (or "Truck the marble in the put") it is not clear what options there actually were as far as the child was concerned. It is uncertain, on the basis of this study, whether the children who did not use syntax themselves could carry out instructions based on information from several lexical items, or whether they could use word order when it was critical to the interpretation of a message. As we saw, Craig combined information from several lexical items, as well as using syntactic cues at a time when he could barely speak at all.

Recently, Chapman and Miller (1973) proposed that even young children who produce sentences themselves may use a comprehension strategy based solely on the meanings of the individual lexical items, assigning plausible relations among the items on the basis of context, etc. Indeed, these authors suggest that the children's production may precede comprehension, in the sense that while their production strategy involves word order (namely, mentioning the actor first), their comprehension strategy ignores the relational meanings encoded in the syntax. Here again, Craig does not fit this pattern. Perhaps the discrepancy is due to the fact that the sentences he understood were made up of very well-known words used in relation to familiar events.

DISCUSSION

Let us examine what the data from Wendy, Craig, and Kristen indicates about how they represent information about objects and events, and how they process linguistic input. The data presented here are preliminary and unquantified, and these children may not constitute a representative sample. Nevertheless, the pilot findings from these children's receptive language enriches the picture of the child's early intellectual development which has evolved from the examination of productive language and of the child's behavior towards objects.

The present data suggest that the child's response to the speech of others may provide a unique way to tap his mental representations of events. Suppose that the small child can represent to himself the properties of objects and events (i.e., that he can recollect what things look like, feel like, etc.) during the period when his own speech involves only single words and before he uses successive single-word utterances to encode thematic material, as described by Bloom (1973). This ability cannot be tested via his productive language. If the child says a word in the presence of an appropriate object, one does not know whether he can think about that object in its absence. If he says that word when the object is absent, one does not know whether he is thinking about the object or just engaging in deferred imitation of the speech sound itself. Making use of the child's receptive language, one can investigate whether he distinguishes particular objects or acts from others and whether or not he can invoke mental representations of objects; one can investigate his knowledge of his surroundings (e.g., whether he stores information about the locations of various objects). It is even possible that the development of receptive language might precede the child's ability to demonstrate his understanding in his observable responses, although I doubt it.

Two aspects of the child's behavior during the second year of life have been treated as important clues to his mental processes. The first has to do with his productive language, namely, with the frequently reported tendency towards overgeneralization in the early usage of words. The explanations that have previously been offered would imply that equivalent overgeneralization should occur in both comprehension and production (e.g., Piaget, 1962; Clark, 1973). I found no evidence for overgeneralization in comprehension, although there was overgeneralization in production for these same children. The second important source of information about the child's mental processes is his behavior with respect to hidden objects as described by Piaget (1954, 1962). The failure of infants to pursue objects that are displaced while out of view (until these infants are approximately 1½ years of age) led Piaget to infer that their concept of object is not complete until that age. The fact that the children reported here sought objects in response to words before one year of age supplements this picture of the child's notions about objects, as we will see below.

It was noted above that the child's systematic response to words necessarily involves *memory for the sound-patterns of certain words, long-term memory for events* (e.g., objects and people), as well as *memory for the relations between particular word-sound patterns and particular types of remembered objects or events*. In examining the children's behavior it has become apparent that there are two other factors to be considered in tracing the development of comprehension during the age period under consideration here. First, there is the child's *memory for the current state of affairs* that exists around him; namely, the type of information typically referred to as "orientation in time and place"—memory of the locations of various movable objects and people, the momentary spatial relations between himself and various objects, both fixed and movable, which are not in view, etc. In addition, there is the child's ability to *transfer from long-term into active memory the stored information about objects, acts, etc., which is linked to particular word-sounds*. That is, while consistent response to incoming words implies that they activate word-sound schemas which, in turn, activate meaning, there may be various levels in the ability to transfer such information into active memory.

Mental Representation of Events: Early Word Meanings

The earliest words to which the children responded systematically designated individual objects, classes of objects, and perceptible acts. All of these words involved referents that could easily be pointed out by an adult speaker. First of all, they could be pointed out because of their perceptual properties, visual-palpable, or tactual-kinesthetic. Secondly, and perhaps most important, is the fact that the objects and actions which became linked to word-sounds involved aspects of the child's experience that were distinctive and salient to him at the time the words were learned.

My impression of the learning of words is as follows: The child became familiar with certain objects and object classes; among these salient objects were his pets, his bottle, cookies, etc. He learned certain distinctive acts, such as standing up or sitting down, or carrying out particular routines like the games of peek-a-boo or patty-cake. Some of these salient familiar objects, object classes, or acts became linked to the sound-patterns of particular words. These sound-patterns then came to serve as retrieval cues for these salient experiences.

No doubt there are factors other than perceptual salience that are important to the learning of particular word-meaning pairings. For example, the characteristics of the sound-patterns of particular words (e.g., their discriminability) and the frequency with which particular word-sounds were paired with their referents must be important. I did not obtain any insight into these issues from my observations. To estimate the frequency or consistency with which particular objects or acts were paired with particular word-sounds would require extensive time sampling and the use of video-taped records. We are only now starting this type of data analysis.

In sum, I would argue that the "meanings" which became linked to word-sounds formed unitary cohesive elements of experience before that linkage occurred. That is, it seems to me that whatever visual-tactual information went into learning about bottles, and whatever perceptual-motor coordination went into learning peek-a-boo or patty-cake, took place first, and then the child linked this knowledge to a word-sound. The existence of salient unitary "meanings" (schemas) may even have been a prerequisite for the child to attend to the accompanying word-sound.

Occasionally, word-sounds serve only temporarily as retrieval cues for an object or act. For Wendy, certain sound-patterns were linked to particular objects and acts over periods of a few weeks but afterwards produced no systematic response, (e.g., "bangbang" and "Mommy"). It is easy to understand why the linkage between word and referent might disappear in a case like "bangbang." A particular type of activity or object may be important to the child for a limited period of time and, during that period, remains linked to a word. However, as particular acts or objects fade from importance in the child's life, their schemas are no longer salient and thus can no longer be elicited by the sound-pattern. The only exception was Wendy's loss of "Mommy." Mommy remained of central importance. Nor was "Mommy" replaced by some substitute name. The disappearance of Wendy's use of the word "Mommy" as a distress cry might be because it never stood for the person Mommy, although her comprehension of "Mommy" initially seemed to link the word with the person.

Object Words. For all three children with pets, the pet's name was the first word they understood, and two of them said the pet's name months before they used any other word. Indeed, "Cora" has been the only word that Thomas has given any evidence of understanding. The reason for this, I would argue, is that a pet is an especially salient aspect of an infant's experience. Babies frequently seem fascinated with moving animals. A cat, dog, gerbil, mouse, or fish is a relatively small object and thus is more likely to be seen as a perceptual unit by the baby than larger objects like adult human beings. There may also be something about the nature of the movements of animals which attracts the attention of infants. It is also possible that the pet is more frequently named in the baby's presence than are other salient objects. A pet is certainly named more consistently than are people; for example, Mommy may be variously called "Mommy," her own name, and perhaps some designation like "Honey," in addition to the pronouns, "she," "her," "you," "me," and "I."

Many of the children's object words were proper names: Mommy, Daddy, the pet, and various animal words for particular stuffed animals. At least for

Kristen, there were several names for particular stuffed animals, such as "Pink Bunny" and "Bear," in addition to names for Cantebury and Gefian (the dog). With respect to class names, some of them referred to objects that were probably perceptually indistinguishable from one another. For example, different diapers look alike; some socks, undershirts, etc., also look alike. This was not true for all class names, however. While certain subcategories of cookies, bananas, and apples are indistinguishable, many of them clearly look different from one another, at least to adults and surely to the children as well. "Bottle" and "dog" as well as food names stood for different objects which the children could no doubt distinguish from one another, and yet they were categorized together by name. Indeed, when his baby sister arrived, Craig showed clearly that he could distinguish among the different objects to which he responded as "bottle." (That is, he distinguished "Craig's bottle" from "baby's bottle.") Wendy's names for stuffed animals were class names which extended to animals with which she was not familiar and which differ markedly in appearance.

As we noted above, various claims about early word meanings have been based on overgeneralization in children's word production. Piaget has discussed the child's overextensions in the early use of words in terms of shifting unstable word *meanings* which he believes reflect the level of the child's conceptual development during this period. He says (1962) that "these first verbal schemas are intermediary between the schemas of sensory-motor intelligence and conceptual schemas . . . just as . . . deferred imitation is intermediary between sensory-motor imitation and representative imitation [p. 220]." Early words, he notes, "are still essentially sensory-motor in that they are capable of generalization and of application to an increasing number of objects . . . the concept implies a fixed definition, corresponding to a stable convention which gives the verbal sign its meaning. The meaning of words do not constantly change, because the classes and relations they denote involve a conceptual definition determined once for all by the social group [p. 220]."

In her review of the literature on overextensions, Clark (1973) has taken a different approach. Her proposal assumes that these early words the child uses can be analyzed into component attributes or features of meaning, and she suggests that when the child first uses words, he has only "partial entries for them in his lexicon." Thus, the initial meaning of "dog" might be taken as involving only one feature by the child; he might have characterized the word "dog" as meaning "four-legged." This would necessarily involve the child in overextensions since there are many four-legged animals in addition to dogs. This hypothesis relates specifically to word meanings; it is not claimed that the child's perceptual categorizations of objects initially involve few features; e.g., that he cannot distinguish between dogs and horses. (We have not drawn a distinction between early word meanings and perceptual schemas for objects and actions here.)

With respect to comprehension, however, I have noticed no overgeneralization. The children typically did not respond to a word unless they knew its referent (with the exception of Craig's early tendency to hold up objects to the question "Where is the x?" in the period before he understood anything; but that could not be called overgeneralization in the usual sense of the term). While mistakes occasionally occurred, they could not easily be described as overgeneralizations of meaning resulting either from shifting categorizations or from the use of only single features of meaning. They either occurred when the child had some prepotent object or action preference which they made to the wrong verbal input, or, as noted below, when there were several poorly known words within a single cognitive-semantic domain. The most straightforward explanation for these occasional errors is that the child stores a number of specific "meanings" and a number of specific word-sound patterns, and he may confuse which word-sounds are linked to which meanings. Often, errors occurred with long latencies, and the child's facial expression indicated his confusion. Clark suggests that once the child has attached meaning to a word, even though it is an incomplete meaning, "it simply *has that meaning* for him." This was not true for the children reported here; they seemed quite aware of uncertainty even when they apparently knew that the sound-patterns were words, i.e., had meanings.

In production, however, both Craig and Wendy *did* exhibit the classic pattern with respect to animal names. According to his mother's report, Craig called a large number of animals "di," including ducks at a pond and pigs in Old Sturbridge Village. Wendy's mother reported that Wendy alternately called a visiting gerbil "fish" and "bear." I doubt that either of these children confused their dog or fish with these other animals. Nor does it seem likely that they believed that the words "di" or "fish" stand only for one perceptual feature of these animals. The most straightforward test for overgeneralization in comprehension would be to present those objects to which the children overgeneralized in their speech and ask "Where is the x (e.g., fish)?" I did not do this. In a recent lecture, Labov (1973) reported on his daughter's use of "Mommy" at a time when she only produced a very few words. He reported that she said "Mommy" to all family members but, at the same time, if asked "Where is Mommy?" would look only at Mommy and *not* at these other family members. He proposed that she might have two different "meanings" for Mommy, one as a proper name for Mommy and one as a class name for family members. I would guess instead that the overgeneralization in such cases is not due to the nature of word-meanings themselves, but rather to factors specific to production, which we consider below in the discussion of the relation between receptive and productive language.

I would not claim that the developing child never forms categories that are overly general compared to adult categories. For perceptually similar categories, or when category boundaries are drawn arbitrarily along a continuous dimension, ambiguities in categorization surely must arise. Indeed category boundaries vary in different cultures. However, many of the objects these children categorize together, such as cookies, apples, shoes, etc., form sets that are very separate and distinct from one another both in their perceptual properties and in their functions. For these categories, there seems little evidence from the child's object selection that his categories shift, or that his words have fewer features of meaning for him than for adults.

These children's knowledge of object names has been evaluated by asking for the objects under conditions where exemplars of the object-class named as well as of other object-classes were available. Included in these tests were a few striking natural experiments, such as when a dog was added to Kristen's household, making it possible to determine that she knew it wasn't Cantebury, and when a new baby and baby bottle were added to Craig's household, making it possible to determine that he could discriminate different subcategories of bottles. This type of testing would lead to errors if the child has overgeneral classes involving only single features, or if his categories are continually shifting. However, one might argue that the strongest test for overgeneralization might be to ask "Where is the x?" when no member of the target class is available. Then one could see whether the child would substitute some other object, or simply would not respond, thus showing a firm unwillingness to overgeneralize. I have asked for absent objects and had the child look around and reject all the alternatives present. I have not, however, introduced non-class members which varied systematically in their perceptual properties from the target class. Of course, by the time children seek out even hidden objects when asked for them, such a technique becomes unfeasible in any case because the objects for which children have names are typically found in their homes, so they simply go and get them if they are not in view when asked for.

Cognitive-Semantic Domains. The salient experiences of the child that become linked to words seem to be clearly distinguishable from one another. Nevertheless, they almost certainly are *not* stored in memory in a haphazard fashion. That is, *dog* and *bear* are no doubt more closely related to one another in memory than are *dog* and *bottle*. The reasons for believing that object-schemas are systematically organized with respect to one another in the child's memory derive both from the present study and from our pilot studies with slightly older children.

Those confusions that occurred in the children's receptive language were typically within, rather than between, domains of objects. Especially in the domain of words for body parts, the children made several errors as they were learning. Both Wendy and Craig learned names for several body parts, initially with respect to their own bodies. Each of them learned "hair" first. At this point there were no confusions of pointing at the wrong place in response to other words for body parts. These other words were simply unfamiliar and the children ignored them. Subsequently, they both learned "nose" fairly well. Wendy learned "teeth" and "belly button," but less well. Craig learned "mouth" and "ear," but less well. Both of them learned "foot." When one of these less well-known words was used, either child occasionally pointed to the body part named by another word, or to their noses.

Let us consider what these errors indicate about the children's knowledge of their body parts themselves, and of the words linked to them. The least likely hypothesis is that the child confuses his mouth object-schema with his ear object-schema, or is in any way unable to distinguish among his actual different body parts. Nor is it likely that the child believes that any of these words simply means "body part." The best description of what is going on, it seems to me, is that the children are confused about which word goes with which body part.

Another reason for postulating that object-schemas are systematically organized with respect to one another in the long-term memories of small children comes from some of our pilot studies with children from 3 to 3½ years of age (in conjunction with Felicia Lui). We employed a modification of the procedure used by Wickens (1972) with adults. Children were presented with pairs of words of a particular class, and then an interference task was given before the word pair was to be recalled. Three pairs in succession were drawn from a single semantic category, and then the next three pairs were drawn from a different category. For adults, successive sets of words within one category are recalled progressively more poorly, and a category shift may result in markedly better recall. The improvement in recall following a category shift is known as release from proactive inhibition and provides an index that one set of words is in some way psychologically different from earlier sets of words. Using the categories of animals, body parts, clothing, and furniture, we obtained a marked build-up of proactive inhibition and then marked release with category shifts in these young subjects. This result indicates that the words within these semantic categories are more like one another in meaning to these three-year-old children than words from different semantic categories.

There are many reasons why object-schemas within categories such as body parts, foods, eating utensils, etc., might be stored together when they are initially learned. For example, body parts are spatially close to one another and, in addition, their names are frequently taught in temporal proximity. When Mommy asks "Where is your nose?" she frequently follows with "Where are your ears?" (etc.). To take another example, different foods are not only similar in function, but they appear in the same contexts (e.g., while sitting in one's high chair in the kitchen). No doubt the naming of different foods occurs in temporal proximity (e.g., "Here's your meat and potato"). It is not surprising then that the memories for different object classes within certain categories should be closely related to one another in memory. These word-meaning pairings would be closely related both because the object-schemas they designate are themselves closely related, and possibly also because naming of objects within a domain frequently occurs in temporal proximity.

The existence of cognitive-semantic domains does not necessarily imply the existence of superordinate categories like "food," "body part," etc. Different schemas, together with their names, may simply be stored more or less closely to one another in memory on the basis of their perceptual or functional similarity, and if the word-meaning pairings within a domain are stored together, one might expect to find some degree of mutual confusability, etc.

Action Words. The children responded systematically to very few action words, and some of these were names for games like "patty-cake." As indicated in the introduction, the argument might be made that these acts were simply conditioned responses to particular words which serve as discriminative stimuli for these acts. The argument has two parts: first, that no concept of an act is involved when the child makes patty-cake, and second, that the word-sounds are *signals* for these acts, not *symbols* that designate the acts. I will not consider the second issue here; it is examined in detail in Higgins and Huttenlocher (1973). But let us consider the first issue.

Wendy's response to "bangbang" at 10 to 11 months of age could be viewed as a simple S-R sequence; the behavior of banging occurred spontaneously and might have become paired with "bangbang" which Mommy said frequently. Both Craig and Wendy responded to "sit down," but of course sitting down also is a spontaneous behavior. (The issue of production of "sit down" by Wendy is taken up later on.) For these cases, it could be argued that the word is a stimulus which is wired directly to a particular motor plan. Responses to "peek-a-boo" and "patty-cake" which occurred at the same age as to "bangbang" for Wendy, and at 15 months for Craig, are somewhat more complex, because these are not spontaneous behaviors but rather learned imitations. Thus the child not only knew how to carry out such behaviors, but also knew how they appeared when others carried them out. Kristen's "whistle" and "sound like the wind" are still more complex. Whistling was learned in imitation of Mommy; it was not just learned as a particular movement, but in order to make a particular sound. Furthermore, Kristen could not see herself imitating these movements and, as Piaget argues, such imitations involve more complex processes than imitations of behaviors that the child can observe himself making. In none of these cases, however, is it clear whether one should postulate that the child brings to active attention any information about what it would feel like to carry out the act, or about how such an act appears. Nor indeed do these responses provide evidence as to whether the children *could* "think about" such acts.

Craig's words "show" and "give" are quite different in that he responded to them in conjunction with other words. Since Craig listened to a sentence like "Give Jane the apple" and then promptly carried out the command, it seems reasonable to postulate that he formed a mental representation of the action named in relation to the particular object and recipient before carrying out that command. For these early action words (but not, as we argue below, for object words) the more convincing evidence that conceptual representation of the act is involved is when the child responds to them in relation to other words. Even this is not *sufficient*, however, as is pointed out below.

The fact that there are less action words than object words for these children, as well as for the children Meadow saw, may indicate that objects are more salient aspects of the child's experience than the actions carried out by objects. I did not test for actions carried out by anyone but the child himself. It is an interesting possibility, however, that many acts first become differentiated or salient in terms of being carried out by the child himself, and only later when they are observed being carried out by others.

Retrieval of "meanings" into Active Memory. It is easier to deal with the issue of mental representation for object-words than for action-words. As we saw, a regular progression is observed in the children's response to object-words, which seems related to the development of their ability to represent object properties. Piaget argues that children do not possess a firm notion about the permanence of objects until almost 1½ years of age. His argument is based on children's search behavior. Even though the child between 9 and 12 months comes to pursue objects that he watches being hidden, it is not until much later that he will pursue objects that first are hidden and then displaced from view while still hidden (e.g., as when an object first is hidden in one's hand and then placed behind a cloth). The results of these short-term memory tests certainly would not lead to the expectation that the 10–11-month-old child would look for objects on the basis of the objects' names. Yet the child treats his pet as a permanent object by looking for it when asked "Where's Candy (Cora, Cantebury)?" However, the progression in the child's behavior with respect to object names certainly is in accord with the notion that the child's ability to represent object properties may evolve in the period between 10 and 18 months.

As we have noted, the very fact that the child makes systematic responses to object names indicates that he must have stored information about word-sounds, as well as information about object properties, and that he can use that word-sound to retrieve information about the object properties. The most straightforward explanation for the fact that the child looks around for a particular object when asked "Where is the x?" is that the word leads him to transfer to active memory information about the properties of the object. However, a weaker explanation of the mental processes required for this behavior is possible. That is, rather than the word leading the child to transfer information about object properties into active memory, he might only remember the word-sound itself while he looks around, and only when he sees the object that is linked to that word-sound does he recognize that object to be the appropriate one.

The case for the child's actually representing object properties to himself is stronger when the child responds to a word by going directly to the object even though it is out of view. This type of response appeared first for objects which occupied fixed positions in the child's home. For example, we asked Wendy "Where are the fish?" and she crawled some 15 feet around a large barrier to find them. We asked Craig to "get a cookie" when he was in the living room and he went to the kitchen and returned some minutes later with a cookie. One could argue that Wendy just knew the name of the fish-place and that the question "Where are the fish?" led her to take a route to a particular place without thinking about the properties of fish at all. This is a doubtful argument. First, Wendy does not respond to any words for places; as, for example, names for rooms. Second, Wendy *did* devote a great deal of attention to the fish themselves. She sat looking at the fish for long periods of time. Recall that, according to her mother, when the gerbils from her brother's class spent the weekend at her house, Wendy said "fish" and "bear" to them, suggesting that "fish" referred to the characteristics of fish as animal creatures, not to a particular fish-place. The same argument applies even more strongly to Craig and the cookies. For one thing, he did not simply go to the kitchen when asked for a cookie, but actually returned with a cookie. Furthermore, Craig's mother repeatedly tried to teach him the word "kitchen" with no success. Thus while Craig knew a path to "cookie" which occupied a fixed place, the place itself does not seem to have been an entity to Craig. The likeliest hypothesis is that when Craig was asked for a cookie, he retrieved both information about the properties of cookies and about where the cookies were kept.

The argument that words lead the child to recall the properties of objects in the absence of those objects is strongest in the case where the object named occupies a temporary position out of view. For example, consider the time when Craig spilled cookies on his living room floor. When we were in the kitchen later, we asked Craig for a cookie and he went directly to the living room and got them. To do this, I would argue, he must first have recalled information about *cookies,* and second have recalled the *location* of those particular cookies. Similarly, consider the time Wendy, when asked, went directly to her blanket which was on the couch but out of view. Again, the object word must have served as a retrieval cue to bring to active memory, first, the blanket, and second, information about the short-term spatial location of that blanket.

Mental Representation and Relational Meaning. We have only obtained a very limited amount of data concerning the development of comprehension of relational meaning based on combining meanings from several lexical items. Let us briefly consider the mental processes involved in Craig's ability to carry out a command of the form "Give (show) Jane (Mommy, etc.) the baby's (Craig's) bottle" or, earlier, "Give (show) Jane (Mommy, etc.) the bottle (apple, cookie, etc.)" and Kristen's ability to point out "Mommy's (Kristen's) nose (shoe)." There are two issues involved. The first is whether or not the child must take account of those relational meanings encoded in the syntax in order to respond appropriately. Kristen's responses do not require us to make such an assumption. Since there is no evidence that Kristen could assign any relational meaning to "Mommy" in a sentence context other than that of possessor, there is no reason to argue that she interprets this syntactic form differently from the way she would interpret "nose Mommy." Indeed, it is not clear that she is explicitly aware of "Mommy" as a potential actor or recipient, much less that she knows how such notions can be encoded syntactically in a sentence. The same may be said of Craig's response to the three-part commands involving *act, object,* and *recipient.* These three terms are not potentially confusable in terms of what relational meanings they should be assigned. However, Craig finally became able to assign to *Mommy* and *baby* both the roles of *possessor* and of *recipient.* Thus he could show the baby's bottle to Mommy, his bottle to the baby, etc.

The second issue is what sort of representation of events is required for a child to respond to a set of words taken in combination, whether or not these words can be interpreted as having variable relational meanings depending on their syntactic roles in a sentence. When the child points out different noses or shoes, depending on whose name is mentioned with it, or carries out an act with respect to a particular object or person, he shows us the following: First of all, in demonstrating a knowledge that noses (shoes) are objects that belong to particular people, he shows that his knowledge of *both* the items *and* the people involves more than simple stored object-schemas. People are known to have various body parts, to wear shoes, etc., and these objects are known as objects that are possessed and/or used by particular people. In addition, the mental processes at work in interpreting such sentential meanings involve the ability to construct in active memory a representation which involves more than mere retrieval of information linked to individual word-sounds. That is, even in cases when syntax is not necessary for sentence interpretation, it seems unlikely that the child merely calls to mind *baby* and *bottle* or *Mommy* and *shoe*. Rather, he almost certainly calls to mind some relation between them. One must, of course, be cautious. If the child has only experienced *Mommy* in one relation to *bottle*, then he might call them to mind separately, and then relate them in action in the only way familiar to him.

With respect to the particular relational meanings that Craig has mastered, Mommy (or Julie or myself) as recipient clearly is among the first. It is interesting to note that when children start to produce two-word utterances, they use "Mommy," etc., as actor frequently in their speech, but *not* as recipient (e.g., Bloom, 1970). We do not know, of course, whether Craig will follow this same pattern. If he does, this would provide one piece of evidence that the child's comprehension of particular linguistic forms is not the only factor determining what he says.

Relation between Receptive and Productive Language

The picture that evolves from these observations of Wendy, Craig, and Kristen is one of an asymmetry between receptive and productive language. This is evident, first, with respect to quantity; the children responded systematically to many more words than they produced. Second, the few words the children did produce were not a random selection of those words to which they responded systematically. Wendy's only frequent word when I met her and throughout these observations was "see." The only noun words she produced at all were "fish" and "bear," and these were infrequent and overgeneralized in use. Craig's only frequent word was "uh-uh," and all of his other words were the names of his parents, grandparents, and two neighbor children. Kristen used no words. The Meadow data on the development of receptive and productive vocabularies suggest that such asymmetry may be the usual case. There are two types of explanation for this asymmetry: one is that it is due to processes related to the perception or production of word sounds *per se* and the other is that it is due to processes related to the linkage between word-sounds and meaning.

With respect to the first alternative, it is possible that although the child can perceive speech sounds he simply cannot produce them. While certain speech sounds occur spontaneously in babies, the child may not have voluntary control of speech-sound production. Indeed, the determining factor in which words the child produces first could be the sound-patterns they involve; that is, the early words might involve only those sounds that babies make spontaneously (e.g., da, ba). However, an inability to produce word-sounds does not tell the whole story as to why these children do not talk. While Craig did not produce clearly enunciated word-sounds except for "uh-uh," and his attempts to imitate only crudely approximated what he heard, Wendy did not have difficulty in producing word-sounds. What she said was enunciated clearly, as with "see," "hi," and especially "sit down." Craig's words, including "baba," "mama," "dada," "nana," "papa," and "di" or "da" for Candy, in addition to "uh-uh," consisted almost entirely of the sounds produced spontaneously by babies. The morphemes he understood but did not say are often harder to produce. However, Craig did not hesitate to say the two-syllable word "Candy" in an incomplete fashion.

The gap between receptive and productive language might derive from *incomplete storage of the sounds* of the words. That is, certain words might be sufficiently familiar to be recognized but not to be produced. It is true that the words the children produced generally involved simple sound-patterns that had been said to them with strong intonation and frequently used in isolation. Thus they might be more completely known perceptually than other words. This includes Wendy's words "see" and "hi." Her one more complex word combination, "sit down," was said with stress and in isolation. This explanation, however, cannot be complete either. While Wendy said "sit down" perfectly when she could not get down herself, she *stopped* saying it when she learned to sit down, even though she continued to demonstrate that she knew what it meant. Thus *neither* perceptual nor production difficulties can explain why Wendy stopped saying "sit down."

If explanations having to do with the perception and production of speech sounds are not sufficient, then the gap between receptive and productive language must be related to asymmetries between the processes of decoding and encoding. This asymmetry clearly involves a difference between the number of words comprehended and the number produced. It may also involve a difference between the *types* of words the child comprehends and those he produces, although more data from more children are needed before one can draw any firm conclusions about this. Bloom (1973) has noted that the first words the child produces frequently are not typically object names. In explaining why this might be the case, she proposed that the mental representation of object properties may develop later than the mental representation of notions like those encoded by "more," "no," etc. On the basis of the comprehension data from the present study, it certainly appears that children may possess a considerable capacity for mental representation of object properties in the period before they name many objects. While it is possible that the mental representation of the notions encoded in the words the child first produces are simpler than those encoded in the words he understands but does not say, let us consider some alternative explanations.

One possibility is that the very small child tends to become *totally preoccupied with objects and events*. Given the multiple associations that exist among the various objects and events which the child experiences, the link to words may seem unimportant initially. For this reason, he might not encode his experiences in words, even though he is capable of doing so, in the sense that he has stored the necessary information. An allied possibility is that the appearance of productive language depends upon the *maturation of a communicative function*, that is, on the child's realization that the words that have been associated with his experiences can be used by him to communicate with other people. In this case, one might explain why a child might say "more" and "no" before he names objects by postulating that the communicative functions underlying requests, demands, etc. mature earlier than those underlying naming and description.

A rather different explanation is that children initially have *difficulty retrieving words;* namely, that it is easier to retrieve object-information on the basis of a word than it is to retrieve word-information on the basis of an encounter with an object. This could be true even given the simplifying assumption that, for these small children, only one word is linked with any object- or action-schema stored in memory. The argument involves two assumptions; first, that there are differences in the relative distinctiveness of memories for events versus memories for words, and second, that there are differences between the mental processes involved in recognition and those involved in recall.

Let us consider the first assumption in terms of the sort of spatial model which is currently used in discussions of conceptual memory. That is, we will assume that each schema occupies a distinct location in memory and that these schemas are organized according to various principles. The critical points are these: Memories for objects and actions are organized into domains according to similarity of appearance, function, etc. Some of these perceptual schemas are linked to words. Word-schemas are stored together in a different location from the perceptual-schemas. These word-schemas are themselves organized according to (*a*) the properties of the object- and action-schemas to which they are linked, (*b*) their own sound properties such as initial phoneme, stress pattern, etc., and (*c*) frequency of usage. Finally, the area where object- and action-schemas are stored is larger than that where word-schemas are stored. (That is to say, objects and acts are more distinctive from one another in memory than are words.)

The second assumption also is a common one; namely, that *recognition* of incoming stimuli involves direct access to stored traces in memory, while *recall* requires search among various traces stored in memory. Given these two assumptions, encoding should be more difficult than decoding. That is, if recognition involves direct access to a stored schema, whereas recall requires a search process, and there are differences in "crowding" (i.e., in distinctiveness) of perceptual versus word schemas, *recognition* of events and of words might be equal in difficulty, but the recall of perceptual schemas (required in decoding) would be easier than the recall of word schemas (required in encoding).

Within such a framework, it would be possible to account for *differences between the types of words the child comprehends and those he produces,* as well as for there being *overgeneralizations in production but not in comprehension.* Word retrieval would be especially difficult in a conceptual domain which involves several similar object or action schemas, many of which are linked to words, because these words would be stored in close proximity. As we have noted above, the child encounters many different objects which fall into distinct yet similar categories, e.g., various types of animals or foods. Many of the objects within a domain are named frequently by the mother and thus tend to become linked to words. For this reason word retrieval problems might be greatest for object names. Domains involving the notions encoded in words like ''see,'' ''more,'' or ''no'' may well involve fewer closely related conceptual notions and thus fewer closely related word-schemas, so that word retrieval problems would be less marked for these notions. In a domain with many words of closely related meaning, the child may tend to retrieve the most frequent word, thus leading to overgeneralization in production.

It is certainly not possible at present to decide among these alternative explanations for the asymmetry between comprehension and production in the initial stages of language acquisition. However, it does seem clear that the early stages of comprehension can be investigated systematically, and that the relation between comprehension and production in early childhood will ultimately be clarified.

REFERENCES

Bloom, L. *Language development: Form and function in emerging grammars.* Cambridge, Mass.: M.I.T. Press, 1970.

Bloom, L. *One word at a time.* The Hague: Mouton, 1973.

Bloom, L., Higgins, L., & Hood, L. The influence of form and content of adult messages on child-adult discourse. Unpublished manuscript, Teachers College, Columbia University, 1973.

Bowerman, M. Structural relationships in children's utterances: Syntactic or semantic? In T. E. Moore (Ed.), *Cognitive development and the acquisition of language.* New York: Academic Press, 1973.

Burke, D., & Huttenlocher, J. Intonation and the recall of ordered item information. Unpublished manuscript, Teachers College, Columbia University, 1973.

Chapman, R. S., & Miller, J. F. Word order in early two and three word utterances: Does production precede comprehension? Unpublished manuscript, University of Wisconsin, 1973.

Clark, E. What's in a word? On the child's acquisition of semantics in his first language. In T. E. Moore (Ed.), *Cognitive development and the acquisition of language.* New York: Academic Press, 1973.

Donaldson, M., & Wales, R. On the acquisition of some relational terms. In J. R. Hayes (Ed.), *Cognition and the development of language.* New York: Wiley, 1970.

Friedlander, B. Receptive language development in infancy. *Merrill Palmer Quarterly,* 1970, **16,** 7–51.

Glucksberg, S., Krauss, R. M., & Higgins, E. T. The development of referential communication skills. In F. Horowitz & G. Siegel (Eds.), *Review of child development*. In press.

Higgins, E. T., & Huttenlocher, J. Symbols and other signs. Unpublished manuscript, Teachers College, Columbia University, 1973.

Huttenlocher, J., & Burke, D. The development of short-term ordered recall. Unpublished manuscript, Teachers College, Columbia University, 1973.

Huttenlocher, J., Eisenberg, K., & Strauss, S. Comprehension: Relation between perceived actor and logical subject. *Journal of Verbal Learning and Verbal Behavior*, 1968, **7**, 527–530.

Huttenlocher, J., & Higgins, E. T. Reasoning, congruence, and other matters. *Psychological Review*, 1972, **79**, 420–427.

Huttenlocher, J., & Higgins, E. T. Languages of thought. Unpublished manuscript, Teachers College, Columbia University, 1973.

Huttenlocher, J., & Presson, C. Understanding descriptions of transitive relations. Unpublished manuscript, Teachers College, Columbia University, 1973.

Huttenlocher, J., & Strauss, S. Comprehension and a statement's relation to the situation it describes. *Journal of Verbal Learning and Verbal Behavior*, 1968, **71**, 300–304.

Huttenlocher, J., & Weiner, S. Comprehension of instructions in varying contexts. *Cognitive Psychology*, 1971, **2**, 369–385.

Labov, W. Paper presented at Teachers College, Columbia University, May, 1973.

Meadow, S. Comprehension and production of the single word in the two year old. Unpublished manuscript, University of Pennsylvania, 1972.

Palmero, D. More about less: A study of language comprehension. *Journal of Verbal Learning and Verbal Behavior* 1973, **12**, 211–221.

Piaget, J. *The construction of reality in the child*. New York: Basic Books, 1954.

Piaget, J. *Plays, dreams and imitation in childhood*. New York: W. W. Norton, 1962.

Posner, M., & Warren, R. Traces, concepts, and conscious constructions. In A. W. Melton & E. Martin (Eds.), *Coding processes in human memory*. New York: Halsted Press, 1972.

Seligman, M. E. P., Seligman, K., & Weber, E. Noun comprehension and production of the two year old: The myth of the passive vocabulary. Unpublished manuscript, University of Pennsylvania, 1971.

Shipley, E., Smith, C., & Gleitman, L. A study in the acquisition of language: Free responses to commands. *Language*, 1969, **45**, 322–342.

Slobin, D. I. Cognitive prerequisites for the development of grammar. In C. A. Ferguson & D. I. Slobin (Eds.), *Studies of child language development*. New York: Holt, Rinehart & Winston, 1973.

Stern, D. Mother and infant at play: The dyadic interaction involving facial, vocal and gaze behaviors. In M. Lewis & L. Rosenbloom (Eds.), *The Origins of Behavior*. Vol. 1. New York: Wiley, 1973.

Wetstone, H. S., & Friedlander, B. Z. The effect of word order on young children's responses to simple questions and commands. Paper presented at the meeting of the Society for Research in Child Development, Philadelphia, March, 1973.

Wickens, D. Characteristics of word encoding. In A. W. Melton & E. Martin (Eds.), *Coding processes in human memory*. New York: Halsted Press, 1972.

14

DISCUSSION: SECTION II

Following the formal presentation of an abstract of the preceeding five chapters, an informal discussion was held. This section contains the edited transcript of that discussion. The discussion members were:

Lyle Bourne
University of Colorado

James Erickson
Ohio State University

Janellen Huttenlocher
Columbia University

Marvin Levine
State University of New York (Stony Brook)

Elizabeth Loftus
University of Washington

Frank Restle
Indiana University

Frank Slaymaker
Loyola University of Chicago

Gene E. Topper
Loyola University of Chicago

LOFTUS: I would like to begin this discussion by going back to a question that was raised yesterday by Bob Solso, regarding the idea of structure. It seems that this notion of structure has entered into quite a few of the presentations not only today but yesterday as well.

Frank Restle, this morning, for example, said something about the "knowledge structure" a person has. He talked about a "highly organized system." He even said, I am happy to say, that "hierarchal or tree structures seem to be very natural." He said, "Later on we'll have to find out what the cognitive structure is." Yesterday, Dick Atkinson said something about knowledge structures, and he has coined the term, "EKS" to stand for "event knowledge store." Shepard and Metzler even admitted to some structure yesterday. Bob Solso, of course, has an associative structure in mind and discussed how cues relate to recall of things in memory structure. Jim Jenkins said that his experiments were trying to get at the interaction between materials, tasks, and the subject's store of knowledge. Lyle Bourne talked about inferences being a part of the subject's store of knowledge. Even Janellen, in her discussion of language development in children, talked about semantic domains, and about the fact that children seem to have category items grouped together in some sense.

The question I would like to ask is, if there is a semantic memory or structure, a knowledge store, some store of concepts, the information involved must have gotten there somehow. How these concepts, how this knowledge is acquired is certainly an interesting and important question. I am wondering if the research on concept formation can tell us anything about how these natural language concepts got into this highly organized system. I think maybe we'll start with Lyle, if you will . . .

BOURNE: The question I had hoped you would ask is a question about what I think, or what the participants think, is the best way to characterize knowledge or memory. How do you best describe it? My answer to that question, although I don't know yet how knowledge comes about, is to say that it is conceptual; knowledge or memory is best thought of as a system of concepts. If you want to talk about things like event knowledge stores, long-term memory, or semantic memory, then the best description, the best guess, that I can give is that it consists of concepts. There may be words, representations of words, and images in memory. Words in a sense are there to identify the concepts that a person has, and the images seem to be representative of concept particulars. And memory may be organized in such a way that you can get from word to concept or concept to word or concept to image. But my best guess about what the important nature of knowledge or memory is, is that it consists of concepts.

Now, how do concepts get into one's store of knowledge? I don't know. Marvin talked as if it's sort of already there. In the context of describing a lot of different transfer phenomena, what it seemed to me he ended up saying is that you reshuffle things or you come to focus on a particular part of what is there already. You limit your selection of hypotheses, responses, or whatever, to some subdomain within a bigger knowledge structure that already exists. I don't know whether that is true or not, but I guess that's how I am going to pass the ball on down the line to him.

Before doing that, however, let me quickly add that a lot of the experiments that are done in concept formation with adult subjects who solve a number of problems based on a variety of different rules are learning-set type experiments, and they give you learning-set type, quantitative data if that's what you're interested in. I think the interpretation has to be that new concepts come to exist in memory. It seems implausible to me that you have a big domain which gets shuffled around and that you end up focusing on some subset of things in that domain. But I don't know, maybe my experiments are so limited that they fail to represent a very general case. So, there you go Marvin . . .

LEVINE: Let me respond to the original question. I really have two things to say. I see a hiatus in my work between the kind of theorizing that I do and the kind of theorizing that involves the knowledge of (what I think of as) structure—I will elaborate on that in just a minute. My type of experiment is traditionally called concept learning, but I think of it as a problem-solving task. My theory is a theory of problem solving. As you can gather from the talk today, I am striving to generalize this theory. For 10 years I have worked within this one restricted task, but I am striving to generalize the theory as much as I can. For the life of me, however, I don't see how I can take this theory that I have been working with and apply it to tasks like Maier's (1930) pendulum problem, or the Maier coat-rack problem, or these natural-world problems. This is where the hiatus comes in . With these latter problems you are tapping into the subject's geometric sense of the environment around him and his knowledge of what happens when you put pieces of wood together or of how pendulums behave. Theorizing about these problems requires some understanding about the subject's representation of his environment as a structure and about his ability to derive the implications from that representation. That is where I see the gap between the theory of "concept learning" and the theory of knowledge as structure. If I could solve that problem, I would be ten steps ahead.

I can put that same issue in a more schematized way, from Tolman's writings. Tolman had two cognitive constructs in his writings that deal with the impact of the stimulus on the organism. One is that, in contrast to the S–R position, learning is S–S, i.e., that organisms learn sequences of stimuli. Pavlov's dog is learning, essentially, that food follows the tone. Or the rat learns that if he turns to the right at this point, he will receive food. That was one cognitive idea, i.e., you don't have to have a response—the response only makes the learning manifest. The other cognitive construct was that the rat had a cognitive map. But he never tells us how you get from the learning of the little S–S links to the map.

I see that as a fundamental problem. I see that as the distillation of the problem you are raising. Between the subject's ability to learn a concept and his ability to deal with environmental (and symbolic) structure is a void. All I can do at this time is note this hiatus.

LOFTUS: It seems as if both of you feel that the concept learning that you study may have *nothing* to do with the learning of concepts that is involved in building up a semantic structure.

LEVINE: Right.

ERICKSON: Yes, that is quite clear. We don't know anything about how the concepts are formed or how they get in there. Like Lyle's studies, my studies and Marv's studies basically relate to how you use information you already have in solving a particular problem that the experimenter gives you.

LOFTUS: So perhaps they shouldn't be called the same thing? They shouldn't both be called, "concept learning." What are the developmental psychologists saying about this problem, Janellen?

HUTTENLOCHER: Would you state the problem again?

LOFTUS: If our concept learners all agree that their concept learning doesn't have anything to do with the learning of concepts . . .

LEVINE: The learning of *structure*, please! How you get from concept to structure is like Tolman's problem of how you get from stimulus to map.

LOFTUS: Do the developmental psychologists know anything about the learning of natural language concepts?

HUTTENLOCHER: Of course that has been my motive in studying the origins of systematic behavioral responses to natural language input. I cannot say that I have found out how natural language concepts are acquired. Certain notions seem to be acquired very early. Objects all clumped together in certain categories by their perceptual properties, shape, etc., and by function; no, I am not prepared to say where they come from.

BOURNE: Do they happen just as Marvin says, do they just exist? Maybe all of a sudden they are there, or maybe they were there all the time and we weren't somehow able to make contact with them, *or* is there a process by which they evolve and develop?

HUTTENLOCHER: Certainly many kinds of notions, for example, many relational notions, are not there at all in the children I have seen.

BOURNE: So they must evolve by some process or other. Do we know anything about that?

RESTLE: Why do you say they *must* evolve?

LOFTUS: Either they are there or they evolve!

RESTLE: All right. If those are the only two alternatives, then they evolve; but that's a pretty broad meaning to evolve.

BOURNE: Well, what would *you* say?

RESTLE: I was just kind of curious if those were the only two possible alternatives—if they were there or they evolve.

LEVINE: I think you, Lyle, are reacting to the system of the hypothesis universe that I presented. Is this correct? There is, I suppose, the implication that the subject comes to the task with these domains in his head. However, I don't really believe that. That is a sort of schematic approximation. I am very happy to see your documentation that subjects will construct rules and construct categories. I am sure that goes on. I don't think, however, that for the extensions I presented today that I need to get into that complication. I see your work as one step up, not ten steps away, but one step away from where I am now. I begin to see the possibility that there is something of mutual interest there; something that we could both deal with. Certainly, one of the things is how do you get into rule construction? . . . How's that for a namby-pamby answer?

BOURNE: I don't understand. But Frank, either they evolve or they are already there.

LOFTUS: They could arrive spontaneously, I suppose, rather than evolve.

BOURNE: That's a form of evolution, or are we quibbling about words?

LOFTUS: No. He seems to have another alternative in mind.

BOURNE: But he won't tell.

RESTLE: I was trying to see the possibility. The trouble, I feel, is that in this kind of experiment whenever we look for the acquisition of knowledge, we find it is already there, i.e. the kind of information a person needs to solve experimental problems is always twofold. First there is general knowledge about the situation or the possibilities, what the game is in the concept learning experiments, or what the structure of the world is in Huttenlocher's observations. Second there are certain specific facts inserted by the experimenter to make the system. The experimenter wants to understand an underlying structure, and he gives the subject some special knowledge which then enables the subject to trace the operation of the structure. Arbitrary concept problems, I think, have this characteristic. The arbitrary stimuli and rules make no sense at all, but the subject absorbs them into a structure he already has ready. The experiment does not reveal learning of the kind you want. The arbitrary stimuli become absorbed into the subject's cognitive system, and we can then observe combinational and transformational properties of that system. Still, I am not convinced that Lyle Bourne's subjects develop any new conceptual possibilities in the couple of hours of the experiment. That is my sense of the problem here when we talk about the development of knowledge. Arbitrary markers are learned quickly, but that is trivial. The markers enable us to see a cognitive structure, we don't see the structure growing.

LOFTUS: I want to tell you about an experiment and see what you think. It is a different approach to studying the acquisition or development of structure. I took some subjects who were in the process of learning new material, i.e., adding to their current store of knowledge. These subjects were some of my graduate students at the New School. They were learning, among other things, the names of psychologists. Without going into the details of the experiment, I find that people who are in the beginning of their graduate career (and these are inferences based on the reaction-time data I collected) have "a list" of psychologists in mind (they know Freud, Skinner, Piaget), and if you ask them a question such as, "Give me the name of a psychologist who is associated in your mind with the field of learning whose name begins with 'S'," they are going to give you Skinner. They would give Skinner if you asked for a "perception" psychologist. They have a few names in mind, and that is all they can give. You take advanced graduate students, and something very different happens. Again, without taking the time for too much detail, the advanced graduate students have a very different structure. They don't have a list. They have a group of psychologists who are associated with learning, and a different group of psychologists who are associated with social psycology, etc. Their knowledge structure is more elaborate and is reflected, I feel, in the reaction time that I collect. I don't know, is this going to work in terms of understanding how material becomes added to the structure?

RESTLE: You mean that if an experiment deals with a big enough structure and lasts a long enough time, that knowledge is actually acquired by subjects?

LOFTUS: Yes.

RESTLE: That makes a great deal of sense to me. I was hoping Janellen was going to find such things, because she was taking a period of six months in a period of rapid cognitive growth in the child.

HUTTENLOCHER: The main change in these children was not so much the evolution of object categories as the evolution of mental process. While they could seek the same types of objects on the basis of a word early on, however, there was a difference in their behavior in retrieving objects during this period. At first they would look around, apparently at random, and find an object that fit with that word. In a later period, when you asked for something that wasn't there they had to take a long route to get to it and come back with it, finally even going directly to a temporary place for the object. Two things can be said about this. First, they were learning where things were kept. Secondly, they weren't just walking, holding the word-sound in mind waiting till they ran into the object, but no doubt were thinking about the object's properties.

LOFTUS: They were *not* holding the word in mind?

HUTTENLOCHER: I would argue that they were thinking of the properties of the objects themselves when they went. It seems to me that if you ask a child for something like a cookie, and he goes to where the cookies have recently been put, but are not normally kept, like Craig with the spilled cookies, such a child must be able to recollect the properties of these objects as well as their location; otherwise, I don't know why a child would take a direct route to a short-term object location. This development of the ability to represent information about objects and places matches very closely with the kind of thing Piaget talks about with respect to sensory motor development. If they can represent object properties and they look for objects in their absence, I wonder why they don't talk. I don't know the answer to that.

LEVINE: Consider this situation of telling a child, "Bring me a cookie." The suggestion that the word "cookie" elicits some sort of knowledge index or an image of a cookie is the S–S idea of Tolman. It is a minimal sense of structure. If, however, the child can negotiate the house and go from one room to another in search of the cookie, and if it is not up above he looks down below, and if, when he finds the cookie, he brings it directly to you, then he has that conception of the space around him. That is a richer sense of structure, and that is a much bigger mystery.

LOFTUS: It also raises the question of visual versus verbal structure and how the two fit in with each other. Are either of you two doing any work on that problem?

SLAYMAKER: I don't know how we ended up in language but, with regard to structure as Lyle was talking about it, I would like to bring the discussion back to the specific structure that he mentioned with regard to the four inferences with which a subject approaches these concept learning problems. Now, if we can relate this to Marvin's concepts, I imagine these four inferences would have to gain habit strength by instruction (Marvin seems to indicate that instructions are equivalent to practice) or by simply throwing the subject into the task where eventually he will learn a set of dominant inferences. Lyle's data clearly indicate that subjects can assimilate these various rule structures and eventually learn a biconditional very rapidly. Apparently, there has to be some kind of (if nothing more than transient) alteration in role structure. In terms of the inferences Lyle proposes it would be very simple to go through and change the nature of either 1, 2, 3, or 4 of those inferences and make a biconditional the most likely concept to be learned. Then you could make predictions from that basis as to how difficult it would be to learn a simple conditional proposition once a subject is restricted by a biconditional frame. This is, once again, what Marvin was talking about as structure, in terms of specifically whether a subject is operating within one domain or another domain, and how he might transfer from one to another. I think Lyle is really speaking about the structure of conceptual behavior in terms of a set of rules and the relationships among them.

ERICKSON: I don't think that Lyle's data show that subjects know what a biconditional rule is. They show that subjects can learn to sort things according to a biconditional rule, for example, but do not show that subjects really know what such a rule means. To be able to say that, you would need data showing transfer from some sort of rule learning task to other tasks in which conditional or biconditional rules are needed. I am thinking of tasks like those used by Wason and Johnson-Laird (1972), where they show how much difficulty subjects have with very simple sorts of conditional rules. I would like to ask Lyle if he knows of any such data. For example, has John Taplin gathered any data showing transfer from conditional rule learning tasks to conditional reasoning tasks?

BOURNE: John Taplin, now at Claremont Graduate School, has tried to train people to reason consistently with sentences according to some rule. It is my impression that he has done that with biconditionals and conditionals, as well as other rules from the propositional calculus. He hasn't examined, to my knowledge, the nature of the subject's understanding of the complete calculus nor how rules transfer from one to the other. I understood you to say that my data do not indicate that the subject has any understanding of the biconditional rule; I guess there is a sense in which that is true and a sense in which it is not. It depends on how you identify the subject's knowledge, what he is capable of doing with it, and what kind of cognitions and concepts come about as a consequence of solving a series of rule learning or linguistic deduction problems. In one sense the subject knows the rule very well, because, after a series of problems, he merely grinds out answers, quickly and with minimal information. In that sense he knows the rule. But, does he have a nice, neat, formal linguistic expression that identifies what he knows, that identifies his new knowledge? The answer is "no." You can train him on sorting problems till you are blue in the face, and he is not going to describe what he knows very well. You can help him to do that but that is another kind of training. Now, does a newly-learned rule transfer? I wish I knew. Unfortunately, transfer experiments, again despite what Jim said, take a long time to do. Getting transfer from knowledge of one rule to performance with another one is very hard, because it takes a long time for subjects to become proficient. We have done the gross experiment to look for *any* degree of interrule transfer, and there is some. But there is a lot more that has to be done to work out the details.

LEVINE: Have you looked at transfer from two-valued stimuli to three-valued stimuli for something like the biconditional?

BOURNE: There are some experiments like that, but they are few and far between. A student who just finished a degree in my lab trained subjects on a variety of rules in the usual multiple rule-learning paradigm. At the end of a series of problems, subjects were pretty good at problems with two terms and three values per dimension. He tried a variety of transfer or generality tests to determine how well subjects could do when there are three terms combined by the same rule, how well they could do when there are three terms and two rules (one between the first two terms and another between the second two), how well they do when transfer is to more meaningful kinds of stimuli, and how well they do when you give them a word problem that nonetheless corresponds to one of the rules they just learned. The problem of generality is being examined, but I can tell you little about the data. We simply don't understand this process very well at this time.

LOFTUS: Before we end, I just want to ask Gene if you have any "lectures" you are dying to give?

TOPPER: No lectures, but a question for Dr. Bourne. Do you object to the use of hypotheses as mediators?

BOURNE: I don't think so, but I don't think that is what I was talking about either. I would understand the term hypothesis as being something like the possible solution to the problem. That is not what I was talking about. I was talking about skills or mechanisms for getting to an hypothesis or getting to a possible solution. I don't like mediators, and I don't like hypotheses *too* well either. But both concepts are okay if you know how to use them.

LOFTUS: Any other comments?

AUDIENCE (Jenkins):   Could we offer a tribute to Loyola on behalf of the participants and spectators! (applause)

REFERENCES

Maier, N.R.F. Reasoning in humans, I: On direction. *Journal of Comparative Psychology*, 1930, **12**, 115–143.

Wason, P.C., & Johnson-Laird, P.N. *Psychology of reasoning: Structure and content*. Cambridge, Mass.: Harvard University Press, 1972.

AUTHOR INDEX

Numbers in italics refer to the pages on which the complete references are listed.

A

Adams, P. A., 11, *20*
Allen, T. W., 82, 84, 86, 91, 96, 97, *97*
Anderson, J. R., 48 *72*, 94, 96, *97*, 143, *144*
Anderson, R. C., 262, *286*
Andrews, O. E., 299, *302*
Anisfeld, M., 49, *72*
Archer, E. J., 293, *302*
Arnheim, R., 18, *20*
Atkinson, R. C., 63, 64, *72*, 83, *97*, 102, 105, 108, 114, 116, 118, 120, 122, 126, 128, 131, 132, *144, 145, 146,* 203, 205, *217,* 236, 237, *255*
Attneave, F., 194, *198*
Austin, G. A., 238, 240, *256,* 260, 261, 262, 264, 265, 269, 273, 274, 275, 279, *287*

B

Bahrick, H. P., 28, *42*
Bamber, D., 197, *199*
Barbizet, J., 198, *198*
Barch, A. M., 55, *72*
Barclay, J. R., 222, *230*

Barker, D., 68, *73*
Bartlett, F. C., 46, *72*
Baylor, G. W., 198, *198*
Beale, I. L., 187, *199*
Begg, I., 307, *329*
Beito, A., 71, *75*
Benjafeld, J. G., 274, *287*
Berg, E. A., 300, *303*
Berian, K. M., 82, *99*
Biersdorff, K., 30, *43*
Bjork, R. A., 45, *73,* 82, 84, 86, 91, 96, 97, *97*
Block, R. A., 48, *73,* 78, 80, 82, 84, 86, 90, 92, 95, *98*
Bloom, L., 332, 333, 354, 364, 365, *367*
Bock, R. D., 188, *198*
Bogen, J. E., 188, 198, *199*
Bohm, A. M., 11, *20*
Boies, S. J., 191, *200*
Boka, J. A., 68, *73*
Bourne, L. E., Jr., 233, 238, 249, 250, 252, *255, 256,* 257, 258, 259, 260, 261, 262, 265, 273, 279, *286, 287, 288,* 293, 300, *302, 303*
Bower, G. H., 32, *42,* 48, *72,* 91, 94, 95, 96, *97,* 143, *144,* 198, *199,* 207, *217,* 262, *286, 288,* 292, *303*

Bowerman, M., 332, *367*
Bransford, J. D., 209, *217, 222, 230*
Bregman, A. S., 198, *200*
Briggs, G. E., 117, *145, 146*
Broadbent, D. E., 108, *145*
Brooks, L. R., 198, *199*
Brown, G. G., 293, *302*
Brown, R., 198, *199*
Bruder, G., 63, *72*
Bruner, J. S., 103, *145,* 238, 240, *256,* 260, 261, 262, 264, 265, 269, 273, 274, 275, 279, *287*
Burke, D., 339, *367, 368*
Burnham, C. A., 197, *199*
Buschke, H., 63, 64, *72*
Bush, C. T., 78, *99*
Byers, J. L., 264, *287*

C

Carpenter, P. A., 198, *199*
Carter-Sobell, L., 67, *74*
Ceraso, J., 308, 319, 320, 324, *329*
Cermak, G., 63, 64, *72*
Chapman, J. P., 308, 325, 326, *329*
Chapman, L. J., 308, 325, 326, *329*
Chapman, R. S., 333, 353, *367*
Chase, W. G., 142, *145,* 187, *199*
Chen, S. S., 198, *200*
Chipman, S., 150, 189, 198, *200*
Chisholm, D. C., 25, *43*
Clark, E. V., 198, *199,* 338, 354, 357, *367*
Clark, H. H., 142, *145,* 187, 198, *199*
Cohen, J. C., 24, 25, 26, *42*
Collins, A. M., 32, *42,* 209, *217*
Cooper, F. S., 203, *217*
Cooper, L. A., 148, 150, 186, 187, 188, 189, 194, 198, *199*
Coots, J. H., 92, 93, *98*
Corballis, M. C., 187, *199*
Cost, J. R., 293, *303*
Craik, F. I. M., 17, *20,* 51, 62, *72,* 106, *145,* 206, 207, *217*
Cramer, P., 55, *73*

D

D'Agostino, P. R., 79, 87, 88, 92, 93, 96, 97
DaPolito, F., 68, *73*

Davidson, R. E., 264, *287*
Dean, M. F., 68, 71, *73*
Denny, J. P., 274, *287,* 307, *329*
Denny, N. R., 261, *287*
DeRemer, P., 79, 87, 88, 92, 93, 96, 97
Dodd, D. H., 252, *256*
Doherty, M. A., 276, *287*
Dominowski, R. L., 38, *42,* 257, 260, 261, 262, 264, 265, 273, 279, *286, 287*
Donaldson, M., 338, *367*
Donaldson, W., 204, *217*
Dovel, J. C., 88, *97*
Doyle, A. C., 40, *42*
Dreissen, E., 298, *303*
Duarte, A., 92, *98*
Duncan, C. P., 38, *42*

E

Eagle, M., 55, 60, *73*
Ebbinghaus, H., 2, *20,* 46, *73*
Eberlein, E., 55, *73*
Eichelman, W. H., 191, *200*
Eifermann, R. R., 261, 264, 279, *287*
Eisenberg, K., 337, *368*
Ekstrand, B. R., 23, *43,* 47, 49, 54, 61, 62, 68, *73, 75,* 257, *286*
Ellis, H. C., 22, *42*
Elmes, D. G., 87, 88, *97*
Erickson, J. R., 300, *302,* 313, *329*
Eschenbrenner, A. J., Jr., 58, 68, *73*

F

Feng, C. A., 148, 187, *200*
Festinger, L., 197, *199*
Filbey, R., 188, *199*
Fillenbaum, S., 104, *145*
Fingerman, P., 293, 296, *302, 303*
Fischler, I., 122, 131, *145*
Fishbein, H. D., 299, *302*
Fishkin, A., 300, *303*
Flanagan, J. L., 56, *74*
Flickinger, R. G., 92, 93, *98*
Franks, J. J., 209, *217,* 222, *230*
Frase, L. T., 307, *329*
Freedman, J. L., 32, *42*
Friedlander, B. Z., 332, 353, *367, 368*
Fulkerson, F., 55, 58, 62, 68, *73*
Furth, H. G., 198, *199*

G

Garron, D. C., 188, *199*
Gartman, L. M., 93, 94, *98*
Gazzaniga, M. S., 188, 198, *199*
Geisler, W. S., 31, *43*, 205, *217*
Gholson, B., 294, *303*
Giambra, L. M., 264, *287*
Gibson, A. R., 188, *199*
Gibson, J. J., 16, *20*
Glanzer, M., 92, *98*
Gleitman, L., 339, *368*
Glucksberg, S., 133, *146*, 336, *368*
Goldstein, S., 261, *286*
Goodnow, J. J., 238, 240, *256*, 260, 261, 262, 264, 265, 269, 273, 274, 275, 279, *287*
Grant, D. A., 293, 300, *303*
Greenbloom, R., 25, *43*
Greener, W. I., 87, *97*
Greenfield, P. M., 198, *199*
Greeno, J. G., 24, 25, *42*, 45, *73*, 78, 87, 93, *98*
Gregg, L. W., 263, 264, *287*
Gregory, R. L., 204, *217*
Grossman, L., 55, 60, *73*
Gumer, E., 299, *303*
Guthrie, J. T., 262, *286*
Guy, D. E., 238, *256*, 259, 261, *286*

H

Halpern, J., 298, *303*
Ham, M., 23, *43*
Harbert, R. L., 261, 262, *287*
Harrington, A. L., 26, *42*
Hartlage, L. C., 188, *199*
Hawkins, H. L., 237, *256*
Haygood, R. C., 233, *256*, 258, 259, 261, 262, *287*, 293, *303*
Henle, M., 308, *329*
Herrmann, D. J., 142, *145*
Higgins, E. T., 333, 334, 336, 361, *368*
Higgins, L., 333, *367*
Hillner, K., 80, *99*
Hintzman, D. L., 48, *73*, 78, 79, 80, 82, 84, 85, 86, 90, 92, 93, 95, 96, *98*
Höffding, H., 46, *73*
Hollingworth, H. C., 46, *73*
Homa, D., 132, *145*
Hood, L., 333, *367*

Hopkins, R. H., 61, *74*
Horowitz, L. M., 91, *98*
Houston, J. P., 24, *42*
Hovland, C. I., 238, *256*
Hubel, D. H., 189, *199*
Humphreys, L. G., 296, *303*
Hunt, E. B., 262, *287*
Huttenlocher, J., 192, 198, *199*, 333, 334, 337, 339, 361, *367, 368*
Hyde, T. S., 10, 12, 13, *20*

I

Ingison, L. J., 61, *73*

J

James, C. T., 24, 25, *42*
James, W., 46, *73*
Jeeves, M. A., 261, 264, *288*
Jenkins, J. J., 3, 10, 12, 13, 14, 15, *20*, 25, *42*, 307, *329*
Jesse, F., 47, *75*
Johnson, D. M., 301, *303*
Johnson, J. E., 58, *73*
Johnson, N. F., 93, 94, *98*, 212, *217*, 223, 230
Johnson, P. J., 240, 248, *256*, 300, *303*
Johnson-Laird, P. N., 305, *329, 375, 376*
Johnston, C. D., 10, *20*
Johnston, W. A., 92, 93, *98*
Jost, A., 77, 78, 79, *98*
Juola, J. F., 102, 108, 114, 116, 118, 120, 122, 128, 131, 132, 141, *144, 145*
Just, M. A., 198, *199*

K

Kanak, N. J., 56, 58, 71, *73, 74*
Karchmer, M. A., 68, 69, *75*
Karpf, D., 264, *287*
Kausler, D. H., 49, 55, 58, 61, 62, 63, 64, 65, 66, 68, *73, 74*
Keppel, G., 4, *20*
King, W. L., 255, *256*
Kinsman, R. A., 252, *256*
Kintsch, W., 46, 48, 61, *74*, 78, *98*, 101, *145*
Kirkpatrick, E. A., 46, *74*
Kirkpatrick, M., 80, *99*
Klatzky, R., 120, *145*

Klipp, R. D., 252, *256*
Knapp, M. E., 49, *72*
Köhler, W., 198, *199*
Kolakowski, D., 188, *198*
Kollasch, S. F., 49, *74*
Koopmans, H. S., 108, *145*
Kosslyn, S. M., 198, *199*
Krauss, R. M., 336, *368*
Kuhn, T. S., 45, *74*

L

Labov, W., 358, *368*
Lakoff, G., 104, *145*
Landauer, T. K., 32, *42*, 81, *98*
Laughlin, P. R., 261, 264, 276, *287*
Lenon, R., 63, *72*
Levine, M., 260, 262, 263, 264, 265, 266, *287*, 291, 292, 294, 295, 296, 299, *303*
Levinthal, C. F., 299, *302*
Levison, M. J., 265, *287*
Levy, J., 188, 198, *200, 201*
Liberman, A. M., 203, *217*
Light, L. L., 67, *74*
Lindsay, P. H., 143, *146*
Link, W. E., 261, *286*
Lively, B. L., 134, *145*
Lockhart, R. S., 17, 20, 24, *42*, 51, 62, *72*, 106, *145*, 206, 207, *217*
Loftus, E. F., 32, *42*
Loftus, G. F., 32, *42*, 86, *98*
Lovelace, E. A., 55, 61, 63, *74*
Luh, C. W., 46, *74*

M

McCarthy, S. V., 55, *74*
McClelland, D. C., 47, *74*
McCormack, P. D., 101, *145*
McDougall, R., 46, *74*
Macey, W. H., 38, 39, *43*
McGuigan, F. J., 40, *42*
Mackworth, N. H., 195, *200*
McLaughlin, J. P., 142, *145*
Madigan, S. A., 1, *20*, 28, *43*, 80, 91, 92, 93, 94, *98*
Maier, N. R. F., 371, *376*
Mandler, G., 108, *145*, 207, *217*
Martin, E., 45, *74*, 91, 93, *98*, 143, *145*
Martin, J., 262, *287*
Meadow, S., 352, *368*
Melton, A. W., 45, *74*, 78, 79, 81, 91, *98*,

143, *145*
Metzler, J., 147, 148, 153, 156, 176, 178, 184, 186, 187, 188, 189, 193, *200, 220, 230*
Meyer, D. E., 131, *145*
Meyer, H., 68, *74*
Meyers, L. S., 298, *303*
Miller, J. F., 333, 353, *367*
Miller, P., 299, *303*
Miller, R. R., 81, *98*
Millward, R. B., 273, 279, *287, 293, 303*
Minturn, A. L., 103, *145*
Moeser, S. D., 198, *200*
Mohs, R. C., 126, *146*
Morin, R. E., 117, *146*
Mueller, J. H., 55, 56, *74*
Müller, G. E., 46, *74*
Murdock, B. B., Jr., 113, *146*
Musgrave, B. S., 24, 25, 26, *42*

N

Nahinsky, I. D., 263, 279, *287*
Nappe, G. W., 71, *75*
Naus, M. J., 132, 133, *146*
Neisser, U., 198, *200, 239, 256, 261, 287*
Nelson, K., 198, *199*
Neumann, P. G., 300, *303*
Newby, R. W., 56, 58, *74*
Newell, A., 197, *200, 260, 276, 287*
Newman, W., 91, *98*
Newman, W. M., 154, *200*
Noll, A. M., 154, *200*
Norman, D. A., 39, 40, *42*, 48, *74*, 143, *146*, 236, *256*

O

O'Banion, K., 262, *286*
Olson, R. D., 62, 63, *73*
Omler, J. A., 261, 262, *287*
Ono, H., 197, *199*
Ornstein, P. A., 133, *146*
Osler, S., 27, 28, *43*

P

Paivio, A., 61, *74*, 198, *200, 207, 217*
Palermo, D. S., 55, *74*, 338, *368*
Pavur, E., 65, *73*
Pearlstone, Z., 27, *43*, 108, *145*
Peixotto, H. E., 47, *74*

Penfield, W., 198, *200*
Peterson, L. R., 78, 80, 81, *98, 99*
Pezzoli, J. A., 307, *329*
Phillips, S., 294, *303*
Piaget, J., 198, *200, 354, 355, 357, 368*
Posner, M. I., 90, *99,* 141, *146,* 191, *200,*
  235, *256,* 260, *287,* 335, *368*
Postman, L., 4, 10, 11, *20, 25, 43,* 47, *74*
Potts, G. R., 209, *217*
Premack, D., 198, *200*
Presson, C. C., 192, *199,* 337, *368*
Provitera, A., 308, 319, 320, 324, *329*
Psotka, J., 198, *201*
Pulley, S. J., 61, *74*

Q

Quillian, M. R., 32, *42,* 209, *217*

R

Ranschburg, P., 46, *74*
Rapoport, A., 104, *145*
Raser, G. A., 64, *74*
Raskin, D., 55, *73*
Rawlings, E. I., 198, *200*
Rawlings, I. L., 198, *200*
Reicher, G. M., 78, *98*
Remington, R. K., 71, *75*
Restle, F., 204, *217,* 223, *230,* 265, *287*
Richardson, A., 198, *200*
Richardson, J., 23, 25, *43*
Rips, L. J., 104, *146*
Robbins, D., 78, *99*
Roberts, L., 198, *200*
Rogers, M. K., 79, 84, 85, 86, 90, 93, 96,
  98
Rokeach, M., 215, *217*
Rollins, H., 187, *201*
Ross, B. M., 47, 60, *74*
Rothstein, L. D., 117, *146*
Rowe, E. J., 61, *74*
Rumelhart, D. E., 80, *99,* 143, *146*
Rundus, D., 83, 95, *99*
Russell, I. S., 68, 69, *75*

S

Saltzman, D., 80, *99*
Saltzman, E., 198, *199*
Sanders, L. W., 88, *97*
Sanford, B. J., 134, *145*

Sardello, R. J., 58, *73*
Sawyer, C. R., 240, 248, *256*
Schank, R. C., 141, 142, *146*
Schnorr, J., 63, 64, *72*
Schulz, L. S., 55, 63, *74*
Schulz, R. W., 22, *43,* 61, *74*
Schvaneveldt, R. W., 131, *145*
Schwartz, S. H., 260, 279, *288*
Segal, S. J., 198, *200*
Selfridge, O. G., 189, *200*
Seligman, K., 352, *368*
Seligman, M. E. P., 352, *368*
Sells, S. B., 307, 328, *329*
Settle, A. V., 55, *73*
Seward, G. H., 47, *75*
Shaffer, W. O., 84, 85, *99*
Shankweiler, D. P., 203, *217*
Shannon, C. E., 37, *43*
Shaughnessy, E., 187, *201*
Shaughnessy, J. J., 55, 68, 71, *75,* 86, 87, *99*
Sheehan, P., 198, *200*
Shepard, R. N., 47, 48, 61, *75,* 93, *99,* 147,
  148, 150, 153, 156, 187, 188, 189, 194,
  197, 198, *199, 200,* 220, *230*
Shiffrin, R. M., 31, *43,* 83, 84, 85, *97, 99,*
  101, 105, *145, 146,* 203, 205, 209, *217,*
  236, 237, *255*
Shigley, R. H., 237, *256*
Shipley, E., 339, *368*
Shoben, E. J., 104, *146*
Shulman, H. G., 51, *75,* 78, *98*
Siegel, L. S., 265, 279, *288*
Silverman, W., 63, *72*
Simon, H. A., 197, *200,* 260, 263, 264, 276,
  287
Sinclair-de-Zwart, H., 198, *200*
Slobin, D. I., 332, *368*
Smith, C., 339, *368*
Smith, E. E., 104, *146*
Smoke, K. L., 238, *256*
Snyder, C. R. C., 189, *200*
Solso, R. L., 24, 26, 30, 38, 39, *43*
Spear, N. E., 68, *75*
Sperling, G., 237, *256*
Sperry, R. W., 188, 198, *199, 201*
Spoehr, K. T., 273, 279, *287*
Springer, A. D., 81, *98*
Sproull, R. F., 154, *200*
Stafford, R. E., 188, *201*
Steinmeyer, C. H., 299, *303*
Stern, D., 340, *368*
Sternberg, S., 101, 109, 112, 113, 116, 136,

146, 208, *217*, 237, 238, *256*
Stone, P. J., 262, *287*
Strauss, S., 337, *368*
Stromeyer, C. F., 198, *201*
Strong, E. K., Jr., 47, *75*
Studdert-Kennedy, M., 203, *217*
Summers, J. J., 48, *73*, 78, 80, 82, 84, 86, 90, 92, 95, *98*
Sutherland, N. S., 187, 189, *201*
Swanson, J. M., 117, *145, 146*

T

Taplin, J. E., 261, 264, 266, 272, 273, *288*
Taylor, R. L., 187, 191, *200, 201*
Teeters, T. D., 24, *43*
Teghtsoonian, M., 47, *75*
Thomson, D. M., 22, 27, 29, *43*, 68, *75*, 106, *146*
Till, R. E., 14, 15, *20*
Topper, G. E., 38, 39, *43*
Townsend, J. T., 113, *146*
Trabasso. T., 187, *201*, 262, *286, 288*, 292, *303*
Trafimow, E. S., 26, *43*
Tulving, E., 1, *20*, 27, 28, 29, *43*, 68, *75*, 106, 141, *146*, 204, *217*, 236, *256*

U

Ullrich, J. R., 55, *74*
Underwood, B. J., 4, *20*, 22, 23, 29, *43*, 47, 48, 49, 54, 55, 62, 68, 71, *73, 75*, 77, 78, 79, 86, 87, 90, *99*, 131, *146*
Uttley, A. M., 187, *201*

V

Vandenberg, S. G., 188, *201*
Viterna, R. O., 47, *75*

W

Wales, R., 338, *367*

Walker, C. M., 261, *288*
Wallace, W. P., 49, 54, 62, 68, 71, 72, *73, 75*
Walsh, D. A., 12, 13, *20*
Wampler, R., 80, *99*
Warnock, J. E., 154, *201*
Warren, R. M., 90, 94, *99*, 335, *368*
Wason, P. C., 271, *288, 305, 329, 375, 376*
Waters, R. M., 48, *73*
Weaver, F. S., 117, *146*
Weber, E., 362, *368*
Weene, P., 239, *256*, 261, *287*
Weiner, S., 337, *368*
Wertheimer, M., 301, *303*
Wescourt, K. T., 126, *146*
Wetherick, N. E., 261, 264, 274, 279, 280, *288*
Wetstone, H. S., 353, *368*
Whalen, C. H., 55, *72*
Wiant, J., 68, *73*
Wickelgren, W. A., 48, *74*, 82, 99
Wickens, D. D., 29, *43*, 360, *368*
Wickens, T. D., 101, *145*, 293, *303*
Wiesel, T. N., 189, *199*
Wilkins, M. C., 328, *329*
Wilkinson, W. C., 87, *97*
Williams, J. D., 134, *146*
Winograd, E., 68, 69, *75*
Wood, C. T., 122, 131, *145*
Woodworth, R. S., 307, *329*

Y

Yilk, M. D., 198, *200*
Yngve, V., 212, *217*
Young, J. L., 80, 93, *99*
Young, R. K., 24, *43*, 56, 58, *74*

Z

Zavortink, B., 4, *20*
Zeichmeister, E. B., 64, *75*
Zelazny, C., 24, *43*
Zimmerman, J., 55, 68, 71, *75*, 86, 87, *99*
Zusne, L., 187, *201*

SUBJECT INDEX

A

Anagram(s), 38–39
Action-schema, 334
Aristotelian syllogism, 306–307, *see also* syllogistic reasoning
Associative clustering, 10–11, 13, 15
Associative continuity hypothesis, 28
Associative learning, 22, 27
Associative response hypothesis, 56
Atmosphere effect, 307, 310, *see also* Syllogistic reasoning
Attention (Children's), 339–340
Attribute identification, 261–263, 265, 269
    Paradigms, 262

B

Bayes' theorem, 305
Bigram frequency, 38–39
Bigram versatility, 38–39
British associationists, 2, 45

C

Children's language
    protocols, 341–352

Class concept, 258
Code, 17–18, 143, 189, 204, 235, 254, 332, 336
Cognition, 221, 224, 225, 231
Cognitive maps, 226
Concept, 231–232, 257
Concept formation, 203
Concept identification, 259, 260, 276–279
    protocols, 281–286
Conceptual behavior, 257–263, 371, 372
Conceptual code(s), 104
Conceptual problems, 231, 253
Conceptual problem solving, 234–238
Conceptual rule learning, 231–256, 232–233
    subordinate operation, 236–237
Conceptual Store (CS), 104–109, 131, 141–142, 143
Conceptual tasks, 232, 269
Creativity, 32
Cross-structural associative cuing, 34
Cryptic messages, 37
Cue(s), 68
    efficacy, 22, 27, 30, 40, 42
    and memory, 21–44, 27, 30, 370
    multiple, 30–31, 36, 42
    retrieval, 22, 28
    selection, *see* Stimulus selection

D

Decoding, 32, 41

E

Einstelling, 289, 294–296
Encoding, 27–28, 34, 36, 92, 94, *see also*
  Spacing effect; Encoding variability
  multiple, 29–32
  specificity hypothesis, 27–29
  variability hypothesis, 92–93
Event Knowledge Store (EKS), 104–105,
  106–109, 119–122, 124, 126, 127, 128,
  129, 141–142, 143, 144, 220, 370

F

Featural components, 49, 63, 72
Forgetting, 3–9
Free recall, 46, 47, 95
Frequency judgments, 95
Frequency theory, 54–56, 67, 71, 220

G

Gestalt psychology, 8, 204, 227

H

Hologram, 228
Homonym, 51, 63
Hypothesis (H) Theory, 289, 300

I

Implicit Associative Responses (IAR), 31, 33,
  36, 38, 41, 55, 63, 225
Information Flow
  in memory, 209–214
Information processing, 225
  Perceptual, 235
Interference theory, 46
Intra-Structural Associative Paradox (ISAP),
  36–41, 42
Isomorphism, 150

K

Knowledge, 2–3, 369, 370, 371, 373

L

Language comprehension
  origins, 331–367
Learning, 5, 6, 8, 9,
  concept, 203
  incidental, 9, 12
  intentional, 9, 12, 16
  serial pattern, 203
  and stimulus selection, 26
  tactics, 26
Learning set, 293–294
Learning-to-learn, 289
Linguistic code, 333
Logic, 305–306
Long-Term Memory (LTM), 102–103, 104,
  203, 204–206
Long-Term Store (LTS), 102–104, 141–142,
  143, 144, 220

M

Meaning, 18
Meaningfulness, 3
Memory, 16, 47, 69, 77, 220, 221, 225, 229,
  254, 279, 370, *see also* Sensory register,
  Memory structure, Short-Term Store, and
  Long-Term Memory
  associative, 2, 22
  attributes, 29
  in children, 9
  in concept problems, 236–237
  episodic, 203, 204, 207
  iconic, 205, 207
  levels of, 204–209
  models, 32–33, 224
  networks, 143–144
  organizational factors, 95, 206–207,
    209–214, 214–215
  permanent, 49, 52–53
  retrieval, 46, 208
  scanning, 101
  search, 109–117, 117–125, 125–129,
    129–134, 134–139, 221
  semantic, 203, 204
  set, 135
  system, 102–103
  theory(s), 32–33, 204
  trace, 22
  working, 203
Memory structure, 22, 32–36, 41, 104,
  142–143, 203–217, 220, 223, 369

Mental chemistry, 32
Mental forestry, 32, 215
Mental representation of events
    early word meanings, 355–364
    relational meaning, 363–364
Mental rotation, 150–151, 220, *see also* Three
    Dimensional Objects
    cognitive processes, 197–198
    complexity of objects, 187–188
    inclination of axis, 187
    reaction time, 161–163, 168, 172–175,
        176, 181
    same vs. different objects, 186–187
    search, 176
    sex and handedness of subjects, 188–189
    theory, 189–198
Mental transformation, 150–157
    analog nature, 150–151
Mnemonic, 1, 16

N

Neo-cognition, 220
Nonsense syllables, 2, 5–7, 45, 207

O

Orienting tasks, 16
Orthography, 10, 12, 17, 64–65

P

Paired associative learning, 48
Paradigm shift, 45
Partial Reinforcement Extinction Effect
    (PREE), 289, 296–298
Password, 21
Perceptual code, 103–104
Phonemic features, 63–64
Piaget-type tasks, 332
Proactive interference, 4, 8, 29
Problem solving, 251, *see also* Conceptual rule
    learning and Rule learning
Productive language, 354, 364–367

R

Reasoning, 305, *see also* Syllogistic reasoning
Recall, 4, 13, 16, 17, 19, 61
    cued, 88
        of words, 335

Receptive language, 336–338, 352, 353,
    364–367
Recognition learning, 45–72, 46, 48, 54, 61,
    64, 67, 71, 72, 93, 224
    memory, 117, 139–140
    of words, 335
Remembering, 1, 8, 20, 220
Response-response, 3
Retrieval, 204
Retrieval index, 37
Retroactive inhibition, 68, 71
Retroactive interference, 208
Reversal-nonreversal shift, 298, 298–300, 301
Rule difficulty, 238–239
Rule learning, 231, 248, 254–255
    multiple, 250

S

Search and match, 28, 26, 38
Semantic features, 67
Semantic processing, 13
Sensory buffer, 204–206
Sensory Register (SR), 102
Sentence
    comprehension, 353
    topic, 19
Serial learning, 223
Short-Term Store (STS), 102–109, 109–110,
    112, 115, 117, 120, 122, 126, 127, 128–129,
    135, 138
Spacing effect, 77–97, 224
    asymptote, 78–81
    consolidation, 81–83, 97
    encoding variability, 91–95, 96
    habituation, 90–91, 97, 220
    rehearsal, 83–86, 96
    voluntary action, 86–89, 97
Stimulus *see also* Perceptual code
    associations, 33–36
    filter, 33–36
    functional, 22, 46
    learning, 23
    and learning, 21–22
    meaningfulness, 22–25
    nominal, 22
    retrieval, 23
Stimulus competition, 25–27
Stimulus selection, 22–27
    and meaningfulness, 23–25
    and memory structure, 24–25
    new look, 22–23, 41

and position, 25
and stimulus competition, 25–27
Subjective organization, 6–7
Syllogism *see also* Logic, Reasoning
Syllogistic reasoning
    analysis, 308–313
    applications, 313–322
    complete combination model, 312–327
    compromise model, 322–327
    inference, 308–309
    model for invalid syllogisms, 322–326
    random combination model, 312–327
    research, 307–308
    set analysis theory, 311
Syntactic rules, 332

T

Tags
    features, 58
    frequency of response, 49–56, 69
    process, 58
Thinking, 305
Three dimensional objects, 147–197, *see also*

Mental rotation
    internal representation, 151–153
    experiments of, 153–169, 169–176
TOTE, 211
Transfer, 289
Transfer hypothesis, 291, 292–293, 294, 295–296, 297, 298, 301

V

Variance, 3
Verbal Discrimination Learning (VD), 47, 58, 60, 68, 72

W

Why Didn't I Think of That (WDITOT), 32, 39
Within-structural associative cuing, 34–36
Word-schema, 334

Y

Yes I Know (YIK), 32, 39